THE GLOBAL CAPITALIST CRISIS AND ITS AFTERMATH

Globalization, Crises, and Change

Series Editor

Professor Berch Berberoglu
University of Nevada, Reno, USA

Careful sociological analysis of the dynamics and contradictions of neoliberal globalization is sorely needed in order to assess the social consequences of this process on affected populations and develop appropriate responses to overcome the current global economic, political, and social crises.

Volumes in the series will focus on three interrelated processes that are the product of the latest phase of global capitalist development at the end of the twentieth and the beginning of the twenty-first century:

1. The nature and dynamics of neoliberal globalization;
2. the worldwide contradictions and crises of neoliberal globalization;
3. the responses to neoliberal globalization with focus on social change and transformation including popular social movements based on grassroots people's organizations, mass protests, rebellions, and revolution.

Taken together, these provide a comprehensive analysis of the nature, contradictions, and transformation of globalization through its inner logic that ultimately leads to the changes wrought by this process on a global scale. The significance of this series is that it provides the opportunity to examine this multifaceted phenomenon that has had (and continues to have) a major impact on society and societal development in our time.

Also in the series

Imperialism and Capitalism in the Twenty-First Century
A System in Crisis
James Petras and Henry Veltmeyer
with Raúl Delgado Wise and Humberto Márquez
978-1-4094-6732-8

Beyond the Global Capitalist Crisis
The World Economy in Transition
Edited by Berch Berberoglu
978-1-4094-1239-7

The Global Capitalist Crisis and Its Aftermath

The Causes and Consequences of the Great Recession of 2008–2009

Edited by

BERCH BERBEROGLU
University of Nevada, Reno, USA

Routledge
Taylor & Francis Group
LONDON AND NEW YORK

First published 2014 by Ashgate Publishing

2 Park Square, Milton Park, Abingdon, Oxfordshire OX14 4RN
52 Vanderbilt Avenue, New York, NY 10017

Routledge is an imprint of the Taylor & Francis Group, an informa business

First issued in paperback 2020

British Library Cataloguing in Publication Data
A catalogue record for this book is available from the British Library

The Library of Congress has cataloged the printed edition as follows:
Berberoglu, Berch.
The global capitalist crisis and its aftermath : the causes and consequences of the Great Recession of 2008–2009 / by Berch Berberoglu.
pages cm. -- (Globalization, crises, and change)
Includes bibliographical references and index.
ISBN 978-1-4724-1727-5 (hardback) 1. Global Financial Crisis, 2008-2009. 2. Economic policy. I. Title.
HB37172008 .B46 2014
330.9'0511--dc23

2014016419

ISBN 978-1-4724-1727-5 (hbk)
ISBN 978-0-367-60019-8 (pbk)

Contents

List of Figures and Tables

Figures

Tables

Notes on Contributors

Berch Berberoglu is Professor of Sociology, Department Chair, and Director of Graduate Studies in Sociology at the University of Nevada, Reno, where he has been teaching for the past 36 years. He has written and edited 30 books and many articles. His most recent books are *Political Sociology: An Introduction to the State and Society* (2013), *Beyond the Global Capitalist Crisis: The World Economy in Transition* (2012), and *Globalization in the 21st Century: Labor, Capital, and the State on a World Scale* (2010). He is series editor for Ashgate for the book series "Globalization, Crises, and Change" and for Palgrave Macmillan for the book series "Social Movements and Transformation." His latest book *America after Empire: The Promise and a Vision for a New America in the 21st Century* will be published by Paradigm.

Luis Arizmendi is Director of the international review *Mundo Siglo XXI* at the Center for Economic, Administrative, and Social Research of Instituto Politécnico Nacional (IPN) in Mexico. He has given keynote lectures at universities and research centers in India, Venezuela, Spain, Bolivia, Ecuador, and Mexico. He has translated the works of prominent social scientists into Spanish, and has published many articles and books. He has worked as Professor of Political Economy at the Universidad Nacional Autónoma de México (UNAM) for the past 25 years.

Patrick Bond is Director of the Center for Civil Society at the University of KwaZulu-Natal in Durban, South Africa. He previously taught at Wits University in Johannesburg and drafted policies for the first democratic South African government. His doctorate in economic geography was with David Harvey at Johns Hopkins University, and he moved to southern Africa in 1989. His books include *Elite Transition* (2014), *South Africa—Present as History* (co-authored with John S. Saul, 2014), *Looting Africa* (2006), and *Against Global Apartheid* (2003).

Chris Chase-Dunn is Distinguished Professor of Sociology and Director of the Institute for Research on World-Systems at the University of California-Riverside. He is the author of numerous books and articles related to the world-system. His recent research focuses on the causes of waves of empire and urban expansion and collapse over the last 5,000 years. His studies of structural globalization and global state formation have been supported by the National Science Foundation.

David Elliott is Adjunct Associate Professor at University of Maryland University College and retired from a full-time career in higher education as both a faculty member and administrator at several institutions. He received his Master of Social Science degree from the Institute of Social Studies in The Hague, the Netherlands and his PhD in Sociology from the University of Oregon in 1984. He has published two books and a number of articles on international political economy, development, and related areas.

David M. Kotz is Professor of Economics at the University of Massachusetts Amherst and Distinguished Professor in the School of Economics at the Shanghai University of Finance and Economics. His recent and forthcoming books include *The Rise and Fall of Free-Market Capitalism* (2014), *Contemporary Capitalism and Its Crises* (2010), coedited with Terrence McDonough and Michael Reich, and *Russia's Path from Gorbachev to Putin: The Demise of the Soviet System and the New Russia* (2007), with Fred Weir. He has published articles in *Review of Radical Political Economics*, *Science and Society*, *Monthly Review*, and various Chinese and Russian journals.

Bill Lucarelli is Senior Lecturer in the School of Economics and Finance at the University of Western Sydney, Australia. He received his PhD in economics from the University of Sydney in 1996. He is the author of numerous books, including *Monopoly Capitalism in Crisis* (2004), *The Economics of Financial Turbulence* (2011), and *Endgame for the Euro: A Critical History* (2014). He has published articles in *Journal of Contemporary Asia*, *Contributions to Political Economy*, *Journal of Post-Keynesian Economics*, and *Review of Radical Political Economics*, among others.

David Thurston Martin is a doctoral candidate in the International Development Studies program at Saint Mary's University in Halifax, Nova Scotia, Canada and in the Development Studies program at the Autonomous University of Zacatecas in Mexico. He is currently researching the impact of the decline of US hegemony and the rise of China in Latin America with particular focus on extractive industries.

Martin Orr is Associate Professor and Chair of the Department of Sociology at Boise State University. He received his PhD in Sociology from the University of Oregon in 1992. His research and teaching interests include social inequality, social movements, the environment, political sociology, and global political economy. He has published numerous articles on these and related issues focused on the crisis of global capitalism.

James Petras is Professor of Sociology (Emeritus) at the State University of New York at Binghamton and Adjunct Professor at St Mary's University, Halifax, Nova Scotia, Canada. His areas of specialization include the political economy of the US Empire, social movements, and Latin America. He has published 65 books in 29 languages and over 500 articles. He is the author of *Global Depression and Regional Wars*, and co-author (with Henry Veltmeyer) of *Globalization Unmasked: Imperialism in the 21st Century, System in Crisis, Multinationals on Trial*, and other books.

Anthony Roberts is a doctoral candidate in the Sociology Department at the University of California-Riverside. His research interests are income inequality, globalization, and labor. As a research assistant for the Institute for Research on World-Systems at UCR, he is currently conducting cross-national research on the global determinants of the institutionalization of labor since the 1960s.

William I. Robinson is Professor of Sociology, Global Studies, and Latin American Studies at the University of California, Santa Barbara. His scholarly research focuses on macro and comparative sociology, globalization and transnationalism, political economy, development and social change. He is the author of *Transnational Conflicts: Central America, Social Change, and Globalization*, and *A Theory of Global Capitalism: Production, Class, and State in a Transnational World.* His latest book is *Latin America and Global Capitalism: A Critical Globalization Perspective.*

Alvin So is Professor in the Division of Social Science at Hong Kong University of Science and Technology. He received his PhD in sociology from the University of California at Los Angeles in 1982. His research interests include social classes and the development of China and East Asia. He is the author of *Social Change and Development*, *East Asia and the World Economy*, and *Class and Class Conflict in Post-Socialist China.* He is the editor or co-editor of several volumes, including *China's Developmental Miracle: Origins, Transformations, and Challenges*, and *Handbook of Contemporary China.*

Henry Veltmeyer is Professor of Sociology and Development Studies at St Mary's University, Halifax, Nova Scotia, Canada and the Universidad Autónoma de Zacatecas in Mexico. He is author, co-author, and editor of over 40 books, including *Transcending Neoliberalism* and *Dynamics of Social Change in Latin America*, and (with James Petras), *Globalization Unmasked: Imperialism in the 21st Century, System in Crisis, Multinationals on Trial*, and, most recently, *Social Movements in Latin America* and *Beyond Neoliberalism.*

Levin Welch is Adjunct Professor of Sociology at Los Angeles Valley College and California State University, Stanislaus. He received his MA in sociology from the University of Nevada, Reno, in 2013. He conducted research on the Occupy Wall Street Movement for his thesis project. His areas of interest include political economy, economic crisis, and social movements in the United States and around the world aimed at resisting global capitalism.

Gordon Welty is Professor Emeritus at Wright State University and is currently Lecturer in Social Sciences at Adelphi University. He has published numerous articles in various journals, including *Political Studies*, *Antioch Review*, and *Mundo Siglo XXI.* His areas of research and writing interest include social theory, political economy, development, and Latin American studies, among others.

Preface and Acknowledgements

Global capitalism is in crisis. Going through the worst economic downturn in recent history—the worst since the Great Depression of the early twentieth century—it has set into motion forces that have unleashed an all-out attack on working people, resulting in an unprecedented level of inequality in recent history. In this seventh year of the collapse of the global capitalist economy that started to unravel in 2008, the long-term effects of this great calamity in the aftermath of the initial collapse are beginning to be felt now as we move deeper and deeper to the onset of an even greater crisis that is in the making—one that will inevitably characterize the Great Recession of 2008–09, which is continuing in full force across the capitalist world today in 2014, as the precursor or beginning point of the Great Depression of the early twenty-first century!

This book sheds much light into this recent turbulent history of global capitalism that has turned the crisis of the global capitalist system into a crisis for labor and for society in general to such an extent that progressive forces throughout the world are calling for the transformation of this moribund, defunct, and retrograde system and its replacement by a new one that is more in line with the needs and aspirations of working people across the globe. This, in essence, is what many hope and expect will occur in the aftermath of the global capitalist crisis and collapse in the early twenty-first century.

It gives me great pleasure, as editor of this book, to present to you 13 powerful chapters produced by some of the world's foremost authorities and experts in their respective fields of study. This superb team of critical scholars who have produced these impressive pieces of research and analysis on the predicament of the global capitalist economy and its crises, make a great contribution to our understanding of the nature and contradictions of global capitalism and its transformation in the period ahead.

I would like to thank each of the contributors to this book as partners in an important project that is designed to expose the inner workings (and failures) of a system that has caused so much misery and oppression amidst plenty that has been misappropriated, abused, and unequally distributed. Whereas much of this wealth is distributed to those in the top 1 percent of society who did not create it and who do not deserve it, the real creators of wealth—labor—who constitute the great majority of society, have gone without, as exploited wage-slaves of wealthy capitalists and their corporations. But, just as slavery in its brute form was abolished through civil wars, rebellions, and revolutions, so, too, one hopes, working people will one day abolish capitalism and wage-slavery so that labor, and humanity in general, can rid itself of this insanity that has inflicted so much pain and misery on working people across the world throughout much of recent human history.

Several of the chapters included in this book were first published in a special issue of the journal *International Review of Modern Sociology*, 38(2) (Autumn 2012), which I edited as guest editor; they appear here in revised and updated version. Several other chapters of this book were commissioned especially for this volume and are original contributions that are being published here for the first time. I would like to thank Dr Sunil Kukreja, editor-in-chief of the above-named journal, for granting permission to reprint the articles in revised form. I would like to thank colleagues and comrades who have provided me valuable insights into the various aspects of the ongoing global capitalist crisis, in particular Alan Spector and Walda Katz Fishman, among others, as well as some of my graduate students, in particular Levin Welch and Jason King, who assisted me in obtaining data that I was able to use to update some of the charts included in my chapter in the book. Finally, I would like to thank my commissioning editor at Ashgate, Claire Jarvis, for allowing me the freedom to pursue this important project and Aimée Feenan for her meticulous professional work in every stage of the copy-editing process. It was a pleasure working with her on this book.

Introduction: The Global Capitalist Crisis and Its Aftermath on a World Scale

Berch Berberoglu

As we enter the seventh year of the continuing global capitalist crisis that began with the September 2008 financial meltdown on Wall Street and other centers of global capitalism, the prospects for a rapid recovery of the economies of the United States and Europe, as well as those integrated into the global capitalist system, appear to be dim. While stock markets across the globe have made a big turnaround over the past six years, from their lows in late 2008 and early 2009 to their pre-recession highs and beyond by mid 2014, unemployment rates have continued to remain near double-digit levels in most advanced capitalist economies, with depression-level rates in countries suffering from the sovereign debt crisis, such as Greece, Spain, Portugal, and Italy. The grim economic situation that has cast doubt over chances of a rapid recovery anytime soon, was made worse with the new wave of mortgage foreclosures that the banks unloaded in the past few years—a situation that has relegated the US and global economy into greater uncertainty.

Robert J. Samuelson, writing in the February 16, 2014 issue of *The Washington Post*, under the title "Economists in the Dark," deals a heavy blow to the high priests and practitioners of the "dismal science" when he states: "These are hard times for economists. Their reputations are tarnished; their favorite doctrines are damaged. Among their most prominent thinkers, there is no consensus as to how—or whether—governments in advanced countries can improve lackluster recoveries" (Samuelson, 2014: 1). "The Great Recession and financial crisis changed behavior in fundamental ways that economists have yet to incorporate fully into their models and theories" he continues. "The widespread faith that modern [capitalist] societies were sheltered from deep and sustained economic setbacks has been shattered" he adds. "The faith in economics [i.e., the capitalist economy] was, in many ways, the underlying cause of both the financial crisis and Great Recession—it made people overconfident and careless during the boom—and the basic explanation for the weak recovery, as stubborn caution replaced stubborn complacency." Thus, Samuelson concludes: "to regain relevancy, economists are searching for a new light bulb—or better use of the old one. Meanwhile, most are still sitting in the dark" (Samuelson, 2014: 2).

Analysis of the causes and consequences of the Great Recession of 2008 and the subsequent global capitalist crisis and its aftermath does not require the assistance of bourgeois economists that Samuelson so poignantly criticizes and discredits.

The contributions of Marxist-oriented political economists that constitutes the bulk of the chapters included in this book, on the other hand, go a long way toward providing an understanding of the dynamics and contradictions of the global capitalist crisis and its aftermath as millions around the world struggle against the effects of this great depression of the early twenty-first century that continues to inflict pain on working people across the globe.

Writing about the continuing capitalist crisis and its aftermath in my latest book *Beyond the Global Capitalist Crisis: The World Economy in Transition*, published in early 2012, and pointing out that "Global capitalism is in serious crisis, and the current continuing severe global recession is the worst economic downturn since the Great Depression of the early twentieth century," I added "as the global capitalist crisis takes on depression-era characteristics," and "as millions of unemployed working people look for a job to pay for their basic necessities, capitalist states throughout the world have spent hundreds of billions of tax dollars to bail out failed commercial and financial institutions," with more than a trillion dollars spent by the US government alone "to save the global capitalist system from total collapse" (Berberoglu, 2012: 1). It turns out that the total bailout money that was spent to save the system from collapse was much more than officially reported at the time; in fact, according to a US Government Accountability Office (GAO) Report released in July 2011, the bailout money used to rescue dozens of corporations and banks across the globe was in excess of $16 trillion! (GAO, 2011: 131). Moreover, according to Sanjeev Ghotge, in 2009 while US economic output was $12 trillion and US savings was $2.4 trillion, the amount of debt accumulated from derivatives by the private sector was $473 trillion (Ghotge, 2009: 85–6)—an alarming situation that could lead to an economic catastrophe if this sector of finance capital were to unravel in another future financial meltdown (Sherman, 2010; Bivens, 2011).

Given the severity of the 2008–09 global capitalist crisis and its magnitude, I argued boldly and in no uncertain terms, that what we have been facing is "a systemic crisis that is permanent and irreversible" (Berberoglu, 2012: 179). Thus, any attempt to rescue the system from total collapse, I insisted, would be a futile exercise that is palatable only to those who operate under the illusion that capitalism once again will be rescued and will survive—and this, despite the massive role of the capitalist state in intervening in the global economy to reverse its decline and fall. If six years after the great catastrophe we continue to suffer from the effects of the crisis across the world, it most certainly tells us that we are in fact at a major turning point in recent world history—an epochal transformation of world systemic proportions in the early twenty-first century, i.e., the impending transformation of global capitalism (Calhoun and Derluguian, 2011).

This important book on the global capitalist crisis and its aftermath brings together the work of prominent scholars in the field who are keenly aware of the origins, nature, and contradictions of the global capitalist system and the crises of global capitalism, past and present. Their deep observations and analyses of the forces at work at the global level make them an ideal source uniquely positioned to examine the evolution and transformation of capitalism on a world scale. Their contributions to this effort to understand the dynamics and contradictions of the process that has led to the biggest economic calamity of the past century since the Great Depression, will go a long way toward untangling the complex web of economic, political, and social realities that have come to define the contours of global capitalism and the global capitalist crisis of the early twenty-first century.

David Martin in his review of recently published accounts of the crisis, provides a critical analysis of various theories of late twentieth and early twenty-first century capitalist dynamics. He argues that while each of the authors he discusses make an important contribution to our understanding of neoliberal globalization and the global capitalist crisis, they fall short of providing a comprehensive analysis of all the factors that are involved in explaining the nature and causes of the crisis that culminated in the financial meltdown of 2008–09 that continues to this day. Taken together, Martin argues that these analyses are an important addition to our understanding of the inner workings of neoliberal capitalist globalization that led to the global catastrophe that we are continuing to experience today.

In the next chapter, I provide an analysis of the ongoing global capitalist crisis and outline its dynamics and impact on the US economy and society. I show that the crisis, which originated in the United States during the "Great Recession" of 2007–09, and which continues unabated to this day, is characterized by high rates of unemployment, low purchasing power, rising personal and institutional debt, home mortgage foreclosures, personal and corporate bankruptcies, increasing income and wealth inequality, lower living standards, and rising poverty. I contend that the source of the continuing capitalist crisis is to be found in the growing polarization between labor and capital (i.e., between wages and profits) over the past several decades. The rising productivity of labor during this period has not translated into rising incomes for working people.

The accelerated globalization of capital and further outsourcing of production, speculative financial markets, mushrooming bank loans, and rising institutional and consumer debt, a dramatic increase in the price of oil, and a consequent decline in consumer spending, have triggered massive layoffs, hence rising unemployment, and led to major disruptions and dislocations in various sectors of the US and global economy. Given the systemic nature of the crisis, I conclude that any long-term solution to the crisis of the US and world economy will need to come from a thorough transformation of global capitalism.

William I. Robinson eloquently discusses the scope and depth of the "Great Recession" within the context of an analysis of the nature and various dimensions of the global capitalist crisis. He argues that over the course of the past several decades, capitalism has gone through a qualitative transformation, such that previously nationally-based accumulation has now become transnational, hence giving rise to a transnational capitalist class. Referring to the leading imperial state, the United States, he contends that it constitutes the leading force behind the transnationalization of capitalism and has come to shoulder the burdens of empire to regulate and run a global capitalist system on behalf of the transnational capitalist class and all that is encompassed under global capitalism.

Robinson situates the causal origins of the global capitalist crisis in a combination of factors centered on over-accumulation and contradictions of state power. He argues that this twenty-first century capitalist crisis is unprecedented in terms of its magnitude, its global reach, the extent of ecological degradation and social deterioration, and the scale of the means of violence. Pointing out that the global capitalist economy experienced a period of hyper-accumulation in the 1980s and 1990s as a result of capitalist globalization but stagnated by the turn of the century, Robinson explains that transnational capitalists and elites turned to two major mechanisms for unloading surplus and sustaining accumulation in the face of chronic stagnation: financial speculation and militarized accumulation.

After a careful analysis of the causes and consequences of the continuing global capitalist crisis and its political implications, Robinson points to the catastrophe that neoliberal capitalist globalization has brought in its wake in this latest round of worldwide capitalist crisis, and rings the alarm bells of the situation's urgency, which he warns if not addressed, it may lead to the collapse of world civilization as we know it. He points out that, while reform-oriented elites have responded to the crisis by calling for a neo-Keynesianism from above and mechanisms for transnational regulation, popular and working classes have resisted attempts to transfer to them the burdens of the crisis through austerity, wage cuts, and unemployment. Robinson goes into great lengths to show that the crisis we are in is not cyclical or structural, but is at core *systemic*, and thus it may threaten to bring about the end of the global capitalist system. He warns us of the grim future that awaits us in the coming years if nothing is done to stop global capitalism in its tracks.

James Petras and Henry Veltmeyer are veterans of global capitalist crises and have spent a lifetime exposing the inner workings of the global capitalist system and its contradictions across the world. In the chapter that follows, they point out that with the onset of the global financial crisis in 2008, the world capitalist system suffered a shock that shook its very foundations, threatening the functioning of key financial institutions and the economies at the center of the system. However, the crisis, they argue, merely served to restructure the system, destroying capital in the process but also regenerating conditions for a new round of accumulation based on large-scale investments in the natural resource wealth of countries on the periphery of the global capitalist system.

Finance capital, the major force behind the financial meltdown, recovered from its losses, and the capitalist class in its financial core was strengthened by a bailout of the financial institutions with public funds. Thus, Petras and Veltmeyer argue, the crisis has been used to the strategic advantage of capital in its class war against labor, to further the accumulation of capital and the consolidation of capitalist rule. The point is that, the crisis, they argue, is functional for the leading elements of the capitalist class, allowing them to profit from the crisis while passing on the costs to the working class—to convert a systemic crisis (of capital and the state) into a crisis for labor. Thus, the global capitalist crisis is not a crisis of capital or of capitalism itself, but is a crisis that has affected working people the most, hence it has become a crisis for labor.

Levin Welch, providing a wealth of data on the 2008 financial meltdown and its aftermath, argues in the next chapter that the global capitalist crisis, focused on the United States, provided a great opportunity for capitalists to accumulate immense wealth through the restructuring of industrial, commercial, and financial capital. While the workers and marginalized populations suffered the consequences of the crisis, corporate profits (including especially those of the big banks) soared during the past six years, as witnessed by the performance of the stock market over this period.

Welch argues that the main cause of the 2008 meltdown was the uncontrolled and unregulated expansion of finance capital through speculative and corrupt financial activities in what has become known as "casino capitalism." Thus, privatization, deregulation, "free" markets and other neoliberal policies and practices adopted during the previous three decades came to a head in a multiple way beyond the housing bubble that burst in the opening salvo of the "great recession," signaling the beginning of the global capitalist crisis.

In looking at the impact of the crisis on different segments of society, Welch documents the immense inequality between labor and capital that this recession has produced, with enormous wealth at one pole and poverty and misery at the other, which he argues points to the necessity for the working class to bring about much needed change through collective social and political action.

David Elliott, in his chapter on the eurozone crisis, explains why it differs from that of the United States and what its impact has been upon working people in Europe. He argues that one key difference is the stronger monetarist policy in the eurozone, taking actions that adversely impact some countries (i.e., those in the periphery of the European Union), but the economic forces that have been making the key decisions are not directly accountable to these countries. Germany, the European Central Bank (ECB), and the IMF have stressed monetary as opposed to fiscal tools, thus leaving the less powerful eurozone countries at their mercy. As a result, the concentrated economic power of key states like Germany across the eurozone means that monetary policy exercised by the ECB is often in conflict with the fiscal policies and interests of the more seriously crisis-impacted nations: Portugal, Italy, Ireland, Greece, Spain, and Cyprus.

Elliott points out that the fundamental cause of this crisis was the global financialization of capital. While securities fraud, home loan issues, debt fraud and mismanagement, and export of consolidated risky assets from the US triggered the collapse, such activities were found across the capitalist world. The impact of these issues on Portugal, Italy, Ireland, Greece, Spain, and Cyprus, he contends, requires an examination of the relationship of these countries with the eurozone of which they are a part: as one arm of the European Community, the ECB manages the euro as the currency for the 17 members of the eurozone and operates its neoliberal monetary controls under the influence of Germany (the largest economy) but largely outside the influence of smaller eurozone members. The ECB does not control individual nations' fiscal policies (government spending and taxation) so its power to directly influence the eurozone economy is largely in the realm of currency in circulation, interest on debts, and packaging loans to ailing members of the eurozone. But this is done under conditions often seen as punitive or unfair by the stricken countries.

Elliott points out that the reasons for each country's predicament were largely rooted historically in European and world politics and economy that had not been addressed when the euro was developed in the 1990s. Some of the problems experienced by these countries were the unintended consequences of ECB monetary interventions and its conditions. He goes on to argue that Germany's extraction of surplus value by greater exploitation of its workers (especially vis-à-vis many of the other eurozone members), alongside its larger economy, placed Germany in a position to not only influence the ECB but to further grow its economy at the expense of countries that for historical reasons were not as competitive in the world economy.

To sum up, Elliott contends that the continuing eurozone crisis is the result of the nature of contemporary global capitalism: financialization. The crisis struck Portugal, Italy, Ireland, Greece, Spain, and Cyprus with greater force, he concludes, because of their giving up individual monetary policy in favor of the ECB and because of the role that Germany played in the neoliberal policies of the Bank, arguing that EU leading perspectives were characterized by the use of national units of analysis or points of view rather than, for example, the eurozone as a transnational system. Thus, Elliott contends, the European Community, including the eurozone, is trapped in a stalemate: a web of nationalist, neoliberal, monetarist economic policy spun by Germany, the IMF, and the ECB, supported by Britain and other non-euro members of the EU versus the fragmented working classes in the countries of Europe's periphery. Focusing on the long economic stagnation in Japan and the impact of the global capitalist crisis on the Japanese economy, Bill Lucarelli in the next chapter examines the dynamics of the business cycle in Japan within the context of the global economy and the crisis that has been affecting that country. He argues that the accumulation of debt in Japan has acted as a powerful trigger in the inversion of the business cycle and has set in train a phase of severe liquidation of assets and financial retrenchment. The stress-selling of assets also culminated in a contraction of deposits and a fall in the velocity of circulation of money. As asset prices tumbled, he writes, the process became cumulative and self-reinforcing: in the absence of Central Bank intervention to inject liquidity into the system, the rate of bankruptcies escalated, which was then amplified by a profitability crisis and the subsequent curtailment of investment. Thus, rising unemployment and a fall in aggregate demand were transmitted through the multiplier effects of a decline in aggregate income.

Despite near zero short-term interest rates, Lucarelli points out, Japanese corporations not only curtailed their demand for credit but accelerated their repayment of existing loans in order to restore their respective balance sheets.

Indeed, the Japanese experience of debt-deflation, he argues, could now be spreading to the United States and Europe. Successive stimulus measures through public works programs and the bail-out of insolvent banks, he adds, had blown out the budget deficit to over 10 percent of GDP, while the ratio of government debt was estimated at over 240 percent of GDP in 2010. If the Japanese authorities were to succumb to western demands from the OECD and the IMF and launch a neoliberal strategy of market liberalization, writes Lucarelli, the short-term impact would be disastrous: a depressive spiral of bankruptcies and growing unemployment, not witnessed since the Great Depression, could be set in motion. Despite these domestic problems of deflation and a liquidity trap, Japan, we are told, continues to accumulate a current account surplus, most notably with the United States; a large proportion of this trade surplus has been accomplished by falling imports as a result of the stagnation of domestic demand. Lucarelli argues that the problem of excess capacity will compel Japanese corporations to expand their exports in order to counteract a falling profitability on the domestic market. The burgeoning trade deficit in the US, however, could provoke retaliatory protectionist measures, he adds. Thus, the conditions are therefore quite favorable, he says, for the outbreak of a classical Keynesian trade war. Lucarelli concludes his chapter by shedding some light on these tendencies toward inter-state trade and currency wars through competitive devaluations and the more recent resort to quantitative easing as a means of currency devaluations between the competing nation states and regional blocs.

Shifting to China in the next chapter, Alvin So attempts to examine the impact of the global capitalist crisis on the Chinese economy and the responses of the Chinese state to the continuing crisis. He states that in the initial period immediately after the outbreak of the crisis its impact on China was highly positive, with China emerging from the crisis considerably strengthened, as the crisis not only provided the opportunity to strengthen its "state-developmentalism," but also the chance to expand its power in the inter-state system. Thus, the crisis had increased the probability of the rise of China as a global power as well as the shift in the center of global capital accumulation from the West to the East in the twenty-first century.

Several years later, however, the situation has substantially changed, according to So: With the deepening of the continuing crisis since 2012, China's hyper-growth economy has eventually slowed down as the state has silently discarded its "*developmentalist* model." The state has no longer provided a massive stimulus package to jumpstart the economy as it did in 2008; instead, the new leaders have opted for the tightening of credit, the strengthening of market discipline, market liberalization, streamlining the state bureaucracy, and the opening of the state sector to foreign investment.

Nonetheless, So points out that despite adopting a more pro-market policy, China is not moving in the direction of naked neoliberalism. Instead, it is moving along a new path that So calls "*state-neoliberalism*." This "state-neoliberalist model" in China, he argues, is different from the *neoliberal state* in the West. First, whereas the Western neoliberal state is aimed at serving the interests of the capitalist class, state-neoliberalism in China is aimed at serving the central role of the "communist party-state" when it was threatened by the deepening global capitalist crisis. Second, whereas the Western neoliberal state has shown signs of retreat from the economy, the Chinese state continues to intervene into the economy with long-term planning and urbanization projects. Third, whereas the Western neoliberal state is weakened by public management reforms to downsize the state bureaucracy, the Chinese state is strengthened, not weakened, through its mass-line education and anti-corruption campaigns. Finally, whereas the Western neoliberal state advocates globalization and the opening of the domestic economy to transnationals, the Chinese state has taken an aggressive stand to protect its strategic sectors from the assault of the transnationals and to heighten its national credentials in territorial disputes in the South and East China Seas. Although the transnationals are now allowed to enter the strategic sectors, So admits, the Chinese state also wants to upgrade and to strengthen Chinese companies so they can compete with the transnationals in both the Chinese market and the world economy.

If the Chinese developmental experience is characterized by trial and error, mid-course corrections, and reversals of policies, what is the future trajectory of state-neoliberalism in China? So asks. He responds to this by saying the consolidation of state-neoliberalism is the most likely scenario, and China could end up in a position that Silver and Arrighi had envisioned two decades ago: "China appears to be emerging as the only poor country that has any chance in the foreseeable future of subverting the Western-dominated global hierarchy of wealth." Whether China succeeds in achieving this, So concludes, will depend on, to a large extent, how global capitalism is able to deal with the unfolding worldwide economic and financial crisis that is now threatening its very survival.

Russia is among the countries significantly affected by the global capitalist crisis that broke out in 2008. David Kotz in his chapter on the impact of the crisis on Russia takes up an analysis of this impact at great length. He first examines the political economy of post-Soviet Russia, including the manner of its insertion into the global capitalist system, in the period prior to the start of the global capitalist crisis. He then considers the impact of the crisis on Russia including the likely long-term effects of the continuing global capitalist crisis of capitalism over the coming years.

Kotz points out that in 1992 the post-Soviet Russian state under President Boris Yeltsin rapidly dismantled the institutions of state socialism, aiming to replace it with a capitalist system. The state followed the neoliberal strategy for achieving this transition, which included immediate freeing of markets, rapid privatization, and tight monetary and fiscal policies. There followed an 8-year-long deep depression as well as a breakdown of public order, as a criminalized oligarchic form of capitalism took root. Russia's economy was deindustrialized and became dependent on the export of raw materials, particularly oil and natural gas.

After the Yeltsin regime was replaced by that of President Vladimir Putin in 2000, state power expanded and was centralized once again in the Kremlin.

The chaos of the 1990s, Kotz points out, was replaced by a restoration of public order; however, the expansion of state power was not accompanied by a shift in economic strategy. Kotz presents evidence that the Putin regime has continued the neoliberal economic strategy rather than shifting to a developmentalist state. This produced a deepening of Russia's dependence on oil and natural gas exports through the eve of the global capitalist crisis. Rising oil prices in the years prior to the crisis brought a big capital inflow and rapid GDP growth.

Kotz shows that the onset of the crisis in 2008 led to a collapse of oil prices, a sharp drop in Russia's exports, and a large outflow of capital. There followed a decline in GDP of 7.8 percent in 2009, the steepest of any major economy. He points out that the Russian state used its huge stabilization fund to finance a bailout of the big companies and banks controlled by the oligarchs, while small companies and banks were allowed to fail and the working class suffered big layoffs. After 2009 the price of oil recovered, buoyed by continuing rapid growth in China, which led to a resumption of modest economic growth.

Given this situation, Kotz argues that the future prospects for working people in Russia are dim, if the current regime remains in power. Despite talk about rebuilding Russian industry, there has been no shift away from the neoliberal strategy. Thus, Russia remains a petro-state. However, if oil prices remain high in the coming years, Kotz points out, the Putin regime has a good chance to hold onto power in the immediate future. Finally, Kotz considers various developments that might derail the retrograde system in Russia, including low investment in new sources of oil, worsening stagnation in the global economy which might reduce oil exports, possible divisions among the oligarchs, and the possible development of significant working class opposition to Russia's economic direction.

Next, moving on to the periphery of world capitalism, Louis Arizmendi and Gordon Welty examine the impact of globalization and neoliberalism on Latin America in the context of the epochal crisis of global capitalism. They point out that since the late 1990s a number of Latin American countries have begun to question the ideology and practices of the neoliberal state.

Arizmendi and Welty identify three types of Latin American states that have questioned neoliberalism. The specifically post-neoliberal states include Bolivia, Ecuador, and Venezuela; the limited post-neoliberal states include Argentina, Brazil, and Uruguay; the ambiguous post-neoliberal states include El Salvador, Guatemala, and Nicaragua. They go on to identify a fourth type of state, one that is opposed to the post-neoliberal trend—the neoauthoritarian state. This includes Colombia, Honduras, and Mexico. The several post-neoliberal trends collide with the neoauthoritarian trend in contesting the definition of contemporary capitalism.

The post-neoliberal states of Latin America were not as deeply affected as the United States and the eurozone states, argue Arizmendi and Welty. As during the Great Depression of the 1930s, which provided an opening for autonomous national development de-coupled from the advanced capitalist states mired in deep economic crisis, the post-neoliberal states of Latin America by disassociating with the failed neoliberal policies of global capitalism were able to preempt the effects of the most recent crisis and minimize its impact.

Arizmendi and Welty assess this impact within the context of the globalization of capital and the epochal crisis of global capitalism by focusing on several key countries in Latin America—Bolivia, Brazil, Ecuador, Mexico, and Venezuela. First, the focus is on Mexico, which illustrates the subordination of a peripheral country to the center, on an even deeper level than seen before. Not only does the center extract a technological rent from peripheral countries such as Mexico, but it drags them into a debt trap as well. In order to service this debt and pay the technological rent, the peripheral country must relinquish control of the nation's strategic natural resources to the center, and also ensure that the nation's workforce will be available to the transnational corporations at a near-subsistence level. In the case of Mexico, these processes of subordination are illustrated by the fate of Pemex and by the loss of food sovereignty, particularly maize.

Arizmendi and Welty next discuss Brazil, which has avoided global subordination in two ways: by reorienting itself towards China, it has been able to provide a buffer against US hegemony, and it has advanced a project of regional sub-imperialism. Brazil continues to be a global leader in agriculture and extractive industries: its soybean production is second highest in the world, behind the US, especially in terms of genetically modified organisms. However, Arizmendi and Welty point out that Brazil lacks one major characteristic of fully post-neoliberal states: it lacks a substantial anti- or trans-capitalist project. This results in a certain level of ambivalence on Brazil's part toward globalization. That ambivalence, combined with its regional sub-imperialist aspirations, result in an overall weakness of Brazil in countering the global hegemon and its aggressions.

Finally, Arizmendi and Welty discuss Bolivia, Ecuador, and Venezuela, each of which, they argue, are striving to develop a post-neoliberal transcapitalism. This has involved mobilizing the urban and rural poor on behalf of the self-determination of the state and an ending of the over-exploitation of the labor force by global capitalism, as well as putting an end to the plundering of their strategic natural resources by the transnationals.

Patrick Bond in his chapter on the impact of the global capitalist crisis on Africa, criticizes establishment sources for praising the continent for having turned to neo-liberal policies of its own volition. Yet there is nowhere more indicative of the strengths and sometimes debilitating weaknesses of crisis-resistance, he says, than Africa. Bond goes on to argue that the crisis hit Africa very hard, with the 2008 minerals and petroleum commodity prices crashing and national budget deficits growing. He shows that much of the superficial growth can be attributed to the 2002–08 commodities boom, the recovery of several countries from civil war, and a surge in temporary consumer buying power fueled by relaxed credit conditions. Thus, the subsequent hype about "Africa Rising," he cautions us, requires yet more analysis, because in most cases, if one corrects GDP for non-renewable resource depletion, the "net adjusted savings" is negative.

The case of Nigeria is illustrative because in late 2013, it was touted as a 'fast growth' economy alongside Mexico, Indonesia and Turkey (comprising the "MINTs," in Goldman Sachs acronym-speak), and because its GDP doubled in 2014 because of a technical correction, making it Africa's largest in terms of income (as oil continues to serve as the country's primary export commodity). Yet as Bond shows, all the underlying power relations associated with the neocolonial world division of labor makes Nigeria, in reality, Africa's fastest-*shrinking* economy, in terms of its wealth.

Indeed for Africa as a whole, Bond continues, the more the "Africa Rising" narrative is utilized to describe the continent's healthy GDP rates, the more the actual wealth shrinks, especially in countries dependent upon minerals and petroleum. He points out that in other minerals or oil-rich countries such as Australia, Norway and Canada, the corporations doing the extraction mainly operate from their home base, and there is subsequent redirection of surpluses into physical infrastructural investment, so the net adjusted savings are positive, as they are for Asia and Latin America; only Africa and the Middle East have consistently recorded net negative wealth creation, despite their enormous wealth in natural resources, like oil. What this means, Bond argues, is that the crisis conditions are now increasingly displaced to future generations of Africans who will be victimized first by the lack of public goods investment from the resource rents, and second by the wasting of this wealth.

Another outcome, Bond points out, is political degeneration, in which venal elites remain in power, their overall obedience to the dictates of imperialism means more suffering and, as a result, unstable local power relations often lead to battles between rival forces in resource-rich areas. These can be devastating, such as in the eastern Democratic Republic of the Congo where many have been killed in the search for mineral profits.

But resistance is rising, Bond informs us, both in micro-settings where extraction is too painful for local residents to bear, and in many macro-settings that require democratization and more egalitarian social policies. Three North African countries began a process in 2011, in which the mass anger that periodically explodes into "IMF Riots" was channeled into popular coalitions to overthrow authoritarian regimes in Tunisia, Egypt, and Libya, among others—and in each site, in varying degrees, the result was unsatisfactory with reactionary forces defeating a resistance that lacked mass democratic organization and a coherent strategy of taking state power. Bond's analysis of the situation elsewhere in the continent suggests that the deteriorating condition of the masses across the region may lead to further uprisings in Africa in the years ahead.

Chris Chase-Dunn and Anthony Roberts next contextualize the global capitalist crisis within the framework of the world capitalist system, discussing the structural crisis of global capitalism and the prospects for systemic transformation in the next several decades in world-historical perspective. As in previous epochs of global economic turbulence, this period of worldwide economic crisis has generated movements that are mobilizing against neoliberal capitalist globalization. Chase-Dunn and Roberts consider the contemporary network of global counter-movements and progressive national regimes that are seeking to transform the global capitalist system into a more humane, sustainable and egalitarian civilization. Thus, it is within this context of the global reach of capital and the capitalist system that they see the formation and mobilization of a wide array of progressive forces on the Left to take part in the coming world revolution in the twenty-first century.

Going into some detail on the nature of these movements that are coming together on a global scale, Chase-Dunn and Roberts point to the "pink tide" in Latin America, the Arab Spring, Occupy Wall Street, and anti-austerity movements in Europe as a way forward when democratic people's movements across the globe will increasingly coalesce and develop the necessary strategies and tactics to wage struggle against capital and the global capitalist system, and take back the planet from the dominant ruling classes that have been enslaving much of humanity to this day.

Martin Orr's chapter next traces the rise and fall of the United States as an imperial power. Although the international influence and reputation of the United States is at its lowest point in modern history, many still cling to the notion that somehow the United States is "exceptional." While there are characteristics that distinguish it from other nations, and from other empires, the US project has still been subject to the same laws of social development. Orr points out that imperial power is dependent on material bases, and that in the case of the United States an empire was built on its vast natural wealth. Foremost of these resources was oil. The world wars of the twentieth century enabled the United States to cash in its oil wealth for international power. By supplying the petroleum essentially for industrial warfare, the United States was able to amass huge fortunes and to dictate the terms of the post-Second World War *Pax Americana.*

This natural wealth turned out to be finite, however, and by the early 1970s US crude oil production—and the empire—was in decline. Over the course of the 1970s and 1980s the US became more inegalitarian, less democratic, and more repressive. Despite possession of the most powerful military in world history, defeat in Vietnam was followed by stalemate after stalemate. With the collapse of the Soviet Union and absent its restraining influence, the US Empire was given new life.

Given this opportunity, the US government sought to advance and perpetuate global domination by foisting neoliberal "free trade" agreements upon the world's nations. Through the establishment of international bodies like the World Trade Organization, the United States sought to legitimize punitive sanctions upon any government that would interfere with the interests of transnational multinational corporations through taxation, regulation, or other constraints upon predatory behavior. As these attempts stalled due to domestic and international opposition, the US augmented these efforts with neoconservative unilateralism—the attempt to make clear that challenging corporate and banking interests would be met not only by trade sanctions, but by the wanton destruction of the infrastructure of the offending society, and the murder of its people. To the genuine surprise of the architects of this policy, wholesale slaughter aroused international opposition. As it became clear that the United States was not destined to have its own way, the bottom fell out in the Great Recession.

The assault upon the domestic population since the early 1970s had led to stagnant wages and growing indebtedness among US workers. Amid rising productivity, a crisis of overproduction was triggered. Financial fraud and inflation of basic necessities, especially energy, contributed to the crash. Governments, burdened by rising costs and declining revenues, were unable to bridge the gap in demand. The United States government is now deeply in debt, held in contempt at home and abroad, and incapable of even intimidating other nations, let alone subjecting them to its will. With the rise of other economic and military powers, the United States is now, at best, just one nation among many.

Taking the liberty as editor of this book to make my own concluding observations on the global capitalist crisis and the prospects for transformation of the world capitalist system, I argue in the closing essay that the era of neoliberal capitalist globalization has come to an end, and that the political and military maneuvers of US imperialism have not been able to overcome its economic decline on a national level, though its dominant classes have reaped immense profits through their activities across the globe. However, while such plunder might in the short-run save the day for the US Empire, the long term prospects for empire of high finance and global supremacy is problematic. In fact, as others have also argued in various chapters of this book, the decline and fall of the US empire—much as its British predecessor—is an eventuality that is both inevitable and impossible to reverse (Petras 2007, 2009; Parenti 2011). In short, I argue that we will soon be witnessing epochal transformations of global proportions across the world.

Together, the thirteen chapters that make up this book are intended to generate discussion and debate on this important topic, as the nature and causes of the global capitalist crisis and its aftermath are examined and analyzed in great detail in an effort to understand the nature, contradictions, and crises of contemporary global capitalism and its impact on society in the early twenty-first century.

References

Berberoglu, Berch. (ed.). 2010. *Globalization in the 21st Century: Labor, Capital, and the State on a World Scale*. New York: Palgrave Macmillan.

Berberoglu, Berch. (ed.). 2012. *Beyond the Global Capitalist Crisis: The World Economy in Transition*. Farnham: Ashgate Publishing.

Bivens, Josh. 2011. *Failure by Design: The Story Behind America's Broken Economy*. Ithaca, NY: ILR Press.

Calhoun, Craig and Georgi Derluguian. (eds). 2011. *Aftermath: A New Economic Order?* New York: New York University Press.

Ghotge, Sanjeev. 2009. "Financial Meltdown: An Intriguing Silence at the Core." *Capitalism, Nature, Socialism* (December) 20(4), 85–88.

Parenti, Michael. 2011. *The Face of Imperialism*. Boulder, CO: Paradigm Publishers.

Petras, James. 2007. *Rulers and Ruled in the U.S. Empire*. Atlanta: Clarity Press.

Petras, James. 2009. *Global Depression and Regional Wars*. Atlanta: Clarity Press.

Samuelson, Robert J. 2014. "Economists Sitting in the Dark." *The Washington Post* (February 16), http://www.washingtonpost.com/opinions/robert-samuelson-economists-face-hard-times/2014/02/16/70991824-9599-11e3-afce-3e7c922ef31e_story.html.

Sherman, Howard. 2010. *The Roller Coaster Economy: Financial Crisis, Great Recession, and the Public Option*. Boston: M.E. Sharpe.

United States Government Accountability Office. 2011. *Federal Reserve System: Opportunities Exist to Strengthen Policies and Processes for Managing Emergency Assistance*. Washington, DC: US Government Accountability Office.

Chapter 1
The Contours of the Marxist Debate on the Global Capitalist Crisis

David Thurston Martin

Introduction

The global capitalist crisis has generated much debate among scholars about its causes and consequences, but the debates within the tradition of Marxist political economy has been some of the most prolific and insightful, given the tradition's focus on the structures and dynamics of capitalism, rather than individual actors, policies, and institutions. In contrast to scholars of the neo-classical or Keynesian traditions, these scholars stress the structural nature of financial crises and look for underlying causes in the realm of production. As a result, most Marxist scholars locate the roots of the current crisis to the 1970s, when capitalism's post-Second World War boom entered a crisis. But that is the extent of the consensus; these scholars disagree over whether the period since the 1970s has been characterized by stagnation or expansion, overproduction or underconsumption, rising or falling rates of profit, and increasing or decreasing real wages. While these disagreements at face value appear irreconcilable, taken together, the strengths of one argument is complemented by the weaknesses of the others, generating a comprehensive understanding of the structural dynamics of the current global capitalist crisis in the context of the dialectical nature of the uneven development of global capitalism. This chapter will summarize, critique, and synthesize the works of leading authors in the various schools of Marxist political economy to explore the emerging contours of the Marxist debate on the global capitalist crisis.

Stagnation

John Bellamy Foster and Fred Magdoff, editor of *Monthly Review* and son of a former editor of that journal respectively, carry forward the Monopoly Capital school of Marxist political economy, developed in the works of Paul Baran, Paul Sweezy, Harry Magdoff, and Harry Braverman in the 1960s and 1970s, to analyze the current crisis in their 2009 book, *The Great Financial Crisis*. In that book, they compile a selection of essays from *Monthly Review*, dating between 2006 and 2008, and add a new introduction that provides a clear and concise statement of the argument of the Monopoly School on the global capitalist crisis.

This school argues that capitalism has gone through several stages: competitive capitalism from roughly 1770 to 1870, monopoly capitalism from 1870 to 1970, and monopoly-finance capitalism from 1970 to the present. Their argument is that as capitalism matures, it tends to stagnate and, therefore, requires ever larger external stimuli to boost growth. Those external stimuli can come in the form of technological innovations, military spending, the sales effort, and, last, but certainly not least, speculative finance and debt. Thus, for example, the invention of the automobile provided an external stimulus for the massive expansion of capitalism in the mid-twentieth century, but, since the 1970s, the information and communication technology (ICT) revolution has failed to provide a similar stimulus, and the stagnation tendency of monopoly capitalism took hold. As a result, since the end of the long post war boom in the crisis of the 1970s, speculative finance has become a "secondary engine for growth, given the weakness of the primary engine, productive investment" (Foster and Magdoff, 2009: 18). That is, financial speculation and debt are the principal "external stimuli" in the age of monopoly-finance capital by propping up demand through debt expansion and increasing profits through speculation.

The stagnation tendency of monopoly capitalism derives from the overproduction of capital, or, as Marx put it, "the real barrier to capitalist production is capital itself" (Foster and Magdoff, 2009: 20). While expanding the productivity and productive capacity of capitalism, the rise of corporations (first national and now transnational) also created monopolistic control over markets, in which the corporations colluded to keep prices high and production low. This tendency generated massive profits and, at the same time, much underutilized productive capacity. Since the 1970s, the finance sector has absorbed much of this surplus capital, leveraging it into a debt-fueled expansion of effective demand as real wages have leveled under the weight of stagnating productive investment. Since real wages stagnated as productivity increased since the 1970s, monopoly capital faced a growing realization problem for its production. The expansion of consumer credit and household debt intervened to resolve this realization problem.

Therefore, Foster and Magdoff argue that the ascendency of finance capital since the late 1960s is "symptomatic of the underlying stagnation tendency" of monopoly capitalism, producing a "symbiotic embrace" between stagnation and financialization (20). The period since the late 1960s has seen the "'financialization of the capitalist class' in the sense of a shift in the primary sources of wealth accumulation at the very top of society from production to finance" (Foster and Holleman, 2010). In the United States, the finance capital fraction of the capitalist class became increasingly dominant as evident by its accumulation of wealth, profits, and power (Phillips, 2008). Other fractions of capital colluded in this ascendency due to finance's ability to absorb surplus, realize production, and discipline labor and the state. Finance "ascended" to invest surplus in more liquid forms than production and generate speculative profits under conditions of an overproduction crisis, to prop up effective demand through the expansion of household debt, and to discipline labor through financial and fiscal crises.

Foster and Magdoff argue that as a result, rather than a "modest helper" in the accumulation process, "the expansion of debt and speculation that characterized the US economy … since the late 1960s represented the main means by which the system managed to avoid sinking into a deep slump" (19). In other words, finance capital's expansion of credit helped productive capital realize its production without raising wages, and workers increased their consumption through higher levels of household debt, not wages. Raghuram Rajan, former chief economist at the International Monetary Fund, described this strategy as "let them eat credit" (2010). That is, capital "solved" the realization problem of the overproduction crisis through the explosion of household debt.

While this "external stimulus" of debt expansion served as a secondary engine of growth in face of underlying stagnation, it also created the conditions of more volatility as growth came to depend on the speculative asset bubbles and their inevitable crashes. Foster and Magdoff describe monopoly-finance capital's dependence on debt-fueled growth like a drug addict needing ever larger speculative "fixes": "the system became more and more dependent on a series of financial bubbles to keep it going, each one bigger than the last" (18). This drive for ever-bigger bubbles to stimulate growth explains the geographic movement of the series of financial bubbles (and crises) from the periphery of capitalism to the center, that is, from the periphery in the Third World debt crisis of 1982 to the center in the Wall Street crisis of 2008. Only financial markets as "deep" and "sophisticated" as those found on Wall Street could generate an $8 trillion housing bubble at the center of the Great Financial Crisis (Baker, 2009). Given the financialization of the capitalist class and the breaking of the power of labor, the "solution" to this crisis within the current structure of power is to be found not in the nationalization of the banks and their conversion into public utilities, but in the bailout of Wall Street banks with trillions of dollars from state intervention to fuel the "junkies" search for another speculative "fix."

A Critique of Foster and Magdoff

First and foremost, the notion that technological innovation, war, imperialism, sales effort, advertising, financial speculation, and household debt are "external stimuli" to capitalism, that is, "external to the logic of capitalism," ignores the history of capitalism itself, in which innovation, wars, imperialism, military spending, speculative bubbles, financial crises, and debt expansion have all played a central role in overcoming the "real barrier" of "capital itself" by destroying and devaluing capital, and jumpstarting new waves of capitalist expansion. In other words, in order to make the argument that, as capitalism matures, it also stagnates, Foster and Magdoff have categorically excluded as "external stimuli" the very social forces, which capitalism has historically used to overcome the real barrier of the expansion of capital, "capital itself" by destroying and devaluing capital. Innovation/invention, war/imperialism, and debt/financial crises, rather than external, are central to the logic of capitalism in historical perspective. To argue for the stagnation tendency of monopoly capitalism, Foster and Magdoff are forced to claim that the social processes that fuel the dynamism of capitalism are external stimuli. Unfortunately, they are not.

Furthermore, to make the argument that capitalism has stagnated since the 1970s, Foster and Magdoff rely on data only from the United States, arbitrarily excluding the expansion of capitalism into other regions, especially Asia. In this case, they are at least more self-conscious about this selective use of data and argue that their focus on "almost exclusively on the development of the Global Financial Crisis within the context of the US economy" is justified since the "main contradictions of capitalism are still best perceived … from the standpoint of the preeminent capitalist economy at a given stage of its development" (2009: 21). But globalization has been a principal "escape route" for capital from the stagnation in the United Statea (Bello, 2009). Since the 1960s, US capital has exploited the revolution in information and communications technology, such as computers, satellites, and the internet, and transportation, such as containerization, large-capacity cargo shipping, and jet aircraft. This strategy of capital created an integrated system of global production and finance.

Moreover, capitalism expanded into "semi-capitalist, non-capitalist, or pre-capitalist areas" (Bello, 2009). According to James Petras and Henry Veltmeyer in *Globalization Unmasked*,

> for the greater part of the 20th century, substantial regions of the world were organized in a non-capitalist system, a form of collectivism, which did not operate within the capitalist mode of production. In the last decade, these areas have been incorporated and subordinated to the logic of capital accumulation. (2001: 39)

This geographic expansion of capitalism also greatly accelerated primitive accumulation, "a process in which millions have been wrenched from the means of production, proletarianized, and thrown into a global labor market shaped by transnational capital" (Robinson, 2008: 25). The result was not just a geographic expansion but also a demographic one, as indicated by the doubling of the global labor force from 1.46 billion workers in 1980 to 2.92 billion in 2006 as "workers from China, India and the former Soviet bloc entered the global labor pool" (Freeman, 2006: 1). Given that capitalism is defined by the exploitation of wage labor, this doubling of the wage labor force is one of the most significant developments in capitalism since the 1970s.

In addition, the imposition of neoliberalism through the Third World debt crisis also integrated the Global South into the global system of production and finance by "synchronizing" national policies under the International Monetary Fund (IMF)'s structural adjustment programs (SAPs) (Robinson, 2008: 27). The SAPs simultaneously "de-industrialized" the cities and "de-peasantized" the countryside in the Third World, contributing to the generation of an absolute surplus of labor (Araghi, 1995; Delgado and Marquéz, 2008: 1359). As Transnational Corporations

(TNCs) shifted industrial production to the periphery to exploit this surplus labor, they created a New International Division of Labor (NIDL), in which the periphery increasingly exported manufactured goods, and imported food from the center. This industrialization of the periphery "generally … along lines determined by global corporations centered in the advanced capitalist countries" (Foster and McChesney, 2009) makes an analysis of US data inadequate to the task of grasping the main contradictions of capitalism at this stage of development.

Moreover, Foster and Magdoff's justification for relying on US data since it represents the "preeminent capitalist economy" skirts a central issue of our time: for how long will the United States remain the "preeminent capitalist economy"? In short, Foster and Magdoff's decision to focus on stagnation solely in the United States ignores the world historic expansion of capitalism in China, possibly the most dynamic rise of capitalism in history (Li, 2008). In other words, similar to categorizing innovation, war, imperialism and financial crises as external to the logic of capitalism, they argue that the rise of a dynamic new center of capital accumulation in China is external to "main contradictions of capitalism in its current stage of development." It is not; it is impossible to grasp the main contradictions of capitalism in this era without understanding the role of the dynamic rise of China in them.

As argued above, the "great doubling" of the global working class, in which China has played a central role, is certainly internal to the logic of capitalism, contributing significantly to the main contradictions of capitalism in its current stage of development. The explosive productive investment, low real wages, and massive household savings in China contribute to the excess productive capacity, downward pressure on wages, and low interest rates in the US, which, in turn, also result in sluggish productive investment, stagnating real wages, and exploding household debt in the US, the focus of Foster and Magdoff's argument. It is hard to reconcile the Monopoly School's claim that capitalism has stagnated since the 1970s with the dynamic rise of capitalism in China and the dialectical nature of the uneven development of global capitalism.

The Neoliberal Expansion

Several scholars of Marxist political economy are based at York University in Toronto, Canada, including several editors and contributors of the annual *Socialist Register*. While these scholars have diverse analyses of global capitalism, they generally agree that the period since the structural crisis in the 1970s has been characterized by a dynamic expansion of capitalism, not stagnation. An early and key text of analysis of the current global capitalist crisis to come out of this school was David McNally's *Global Sump: The Economics and Politics of Crisis and Resistance*, which has a global perspective on developments in capitalism.

McNally describes the current crisis as a global slump since "the term is meant to capture a whole period of interconnected crises—the bursting of the real estate bubble; a wave of bank collapses; a series of sovereign debt crises; relapses into recession—that goes on for years without a sustained economic recovery" (McNally 2010: 8–9). That is, the financial crisis that kicked off on Wall Street is not a single crisis but a "mutating" one. Moreover, McNally strongly disagrees with scholars like Foster and Magdoff and Robert Brenner (2002), who characterize the neoliberal period as a period of "stagnation" or a "long downturn" (McNally, 2010: 36). Instead, he argues that the neoliberal restructuring of capitalism jumpstarted a new cycle of growth from 1982–97, producing a new center of capital accumulation in East Asia, particularly China. According to McNally, neoliberalism achieved this expansion principally by intensifying the exploitation of labor worldwide, attacking unions in the Global North, resubordinating national developmental states in the Global South, globalizing the production process through global commodity chains, expanding the global reserve army of labor, and reorganizing work with new information and communication technologies. While neoliberalism entailed "global turbulence," it boosted the rate of profit and sustained a capitalist expansion from 1982 to 1997 (McNally, 2010: 41).

McNally further argues that this neoliberal cycle of growth came to an end with the 1997 East Asian financial crisis, marking the "onset of new problems of overaccumulation" (41). These problems did not manifest themselves as a generalized global crisis in 1997 because "a decade long credit expansion delayed the day of reckoning" until the housing bubble burst in 2006–07 (41). In essence, McNally principally disagrees with the Foster and Magdoff over periodization, arguing that the neoliberal period of 1982–97 is characterized by expansion, not stagnation, but after 1997, the stagnation-financialization dynamic came into effect. After the East Asian financial crisis, a credit expansion inflated asset bubbles, which propped up effective demand through the "wealth effect," in which rising asset values increases consumer spending, as well as the explosion of consumer credit and household debt. This credit expansion after the Asian financial crisis postponed the inevitable global crisis, given global overcapacity, until 2007. In other words, McNally agrees with Foster and Magdoff that the current global crisis has structural roots in overproduction, and that stagnation-financialization dynamic temporarily resolved the realization problem, but that dynamic only dates back to 1997, not the 1970s. According to McNally, the neoliberal restructuring of capitalism generated an expansion from 1982–97, and then inflated asset prices and increasing household debt prevented a global crisis until 2007.

A Critique of McNally

From a global perspective, McNally's definition of the "Global Slump" as a series of interconnected crises from, for example, financial crises to sovereign debt crises, applies not just to the period since 2007, but over the entire neoliberal period since the 1970s. As David Harvey put it, "capitalism never solves its crisis problems; it just moves them around" (2010). The displacement of the overproduction crisis, that arose from the recovery of European and Japanese capital from their destruction during the Second World War, into the financial sector created a series of interconnected financial crises starting in the 1970s.

By arguing that the onset of the problems of over-accumulation started in 1997, rather than the late 1960s, and that a credit expansion prevented a "general" crisis only during the period from 1997 to 2007, not earlier, McNally demonstrates the same parochial perspective that he argues so strongly against, when, for example, he states that the "core capitalist countries are far from the full story of the global economy in our era," and that the world economy is "more than the sum of its largest parts" such as the United States, Germany, and Japan (McNally, 2010: 37). That is, McNally considers a crisis as "general" only when it is centered in the core capitalist countries, specifically on Wall Street with the bursting of the dot-com bubble in 2000 and the housing bubble in 2007. But from the perspective of the world economy, the neoliberal period was a general crisis, or, more precisely, a "mutating series of interconnected crises" that culminated in the global capitalist crisis since 2007.

Rather than arguing that financialization grew out the overproduction crisis that began in the late 1960s as Foster and Magdoff do, McNally locates the rise of financialization in Nixon's decision to "close the gold window" in 1971, ending the Bretton Woods agreement that guaranteed that the conversion of the dollar to gold at $35/ounce. He argues that the resulting "floating non-system" of exchange rates created an explosion of financial instruments as multinational corporations sought ways to hedge their exposure to exchange rate volatility. But here McNally confuses cause and effect. The end of Bretton Woods and the shift to floating exchange rates arose out of the structural pressures created by an overproduction crisis. The overproduction crisis caused the Nixon administration to close the gold window, and the demand for new financial instruments was driven as much by capital's search for speculative profits, since the overproduction crisis reduced profit rates in productive investment, as by the need to hedge against exchange rate volatility, as evident by the scale of foreign exchange trading as well as the explosion of financial innovation, creating financial instruments unrelated to foreign exchange.

With the end of the Second World War, US business interests feared the return of the Great Depression, because if high military spending ended then demand would collapse. The solution was to supply US dollars to European allies (and later Japan) so they could purchase US goods in their reconstruction and maintain demand for US production. The Bretton Woods agreement to peg the dollar to gold allowed this flow of US dollars without devaluing the dollar and hurting the reconstruction efforts. But once European and Japanese capital recovered from the destruction of the war and began to compete with US capital on the world market, the global economy faced an overproduction crisis, and the overvalued dollar created by the Bretton Woods agreement became a burden on US capital (Brenner, 2002).

To compete with their new industrial rivals, US capital either needed to impose an internal devaluation (i.e., cut labor costs) or devalue the dollar by closing the gold window. Given the strength of US labor and social movements in the 1960s, US capital could not afford a "frontal attack" on labor in the late 1960s and instead devalued the dollar, postponing such an attack until "stagflation" had weakened unions by the late 1970s (Arrighi, 2007: 130). According to Giovanni Arrighi, *Adam Smith in Beijing: Lineages of the Twenty-First Century*:

> at the end of the long postwar boom, the leverage of labor was sufficient to make any attempt to roll it back through a serious deflation far too risky in social and political terms ... An inflationary strategy ... promised to outflank workers' power far more effectively. It was, indeed, the great stagnation-cum-inflation of the 1970s—'stagflation,' ... that effectively wore down workers' power. (Arrighi, 2007: 130)

The stagflation of the 1970s, especially the related petrodollar recycling and the Third World debt crisis, captures the interconnectedness of the mutating series of crises that emerged out of the overproduction crisis that began in the late 1960s.

In order to maintain the dollar as the world's reserve currency after devaluing the dollar by closing the gold window, the Nixon administration proceeded to broker a secret deal with the Saudi monarchy and the Shah of Iran to raise the price of oil (Gowan, 1999). According to John Perkins in *The Secret History of the American Empire*, the US "corporatocracy" played an "active role in driving oil prices to these record highs. Although business and political leaders, including oil executives, feigned outrage, they were the puppet masters pulling the strings" (2008: 171). Since oil was only traded in dollars, the high price of oil forced central banks to hold more dollars in reserve, increasing the demand for dollars and substituting a dollar-gold standard with a dollar-oil standard that bolstered "dollar hegemony" (Perkins, 2007: 171). Given US domestic oil production, the spike in oil prices in 1973 gave US capital a relative, competitive advantage over European and Japanese capital at the time, undermined the wages of the working class in the US and placed US finance at the center of the global economy.

The Nixon administration's secret deal to raise the price of oil also included an agreement to recycle the surplus petrodollars, especially Saudi oil profits, into US banks. Perkins called this agreement the "Saudi Arabian money-laundering affair" (2007: 172). As a result, the US banks had surplus capital to invest, but, in the context of the overproduction crisis, they had few places to invest in expanded production. Instead, they turned to Third World governments, and pushed flexible rate loans onto them, as those governments sought to maintain their growth and path to development even as the global economy entered into crisis. According to Arthur MacEwan in *Debt and Disorder: International Economic Instability and U.S. Imperial Decline*, the overproduction in the capitalist center meant that:

> in the advanced capitalist countries, the demand for credit did not keep pace with the burgeoning supply of funds. Faced with a rapid expansion of liquidity that

> could not be absorbed in the center, the banks began to push funds out into the periphery of world capitalism. (1991: 61)

Since petrodollars were not invested in production in the US, but instead recycled to Third World governments, the result was slower job growth and higher unemployment in the US, putting immense pressure on unions in the US. The higher oil prices of the 1970s also undermined union wages as their contracts failed to keep pace with rising prices. The stage was set for a frontal attack on labor.

The dramatic rise in US interest rates, known as the "Volcker Shock" after the US Federal Reserve Chairman Paul Volcker, served not only to generate high unemployment and break the power of US labor, but also resubordinated many Third World governments by provoking a sovereign debt crisis, known at the time as the Third World debt crisis (Bello, 2006). These governments faced a scissors' crisis as they saw their debt service payments skyrocket on the flexible interest rate loans that they had received from US banks during the petrodollar recycling, and their export markets collapsed due to the recession provoked by the same high interest rates. Much like the current wave of sovereign debt crises is being used to impose austerity in countries like Greece, the Third World debt crisis served as the mechanism to impose austerity through the IMF's neoliberal Structural Adjustment Programs (SAPs). These SAPs represented an attempt to overcome the barrier to capital by destroying the national capital of Third World developmental states. Needless to say, the Asian tigers (South Korea, Taiwan, Singapore, and Hong Kong) and China escaped this neoliberal destruction.

To call the imposition of neoliberal austerity and destruction of national capital in the Third World through SAPs a "neoliberal expansion" fundamentally mischaracterizes the nature of the process, because, in fact, the capitalist expansion in the neoliberal era occurred specifically in countries and regions, which avoided the imposition of neoliberalism through the Third World debt crisis (for some, at least until 1997). South Korea, Taiwan, Singapore, Hong Kong, and China did not follow neoliberal programs, and, instead, used state intervention and infant industry protection to develop an industrial base, contradicting neoliberalism's "free trade" policies (Chang, 2002). In economies where the IMF imposed SAPs, neoliberalism destroyed national capital and re-articulated their productive apparatuses to serve the needs of transnational production (Delgado-Wise and Márquez-Covarrubias, 2008). Such destruction of national capital and re-articulation of the productive apparatus is not captured by the phrase "neoliberal expansion," but rather is obscured by it.

By attributing the rise of financialization to the volatility of the exchange rates after the closing of the gold window, McNally ignores the displacement of the overproduction crisis onto the Third World through the SAPs. Instead of focusing on the impact of SAPs throughout most of the Third World, McNally narrowly focuses on the rise of new centers of capital accumulation in East Asia to justify the term "expansion," that is, the expansion occurred in countries that specifically avoided the imposition of neoliberalism. Where the term "neoliberalism" did apply, particularly, in Africa and Latin America, the term neoliberal "destruction" or "crisis" better captures the process, not expansion. By confusing the symptoms, floating exchange rates and inflation, with the disease, the overproduction crisis, McNally can then argue that neoliberalism "cured" the disease with the Volcker Shock of high interest rates, which reduced inflation, broke the power of labor, resubordinated the Third World, and spurred a "neoliberal expansion" in East Asia. But if the disease was an over-accumulation of capital, causing an overproduction crisis, then neoliberalism represented a shift of the burden of "adjustment" (i.e., the destruction of capital) onto the Third World through SAPs. The "expansion" occurred in countries which avoided this "destruction." Mirroring the mistake made by Foster and Magdoff when they generalize stagnation from the US to the global economy, McNally generalizes the capitalist expansion from East Asia to the whole world. Both mistakes are rooted in the failure to recognize the dialectical nature of the uneven development of capitalism on a global scale where stagnation and expansion, not only coexist, but they feed off each other.

McNally's conflation of symptom and disease also leads to an inaccurate periodization of financialization. While the 1971 closing of the gold window certainly contributed to financialization, financialization actually began with the creation of the Eurodollar market in the late 1960s, which enabled multinational corporations to deposit their dollar profits in banks in Europe, since the overproduction crisis meant that few profitable investments remained in the United States. Instead, these corporations chose to hold their profits in liquid dollar accounts in search of speculative profits. Thus, the closing of the gold window and the ensuing volatility in foreign exchange markets provided just such an opportunity to make speculative profits with new financial instruments, unleashing the financialization juggernaut.

In addition, while the Volcker Shock triggered the Third World debt crisis and the imposition of neoliberalism, it certainly did not mark an end of financialization, but instead demonstrated expanding role of financial crises in the destruction of capital under conditions of overproduction. As a result, the neoliberal era is punctuated by a series of financial crises that continues today. To name just a few: the Third World debt crisis, the 1987 stock market crash, the late 1980s US savings and loan crisis, the 1992 pound sterling crisis, the 1994 Mexican peso crisis, the 1997 East Asian financial crisis (principally Thailand, Indonesia, South Korea, and the Philippines), the 1998 Brazil/Russia/Long Term Capital Management crisis, the 2000–2001 dot-com crisis, the 2001 Argentine crisis, and the continuing 2007 "Global Slump." Over this same period, debt (government, corporate, and household) has also exploded in the United States. Thus, contrary to McNally's claims, the ascendency of finance and expansion of debt as the engine of growth began in the 1970s, not post-East Asian financial crisis. In fact, the East Asian financial crisis of 1997 resulted from a speculative bubble and crisis, indicating that it just one more data point in a trajectory of financialization and financial crises reaching back to the 1970s, rather than a turning point from a "neoliberal expansion" to debt-fueled growth.

The 1997 East Asian financial crisis also did not mark the end of the "neoliberal expansion" from 1982 to 1997, since that expansion depended principally on the rise of a new dynamic center of capital accumulation in China, which did not fall victim to the East Asian financial crisis, nor did it stop growing after that crisis. The rise of China neither began in 1982, nor ended in 1997. It started in 1978 and continued with an average annual growth rate near 10 percent until the onset of the global slump in 2008, but Chinese growth continues in the 7 to 9 percent range, significantly higher than core capitalist countries. Given this trajectory of Chinese growth, it does not make sense to date the "neoliberal expansion" from 1982 and ending in 1997, since the neoliberal expansion depended on capital accumulation in China, which began in 1978 and continues until today.

The contrast between the stagnation of capitalism in the United States and its expansion in China signals a hegemonic transition in the center of capital accumulation. According to Arrighi: "if past tendencies are any guide to the present and the future, we could expect that the financial expansion would temporarily restore the fortunes of the leading capitalist agency of the epoch, the United States, but would eventually result in a change of leadership in the center of capital accumulation on a world scale" to China (Arrighi, 2010: 371). The dialectical nature of the uneven development of capitalism manifests in the stagnation of capitalism in the United States and its expansion in China, as well as in the financialization and industrialization of their respective economies.

The Falling Rate of Profit

Debates within Marxist economics have focused on Marx's labor theory of value, and, consequently, the generation of surplus in the production process. These scholars have developed mathematical models to apply these concepts, much like neo-classical and neo-Keynesian economists have done with classical and Keynesian concepts. A leading Marxist economist, Andrew Kliman, has written *The Failure of Capitalist Production: Underlying Causes of the Great Recession*, to apply these concepts and models to the current global capitalist crisis. In that book, he takes a similar approach as Foster and Magdoff in that he examines only US data to argue that the global economy never recovered from the overproduction crisis of the late 1960s. In particular, Kliman argues that Marx's law of the tendency for the rate of profit to fall provides the best explanation for the current crisis since the Wall Street financial crisis turned into the "great recession" as result of the underlying weakness of the productive economy which the financial crisis exposed (Kliman, 2012: 24).

The tendency for profit rates to fall derives from Marx's idea that "the real barrier to capitalist production is capital itself" (Foster and Magdoff, 2009: 20). As capital accumulates and productivity increases, less labor is needed to produce commodities, but this undermines profit rates since the living labor (versus dead labor of capital machinery) is the ultimate source of surplus value. The only way to counter this tendency is through the destruction of capital (either financially or physically) to reboot the process of accumulation and, consequently, restore high profit rates.

Kliman argues that, since the Great Depression, the capitalist class has feared the precipitous fall in the rate of profit and the radicalization of the working class that occurred in that period, so, instead, capital has pushed state managers to use fiscal and monetary interventions to "prevent full-scale destruction of capital value" (3). While ignoring the destruction of capital in the Third World through SAPs, Kliman argues that the failure to destroy enough capital since the onset of the overproduction crisis in the 1970s has caused profit rates to fall. That is, the lack of destruction of capital due to state intervention has created the condition in which employment has increased too slowly in relation to the accumulated capital in the United States, leading to a falling rate of profit. Kliman claims that while he is "not an advocate for full-scale destruction of capital," like the Great Depression, but it would, from his perspective, increase the rate of profit (Kliman, 2012: 201).

Kliman delves into a dense technical explanation of how he came to the conclusion that profit rates have persistently fallen since the 1970s. This conclusion is in direct contradiction of McNally, who argued that the neoliberal restructuring of capitalism since the 1970s restored profitability from 1982 to 1997. This difference arises principally in how Kliman determines the rate of profit. He uses historical cost rather than current cost to value fixed investments in the corporate sector and measure profits (that is, fixed investments are valued at their original cost, not their current depreciated value). By taking such an approach, the increased profits used by McNally and others to claim that there was a neoliberal expansion from 1982 to 1997 disappear. Moreover, Kliman argues that, logically, if profit rates were high during the neoliberal period that that would have spurred productive investment, but, instead, the historical record demonstrates sluggish investment in the US economy during the neoliberal era (Kliman, 2012: 165). Countering McNally, he concludes that profit rates and "the economy never fully recovered from the slump of the 1970s" (Kliman, 2012: 24).

But this is where Kliman's reliance on US data gets his argument into trouble. By the same logic that he applies to the US above, fixed investments in the Chinese economy must earn high rates of profit, since such investments have exploded in China over the last 30 years. Kliman claims to account for this investment through an analysis of profits reported by US corporations on their foreign direct investments and concludes that they still adhere to his conclusion that rates of profit have fallen (Kliman, 2012: 190). The problem with Kliman's approach is two-fold: 1) US multinationals are notorious for hiding their profits in offshore tax havens, which renders any analysis of their reported profits from foreign direct investments meaningless (Shaxson, 2011); and 2) the new center of capital accumulation in China is global in nature, that is, while US capital invests there, so does Japanese, Taiwanese, Korean and, of course, Chinese, so their profits are not captured by looking at US corporate FDI data. Kliman argues that the "key pillars of [China's] success" are the following: "alienated labor, sweatshop conditions, mass unemployment, repression, and poverty-level wages" (190). While this sounds like a living nightmare for workers, it apparently is capital's dream come true, given the massive amount of investment attracted to China. That attraction is high rates of profit.

Like Foster and Magdoff, Kliman claims that the current global capitalist crisis exposed the underlying weakness of the productive economy, dating back to the overproduction crisis arising in the late 1960s. And like Foster and Magdoff, he relied exclusively US data to conclude that capitalism has stagnated since the 1970s. By relying on US data, both miss the dialectical nature of the uneven development of capitalism, as evidenced by the dynamic rise of a new center of capital accumulation in China over that period. In short, profit rates and productive investment in the US may have stagnated over the last 40 years, but that ignores the historic expansion of capitalism on a global scale with growing productive investment and profit rates in Asia, centered in China.

Regardless of Kliman's agreement with Foster and Magdoff on the broader issues, he attacks the Monopoly Capital school and their "under-consumptionist alternative" (e.g. at one point, he compares the Monopoly Capital school to a "religious cult"). While he agrees with Foster and Magdoff that debt expansion artificially boosted profitability and growth, leading to repeated financial bubbles and crashes during the neoliberal era, he rejects their assumption that real wages have stagnated over that period leading to a realization problem as productivity grew. Instead, he claims that "US workers are paid more now, in inflation-adjusted terms, than they were just a few decades ago," if total compensation is included (Kliman, 2012: 12). That is, while "wages and salaries *in the narrow sense* have not risen markedly" (emphasis in original), total compensation as share of national income has not declined due to the costs of employer-provided health care and retirement, and state-funded Social Security and Medicare (Kliman, 2012: 124). In short, the exploding costs of (principally) healthcare and pensions, in the context of the leveling of real wages in the US, have resulted not in higher profit rates, but a shift from "wages to other forms of employee compensation" (124). Kliman argues that stagnating real wages have not lead to an increased rate of profit because total compensation continued to rise.

That argument is difficult one to make since the burden of healthcare and pensions in the United States have been shifted onto the workers through 401K pension plans, higher health insurance deductibles and co-pays, which require ever greater contributions from workers, as fewer workers even have access to these programs. Moreover, the Social Security and Medicare are funded by regressive payroll taxes imposed on workers, and their benefits are being cut. In contrast, Foster and Magdoff use the evidence of stagnating real wages, excluding pensions and healthcare, to claim that worker's effective demand has increased through the expansion of household debt. Given that healthcare and pension benefits do not affect current purchasing power, focusing on real wages rather than total compensation, as a measure of effective demand makes sense. If real wages and productive investment both stagnated in the United States at the same time, then it perhaps indicates that the surplus capital, extracted from labor as their productivity increased but their wages did not, was invested in expanded production abroad, particularly in China (as McNally argues), or in financial speculation (as Foster and Magdoff argue), or both. The dialectical nature of the uneven development of capitalism would suggest that falling rates of profit in the US corporate sector would lead to a shift in investment to where profits are higher, be that industrial production in China or speculative financial instruments on Wall Street. Given the expansion of both the industrialization in China and the financialization in the United States, the empirical evidence leads to the conclusion that that was what simultaneously occurred.

Falling rates of profit in the US corporate sector since the 1970s is not the result of rising total compensation for workers but from overproduction crisis caused by the rise of competing capitals and the increasing barrier to capitalist production, capital itself. US capital responded to this crisis by shifting investment into production abroad and into financial speculation. To argue that rates of profit have fallen in the US does not require the ancillary argument of increasing total compensation for workers. In the context of the dialectical nature of the uneven development of global capitalism, the surplus value generated by stagnating wages and rising productivity was re-invested in the globalization of the production and in financial innovation for speculative profits.

Kliman also argues that "permanent state intervention" since the Great Depression saved capitalism from itself, but at the same time prevented the destruction of capital necessary to restart the accumulation process and restore profitability. But, to make this argument, Kliman treats all state interventions as equal, as if the legalization of unions and the creation of social security and unemployment insurance are the same as the troubled asset relief program, quantitative easing, and pumping trillions of dollars into the financial sector through various Federal Reserve lending facilities. That is, Kliman misses the dynamics of class power inherent in these state interventions. Moreover, while the Great Depression destroyed capital, it took demand creation through unionization, the creation of a welfare state, and an explosion of military spending, as well as the physical destruction of rival capitals through war, to jumpstart growth and restore profitability after the Great Depression. When the recovery of German and Japanese capital created the conditions of an overproduction crisis, the capitalist class did not set about to "solve" the crisis through demand creation, but instead reoriented state intervention to increase the rate of exploitation of workers by busting unions and cutting social programs. This outcome represented the correlation of class forces after weakening labor, first through McCarthyism, then through stagflation, and then ultimately through the state attack on labor rights as epitomized by Reagan's firing of the air traffic controllers in 1981. That is, state intervention has a distinctively different class flavor during the Great Depression and the crisis since the 1970s. Conflating the state interventions in the 1930s with the ones since the 1970s under the rubric of "permanent state interventions" and failing to distinguish between state interventions that support workers from those that attack them obscures their distinct class nature and reflection of class power. Rather than demand creation, neoliberal state interventions were geared toward increasing the rate of exploitation of workers and destroying capital, particularly in the Global South, to restart the accumulation process. If these neoliberal state interventions failed to destroy enough capital or reduce social wages enough, as Kliman asserts, then it certainly was not from a lack of trying.

These neoliberal state interventions did succeed in increasing the rate of exploitation in the US, and the surplus was absorbed abroad in a "spatio-temporal fix" in China, while demand in the US was propped up by asset bubbles and consumer credit. Also, the neoliberal state interventions destroyed capital where neoliberalism was successfully imposed but where it was not, state interventions sparked a capitalist expansion and high rates of profit (i.e., China) (Harvey, 2003). Some state interventions have destroyed capital in some places and created capitalist expansions. Just as stagnating real wages and the falling rate of profit in the United States are not mutually exclusive in a global economy, given the uneven development of capitalism, so are state interventions and rising rates of profit not mutually exclusive. The state interventions in the golden age of capitalism from the 1950s to the late 1960s supported high profit rates just as the state interventions in China, such as capital controls, technology transfer, infrastructure and education investments, have supported a world-historic capitalist expansion there. To make his argument that permanent state interventions have prevented the destruction of capital, leading to a falling rate of profit, Kliman ignores the history and class nature of these interventions, and the role of state interventions in creating the conditions for capitalist expansion.

Financialization

In contrast to Kliman, the Social Structure of Accumulation (SSA) School argues that state institutions and interventions are critical to creating stable investment climate for the capital accumulation process to occur. The SSA school attempts to explain "alternating periods of growth and stagnation in capitalist history in terms of new stages of capitalism and their subsequent crises" (McDonough, Reich and Kotz, 2010: 2). So neither the external stimuli of technological innovations, military spending, the sales effort, and speculative finance, as Foster and Magdoff argued, nor the full-scale destruction of capital, as argued by Kliman, are enough to restore profitability and jumpstart the capital accumulation process. Instead, a set of institutions in the broad sense are necessary to channel class conflict and create stable investment climate. According to Victor Lippit, "Capitalists or enterprises require attractive profit rates to invest, but they must also have a high degree of confidence in their expected investment outcomes, a confidence that can be ensured only by a set of institutions that is both stable and favorable. The set of institutions that favors investment is the 'social structure of accumulation,' or SSA" (Lippit, 2010: 46). For instance, the Keynesian SSA grew out the Great

Depression, and the Neoliberal SSA grew out of the stagflation of the 1970s. The contemporary SSA is characterized not only by neoliberalism, but also by globalization and financialization.

William K. Tabb, a leading scholar in the SSA school, argues that "financialization is the central feature of the contemporary social structure of accumulation, that the Anglo-American model of capitalism has grown dependent on financial innovation as a major, if not the, major source of economic growth, and that financialization has dramatically changed the way capitalist production is organized and imparts a systematic risk of great significance" (Tabb, 2010: 149). Given this central role of financialization in the contemporary SSA and the accumulation process, Tabb dedicated a whole book, The *Restructuring of Capitalism in Our Time* (originally titled, *Financialization: The Appropriations of Finance and the Restructuring of Capitalism in Our Time*) to explain the shadow banking system, hedge funds, private equity firms, over-the-counter derivatives, credit default swaps, collateral debt obligation, special investment vehicles and the like. These myriad of financial instruments and institutions are increasingly relevant to an understanding of the dynamics of capitalism at its current stage of development. As mentioned earlier, finance capital has played an increasing role in solving the realization problem through debt expansion, funding the globalization of production, opening up new speculative opportunities through financial innovation, and the devaluation of capital through financial crises.

That latter role has special significance within the context of Kliman's argument that the stagflation crisis and the rise of neoliberalism did not destroy as much capital as the Great Depression and the Second World War, and therefore failed to restart the accumulation process. According to David Harvey, the destruction of capital is precisely the role of the serial financial crises of the neoliberal era have played: they create "vast fields for the absorption of surplus capitals" through the "release of low-cost assets" and provide a "means to visit the costs of the devaluation of surplus capitals on the weakest and most vulnerable territories and populations" (Harvey, 2003: 185). Thus, while the roller coaster of speculative bubbles and crises spells social disaster for the majority of workers, the crises financially destroy capital value and open up new investment opportunities for capital, jumpstarting the capital accumulation process. In this way, financial crises also channel class conflict through the medium of debt. When speculative asset bubbles inevitably burst, then the wealth effect goes in reverse and debt-burdened consumers have to pay down their debts, creating a realization crisis for industrial producers. In turn, they cut production and generate high unemployment. High unemployment reduces tax revenues, as the unemployed stop paying taxes, while the demand for state support increases, as the unemployed need unemployment insurance and other forms of state support. The result is that a financial crisis is transformed into a fiscal, or "sovereign debt," crisis of the state. Then, given the structure of class power, capital uses the fiscal crisis to attack the social wage, increasing the desperation of workers, and thus raising the rate of labor exploitation.

The state interventions in the form of bailouts for the financial sector support this accumulation process while not addressing the underlying causes of the stagnation of capitalist production, and reinforce the domination of finance capital as it becomes ever more concentrated, ever more volatile, and ever more a profit center for capital. In the Great Depression, the Keynesian state intervened in support of workers through public works programs, unemployment insurance and social security, in order "save capitalism from itself" (Kliman, 2012: 185). In the current crisis, the state intervened to support finance capital in order to save finance capitalism from itself. In the "Myths of Neoliberal Deregulation," Leo Panitch and Martijn Konings describe this shift as follows: "Washington's highly pro-active role in containing domestic and international financial crises from the 1980s on was perhaps the most concrete demonstration that the alleged withdrawal of states from markets was an ideological illusion. Financialization enlarged the American state's role both directly and multilaterally, even as it extended the strategic leeway available to capital" (2009: 72). Using this "strategic leeway," finance capital inflates speculative bubbles, and then uses the inevitable financial crises to devalue capital so that assets can be "bought up at fire-sale prices and profitably recycled back into circulation" (Harvey, 2003: 150). Financial speculation and crisis are the mode of accumulation under finance capital as they have "emerged as a primary means by which capitalism perpetually creates its own 'other' in order to feed upon it" (Harvey, 2003: 151).

Moreover, this roller coaster ride of speculative bubbles and financial crises of finance capital is unlikely to end soon. In 2010, Simon Johnson, a former chief economist at the International Monetary Fund, argued that, in the current crisis, "the US financial sector received an unconditional bailout—and is not now facing any kind of meaningful re-regulation. We are setting ourselves up, without question, for another boom based on excessive and reckless risk-taking at the heart of the world's financial system. This can end only one way: badly" (2010). The social structure of accumulation school emphasizes the role of institutions in mediating class conflict to provide a stable investment climate for capital. But, under financialization, capitalism has entered a new stage where capital makes speculative profits from instability and volatility, and state interventions encourage this instability and volatility by providing finance capital with deregulation, bailouts and easy credit. Therefore, the SSA school's emphasis on stability is misguided when finance capital seeks instability and volatility, and financial crises intensify class conflict as the resulting high unemployment and fiscal crises are used as a weapon by capital to attack the workers' real and social wages. Capitalism has increasingly become more unstable as it undermines not only its social basis but its ecological one evident in the ongoing global climate disruption, leaving humanity once again to face the choice: socialism or barbarism? Unfortunately, given the dialectical nature of the uneven development of capitalism on a global scale, the descent into barbarism will be profitable for finance capital—at least until they are confronted by a global working class that is class-conscious, internationally-organized, and powerful enough to take action to advance its own class interests on a global scale.

Conclusion

Foster and Magdoff's argument that monopoly capitalism stagnated since the 1970s missed the dynamic rise of a new center of accumulation in China. McNally's argument that the rise of China represented a neoliberal expansion missed the neoliberal destruction in most of the rest of the Third World under IMF Structural Adjustment Programs. Kliman's argument that state intervention prevented the destruction of capital to restart the accumulation process missed state intervention that destroyed capital under SAPs and created the capital expansion in Asia. Tabb's focus on financialization missed finance capital's role in overcoming "the real barrier to capitalist production" of capital itself by devaluing capital through financial crises. That is, while individually these books miss the dialectical nature of the uneven development of capitalism, taken together they provide a comprehensive analysis of the main contradictions of capitalism in the current global crisis. Stagnation and expansion, overproduction and financialization all coexist due to the uneven development of global capitalism in a never-ending "dance of the dialectic" (Ollman, 2003).

References

Araghi, Farshad. 1995. "Global Depeasantization, 1945–1990." *The Sociological Quarterly*, 36(2), 337–368.

Arrighi, Giovanni. 2007. *Adam Smith in Beijing: Lineages of the Twenty-First Century*. New York: Verso.

Baker, Dean. 2009. *Plunder and Blunder: The Rise and Fall of the Bubble Economy.* New York: Berrett-Koehler Publishers.

Bello, Walden. 2006. "The Capitalist Conjuncture: Overaccumulation, Financial Crises, and the Retreat from Globalization." *Third World Quarterly*, 27(8), 1345–1367.

Bello, Walden. 2009. "The Global Collapse: A Non-orthodox View." *MRZine*, February 20. Retrieved from http://www.monthlyreview.org/mrzine/bello200209.html.

Brenner, Robert. 2002. *The Boom and the Bubble: The U.S. in the World Economy*. NewYork: Verso.

Chang, Ha-Joon. 2002. *Kicking Away the Ladder: Development Strategy in Historical Perspective*. New York: Anthem Press.

Delgado-Wise, Raul and Márquez-Covarrubias, Humberto 2008. "Capital Restructuring, Development and Labour Migration: The Mexico–US Case." *Third World Quarterly*, 29(7), 1359–1374.

Foster, John Bellamy. 2010. "The Age of Monopoly-Finance Capital." *Monthly Review*, February. Retrieved from http://monthlyreview.org/2010/02/01/the-age-of-monopoly-finance-capital.

Foster, John Bellamy and Holleman, Hannah. 2010. "The Financial Power Elite." *Monthly Review*, May. Retrieved from http://monthlyreview.org/100501foster-holleman.php.

Foster, John Bellamy and Magdoff, Fred 2009. *The Great Financial Crisis*. New York: Monthly Review Press.

Freeman, Richard. 2006. "The Great Doubling: The Challenge of the New Global Labor Market." Retrieved from http://emlab.berkeley.edu/users/webfac/eichengreen/e183_sp07/great_doub.pdf.

Gowan, Peter. 1999. *The Global Gamble: Washington's Faustian Bid for World Dominance*. New York: Verso.

Harvey, David. 2003. "The 'New Imperialism': Accumulation by Dispossession." In Leo Panitch and Colin Leys (eds), *The Socialist Register 2004: The New Imperial Challenge* (pp. 63–87). London: Merlin Press.

Harvey, David. 2010. "The Crises of Capitalism." A Keynote Lecture given to the Royal Society for the Encouragement of Arts, Manufactures and Commerce (RSA). London (April 26). Retrieved from http://www.thersa.org/events/vision/vision-videos/david-harvey-the-crises-of-capitalism.

Johnson, Simon. 2010. "Creating the Next Crisis." *Project Syndicate*, June 15. Retrieved from http://www.project-syndicate.org/commentary/johnson9/English.

Kliman, Andrew. 2012. *The Failure of Capitalist Production: Underlying Causes of the Great Recession.* New York: Pluto Press.

Li, Minqi. 2008. *The Rise of China and the Demise of the Capitalist World Economy*. New York: Monthly Review Press.

Lippit, Victor. 2010. "Social Structure of Accumulation Theory." In T. McDonough, M. Reich and D. Kotz (eds), *Contemporary Capitalism and its Crises: Social Structure of Accumulation Theory for the 21st Century*. New York: Cambridge University Press.

MacEwan, Arthur. 1991. *Debt and Disorder: International Economic Instability and U.S. Imperial Decline*. Monthly Review Press: New York.

McDonough, T., Reich, M. and Kotz, D. 2010. "Introduction: Social Structure of Accumulation Theory for the 21st Century." In T. McDonough, M. Reich and D. Kotz (eds), *Contemporary Capitalism and its Crises: Social Structure of Accumulation Theory for the 21st Century*. New York: Cambridge University Press.

McNally, David. 2010. *Global Sump: The Economics and Politics of Crisis and Resistance*. Oakland, CA: PM Press.

Ollman, Bertell. 2003. *Dance of the Dialectic: Steps in Marx's Method.* Champaign, IL: University of Illinois Press.

Panitch, Leo and Konings, Martijn. 2009. "Myths of Neoliberal Deregulation." *New Left Review*, 57, May–June (pp. 67–83). Retrieved from http://www.newleftreview.org//?view=2781.

Perkins, John. 2008. *The Secret History of the American Empire: The Truth About Economic Hit Men, Jackals, and How to Change the World.* New York: Dutton.

Petras, James and Veltmeyer, Henry. 2001. *Globalization Unmasked: Imperialism in the 21st Century.* Halifax, NS: Fernwood Publishing.

Phillips, Kevin. 2008. *Bad Money: Reckless Finance, Failed Politics, and the Global Crisis of American Capitalism.* New York: Viking Press.

Rajan, Raghuram. 2010. "Let Them Eat Credit: How Inequality is at the Root of the Great Recession." *The New Republic*, August 27. Retrieved from http://faculty.chicagobooth.edu/raghuram.rajan/research/articles_files/Let%20them%20eat%20credit%20new%20republic.pdf.

Robinson, William I. 2008. *Latin America and Global Capitalism: A Critical Globalization Perspective.* Baltimore: Johns Hopkins University Press.

Shaxson, Nicholas. 2011. *Treasure Islands: Uncovering the Damage of Offshore Banking and Tax Havens.* New York: Palgrave Macmillan.

Tabb, William. 2010. "Financialization in the Contemporary Social Structure of Accumulation." In T. McDonough, M. Reich and D. Kotz (eds), *Contemporary Capitalism and its Crises: Social Structure of Accumulation Theory for the 21st Century*. New York: Cambridge University Press.

Tabb, William. 2012. *The Restructuring of Capitalism in Our Time*. New York: Columbia University Press.

Wade, Robert and Veneroso, Frank. 1998. "The Asian Crisis: The High Debt Model vs. The Wall Street-Treasury-IMF Complex." *New Left Review* (March–April), 3–23.

Chapter 2
The Global Capitalist Crisis: Its Origins, Dynamics and Impact on the United States

Berch Berberoglu

Introduction

The global capitalist crisis of 2008–09, which continues to unfold in varying degrees across many regions of the world economy as of mid-2014, has had (and continues to have) a devastating effect on millions of working people around the world, while a small minority of wealthy capitalists have profited from the downfall of their economies, bringing to bear their monopoly power over the means of production and destruction through speculative financial misdeeds and military misadventures that have bankrupted their rivals (corporations and countries alike) in their imperial overreach to dominate and pillage the world. They have done this under the cloak of neoliberalism and neoliberal economic policies that promote privatization, "free trade," and foreign investment that have led to the outsourcing of production and jobs—policies that states controlled by capital have championed as a the solution to all their economic problems.

As these misguided neoliberal economic policies have come under mounting criticism and attack in many countries across the world, and as the global capitalist crisis has taken on depression-era characteristics, neoliberalism and neoliberal economic policies have now become thoroughly discredited in countries affected by these policies around the globe. Whereas millions of unemployed people have been looking for a job to pay for basic necessities, governments throughout the world have been spending hundreds of billions of tax dollars to bail out failed commercial and financial institutions, with more than a trillion dollars of economic stimulus program by the United States government alone and several hundreds of billions of dollars by other governments in Europe, China, and elsewhere have been spent to counter the devastating effects of this corrupt system to save the global economy from total collapse (Berberoglu, 2012).

The severity of the 2008–09 global capitalist crisis and its magnitude have led analysts to conclude that this most recent crisis of global capitalism can certainly be classified as the worst and deepest economic downturn and collapse since the Great Depression of the early twentieth century—a predicament that has had, and will continue to have, serious economic, political, and social consequences for years to come. The capitalist state, finding itself in the midst of an economic crisis that is the product of a system it has long supported and cultivated through the protection of private profit at public expense, has found that the heaviest burden of this great economic catastrophe has fallen on its shoulders to resolve. It is in this context that the state has gone to great lengths to bail out failed corporations and financial institutions through the use of the public purse to save the global capitalist system from total destruction—one that came very close to implode through its own misdeeds.

Despite the active role of the state in intervening in the economy to reverse its decline and collapse, corporations and banks, ranging from General Motors and Chrysler to Citigroup and Bank of America, as well as financial and brokerage firms, insurance companies, and real estate underwriters, such as Lehman Brothers, American Insurance Group (AIG), Fannie Mae, and Freddie Mack, have come to a virtual halt, with some declaring bankruptcy, while others threatening to take down with them the entire global capitalist economy (Chossudovsky and Marshall 2010; Sherman 2010). As a result, and with a ripple effect across the US economy, the DOW plunged more than 50 percent from its highs of 14,000 in late 2007 to below 6,500 in early 2009, with more than a trillion dollars of value lost in the stock market—a development that has shaken markets across the globe and resulted in similar losses in stock markets throughout the capitalist world. Although the Dow rose to above 15,000 a little over four years after its worst decline, and hit 17,000 as we move through the seventh year of the crisis in mid-2014, the continuing slump in the eurozone threatens to make things worse, thus derailing any sustained recovery for the foreseeable future. Clearly, the global economy is going through its deepest crisis since the Great Depression of 1929, and this signals serious challenges for global capital over the next decade, especially for the United States (Filger 2010). The best example of this impact and what is in store for us over the next few years, is what has been happening with the sovereign debt crisis in Greece, Portugal, Spain, Ireland, And Italy, as well as the United States (and with what has happened to the once-powerful icons of US big business—General Motors, AIG, Citigroup, and other big corporations and banks).

Let us take a closer look at six of these major US corporate and financial institutions to assess the magnitude of the damage. Figure 2.1 documents the dramatic collapse of the once-powerful financial icon of Wall Street, Lehman Brothers brokerage house, which triggered the panic that, compounded by the enormous housing bubble, led to the banking and financial crisis that resulted in the Great Recession of 2008–09. Although it was officially announced that the recession had actually started in December of 2007, the sharp fall in the stock market, led by the financials, banks, and key industrial corporations, such as General Motors, which declared bankruptcy in June 2009 (see Figure 2.2 for the collapse and liquidation of General Motors, whose stock stopped trading in March 2011 at the level of 4 cents per share), the period 2008–09 marked the beginning of the Great Recession that has been continuing across the globe to this day.

Figure 2.3 shows one dimension of the collapse of the banking system in 2008–09 in what happened to the Citigroup, which went from a $55 stock to one that traded for 96 cents in February 2009, before it went up some to the $2.80 level

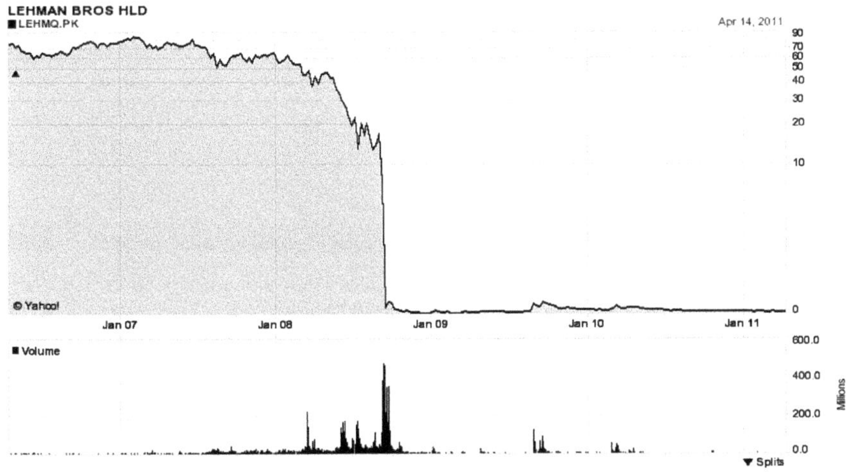

Figure 2.1 Lehman Brothers stock, 2006–11 (in dollars and volume traded)

Source: Yahoo Finance http://finance.yahoo.com retrieved April 14, 2011.

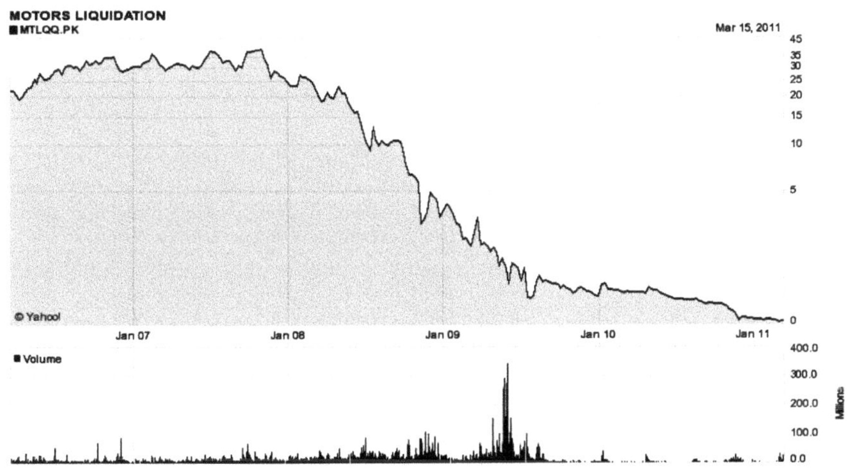

Figure 2.2 General Motors Corporation stock, 2006–11 (in dollars and volume traded)

Source: Yahoo Finance http://finance.yahoo.com retrieved March 15, 2011.

(adjusted for a 1-for-10 reverse stock split in May 2011 that artificially made it a $28 stock in August 2011), which in April 2013 was trading at $45 per share (equivalent to $4.50 before the reverse split). Looking at Citigroup in long-term perspective, and situating its fall in broader context since the 1980s, Figure 2.3a shows its dramatic rise from the mid-1990s through the 2000s (to 2007), followed by its collapse in 2008–09 from which it has not been able to recover as of this writing in mid-2013.

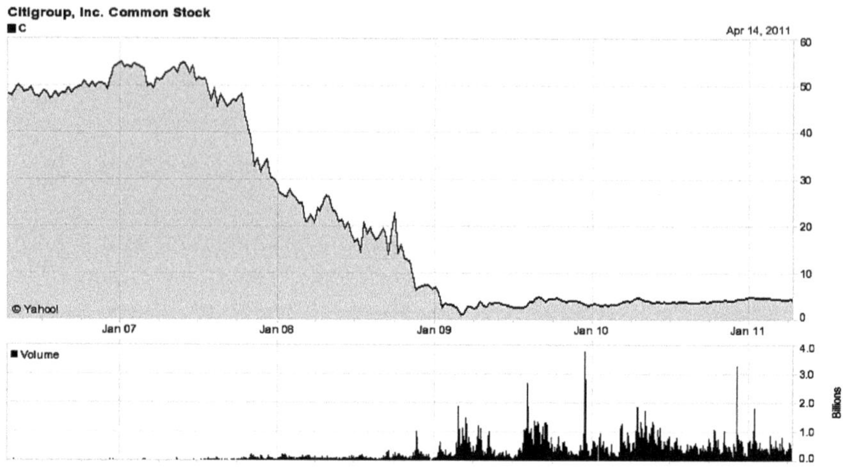

Figure 2.3 Citigroup, Inc. stock 2006–11 (in dollars and volume)
Source: Yahoo Finance http://finance.yahoo.com retrieved April 14, 2011.

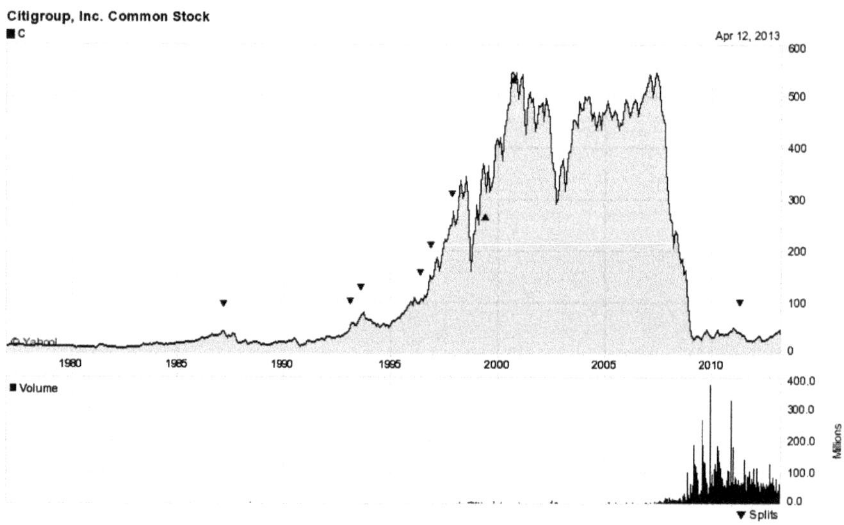

Figure 2.3a Citigroup Inc. stock, 1977–2013 (in dollars and volume)
Source: Yahoo Finance http://finance.yahoo.com retrieved April 12, 2013.

The predicament of the American International Group (AIG) was even more dramatic (see Figure 2.4). The once-giant global insurance company went through a near-collapse, with its stock price crashing from nearly $1,500 a share in mid-2007 down to $63 a share in October 2008. The company was able to avoid bankruptcy through massive government loans and bailout to prevent a meltdown of the entire US economy. Here was a stock which traded at $1,971 per share in

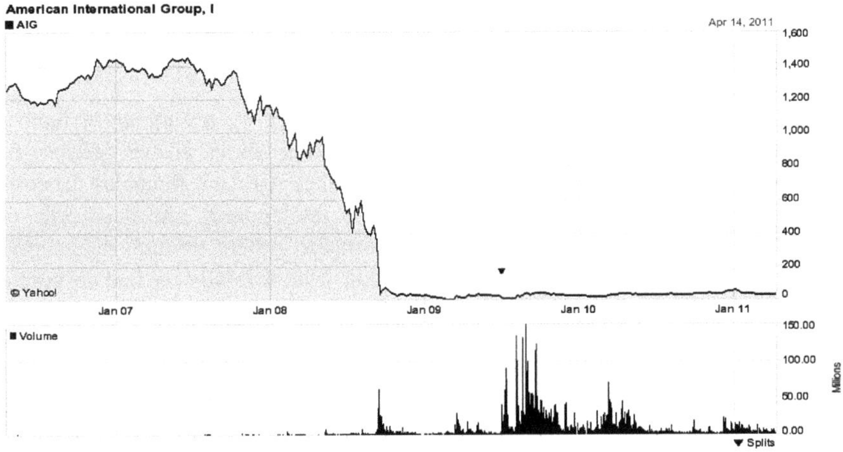

Figure 2.4 American International Group stock, 2006–11 (in dollars and volume traded)

Source: Yahoo Finance http://finance.yahoo.com retrieved April 14, 2011.

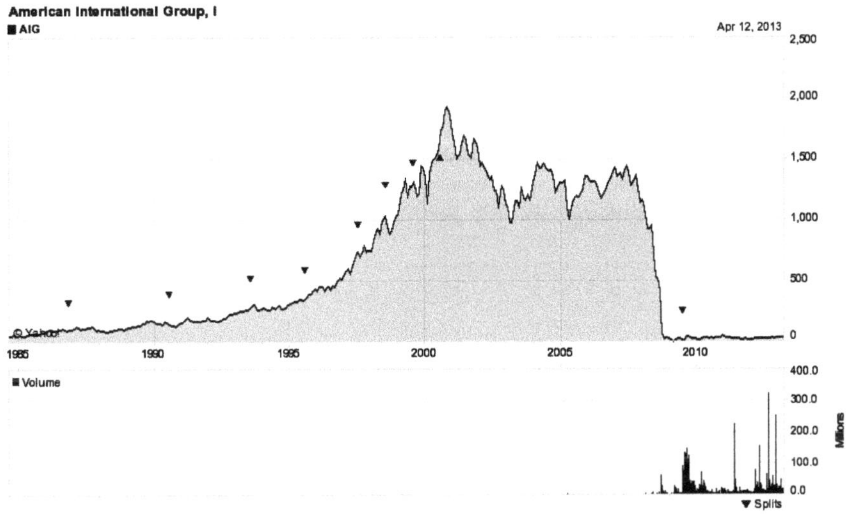

Figure 2.4a American International Group stock, 1985–2013 (in dollars and volume traded)

Source: Yahoo Finance http://finance.yahoo.com retrieved April 12, 2013.

December 2000 had fallen so sharply during the Great Recession that even after five years of "recovery" it had only risen to $48 a share by mid-2013. Looking at AIG stock since the mid-1980s (Figure 2.4a), we see a sharp rise in its price from the mid-1990s to the early 2000s, when it came close to $2,000 a share by early

2001, stabilizing between $1,000 and $1,500 a share until 2007, and then falling off the cliff in 2008 and remaining at the $35 to $40 a share range during the subsequent period from 2008 to 2013.

The Great Recession of 2008–09 was precipitated by a number of factors related to the financial crisis that was in the making, above all the collapse of the real estate and housing market which, together with the financial debacle, was one of the central contributing causes. In this context, one need only to review the total devastation of the home mortgage system through decimation of the popularly known Fannie Mae and Freddie Mac federally-backed corporate mortgage arrangement. As the stock price of both of these giant housing mortgage institutions illustrate, the sharp drop of Fannie Mae stock from the $50 range in mid 2007 to pennies in October 2008, and the similarly devastating drop in value of Freddie Mac stock from the $68 range in mid-2007 to again pennies in October 2008 (see figures 2.5 and 2.6), show the impact of the great recession on the economy, especially the housing and mortgage industry, which without government intervention would have seen the end of it as we have come to know it. By mid-2013, these two stocks were valued at less than $1 a share, with Freddie Mac at 70 cents a share and Fannie Mac at 20 cents a share—a far cry from their heyday not too long ago.

Looking at Freddie Mac stock from a long-term perspective (Figure 2.6a), we see that the stock price greatly increased during the 1990s, stabilized during the early to mid 2000s, and crashed in 2008 (see Figure 2.6a).

Given the failure of the global economy, and as an extension the capitalist system itself (and given the continuation of the recession in the United States, Europe, and elsewhere that may turn into a decade-long depression extending from 2007 to 2017), many are now asking what is in store for the future of the

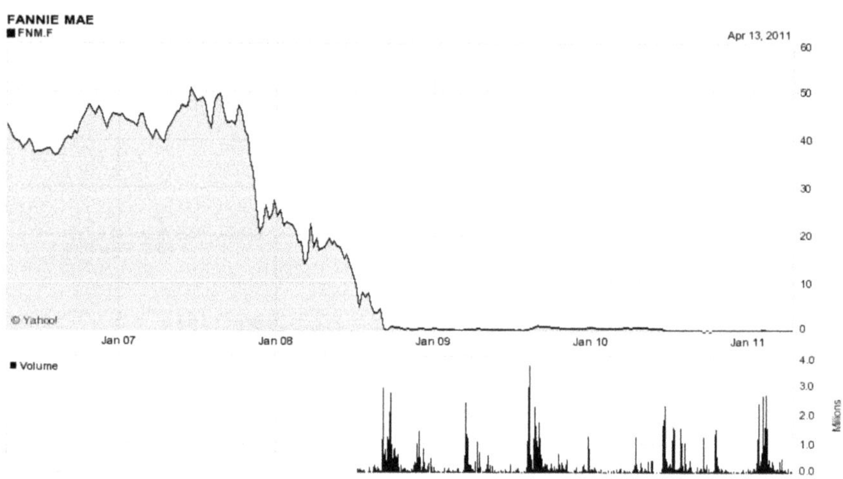

Figure 2.5 Fannie Mae stock, 2006–11 (in dollars and volume traded)
Source: Yahoo Finance http://finance.yahoo.com retrieved April 13, 2011.

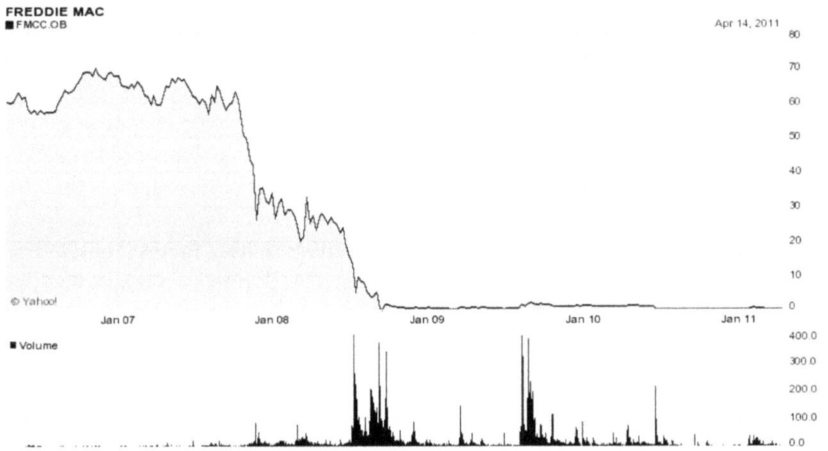

Figure 2.6 Freddie Mac stock, 2006–11 (in dollars and volume traded)
Source: Yahoo Finance http://finance.yahoo.com retrieved April 14, 2011.

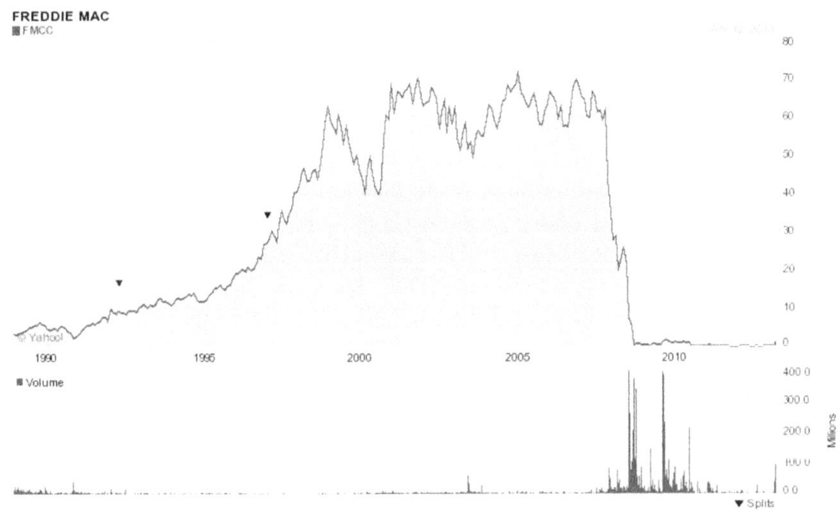

Figure 2.6a Freddie Mac stock, 1990–2013 (in dollars and volume traded)
Source: Yahoo Finance http://finance.yahoo.com retrieved April 12, 2013.

global economy and which direction it will take in the period ahead, i.e., what can we expect in the aftermath of the global capitalist crisis that is continuing unabated so far for more than five years.

The global economic crisis was the main topic of discussion among the leaders of the world's leading economies at the G-20 meetings in London in April 2009, which resulted in guarded optimism that through substantial reforms in global financial institutions and an active interventionist state that monitors the situation with greater regulation of the economy, the evolving economic situation might provide the basis for a mild recovery and a new global economic order. However, today, in 2013, more than five years after the 2008–09 recession had "officially" been declared as "ended," the news about the US and the world economy is such that there is the possibility of a new and more severe recession that would make the situation worse and sink the global economy into another severe slump. That this is a real possibility is now demonstrated by the worsening economic situation in the eurozone, especially in the continent's southern periphery focused on Greece, Spain, Portugal, and Italy, and more recently joined by Cyprus through its banking crisis that may lead to the collapse of the European Union.

What the future of the global economy will look like and what role the United States will play in it are questions that remain open and contingent on the solutions adopted at the national and global level, especially in Europe, East Asia (China), and other emerging centers of global economic power (India and Brazil) in the period ahead. But, clearly, we are going through an important period in the history of the world, and what happens in the next decade will determine the future course of our planet for a very long time (Berberoglu, 2012).

Contradictions and Crises of the Global Capitalist Economy

The development of capitalism over the past hundred years has formed and transformed capitalism in a crucial way, one that is characterized by periodic crises resulting from the business cycle that now unfolds at the global level. The current crisis of the global economy is an outcome of the consolidation of economic power that the globalization of capital has secured for the transnational corporations over this period (Sassen, 2009; Sherman, 2010). This has led to a string of problems associated with the contradiction between the expanded forces of production (technology) and existing social relations, which manifests in a number of ways, including:

1. The problem of overproduction, resulting from the imbalance between wages and prices of commodities fueled by low purchasing power;
2. Increasing unemployment and underemployment resulting from outsourcing of production to low-wage sweatshops in export processing zones abroad, compounded by the continued application of technology in production (i.e., automation);
3. Sub-prime mortgage and credit card debt and rising home foreclosures and bankruptcies as the unemployed become unable to pay off their debts;
4. Intensification of the control of labor through expanded production and reproduction of profits by further accumulation of capital on a world scale;
5. Increased polarization of wealth and income at the national and global level between capital and labor and growth in numbers of the poor and marginalized segments of the population throughout the world.

These and other related contradictions and crises of the global economy define the parameters of capitalist globalization and provide us the framework for discussion on the nature and dynamics of this process that has been unfolding for a number of decades.

Given the logic of global capital accumulation in late capitalist society, and the nature of global capitalist expansion on a world scale, it is no accident that the decline of the domestic economy of advanced capitalist countries over the past three decades corresponds to the accelerated export of capital abroad in search of cheap labor, access to raw materials, new markets, and higher rates of profit. The resulting deindustrialization of the domestic economy has had a serious impact on working people and other affected segments of the laboring population and has brought about a major dislocation of national economies (Phillips, 1998; Berberoglu, 2003; Friedman, Moseley and Sturr, 2009).[1] This has necessitated increased state intervention on behalf of the large corporations and has heightened the contradictions that led to the global economic crisis in the early twenty-first century.

The widening gap between labor and capital (within a deteriorating national economy and the state's budgetary crisis) has led to the ensuing political crisis within the state apparatus and has sharpened the conflicts in a new political direction. As the crisis of the global economy has brought the state to center stage of economic life and revealed its ties to the corporations, thus exacerbating the state's legitimization crisis, the anger of the working people and the masses in general are becoming directed not merely against capital, but against the state itself.

Global Capitalist Crisis and the Crisis of the State

The crisis of the state on the global scene is a manifestation of the contradictions and crises of the global economy, which in the early twenty-first century has reached a critical stage in its development. The massive flow of US transnational investments throughout the world, especially in Western Europe, Japan, and other advanced capitalist regions, has led to the post-Second World War reemergence of rivalry between the major capitalist powers, while fostering antagonisms between them in the scramble for the peripheral regions of the global economy—Latin America, Asia, Africa, and the Middle East (Hart, 1992; Falk, 1999; Halliday, 2001). This has created a situation where the state has become a key player to address and remedy the problems generated by such rivalry in the global economy.

1 This paradox of growth and expansion of capital on a world scale, simultaneously with the decline and contraction of the domestic economy, is a central feature of globalization at its highest and most intense stage of worldwide expansion—a natural outcome of the operations of capitalist imperialism (see Berberoglu, 2003, 2005, 2010).

The current global economic crisis has made the state's role even more difficult, as the latter comes to confront forces that are increasingly hostile to it.

With the integration of the economies of Western Europe into the European Union (EU) and the emergence of Japan as a powerful economic force in the late twentieth century, the position of the United States in the global economy has declined relative to both its own postwar supremacy in the 1940s and 1950s and to other advanced economies since that time. Despite the fact that US capital continues to control the biggest share of overseas markets and accounts for the largest volume of international investments, its hold on the global economy has recently begun slipping in a manner similar to Britain's in the early twentieth century. This has, in turn, led the US state to play a more aggressive role in foreign policy to protect US corporate interests abroad. Its massive deployment in the Middle East in the early 1990s, which led to the Persian Gulf War of 1991, and subsequently its invasion of Afghanistan in 2001 and war against Iraq in 2003, has resulted in great military expenditures that have placed an enormous burden on the American people, who have come to shoulder the colossal cost of maintaining a global empire whose vast military machine encompasses the world (Berberoglu, 1999, 2003, 2005).

In the current phase of the crisis of the US economy and the state, the problems the state faces are of such magnitude that they threaten the supremacy of the United States in the global political economy and by extension the global capitalist system itself. Internal economic and budgetary problems have been compounded by ever-growing military spending propped up by armed intervention abroad (Iraq, Afghanistan, etc.), while a declining economic base at home manifested in the housing and banking crisis, deindustrialization, and a recessionary economy further complicated by the global rivalry between the major capitalist powers that is not always restricted to the economic field, but has political (and even military) implications that are global in magnitude (Harvey, 2003; see also Panitch and Leys, 2003).

Global Economic Rivalry and Capitalist Crises

The growing prospects of economic rivalry between the major capitalist powers, backed up by their states, are effecting changes in their relations that render the global political economy an increasingly unstable character. Competition between the United States, Japan, and European states, and the emergence of China, Russia, India, Brazil and other rival states, are setting them on a collision course for world supremacy, manifested in struggles for markets, raw materials, and spheres of influence in geopolitical—as well as economic—terms, which may in fact lead to a new balance of forces, and, consequently, alliances that will have serious political implications in global power politics. As the continuing economic ascendance of the major rivals of the United States take their prominent position in the global economy, pressures will build toward the politicization and militarization of these states from within, where the leading forces of world economy will press forward with the necessary political and military corollary of their growing economic power in the global system (Hart, 1992; Falk, 1999), as has been the case with the German, French, Russian, and Chinese opposition to war against Iraq in the UN Security Council in 2003.

These developments in global economic and geopolitical shifts in the balance of forces among the major powers will bring to the fore new and yet untested international alliances for world supremacy and domination in the post–cold war era. Such alliances will bring key powers such as Russia and China into play in a new and complicated relationship that holds the key for the success or failure of the new rising centers that will emerge as the decisive forces in the global economic, political, and military equation in the early decades of the twenty-first century (Halliday, 2001; Guthrie, 2006; Stephens, 2009).

The contradictions and conflicts imbedded in relations between the rival states of the globe will again surface as an important component of international relations in the years ahead. And these are part and parcel of the restructuring of the international division of labor and the transfer of production to overseas territories in line with the globalization of capital on a worldwide basis—a process that has serious consequences for the economies of both the advanced and less developed countries. Economic crisis and decline in advanced centers (manifested in plant closings, unemployment, and recession) and super-exploitation of workers in sweatshops abroad (maintained by repressive authoritarian regimes) yield the same combined result that has a singular global logic: profits. It is in this context of the changes that are taking place on a world scale that the state is beginning to confront the current crisis of global capitalism.

Origins and Nature of the Current Global Capitalist Crisis

The periodic crises resulting from the capitalist business cycle now unfolds at the global level, and as a result the current crisis of the global capitalist economy is an outcome of the consolidation of economic power that the globalization of capital has secured for the transnational corporations on a world scale. This has led to a string of problems associated with the financial, banking, real estate, and productive sectors of the economy that have triggered the current global capitalist crisis.

The central problem of the world capitalist system is the recurrent business cycle which is now operating at the global level. It manifests itself in a number of ways, including:

- The problem of overproduction
- Increasing unemployment and underemployment
- Decline in real wages and rise in super-profits
- The sub-prime mortgage and credit card debt

- Speculative corporate financial activities
- Increased polarization of wealth and income.

These inherent contradictions of the capitalist system, now operating at the global level, are part and parcel of the capitalist system and are now manifested on a grand scale across the globe. One important outcome of this process that unfolds on a world scale is extreme income and wealth inequality. Thus while half the world's population lives on $2 a day and quarter of the world's population lives on $1 a day, the level of poverty and inequality in the advanced capitalist countries is also quite significant, as some 44 million Americans (1 in 7) live below the poverty line, and that the share of aggregate income received by the lowest and highest fifth of the US population indicate a widening gap that has been persistent throughout much of recent US history.

Table 2.1, which provides data on the share of aggregate income received by each fifth of households between 1975 and 2009, shows a consistent pattern of income inequality that is a permanent feature of US society that has important implications for the economy and society in the early twenty-first century. A more serious situation exists in the distribution of wealth. Highly concentrated in the top tier of the class structure, the wealthy owners of capital who have accumulated their fortunes over generations have come to account for the lion's share of the total wealth, such that in 2007 in the United States, the top 1 percent of the US population owns nearly half of all wealth, and the top 10 percent of the US population owns nearly 90 percent of total wealth—a situation that places the United States among nations with the greatest income and wealth inequality in the world (see Table 2.2).

Table 2.1 Share of aggregate income received by each fifth and top 5 percent of households, 1975–2009 (in percentages)

Year	Lowest	Second	Third	Fourth	Highest	Top
	20%	20%	20%	20%	20%	5%
1975	4.3	10.4	17.0	24.7	43.6	16.5
1980	4.2	10.2	16.8	24.7	44.1	16.5
1985	3.9	9.8	16.2	24.4	45.6	17.6
1990	3.8	9.6	15.9	24.0	46.6	18.5
1995	3.7	9.1	15.2	23.3	48.7	21.0
2000	3.6	8.6	14.6	23.0	50.4	22.2
2005	3.4	8.6	14.6	23.0	50.4	22.2
2009	3.4	8.6	14.6	23.2	50.3	21.7

Source: US Bureau of the Census, *Current Population Reports*, P60-235, August 2008; *Statistical Abstract of the United States, 2011*, Table 693, p. 454; *2012*, Table 694, p. 454.

Table 2.2 Distribution of wealth in the United States, 2007, by type of asset (in percentages)

Investment assets	Top 1%	Top 10%	Bottom 90%
Stocks and mutual funds	49.3	89.4	10.6
Financial securities	60.6	98.5	1.5
Trusts	38.9	79.4	20.6
Business equity	62.4	93.3	6.7
Non-home real estate	28.3	76.9	23.1
Total for group	49.7	87.8	12.2

Source: Edward N. Wolff, "Recent Trends in Household Wealth in the United States: Rising Debt and the Middle Class Squeeze," *Working Paper No. 589* (March 2010), p. 51.

Focusing on the most recent economic crisis in the United States—the Great Recession of 2008–09—Richard D. Wolff (2009), Professor of Economics at the University of Massachusetts at Amherst, points out that, from 1820 to 1970, every decade US workers experienced a rising level of wages; in the 1970s, however, this came to an end, as real wages stopped rising and they have never resumed since. US workers became more productive, but got paid the same; wages began to stagnate and decline, while the profits of the capitalists multiplied many-fold. Thus, the gap between labor and capital grew bigger, especially since the 1970s (Figure 2.7).

This translated into a higher rate of surplus value, hence a higher rate of exploitation of labor (see figures 2.7, 2.8, and 2.9a). While during the first half of the twentieth century the rate of surplus value in US manufacturing averaged around 150 percent, in the postwar period it sharply increased, reaching 580 percent in 2011 (see Figure 2.9a).

With continuing rise in productivity, and thus higher returns on investment, the situation was the reverse for the workers whose share declined to a mere 14.7 percent in 2011 (see Figure 2.9b).

Given this process which favored capital, and capitalists over labor, the large corporations made huge profits and had much money at their disposal. They bought other corporations (through mergers and acquisitions) and they put their money into banks. The banks loaned that money (with interest!) to workers who didn't have money to consume. This was done to raise the workers' purchasing power because their wages weren't enough to buy things. Since employers no longer raised workers' wages, the workers had to go into debt to survive. Debt began to rise and things got out of control. As corporations increasingly began to invest abroad (outsourcing production and services), US workers lost their jobs, and this led to greater unemployment and underemployment (Wolfe, 2009). Unemployed workers with a lot of debt were unable to make their mortgage and credit card payments, and were forced to go into foreclosures and bankruptcies. This, in turn, led to the collapse of the banking system, necessitating a government

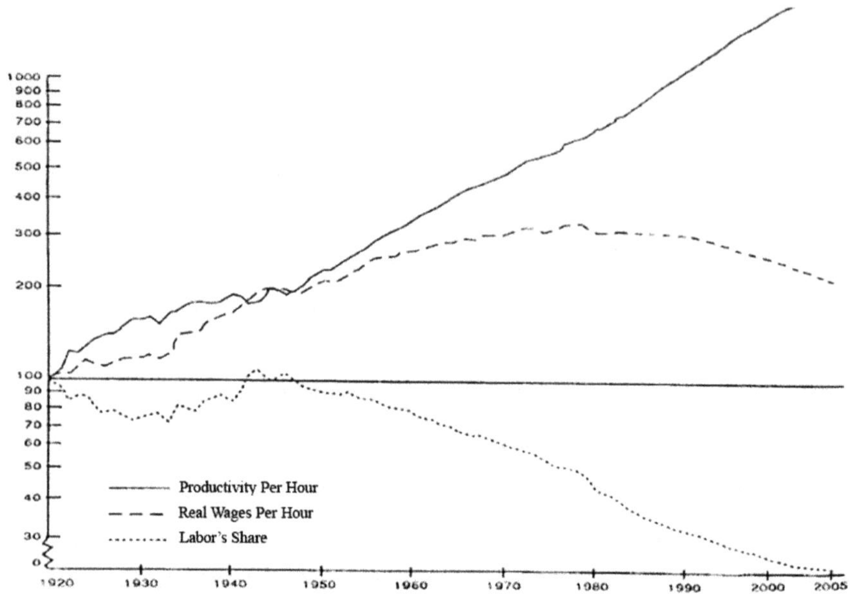

Figure 2.7 Productivity per hour, real wages per hour, and labor's share in US manufacturing industries, 1920–2005, index numbers (1919 = 100)

Source: Victor Perlo, *Super Profits and Crises* (New York: International Publishers, 1984), p. 66. Data for 1984–2005 updated by the author, with the assistance of Jason King.

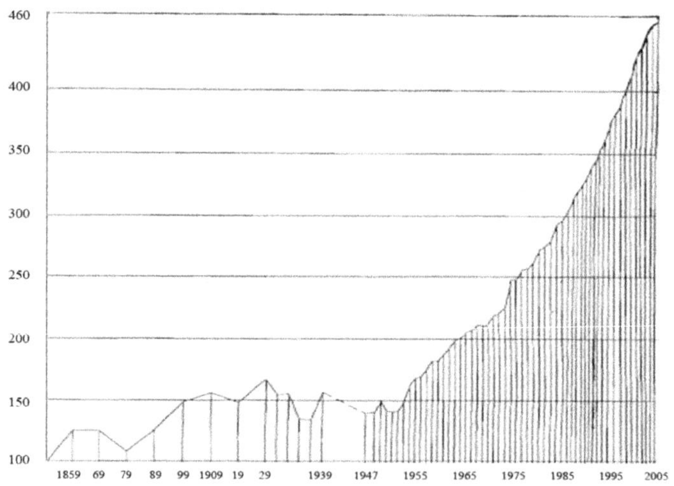

Figure 2.8 Rate of surplus value, US manufacturing industries, 1859–2005

Source: Victor Perlo, *Super Profits and Crises* (New York: International Publishers, 1984), p. 46. Data for 1984–2005 updated by the author, with the assistance of Jason King.

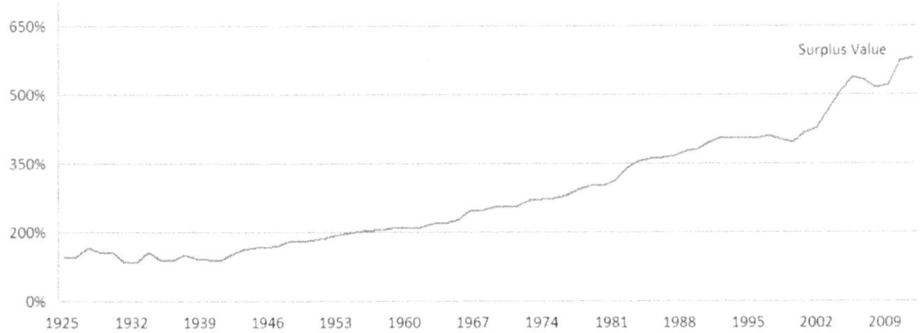

Figure 2.9a Rate of surplus value, 1925–2011
Source: Victor Perlo, *Super Profits and Crises* (New York: International Publishers, 1984), p. 43. Data for 1984–2011 updated by the author, with the assistance of Jason King.

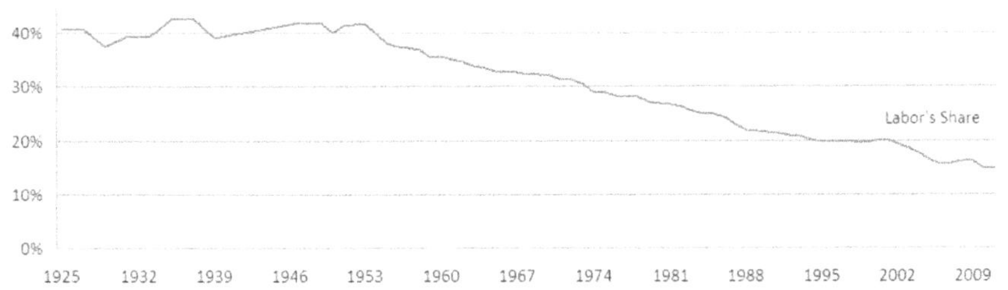

Figure 2.9b Labor's share in production, 1925–2011
Source: Victor Perlo, *Super Profits and Crises* (New York: International Publishers, 1984), p. 43. Data for 1984–2011 updated by the author, with the assistance of Jason King.

bailout of the banks. Wolfe points out that, it is only through the nearly trillion dollar stimulus funds that the US government poured into the economy to save the banks from default, that a financial collapse like that of the Great Depression was averted.

Extent of the Current Capitalist Crisis in the United States

The continuing global capitalist crisis has been deep and widespread, especially in the United States, in the epicenter of the crisis. At the height of the Great Recession, unemployment reached unprecedented levels, from 7 million in December 2007 to 16 million in October 2010; counting the discouraged and part-time workers, the unemployment rate reached 18 percent in 2010. Foreclosures were running over 1 million a year. Poverty rose to 44 million, as 1 in 7 Americans lived at or below the poverty line.

The decline in manufacturing through shifts in production to overseas territories where cheap labor is employed in sweatshops across east and southeast Asia and the increase in finance capital has resulted in much lower levels of employment compared to earlier periods going back to the 1950s to the 1970s (see Figure 2.10). Gone are the days of the auto and steel industries and the smoke-stacked factories of the industrial age through the twentieth century, replaced by a service industry that is based on low-wage, low-skill, non-union, contingent labor, which enriches wealthy capitalists and impoverishes working men and women in the United States and around the world.

With the steady decline of the manufacturing sector in the United States through outsourcing of production to cheap labor areas abroad, 2.9 million well-paying manufacturing jobs have disappeared in the period 2005–2008 alone. And that's on top of a loss of more than 3 million jobs in manufacturing from 1998 to 2003, with millions more lost in the entire postwar period. This has greatly transformed the labor force structure in the United States from a traditionally industrial economy to a new service economy, with all the associated implications for labor, the central one of which is its impact on employment.

In looking at unemployment data for 2007 through 2010, we see that the unemployment rate was 4.6 percent in 2007, 5.8 percent in 2008, rose sharply to 9.3 percent in 2009, and remained at 9.6 percent in 2010 (see Figure 2.11). During the two years following the onset of the recession, the unemployment rate continued to hover above the 9 percent level.

Writing in July 2011 on the deteriorating unemployment situation in the United States, Associated Press economics writer Paul Wiseman observed: "booming profits have allowed Corporate America to leave the Great Recession far behind. But millions of ordinary Americans are stranded in a labor market that looks like it's still in recession" (2011). He went on to point out that "unemployment is stuck at 9.2 percent, two years into what economists call a recovery. Job growth has been slow and wages stagnant" (Wiseman, 2011). Citing recent research by Andrew Sum, Director of the Center for Labor Market Studies at Northwestern University, Wiseman reported that:

> wages and salaries accounted for just 1 percent of economic growth in the first 18 months after economists declared that the recession had ended in June 2009 … In the same period after the 2001 recession, wages and salaries accounted for 15 percent. They were 50 percent after the 1991–92 recession, and 25 percent after the 1981–82 recession. Corporate profits, by contrast, accounted for an unprecedented 88 percent of economic growth during those first 18 months. That's compared with 53 percent after the 2001 recession, nothing after the 1991–92 recession and 28 percent after the 1981–82 recession. (Wiseman, 2011)

In elaborating on this theme in his article "A Boom in Corporate Profits, a Bust in Jobs, Wages" which he called an "economic disconnect" in referring to

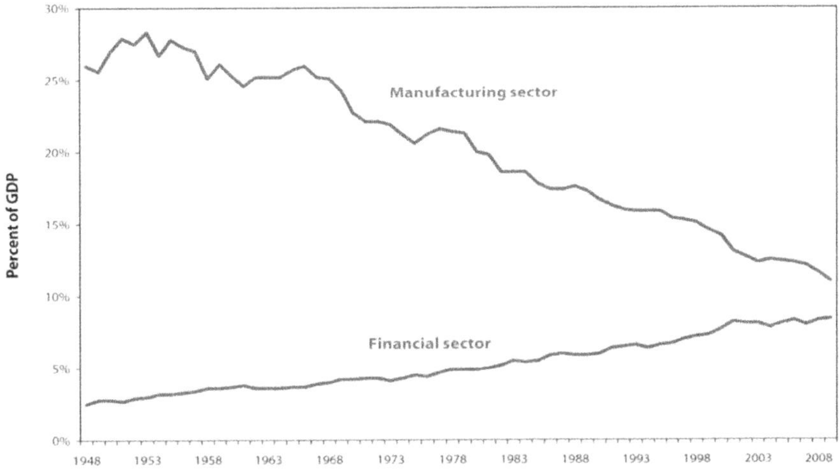

Figure 2.10 Manufacturing and finance sectors as share of overall economy, 1948–2008

Source: Bureau of Economic Analysis data compiled by the Economic Policy Institute.

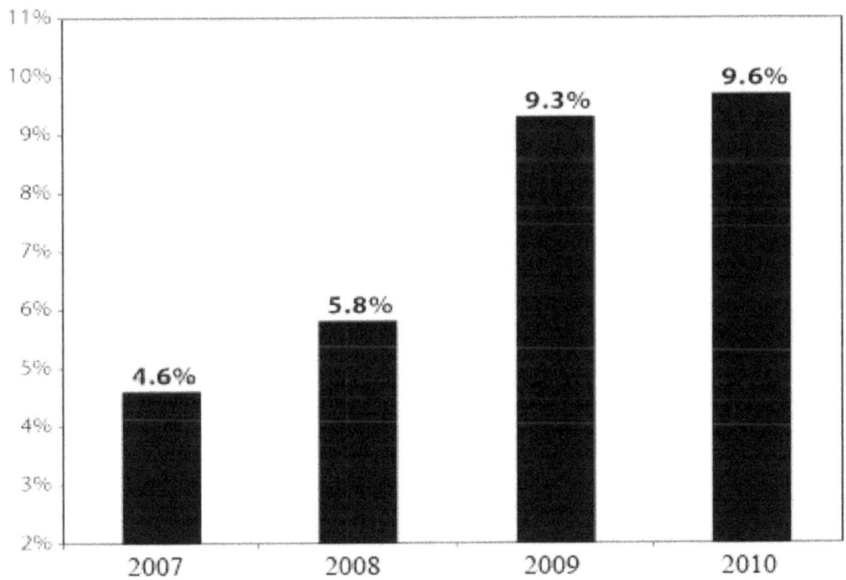

Figure 2.11 Average annual unemployment rate, 2007–10 (in percent)

Source: Bureau of Labor Statistics.

the surge in corporate profits, while jobs and wages remained at recession levels, Wiseman listed several factors that contributed to this predicament:

- US corporations are expanding overseas, not so much at home ... In the 2000s, they added 2.4 million jobs in foreign countries and cut 2.9 million jobs in the United States, according to the Commerce Department.
- Back in the US, companies are squeezing more productivity out of staffs thinned by layoffs during the Great Recession. They don't need to hire. And they don't need to be generous with pay raises; they know their employees have nowhere else to go.
- Companies remain reluctant to spend the $1.9 trillion in cash they've accumulated, especially in the United States, which would create jobs.

The grim economic situation affecting millions of workers across the nation has prompted others, like Simon Johnson, the former chief economist at the International Monetary Fund, to ask: "A Second Great Depression, or Worse?" Writing in *The New York Times* of August 18, 2011, Johnson warned of a prolonged period of economic crisis that may severely affect the US economy: although "the main features of the Great Depression have not yet manifested themselves and still seem unlikely," he wrote, "it is increasingly likely that we will find ourselves in the midst of something nearly as traumatic, a long slump of the kind seen with some regularity in the 19th century" (Johnson, 2011).

Recent data on unemployment, released in September, 2011 by the Bureau of Labor Statistics and reported by the Economic Policy Institute, reveal that the unemployment rate in August 2011 was 9.1 percent (still above 9 percent). This amounted to 14 million workers who were still unemployed (6.3 million more than in December 2007), many of whom concentrated in 11 states with double-digit unemployment rates. The underemployment rate (i.e., those who are unemployed, marginally attached, or working part time involuntarily) was 16.2 percent. Altogether, there were 25.3 million workers who were either unemployed or underemployed in August 2011. Whites had an unemployment rate of 8.0 percent, blacks 16.7 percent, and Hispanics 11.3 percent. In July 2011, seasonally adjusted underemployment was 13.2 percent for whites, 25.3 percent for blacks, and 22.0 percent for Hispanics. And the youth unemployment rate for all 16–24 year olds was 17.7 percent, and for all 16–19 year olds it was 25.4 percent, while for 16–19 year old blacks it was 46.5 percent, and for 16–19 year old Hispanics it was 37.4 percent in August 2011 (Economic Policy Institute, 2011: 1–2).

Looking at the unemployment situation in broader perspective, data for the period 2005 to 2010 shows that the gap in the labor market due to the rise in unemployment from the fourth quarter of 2007 to the fourth quarter of 2010—the worst period of the great recession—amounted to 11.5 million jobs. Thus while jobs needed to match population growth would have put employment at the 141 million level in September 2010, the actual number of people working in September 2010 (129 million) put the total *deficit* in jobs at 11.5 million (see Figure 2.12).

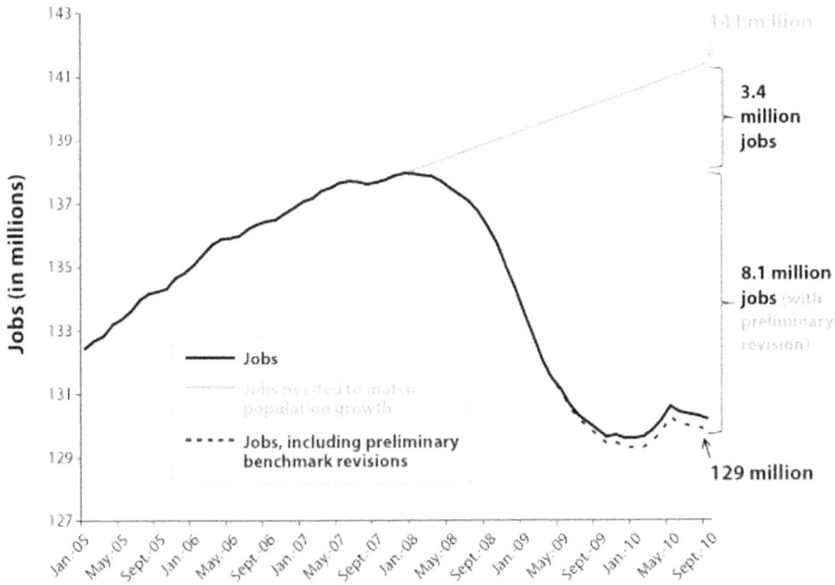

Figure 2.12 Payroll employment and gap in labor market, 2005–10
Source: Bureau of Labor Statistics data compiled by Economic Policy Institute.

Despite the slight improvement in the unemployment rate by August 2011, down to the 9.1 percent level, the economy still needed 11.2 million jobs to regain its pre-recession level of unemployment. With the recession continuing into 2012 and beyond, the economic situation is bound to get worse, and the unemployment and underemployment rates are bound to stay at high levels for at least several more years.

Impact of Globalization on the Current Global Capitalist Crisis

The global expansion of capital has had a great impact on the current global capitalist crisis. This impact is the result of the globalization process which has undermined national economies in the interests of transnational capital that profits from its global operations on a world scale. This has brought about contradictions at a dual level. At the global level, it has meant first and foremost the ever-growing use of cheap labor across the world, hence high rates of exploitation of labor. In addition, it has caused a depletion of resources that could be used for national development; environmental pollution, and other health hazards; a growing national debt that tie many countries to the World Bank, the International Monetary Fund, and other global financial institutions; and a growing militarization of society through endless wars and the imposition of military and civilian dictatorships that violate basic human rights. The domination and control of countries for transnational profits through the instrumentality of the imperial state has at the same time created various forms of dependence on the center that has become a defining characteristic of globalization today (Amaladoss, 1999; Sklair, 2002).

Domestically, the globalization of capital and global economic expansion has had immense dislocations in the national economies of center states. Expansion of manufacturing industry abroad has meant a decline in local industry, as plant closings in the United States and other advanced capitalist economies have worsened the unemployment situation. The massive expansion of capital abroad has resulted in hundreds of factory shutdowns with millions of workers losing their jobs, hence the surge in unemployment in the United States and other advanced capitalist states (Wagner, 2000). This has led to a decline in wages of workers in the advanced capitalist countries, as low wages abroad have played a competitive role in keeping wages down at home. The drop in incomes among a growing section of US labor has thus lowered the standard of living in general and led to further polarization between labor and capital in the United States (Berberoglu, 1992a, 2002, 2009).

The globalization of capital and the integration of national economies into the global system, a process that has been developing over the past several decades, and its intensification under neoliberal policies over the past 20 years, had a direct impact on the extent and depth of the current global economic crisis. Previously nationally-based economies, now under the control of transnational corporations and international financial institutions, have become appendages of the global economy that operates under the logic of global capital accumulation for the benefit of the transnationals, while at a great cost to those who have become its victims.

A major global economic crisis, such as the one we are experiencing today, greatly affects the economies of those nations that have become part of the global capitalist system. Thus, all the known consequences of such economic downturn (rising unemployment and underemployment, declining purchasing power, growing consumer debt, home mortgage foreclosures, bankruptcies, and a host of other economic problems) are the very ingredients of a system-wide crisis that has affected not only the advanced capitalist countries (where the current crisis originated), but all others integrated into the global capitalist system—and more so the latter, as they are more vulnerable to the forces of the global economy and its periodic crises.

The contradictions of global economic expansion, which have caused so many problems in both the periphery and the imperial centers, have in turn created the conditions for the decline and fall of the global economy. Economically, these contradictions have afflicted the system with recessions, depressions, and an associated realization crisis; politically, it has set into motion an interventionist state that through its presence in every corner of the world has incurred an enormous military expenditure to maintain an empire, while gaining the resentment of millions of people across the globe who are engaged in active struggles against it.[2]

The imperial state, extending its rule across vast territories, has dwarfed the militaristic adventures of past empires many times over. Through its political and military supremacy, it has come to exert its control over many countries. As a result, acting on behalf of capital, it has reinforced the domination of capital over labor across the globe. This, in turn, has greatly politicized the conflict between labor and capital and led to a direct clash between these forces. Such clash takes on special significance during global economic crises, as labor and other affected segments of society increasingly become conscious of their interests and begin to take political action that directly confront capital and the capitalist state.

Which Way Out of the Crisis?

Economic remedies to save the system from collapse are bound to fail so long as they remain within the framework of the existing capitalist system. Changes that are required to revitalize the economy and to turn things around, point to a redistribution of wealth and income to increase mass consumption. This would increase demand for consumer goods, hence increase production, and create jobs for the unemployed, as well as raising revenue for the state. All these would require a restructuring of the economy away from failed neoliberal corporate capitalist policies and toward a new set of priorities that promote the interests of working people. Such restructuring requires the transformation of the capitalist system. This would provide greater rights and benefits to working people, and in turn, benefit society greatly and set us on a prosperous course that would vastly improve living standards and pull us out of the economic crisis. But these are not things that can readily be adopted within the framework of the prevailing capitalist order. As vested economic interests lie at the heart of any class-based system, the capitalist system, too, is based on powerful class forces that control, dominate, and benefit from the policies of the state and major social, economic, and political institutions of society that promote the accumulation of capital and secure the wealth of the capitalist class through the instrumentality of the capitalist state (Berberoglu, 2013). Thus, to change the existing societal order, it becomes incumbent upon

2 While one consequence of neoliberal globalization has been domestic economic contraction and an associated class polarization, a more costly and dangerous outcome of this process has been increased militarization and intervention abroad, such that the defense of an expanding capitalist empire worldwide has come to require an increasing military presence and a permanent interventionist foreign policy to protect and advance the activities of transnational corporations. However, such aggressive military posture has had (and continues to generate) major problems for global capitalism and the imperial state, and thus is increasingly threatening the its effectiveness and, in the long run, its very existence.

the working class and its allies to take charge of their political destiny and carry out the transformation of capitalist society, especially capital's supportive political arm, the capitalist state.

Conclusion

The ongoing global capitalist crisis that we are experiencing today is a product of three decades of neoliberal capitalist policies of privatization, deregulation, tax cuts for the rich, speculative investments, financialization, and profiteering of unimaginable proportions. Through these practices many capitalists became very wealthy and amassed great fortunes during this period, while working people were super-exploited through extremely low wages in the sweatshops of the giant capitalist corporations that have spread their tentacles across the globe.

In 2008, global capitalism came very close to destroying the very system that it had created not so long ago. Cyclical crises of recessions and depressions, economic rivalry, political and military conflict, war, and other forms of disruptions and catastrophes have been the characteristic of global capitalism ever since its inception a few centuries ago. In my latest book *Beyond the Global Capitalist Crisis: The World Economy in Transition*, published in 2012, I pointed out that:

> Tracing the evolution of the capitalist economy and the capitalist business cycle historically, it becomes clear that the ups and downs—'booms and busts'—of the capitalist economy is the result of the 'normal' process of evolution of the capitalist system, and that economic crises (i.e., recessions and depressions) are a recurrent aspect of capitalism at the national and now the global level. (Berberoglu, 2012: 179)

I went on to argue that therefore:

> the crisis-ridden business cycle of capitalism—one that is to be found *only under capitalism*—is the life-blood of the capitalist system in that capitalism cannot grow and prosper without such a 'correction' (crisis) in the economy every few years. And this can be seen as part of the process of capitalist expansion and contraction over its life-course. (Berberoglu, 2012: 179)

The contradictions of the unfolding process of global capitalist expansion and accumulation have brought to the fore new political realities: as the crisis unfolds and leads to further political organizing and mobilization by labor, the institutional forces that support the global capitalist power structure intensify renewed repression at home and abroad to control an increasingly frustrated labor movement in the center states and a militant mass movement of popular forces in the less-developed states of the periphery poised to resist neoliberal globalization (Houtart and Polet 2001). This has occurred most visibly in Latin America, Southeastern Europe, the Middle East, North Africa, and other regions where neoliberal policies have come under sharp attack, and where popular alliances of oppressed classes have managed to come to power, or are in the process of mobilizing their forces for such an eventuality.

The continuation of the economic crisis in the advanced capitalist countries is bound to lead to the emergence of similar movements that will seek a political solution to the persistent economic problems that they now confront in the imperial heartlands. And as the social and economic position of the affected populations become threatened in a more severe way across these regions, one can expect the resurgence of grass-roots political movements to enter center stage and play a critical role in the coming period of crises and conflicts that will continue to unfold in the years ahead. Clearly, the inherent contradictions of global capitalism are making it increasingly difficult for the imperial state to control and manage the global political economy, as the continuing global capitalist crisis is making things worse for the state to halt the process from further decline and decay. At the same time, the unfolding crisis is preparing the conditions for the international solidarity of labor in confronting global capital to address the many social, economic, and political inequities that characterize the global capitalist system.

References

Amaladoss, Michael (ed.) (1999) *Globalization and its Victims as Seen by its Victims*. Delhi, India: Vidyajyoti Education and Welfare Society.

Berberoglu, Berch (1992) *The Legacy of Empire: Economic Decline and Class Polarization in the United States*. New York: Praeger.

Berberoglu, Berch (ed.) (2002) *Labor and Capital in the Age of Globalization: The Labor Process and the Changing Nature of Work in the Global Economy*. Lanham, MD: Rowman and Littlefield.

Berberoglu, Berch (2003) *Globalization of Capital and the Nation-State*. Lanham, MD: Rowman and Littlefield.

Berberoglu, Berch (2005) *Globalization and Change: The Transformation of Global Capitalism*. Lanham, MD: Lexington Books.

Berberoglu, Berch (2009) *Class and Class Conflict in the Age of Globalization*. Lanham, MD: Lexington.

Berberoglu, Berch (2010) *Globalization in the 21st Century: Labor, Capital, and the State on a World Scale*. New York: Palgrave Macmillan.

Berberoglu, Berch (2012) *Beyond the Global Capitalist Crisis: The World Economy in Transition*. Farnham: Ashgate.

Berberoglu, Berch (2013) *Political Sociology: An Introduction to the State and Society*. Boulder, CO: Paradigm Publishers.

Bivens, Josh (2011) *Failure by Design: The Story behind America's Broken Economy*. Ithaca, NY: ILR Press.

Chossudovsky, Michel and Andrew Gavin Marshall (eds) (2010) *The Global Economic Crisis: The Great Depression of the XXI Century.* Montreal: Global Research Publishers.

Dorning, Mike (2011) "The Slow Disappearance of the American Working Man," *Bloomberg Businessweek* (August 25).

Economic Policy Institute (2011) *EPI Fact Sheet: Labor Day by the Numbers.* Washington, DC (September 5).

Falk, Richard (1999) *Predatory Globalization: A Critique.* Malden, MA: Blackwell.

Filger, Sheldon (2009) *Global Economic Forecast 2010–2015: Recession into Depression.* www.GlobalEconomicCrisis.com.

Friedman, Gerald, Fred Moseley and Chris Sturr (eds) (2009) *The Economic Crisis Reader.* Boston, MA: Dollars and Sense.

Guthrie, Doug (2006) *China and Globalization: The Social, Economic and Political Transformation of Chinese Society.* New York: Routledge.

Halliday, Fred (2001) *The World at 2000.* New York: St Martin's Press.

Hart, Jeffrey A. (1992) *Rival Capitalists: International Competitiveness in the United States, Japan, and Western Europe.* Ithaca, NY: Cornell University Press.

Harvey, David (2003) *The New Imperialism.* New York: Oxford University Press.

Houtart, Francois and Francois Polet (eds) (2001) *The Other Davos Summit: The Globalization of Resistance to the World Economic System.* London: Zed Books.

Odekon, Mehmet (ed.) (2010) *Booms and Busts: An Encyclopedia of Economic History from the First Stock Market Crash of 1792 to the Current Global Economic Crisis.* Armonk, NY: M.E. Sharpe.

Panitch, Leo and Colin Leys (eds) (2003) *The New Imperial Challenge.* New York: Monthly Review Press.

Phillips, Brian (1998) *Global Production and Domestic Decay: Plant Closings in the U.S.* New York: Garland.

Sassen, Saskia (2009) "Too Big To Save: The End of Financial Capitalism." *Open Democracy News Analysis*, April 2.

Sherman, Howard J. (2010) *The Roller Coaster Economy: Financial Crisis, Great Recession, and the Public Option.* Armonk, NY: M.E. Sharpe.

Sklair, Leslie (2002) *Globalization: Capitalism and Its Alternatives.* New York: Oxford University Press.

Stephens, Philip (2009) "A Summit Success That Reflects a Different Global Landscape." *Financial Times*, April 3, 9.

Wagner, Helmut (ed.) (2000) *Globalization and Unemployment.* New York: Springer.

Wiseman, Paul (2011) "A Boom in Corporate Profits, a Bust in Jobs, Wages," *Associated Press*, July 22.

Wolfe, Richard D. (2009) "Capitalism Hits the Fan," in Gerald Friedman et al. (eds), *The Economic Crisis Reader.* Boston: Dollars & Sense.

Chapter 3

"The Great Recession" of 2008 and the Continuing Global Capitalist Crisis

William I. Robinson

Introduction

Most commentators refer to the global capitalist crisis in economic terms and date it to the US sub-prime loan debacle that began in mid-2007, followed by the global financial collapse of September 2008 and "The Great Recession."[1] The crisis that exploded in 2008 springs from contradictions in global capitalism that are expressed in immanent crisis tendencies and in a series of displacements over the past three decades that had served to postpone a "day of reckoning." I attempt in this chapter to situate the causal origins of the global crisis in *over-accumulation* and also in *contradictions of state power*. The system cannot expand because the marginalization of a significant portion of humanity from direct productive participation, the downward pressure on wages and consumption worldwide, and the polarization of income have reduced the ability of the world market to absorb world output. This is therefore a crisis of social polarization, that is, of *social reproduction*; the system cannot meet the needs or assure the survival of millions of people, perhaps a majority of humanity. At the same time, given the particular configuration of social and class forces and the correlation of these forcers worldwide, national states are hard-pressed to regulate transnational circuits of accumulation and offset the explosive contradictions built into the system.

Yet I want to evoke here the concept of global crisis in a broader sense. This crisis, in my view, is unprecedented in terms of its magnitude, its global reach, the extent of ecological degradation and social deterioration, and the scale of the means of violence. Moreover, because the system is now global, crisis in any one place tends to represent crisis for the system as a whole. National states face spiraling crises of legitimacy as they fail to meet the social grievances of local working and popular classes experiencing downward mobility, unemployment, heightened insecurity and greater hardships. The legitimacy of the system has increasingly been called into question by millions, perhaps even billions, of people

1 Many works have been published in the aftermath of the 2008 collapse, too vast to list here. Among those that I have found useful (despite my disagreement with their interpretations) are: Konings (2010); Harman (2010); Chossudovsky and Marshall (2010); Marazzi (2011); Meszaros and Foster (2010).

around the world, and is facing expanded counter-hegemonic challenges. Global elites have been unable to counter this erosion of the system's authority in the face of worldwide pressures for a global moral economy. My notion of global crisis is best captured in the notion of a *crisis of humanity*, by which I mean a crisis that is approaching systemic proportions, threatens the ability of billions of people to survive, and raises the specter of a collapse of world civilization and degeneration into a new "Dark Ages."

In historic perspective, this twenty-first century global crisis shares a number of aspects with earlier structural crises of the 1970s and the 1930s, but there are also several features that are unique to the present:

1. The system is fast reaching the ecological limits of its reproduction. We may have already reached a point of no return. The ecological holocaust underway cannot be underestimated … peak oil, climate change, the extinction of species, the collapse of centralized agricultural systems in several regions of the world, and so on (see, inter-alia, Parenti, 2012; Dyer, 2010; McKibben, 2012; Foster, Clark and York, 2011).
2. The magnitude of the means of violence and social control is unprecedented, as is the concentration of the means of global communication and symbolic production in the hands of very few powerful groups. Computerized wars, drones, bunker-buster bombs, star wars, and so forth, have changed the face of warfare. Warfare has become normalized and sanitized for those not directly at the receiving end of armed aggression. At the same time we have arrived at the panoptical surveillance society and the age of thought control by those who control global flows of communication and symbolic production;
3. Capitalism is reaching apparent limits to its *extensive* expansion. There are no longer any new territories of significance that can be integrated into world capitalism, de-ruralization is now well advanced, and the commodification of the countryside and of pre- and non-capitalist spaces has intensified, that is, converted in hot-house fashion into spaces of capital, so that *intensive* expansion is reaching depths never before seen.
4. There is the rise of a vast surplus population inhabiting a "planet of slums,"[2] alienated from the productive economy, thrown into the margins, and subject to sophisticated systems of social control and to destruction—to a mortal cycle of dispossession-exploitation-exclusion;
5. There is a disjuncture between a globalizing economy and a nation-state based system of political authority. Transnational state apparatuses are incipient and have not been able to play the role of what social scientists refer to as a "hegemon," or a leading nation-state that has enough power and authority to organize and stabilize the system.

2 The phrase is from Davis' (2007) excellent study.

In short, we have entered a moment of great upheavals, momentous changes, and uncertain outcomes, fraught with dangers, including the very real possibility of collapse as well as the growing threat of repressive social control systems to contain the explosive contradictions of a global capitalism in crisis. If nothing else, it is clear that global capitalism is a highly unstable and crisis-ridden system. If we are to avert disastrous outcomes to the crisis we must understand both the nature of the new global capitalism and the nature of its crisis.

Situating the Global Crisis: From Nation-State to Transnational Capitalism

Several years after the 2008 collapse, wide ranging debate continues on the ongoing crisis, and more generally on the nature of the twenty-first century global order in which the crisis is situated. I have been centrally concerned with these matters and have written widely on them over the past two decades. I have above all sought to construct a theoretical framework for situating these matters, specifically a theory of global capitalism (see, in particular, Robinson, 2004, 2008, ch. 1). The world in which Karl Marx analyzed capital has radically changed. The global capitalism perspective offers a powerful explanatory framework for making sense of the crisis. Following Marx, we want to focus on the internal dynamics of capitalism to understand the crisis. And following the global capitalism perspective, we want to see how capitalism has qualitatively evolved in recent decades. The system-wide crisis we face is not a repeat of earlier such episodes of crisis such as in the 1930s or in the 1970s precisely because world capitalism is fundamentally different in the twenty-first century.

How, specifically, is world capitalism different now than during previous episodes of crisis? Globalization in my view constitutes a qualitatively new epoch in the ongoing and open-ended evolution of world capitalism, marked by a number of qualitative shifts in the capitalist system and by novel articulations of social power. First is the rise of truly transnational capital and a new global production and financial system into which all nations and much of humanity has been integrated, either directly or indirectly. We have gone from a *world economy*, in which countries and regions were linked to each other via trade and financial flows in an integrated international market, to a *global economy*, in which nations are linked to each more organically through the transnationalization of the production process, of finance, and of the circuits of capital accumulation. No single nation-state can remain insulated from the global economy or prevent the penetration of the social, political, and cultural superstructure of global capitalism.

Second is the rise of a transnational capitalist class (henceforth, TCC) that has drawn in contingents from most countries around the world, North and South, and has attempted to position itself as a global ruling class. This TCC is the *hegemonic fraction* of capital on a world scale. It is grounded in global rather than national markets and circuits of accumulation. Third is the rise of transnational state (henceforth, TNS) apparatuses. Such a TNS is constituted as a loose network made up of trans- and supranational organizations together with national states that functions to organize the conditions for transnational accumulation and through which the TCC has attempted to institutionally exercise its class power. Fourth are novel relations of inequality, domination and exploitation in global society, including the increasing importance of transnational social and class inequalities relative to North-South inequalities geographically or territorially-conceived.

Since the 1970s, the emergence of globally mobile transnational capital increasingly divorced from specific countries has facilitated the *globalization of production*. This involves the fragmentation and decentralization of complex production processes, the worldwide dispersal of the different segments and phases in these processes, and their functional integration into vast chains of production and distribution that span the globe. Values cross borders seamlessly as the move swiftly—often instantaneously—through these new transnational or global circuits of accumulation. This new system is driven, at the strictly technical level, by new information technologies and organizational innovations in capitalist production that have modified how value is created, circulated, and appropriated around the world. National economies have been dismantled and then reconstituted as component elements of this new global production and financial system, which is a qualitatively distinct world economic structure from that of previous epochs, when each country had a distinct national economy linked externally to one another through trade and financial flows. This is a shift from international market integration to global productive integration. At the same time an integrated global financial system has replaced the national bank-dominated financial systems of the earlier period. Global financial flows since the 1980s are qualitatively different from the international financial flows of the earlier period.

The globally-integrated production and financial system underscores the increasing interpenetration on multiple levels of capital in all parts of the world, organized around transnational capital and the giant transnational corporations (TNCs). It is increasingly difficult to separate local circuits of production and distribution from the globalized circuits that dictate the terms and patterns of accumulation worldwide. There are still local and national capitalists, and there will be for a long time to come. But they face ongoing pressures to "de-localize" and link to transnational capital if they are to survive. Territorially restricted capital cannot compete with its transnationally mobile counterpart. Transnational capital is the *hegemonic fraction* of capital on a world scale in the sense that it imposes its direction on the global economy and it shapes the character of production and social life everywhere.

Social Origins of Global Capitalism and the Current Crisis

Capitalist globalization is an ongoing, unfinished, and open-ended *process*, one that is contradictory and conflict-ridden, driven by social forces in struggle; it is *structure in motion*, *emergent*, with no consummated end-state. If we are to understand global capitalism and its crisis, we must train our focus in the first instance on configurations of these contradictory social forces analytically prior to our focus on the ways in which they become institutionalized and expressed in political, cultural and ideological processes.

This globalization stage of world capitalism itself evolved out the response of distinct agents to previous episodes of crisis, in particular, to the 1970s crisis of Fordism-Keynesianism, or of redistributive capitalism. In the wake of that crisis capital went global as a strategy of the emergent transnational capitalist class and its political representatives to reconstitute its class power by breaking free of nation-state constraints to accumulation. These constraints—the so-called "class compromise"—had been imposed on capital through decades of mass struggles around the world by nationally-contained popular and working classes. During the 1980s and 1990s, however, globally-oriented forces captured state power in most countries around the world and utilized that power to push capitalist globalization.

Global mobility gave transnational capital newfound structural power over nationally-based working classes. Globalization and neo-liberal policies opened up vast new opportunities for transnational accumulation in the 1980s and 1990s. What took place, in broad strokes, in these decades? Privatizations facilitated a new round of primitive accumulation as public and community spheres were commodified and turned over to capital. Deregulation, liberalization, and free trade agreements allowed for a wave of foreign direct investment, for a sharp increase in cross-border mergers and acquisitions, and for a heightened concentration and centralization of capital on a global scale. The incorporation of the former Soviet bloc and Third World revolutionary regimes into global capitalism provided vast new markets and investment outlets. The revolution in computer and information technology and other technological advances helped emergent transnational capital to achieve major gains in productivity and to restructure, "flexibilize," and shed labor worldwide. This, in turn, undercut wages and the social wage and facilitated a transfer of income to capital and to high consumption sectors around the world that provided new market segments fueling growth. In sum, globalization made possible a major extensive and intensive expansion of the system and unleashed a frenzied new round of accumulation worldwide that offset the 1970s crisis of declining profits and investment opportunities.

But crises of over-accumulation follow periods of hyper-accumulation. At the structural level, the current global crisis is above all one of overaccumulation, or the lack of outlets for the profitable absorption of surpluses. Global elites giddily declared "the end of History" in the heyday of global capitalism's hegemony in the early 1990s, but by the end of that decade the limits to expansion became clear as global markets became saturated. As privatization programs ran their course, the well of assets to privatize dried up. The initial boom in investment opportunities in the former socialist and revolutionary countries began to taper after they were brought into global markets. Once plants and infrastructures made the switch to computer and information technology the remarkable rate of fixed capital turnover that the initial system-wide introduction of these technologies generated could not be sustained. Investment in high tech slowed greatly in the twenty-first century and in 2008 telecommunication and computer orders were down 50 percent from their late 1990s high (Gosselin, 2009). By the turn of the century it became apparent we were headed towards a structural crisis. The system was generating ever more massive surpluses yet opportunities diminished for the profitable absorption of those surpluses, after the boom of the 1980s and 1990s. Global economic expansion and global market contraction reflect a—perhaps *the*—fundamental contradiction of capitalism: *overaccumlation.*

Crisis theory suggests that overaccumulation may be manifested in different ways (see, inter-alia, Harvey's 2006 discussion). How is it manifested in the current crisis? In the last major crisis, that of the 1970s, it took the form of a falling rate of profit, as "profit squeeze" theorists writing in that decade demonstrated. But a "profit squeeze" does not explain the current situation as profits soared in the period leading up to the crisis (see Figure 3.1). In the 1970s, overaccumulation also took the form of stagflation, or inflation together with stagnation. Working and popular classes fiercely resisted in the early and mid-1970s a transfer of the costs of the crisis to themselves. Neither these classes nor capital were willing to shoulder the costs of crisis; this stand-off is what in my view generated stagflation. But working and popular classes were able to put up resistance precisely because they faced capital within the confines of the nation-state. The gains these classes had made within nation-state capitalism and their ability to resist capital's impositions is precisely what led capital in the first place to go global, that is, to undertake a restructuring of the system through globalization. But stagflation and stand-off does not characterize the current crisis, at least not as I write in mid-2012. As has been amply documented, the portion of value going to workers has dropped sharply and living standards have plummeted since the late 1970s. Instead, it seems clear that overaccumulation is now expressed, as it was in the 1930s crisis, as over-production/under-consumption. In the wake of the 2008 collapse, for instance, the world press was full of images of car lots overflowing with vehicles that could not be marketed as factories shut down and production plummeted. And if there was a "credit crunch" it is not because bankers and investors did not have money to lend but because they could not do so profitably due to consumer insolvency.

The capitalist system, in sum, is again facing the recurrent challenge of how to profitably unload surpluses. The system had been stumbling from one lesser crisis to another since the mid-1990s. First were the Mexican peso crisis of 1995 and its "tequila effect" elsewhere. This was followed by the Asian financial meltdown of 1997–98 that also spread to other parts of the world. Then came the recession of 2001. Between the Asian meltdown of 1997–8 and the recession of 2001 global elites began to sound alarm bells. Billionaire financier George Soros warned of the need to save the system from itself (Soros, 1998). These elites became wracked by divisions and infighting as the more politically astute among them clamored for a "post-Washington consensus" project of reform—a so-called "globalization with a human face" (see, inter-alia, Stiglitz 2003). The neoliberal monolith began to

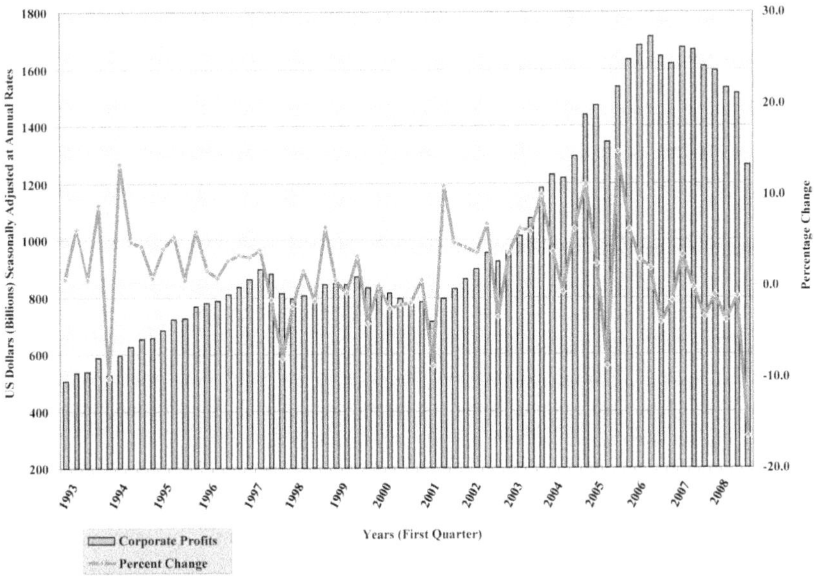

Figure 3.1 Corporate profits, 1993–2008
Source: Bureau of Economic Analysis, National Economic Accounts, NEPA tables.

crack, although it would take several more years before its downfall. By the new century two major mechanisms for unloading surplus would provide a perverse lifeline to the system: financial speculation and militarized accumulation.

Financial Speculation

Globalization has, in large part, been a finance-led process. Deregulation of the financial industry together with the introduction of computer and information technology made possible the creation of a globally-integrated financial system. Transnational finance capital is the most mobile fraction of capital and became the hegemonic fraction on a world scale in the late twentieth century. The "revolution in finance" included over the past few decades all sorts of financial innovations—a vast and bewildering array of derivatives, from swaps, futures markets, hedge funds, institutional investment funds, mortgage-backed securities, collateralized debt obligations, Ponzi schemes, pyramiding of assets, and many more. These innovations make possible a global casino, or transnational financial circuits based on speculation and the ongoing expansion of fictitious capital. Securitization made every pile of money, such as pensions, as well as debt itself, or negative money, a "tradable" and therefore a source of speculation and accumulation. These innovations allowed global speculators to appropriate values through new circuits that were in many respects irrespective of space and irrespective of "real" value or material production.

Transnational finance capital proved to be utterly predatory, seeking out one outlet after another for frenzied speculation. The sequence of speculative waves in the global casino since the 1980s included real estate investments in the emerging global property market that inflated property values in one locality after another, wild stock market speculation leading to periodic booms and busts, most notable the bursting of the dot-com bubble in 2001, the phenomenal escalation of hedge-fund flows and pyramiding of assets (see Figure 3.2), currency speculation, one ponzi scheme after another, and later on frantic speculation in global commodities markets, especially energy and food markets, which provoked a spike in world prices in 2007 and 2008 and sparked "food riots" around the world. Worldwide investment in commodities markets rose from 2006 to 2011 by almost 300 percent, from $141 billion to $431 billion (*The Economist*, 2011: 79).

Subsequently, the speculative frenzy shifted to the global bond market, as governments facing insolvency in the wake of 2008–09 turned to bond emissions in order to stay afloat. Global speculators used the US state's bailouts to channel a new round of speculative investment into the market in state-issued bonds and into bank lending to these cash-strapped states. Once the private banking and financial institutions recovered from the 2008 collapse—in large part thanks to government bailouts—they turned to unloading their surplus into these sovereign debt markets that they themselves helped to create. The global bond market climbed to some US$95 trillion by the start of 2011 and constituted the single biggest market for financial speculation in the wake of the 2008 collapse. In 2011 government bonds accounted for 43 percent of the value outstanding, up from 39 percent a year earlier (for these details, see *TheCityUK*, 2011). Gone are the times that such bonds are bought and held to maturity. They are bought and sold by individual and institutional investors in frenzied 24-hour worldwide trading and bet on continuously through such mechanisms as credit default swaps that shift their values and make bond markets a high stakes gamble of volatility and risk for investors, as I will mention further below. Moreover, the sovereign debt crisis has been presented as caused by working peoples living beyond their means, a convenient smokescreen that conceals the origins and nature of deficits and legitimates the call for social spending cuts and austerity.

The austerity sweeping across Europe (and in the United States) from 2008 and on is particularly revealing; it represents an acceleration of the process of the "Thirdworldization" of the "First World," in which the wealth concentrated at some poles of accumulation in the world is no longer redistributed downward locally towards First World labor aristocracies. Regardless of the outcome of the financial crisis in each individual country, capital wins in both the short and the long term. In the short term, investors cash in on a would-be defaulter with higher bond rates and/or through state bailouts that are channeled into their coffers. In the long run, austerity intensifies the processes of regressive taxation,

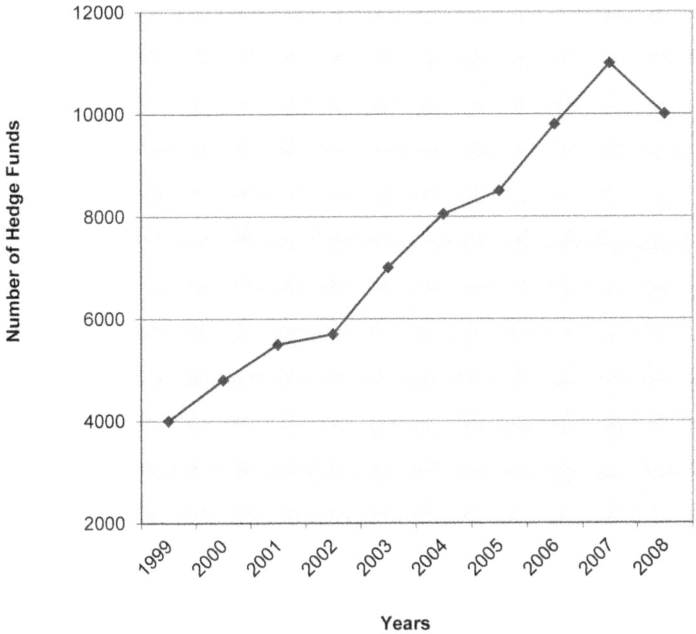

Figure 3.2 Global hedge funds, 1999–2008

Source: International Financial Services London, Report—Hedge Funds 2009 (datasheet) 07/04/2009 [Chart 1, Global Hedge Funds]. Estimates of the size of the hedge fund industry vary due to restrictions imposed on advertising and reporting of performance by hedge funds. As there are no authoritative estimates, we have relied in this report on commercial databases and index providers which rely on information provided voluntarily.

of privatization, and the dismantling of the social wage. Behind massive cuts in education and increases in tuition in both Europe and the United States, for instance, is the steady march of the privatization and commodification of public education. In short, the toxic mixture of public finance and private transnational finance capital in this age of global capitalism constitutes a new battlefield in which the global rich are waging a war against the global poor and working classes.

As speculation in the global financial casino reached a feverish pitch following recovery from the 2001 recession the gap grew ever greater between fictitious capital in this casino and the productive economy, or what the media popularly called the "real economy." This "real economy" was kept afloat momentarily by a massive increase in consumer debt (largely credit cards and mortgages) and federal deficit spending in the United States, which converted that country into the world's "market of last resort" and temporarily postponed the crash. US consumer debt climbed from $355 billion in 1980 to $1 trillion in 1994, to $2 trillion in 2004, and then peaked at $2.6 trillion in 2008, while the US current account went from a surplus in 1992 to deficits of $100 billion in 1998, $700 billion in 2004, and $1.2 trillion in 2008, according to Federal Reserve data. The Federal Reserve decision to reduce interest rates to about one percent in 2003 as a mechanism to overcome the recession also triggered a wave of speculation in the US mortgage market and prompted investors to begin subprime lending, including the infamous "teaser" interest rates aggressively sold to millions of people who would later be unable to meet their mortgage payments once the rates were readjusted to jack up payments. Consumption driven by US consumer credit card and mortgage debt and state deficit financing sustained accumulation worldwide and displaced momentarily the crisis. In the perverse world of predatory transnational finance capital, debt and deficits themselves became new sources of financial speculation.

I want to stress that it was *transnational*—not "US"—capital that relied on US debt and deficits to sustain profit-making around the world. The sub-prime mortgage market, for example, attracted trillions of dollars from individual, institutional, and corporate investors from all continents. It is a mistake to see things in terms of "US capitalism" rather than global capitalism. The US state has acted as an instrument of global capitalism and the United States as a major axis or nodal point for globalized accumulation. US treasury bailouts of the Wall Street-based banks in late 2008 and early 2009, for instance, went to bail out individual and institutional investors from around the world, while the US debt was itself financed by these same investors from all over the world. According to a 2011 report by the US government's General Accounting Office, the US Federal Reserve undertook a whopping $16 trillion in secret bailouts between 2007 and 2010 to banks and corporations from around the world (GAO, 2011).

Global casino capitalism produced an ever-greater expansion of fictitious capital—that is, money thrown into circulation without any base in commodities or in productive activity. Financial speculation fueled industrial production in part, so that the global casino kept the global factory running for a while. But much credit went not to expanded production but to inflate the prices of assets already in place. The gap between the worldwide speculative economy and the productive economy grew to an unfathomable chasm. In 2000, for instance, the worldwide trade in goods and services was less than $10 trillion for the entire year, according to IMF data, while *daily* movements in currency speculation stood at $3.5 trillion, so that in just a few days more currency circulated as speculation than the international circulation of goods and services in an entire year! By the early years of the twenty-first century these massive concentrations of transnational finance capital were destabilizing the system and global capitalism ran up against the limits of financial fixes. The bottoming out in 2007 of the sub-prime mortgage market that triggered collapse a year later of the global financial system headquartered in Wall Street was merely the "straw that broke the camel's back."

Militarized Accumulation

Alongside frenzied financial speculation, the US state militarized the global economy. The cutting edge of accumulation in the "real economy" worldwide shifted from computer and information technology before the dot-com bust to a military-security-industrial-construction-engineering-petroleum complex that also accrued enormous influence in the halls of power in Washington. Military spending skyrocketed into the trillions of dollars through the "war on terrorism" and the invasions and occupations of Iraq and Afghanistan, acting to throw fresh firewood on the smoldering embers of the global economy (see Table 3.1). Spin-off effects of this spending flowed through the open veins of the global economy—that is, the integrated network structures of the global production, services, and financial system. In this way, the US state has mobilized vast resources and political pressures, taking advantage of the dollar's role as the global currency and therefore of the extraordinary power of the US. Treasury, to absorb surpluses and sustain global accumulation by militarizing that accumulation and creating a global war economy.

Table 3.1 US military spending, 2000–2012 (in billions of dollars)

Year	2000	2001	2002	2003	2004	2005	2006	2007	2008	2009	2010	2011	2012
Amount	360	366	422	484	544	601	622	654	731	795	848	879	902*

Note: * Projected.
Source: http://www.usgovernmentspending.com/spending_chart_1997_2012USb_13s1li111mcn_30t_30_Defense_Spending_Chart.

The beneficiaries of US military action around the world have been transnational capitalist groups as a whole. This is the underlying class relation between the transnational capitalist class and the US national state. Despite the rhetoric of neo-liberalism, the US state undertook an unprecedented role in creating profit-making opportunities for transnational capital and pushing forward an accumulation process (the "free market") that left to its own devices would have grounded to a halt much sooner than 2008. The "creative destruction" of war (and natural and humanitarian disasters) generated new cycles of accumulation through "reconstruction." The trillions of dollars invested by the US state in war and "reconstruction" in Iraq and elsewhere has gone to a vast array of investors and sub-contractors that spanned the globe.[3] The picture that emerged was one in which the US state mobilized the resources to feed a vast transnational network of profit making that passed through countless layers of outsourcing, subcontracting, alliances and collaborative relations, benefiting transnationally-oriented capitalists from many parts of the globe as the class relations of global capitalism became deeply internalized *within* every nation-state. The crisis then hit the global system as a whole and is as much political—a crisis of legitimacy—as it is economic.

Responses to the Crisis and Alternative Futures

Is the current crisis cyclical, structural, or systemic? *Cyclical crises* are recurrent to capitalism about once every 10 years and involve recessions that act as self-correcting mechanisms without any major restructuring of the system. The recessions of the early 1980s, the early 1990s, and of 2001 were cyclical crises. In contrast, we are now in a deep structural crisis. *Structural crises* reflect deeper contradictions that can only be resolved by a major restructuring of the system. The crisis of the 1970s was a structural crisis that was resolved through capitalist globalization. And prior to that, the 1930s was a structural crisis that was resolved through the creation of a new model of Fordist-Keynesian or redistributive capitalism. A *systemic crisis* involves the replacement of a system by an entirely new system or by an outright collapse. A structural crisis opens up the *possibility* for a systemic crisis. But if it actually snowballs into a systemic crisis—in this case, if it gives way either to capitalism being superseded or to a breakdown of global civilization—it is not predetermined and depends entirely on the response of social and political forces to the crisis and on historical contingencies that are not easy to forecast. This is an historic moment of extreme uncertainty, in which collective responses from distinct social and class forces to the crisis are in great flux.

Global elites have been scrambling since the Asian crisis of 1997–98 to develop more effective TNS apparatuses or institutions and mechanisms that allow for transnational coordination and supervision. These efforts have intensified since the collapse of 2008. What are the prospects of a "new New Deal"? At the time of writing (mid-2013) there were little signs that capitalist states could foment a shift back from financial to productive accumulation. Global capital has become a leviathan in which capitals from around the world are so deeply inter-penetrated not only across borders but through the overlap of productive and financial circuits that it is not clear how meaningful it is to continue to make a distinction, in the classical way, between the two. The giant global financial conglomerates draw in individual and institutional investors from around the world and in turn circulate unfathomable amounts of capital into productive, commercial and service circuits. There did not appear to be the political will or even the notion among global elites and capitalist state managers in 2013 to restructure the system in any way that would reestablish some boundaries between financial and productive circuits or that would modify the role transnational finance capital has played as the regulator of the circuit of accumulation and the causal agent in the crisis. While some state officials called for a re-regulation of the global financial system, none appeared to challenge in any fundamental way the very structure in which transnational finance capital exercises such utter domination over the world.

Reformist forces from above in the 1930s were able to restructure capitalism by curtailing capital's prerogatives without challenging its fundamental interests. Now, in contrast, I do not see any way a reformism from above could adequately address the crisis without a head-on collision with the interests of global capital—the transnational banks, the oil/energy sector, the military-industrial-reconstruction complex, and so forth. This is to say that the capitalist state in order to salvage the system from its own self-destruction would have to exercise a remarkable degree of autonomy not just from individual capitalists and investor groups but from the leviathan that is the inextricably entangled mass of global capital. Such a role could only come about under a change in the worldwide correlation of class and social forces in favor of popular and working classes. The principle underlying difference between the 1930s New Deal project of reform and restructuring and the twenty-first century conjuncture is this correlation of class and social forces worldwide. There is no socialist-oriented bloc of countries currently that could exercise a critical counterweight to capitalist elites in response to the crisis, and mass socialist and workers' movements, although they are burgeoning, are weak compared to the 1930s.

On the other hand, although these forces are weaker in a comparative historical sense, they are also more coordinated across borders and regions in the new global age and reinvigorated by the crisis. To speak of a global justice movement is not mere rhetoric because resistance and counter-hegemonic forces around the world are acutely aware in a way that we have not previously experienced that local resistance struggles and alternative projects acquire their meaning in the context of and in relation to transnational struggles and projects. In the late 1990s popular resistance forces in different parts of the world calling for transformative projects formed a critical mass, coalescing around an agenda for global social justice. Resurgent left, radical, and anti-capitalist forces worldwide have again placed socialism on the world political agenda. Latin America appears to be the "weakest link" at this time in the global capitalist leviathan. The Venezuelan revolution is attempting to construct a twenty-first-century socialism and to stake out a radical anti-capitalist pole in South America. Everywhere popular forces are in ferment and mass struggles escalating. The organized left has had a renewed presence in many countries.

These counter-hegemonic forces call for the resolution of the crisis through a more far reaching transformation of the global social order. But severe fragmentation of the popular classes brought about by decades of global informalization and flexible accumulation continues to challenge counter-hegemonic forces to find new ways to aggregate dispersed groups into collective projects of transformation. Anarchist-inspired aversions to struggling for state power and the illusion of being able to "change the world without taking power" (Holloway 2005) are under heightened challenge. A radical response from below to the crisis lacks at this time a "post-modern prince" or political vehicles and concrete projects for reordering the world, a deficiency that the global justice movement seems to be more acutely aware of than prior to the crisis. At the close of a 120,000-strong meeting of the World Social Forum in Belem, Brazil, in January 2009, representatives from social movements from around the world declared:

> We are facing a global crisis which is a direct consequence of the capitalist system and therefore cannot find a solution within the system … In order to overcome the crisis we have to grapple with the root of the problem and progress as fast as possible towards the construction of a radical alternative that would do away with the capitalist system and patriarchal domination. We, the social movements, are faced with an historic opportunity to develop emancipatory initiatives on a global scale. Only through the social struggle of the masses can populations overcome the crisis … The challenge of social movements is to achieve a convergence of global mobilization. (Assembly of Social Movements, 2009)

The initiative seemed to pass in early 2009 from global elites to oppositional forces from below. Global elites meeting in January 2009 for the annual summit of the World Economic Forum in Davos, Switzerland, appeared to be rudderless—confused and divided, unable to come up with coherent solutions to the crisis and on the defensive. In contrast, the 120,000 participants from the Belem World Social Forum meeting were clearly on the offensive. In the following years the Arab Spring erupted in the Middle East, Europe became engulfed in anti-austerity strikes and mobilizations, the Occupy movement took the United States by storm, and Chilean student and worker protests underscored the ongoing popular and revolutionary challenges to global capitalism emanating from Latin America. Could such global mobilizations from below push reformist-minded elites further to the left or even push them beyond reformism? Popular forces from below need to convert counter-hegemony into a hegemony within the gamut of social and political responses to the unfolding crisis. This hegemony must involve a radical critique of the crisis. Now is the time to move from opposition to neoliberalism to opposition to the mildly reformist proposals that do not challenge the power of the transnational capitalist class and the global capitalist system.

The Dangers of Neo-Fascism and Collapse

Nation-states will remain for the foreseeable future a fundamental terrain of battle among contending social forces. National states face spiraling fiscal and legitimacy crises. Managers of the capitalist state need to generate conditions for a reactivation of transnational accumulation yet they also must respond to mass popular pressures from below. Many governments will likely collapse, such as happened in Iceland in January 2009, and may happen in Greece, Spain and elsewhere, as states find no way to manage the explosive pressures generated by the crisis. Global elites clearly were unable to counter the erosion of the system's authority. Might states turn to national protectionism in response to pressure from national constituencies to address the crisis? The integrated nature of the global production and financial system makes it difficult for it to be disassembled into national systems. Moreover, it is not in the interests of transnational capital to seal off any national territory, which would undermine the transnational circuits of accumulation that are based on vast and overlapping chains of suppliers and subcontractors across the globe and thoroughly transnational ownership and cross-investment of what appear in namesake alone as "national" corporations.

Apparent protectionist measures in late 2008 and early 2009 sought not to shield national capitals in rivalry with one another, as in the 1930s, but to bail out *transnational* capital within particular nation-states. National constituencies pressing for protectionism were not capitalist groups, who are transnational in character even when headquartered in one nation or another, but popular and working classes. US trade unions, for instance, called for a "buy American" provision to be included in the early 2009 US government bailout of auto firms while the US Chamber of Commerce and other business groups railed out against such provisions (Wallsten, 2009). Such labor protectionism may be progressive in some cases but in others is clearly chauvinist, such as in the United States and England, where it has been directed by privileged, largely white, sectors of the working class against immigrants. And it is this constituency that could form the social base for far-Right responses to the crisis. Crises of state legitimacy and vacuums in institutional power, in this regard, open up space not just for popular forces from below but also for the far-Right forces that compete with reformist and radical responses to crisis.

This proto-fascist Right seeks to fuse reactionary political power with transnational capital, to organize a mass base among historically privileged sectors of the global working class, such as white workers in the North and middle layers in the South, that are now experiencing heightened insecurity and the specter of downward mobility. The proto-fascist response to the crisis involves militarism, extreme masculinization, racism, the search for scapegoats (such as immigrant workers in the United States and Europe), and mystifying ideologies. The need for dominant groups around the world to assure widespread, organized mass social control of the world's surplus population and of rebellious forces from below gives a powerful impulse to a project of twenty-first century global fascism. A twenty-first century fascism could develop police states drawing on new sophisticated systems of surveillance and coercive and ideological control and the mechanisms they make possible for controlling space and exercising more selective repression than what we traditionally associate with early twentieth century fascism. Images of what such a political project would involve spanned from the late 2008/early 2009 Israeli invasion of Gaza and "ethnic cleansing" of the Palestinians, to the scapegoating and criminalization of immigrant workers in the United States, genocide in the Congo, the spread of neo-Nazis and skinheads in Europe, and the incipient breakdown of constitutional order under the George W. Bush administration (for an extended discussion see Robinson and Barrera 2012).

Conclusion

Could global civilization collapse if one or another project is unable to impose its hegemony and stabilize the system? There are many historical episodes of collapse when civilizations are unable to resolve the contradictions that tear them apart (Diamond 2005). When no social or political force is able to prevail and impose a stable system of domination collapse has been the outcome. This was the case, for instance, with the collapse of the Roman and Mayan empires, several Chinese dynasties, and the Easter Island civilization. The current moment is distinct in that this time the collapse would be of global civilization. Ecological constraints also played a role in previous collapses. However, we face the prospects of a more far-reaching systemic implosion in the twenty-first century through ecological crisis—as suggested in peak oil and other resource depletion scenarios, the spiral of species extinctions, and scientific predictions of a collapse of central agricultural systems in China, Australia, the US Midwest and other global breadbaskets in the coming decades. The ecological constraints to a resolution of the global crisis circumscribe the political possibilities for its resolution. Even if global capitalism could manage to stabilize in the next few years, a recovery would be ephemeral without a more fundamental resolution of the fundamentally unsustainable nature of the system. Sociologist Sing Chew has studied "recurrent dark ages" in world history, including mass dying, political chaos and a regression in levels of social organization and productive forces. He has warned that we face the possibility now of a "new dark ages" on a planetary scale (Chew, 2006).

Crises are times of great uncertainty so that short-term predictions are of little value. They are also moments in which political agency may prevail over the structural determinations. Depending on the elements of contingency and agency, crises may tilt the correlation of social and class forces in distinct directions. Crises may therefore also present opportunities for dominant groups, particularly for capital, to utilize unemployment and hardship to carry through further dispossession. In this respect, the 2008 financial crisis was a major turning point. The multi-billionaire Warren Buffet, chairman of Berkshire Hathaway, and one of the richest men in the world, famously stated in 2006 that "There's class warfare, all right, but it's my class, the rich class, that's making war, and we're winning" (as cited in Carroll, 2010: 1).

In fact, the global crisis provided the TCC with an opportunity to intensify this war. As the crisis spread, it generated the conditions for new rounds of massive austerity worldwide, greater flexibilization of labor, steeply rising under and unemployment, foreclosures, furloughs, reduced working hours, amid mounting debt peonage have been some of capital's mechanisms for transferring the cost of crisis onto the masses of popular and working classes. The crisis allowed transnational capital to squeeze more value out of labor, directly through more intensified exploitation and indirectly through state finances. Social and political conflict escalated around the world in the wake of 2008, including, as mentioned above, repeated rounds of national strikes and mass mobilization in the European

Union, uprisings in North Africa and the Middle East, etc. While the TNS failed to intervene to impose regulations on global finance capital, it did intervene to impose the costs of devalorization on labor. By 2010 global corporations were registering record profits and corporate income escalated. After suffering losses in 2008, the top 25 hedge-fund managers were paid, on average, more than $1 billion each in 2009, eclipsing the record they had set in pre-recession 2007 (Freeland, 2011). In 2011 corporate profits in the United States hit their highest level since 1950, while in that same year real wages fell. Between 2009 and 2011, 88 percent of national income growth in the United States went to corporate profits while just one percent went to wages (Garofalo, 2012). The Dow Jones, which had dropped from 14,000 to 6,500 in late 2008 and early 2009, rose to 13,000 in early 2012.

Unless there is effective resistance, global capital is likely to make permanent the further flexibilization of labor and other concessions it is wringing out of workers through the crisis. The bailouts of transnational capital, particularly transnational finance capital, come at the expense of taxation on working classes and therefore represent in themselves a transfer of the devaluation of capital onto labor. Will popular sectors manage to forge a social solidarity of the oppressed, the exploited, and the subordinate majorities across ethnic and national lines? Dominant groups, especially in the heartlands of global capitalism, will try to aggravate existing national and ethnic hierarchies of labor, to scapegoat immigrants, unemployed Black people, and so forth. Gary Dymsky has shown how financiers shifted from redlining African American communities in the United States in their mortgage lending to predatory lending to them, that is, from racial exclusion to racial exploitation (Dymysky, 2009). Since the subprime collapse the dominant discourse attempts to shift blame to these African American families as "irresponsible borrowers." Similarly, anti-immigrant forces in the United States have shifted from a blatant racialist anti-Latino discourse to an economicist discourse of "protecting citizens' employment." These discursive shifts underscore that a major dimension of the battles to come is *whose* interpretation of the crisis will prevail. How majorities in global society understand the threats to their security and survival will shape their social and political agency.

It is at times of crisis rather than equilibrium in a system, to reiterate, that space opens up for new ideas and for collective agency to influence the course of structural change. We are entering a period of turbulence, upheavals, collapse of states, political vacuums and prolonged conflict as we step into the unknown. In my view, resolution of the crisis must involve a radical redistribution of wealth and power downward to poor majorities. Social justice requires, at the minimum, reintroducing a redistributive component into the global accumulation process. This raises the question of what forces in favor of social justice can hope to achieve if and when poor people and popular sectors are able to win state power in particular countries, or at least to place into state agencies people who are responsive to their plight, aware of their needs, and willing to challenge the prerogatives of transnational capital.

Yet this brings us full circle back to globalization and to what makes the early twenty-first century distinct from previous moments in the history of world capitalism. In this qualitatively new stage of global capitalism there are clear limitations to the reintroduction of a redistributive project at the nation-state level. It is not clear how effective national alternatives alone can be in transforming social structures and resolving the crisis. If the (capitalist) state as a class relation is becoming transnationalized then any challenge to (global) capitalist state power must involve a major transnational component. Struggles at the nation-state level are far from futile. They remain central to the prospects for social justice, to progressive social change, and to any resolution of the crisis. But any such struggles must be part of a more expansive transnational counter-hegemonic project, including transnational trade unionism, transnational social movements, transnational political organizations, and so on. And they must strive to establish sets of transnational institutions and practices that can place controls on the global market and rein in some of the power of global capital as the first step in a resolution of the crisis. An alternative to global capitalism must be a *transnational* popular project. The popular mass of humanity in its struggle for social justice must develop a *transnational* class consciousness and concomitant global political protagonism involving strategies, programs, organizations and institutions that link the local to the national, and the national to the global.

References

Assembly of Social Movements. 2009. “Declaration of the Assembly of Social Movements at the World Social Forum,” February 5, from http://www.globalresearch.ca/index.php?context=viewArticle&code=ASS20090204&articleId=12160.

Carroll, William K. 2010. *The Making of a Transnational Capitalist Class: Corporate Power in the 21st Century*. London: Zed.

Chew, Sing C. 2006. *The Recurring Dark Ages: Ecological Stress, Climate Changes, and System Transformation*. Lanham: AltaMira Press.

Chossudovsky, Michel and Andrew Gavin Marshall (eds) 2010. *The Global Economic Crisis: The Great Depression of the XXI Century*. Quebec: Global Research Publishers.

Davis, Mike. 2007. *Planet of Slums*. London: Verso.

Diamond, Jared. 2005. *Collapse: How Societies Choose to Fail or Succeed*. New York: Penguin.

Dicken, Peter. 2007. *Global Shift*, 5th Edition. New York: Guilford.

Dyer, Gwynne. 2010. *Climate Wars: The Fight for Survival as the World Overheats*. Oxford: Oneworld.

Dymsky, Gary A. 2009. “The Political Economy of the Subprime Meltdown,” paper presented at the symposium, Financial Crisis and Globalization, Institute for Global Cooperation and Conflict (IGCC), University of California at Riverside, 13 January.

Foster, John Bellamy, Brett Clark and Richard York. 2011. *The Ecological Rift: Capitalism's War on Earth*. New York: Monthly Review Press.

Freeland, Chrystia. 2011. "The Rise of the New Global Elite," *The Atlantic*, January/February, from http://www.theatlantic.com/magazine/archive/2011/01/the-rise-of-the-new-global-elite/8343/.

Garofalo, Pat. 2012. "Corporate Managers and Profits are Increasing, but Workers' Wages Aren't," *Thinkprogress Economy*, February 22, from http://thinkprogress.org/economy/2012/02/22/430190/corporate-profits-wages- 2012/.

General Accounting Office. 2011. "Federal Reserve System: Opportunities Exist to Strengthen Policies and Processes for Managing Emergency Assistance, GAO-11-696," July, Washington, DC: GAO.

Gosselin, Peter G. 2009. "U.S. economy may sputter for years," *Los Angeles Times*, 19 January, A1.

Harman, Chris. 2010. *Zombie Capitalism: Global Crisis and the Relevance of Marx*. Chicago: Haymarket Books.

Harvey, David. 2006. *The Limits to Capital*. London: Verso.

Holloway, John. 2005. *Change the World without Taking Power*. London: Pluto.

Konings, Hans. (ed.) 2010. *The Great Credit Crash*. London: Verso.

Marazzi, Christian. 2010. *The Violence of Financial Capitalism*. Los Angeles: Semiotics(e).

McKibben, Bill. 2012. "Global Warming's Terrifying New Math," *Rolling Stone*, August 2, from http://www.rollingstone.com/politics/news/global-warmings-terrifying-new-math-20120719?print=true.

Meszaros, Istvan and John Bellamy Foster. 2011. *The Structural Crisis of Capital*. New York: Monthly Review Press.

Parenti, Christian. 2012. *Tropic of Cancer: Climate Change and the New Geography of Violence*. Nation Books.

Robinson, William, I. 2004. *A Theory of Global Capitalism*. Baltimore: Johns Hopkins University Press.

Robinson, William, I. 2007. "Beyond the Theory of Imperialism: Global Capitalism and the Transnational State," *Sociology Without Borders*, 2, 52–56.

Robinson, William, I. 2008. *Latin America and Global Capitalism*. Baltimore: Johns Hopkins University Press.

Robinson, William, I. and Mario Barrera. 2012. "Twenty-First Century Fascism: A U.S. Case Study," *Race and Class*, 53(3), 42–49.

Soros, George. 1998. *The Crisis of Global Capitalism: Open Society Endangered*. New York: Public Affairs.

Stiglitz, Joseph. 2003. *Globalization and its Discontents*. New York: W.W. Norton.

The CityUK. 2011. "Global Bond Market Up 5% in 2010 to Record $95 Trillion," from http://www.thecityuk.com/media/press-releases/global-bond-market-up-5-in-2010-to-record-95-trillion-more-than-two-thirds-the-size-of-equity-market/.

The Economist. 2011. "Back to the Futures." *The Economist*, September 17, 79.
Wallsten, Peter. 2009. "Liberals Watch Obama, and Worry." *Los Angeles Times*, February 16, A1.

Chapter 4
The Global Financial Crisis: A Crisis of Capital or for Labor?

James Petras and Henry Veltmeyer

From the neoconservative far right to the far left we have been deluged by writings about the "crisis of global capitalism." While these writings, according to the ideological predispositions of their authors, differ as to the causes, consequences, prognosis and cures, there is a virtual consensus that "the crisis" threatens to put an end to capitalism as we know it—certainly in its neoliberal form. And there is no doubt that for a short period, from 2008 to 2009, the capitalist system in Europe and the United States suffered a shock that shook the system to its foundations, threatening the functioning and the stability of key financial institutions as well as the capitalist development of economies at the center of the system. However, as is the norm for capitalism, the crisis merely served to restructure the system, to shake out its underperforming and weaker agents and destroy capital in the process but at the same time regenerating conditions for a new round of capital accumulation. As it turned out finance capital, the major force behind and the principal detonator of the financial meltdown and its repercussions, recovered from its losses—over $4 trillion according to the IMF (Landler, 2009)[1]—and the capitalist class in its financial core was strengthened, to no small extent by the bailout of the banks and other financial institutions owned by elite members of this class. With this bailout, which the IMF estimated would require at least $1.1 trillion of public funds—in fact well over $3 trillion—combined with the magic of the market in restoring the value of the elite's financial assets, the tiny group of billionaires at the apex of this elite (some 1,200), not only recovered the pre-crisis value of its financial assets, but it is estimated that their fortunes had increased by at least 25 percent and as much as 37 percent.[2] In addition—and more importantly—the political,

1 The IMF puts the losses from the global economic crisis at $4.1 trillion but this figure only includes losses directly attributable to the major banks and financial institutions.

2 It is estimated that the US billionaires, the 413 individuals (all men) at the center or top of the system and the epicenter of the recent financial crisis, have increased their holdings and fortunes—by some 30 percent since 2008. In Mexico, Carlos Slim, the world's richest man, is reported to have increased his fortune by 38 percent since the end of 2008. Even without any further study it is evident that the state played a much more important role than the market in the restructuring of wealth in the aftermath of the crisis and the "recovery" by the small club of billionaires at the apex of the income distribution. For example, in Canada

social, ideological conditions of "the crisis" served to consolidate the dominance of capital over labor, converting a crisis of capital into a crisis for labor (and to some extent a crisis in the functioning of the state).[3]

In short, the crisis has been used to the strategic advantage of capital in its class war against labor, to further the accumulation of capital and the consolidation of capitalist rule. This class war, like the recession—described by a number of analysts as a "triple crisis"—can be traced back to the production crisis of the early 1970s and beyond to the "Great Depression" at the turn into the third decade of the twentieth century. The result: the concentration of capital, an extension of the fundamental capitalist relation of wage labor exploitation, a deepening of the global divide between capital and labor in the distribution of wealth and income, and an expansion of the global reserves of surplus labor needed to reactivate the accumulation process. However, the focus as well as an overemphasis on the dynamics of financial capital—on the (mal)functioning of the financial institutions and the failure in global governance—has distracted many analysts and activists on the Left, leading them not to see what is happening at a more fundamental level, both at its epicenter (the US and Europe) and in its various peripheries, and to appreciate fully the social and development implications of the crisis. For one thing, the global financial crisis is far from global in its scope and scale, and despite its tri- or multi-dimensional form it is essentially a systemic production crisis. For another, the crisis points to the dynamics and conditions of a major global realignment of economic power (from the US and Europe to the BRICs) and the efforts of financial capitalists at the center of the system to protect their interests and maintain their hegemony over the world capitalist production process. Furthermore, the notion of a homogeneous global crisis of capitalism advanced on both the right and left[4] overlooks profound differences in the social

---

corporate tax rate as an anti-crisis measure was reduced (from 18.5 to 16 percent in the case of Canada), ostensibly so as to promote productive (employment generating) investments. Needless to say, these investments have not taken place. What has taken place is several rounds of bonuses paid out to the CEOs of the financial institutions and corporations that were bailed out or had failed to go under. The rich and super-rich owners of the capital invested in these corporations and institutions were the primary beneficiaries of the anti-crisis policies, bailouts and austerity measures adopted by governments everywhere within the system. Needless to add, the primary losers in this stacked game have been the working class.

3 Vis-à-vis the state the crisis sometimes takes the form of a legitimation crisis, as for example, in the inability of the Latin American state today to justify its policy agenda of neoliberal globalization; it can also take the form of a fiscal crisis, as in the late 1970 when virtually every government in both the north and the south found itself unable to finance the programs of social welfare and economic development, or a debt crisis, as in 2011 when the US government found itself unable to finance its operations because of a debt overhang of $14 trillion.

4 The literature on the crisis is too voluminous to cite or review but see, inter alia, Berberoglu (2012), Foster and Magdoff (2009), Gills (2011) and Konings (2010).

and political dynamics of capitalist development, and the forces and relations of production, within and among diverse regions, countries and classes, in diverse contexts, social formations and staging areas of a global class war. Above all—and to the main point of this chapter—the current literature on the crisis is overly focused on the economics and political economy of the crisis, on the problems that it presents for capital (and its causes, policy prescriptions and strategic responses). As a result, the crisis literature reflects the absence of studies into the functionality of the crisis for restructuring the system, and a relative lack of studies of what we might term the "sociology of crisis."[5]

The Global Crisis Thesis

Advocates of a global crisis thesis argue that beginning in 2007 and continuing to the present the world capitalist system is on the verge of collapse and that sought-for or found signs of a recovery is a mirage or but a temporary refuge. They cite the stagnation and continuing recession (particularly the growing and disturbingly high rates of household and public sector debt, youth unemployment and the slow growth in jobs) in North America and the Eurozone, as well as the unsustainable countermeasures taken in some cases such as Greece. These critics present or cite GDP data hovering between negative to zero growth in production and employment. Their argument is backed up by data citing double-digit unemployment in both regions. They frequently correct the official data which understate the number and percentage of the unemployed by excluding part-time, long-term unemployed workers and others. The "crisis of capital" argument is consolidated by citing the millions of American homeowners who have been evicted by the banks, the sharp increase in poverty and destitution accompanying job losses, wage reductions and the elimination or reduction of social services. The idea of "crisis" is also associated with the massive increase in bankruptcies of mostly small and medium size businesses and regional banks, the erosion of the production apparatus and the inordinate concentration of wealth and income resulting from the policy dynamics of deregulated "free" market capitalism.[6]

5 On a "sociology of crisis" see Veltmeyer (2011).

6 In the US, where this inordinate development and the associated 'structure of social inequality' achieved its maximum expression, the social conditions of free market capitalism have brought about an extraordinarily acute and polarized class division reflected in the following statistics (see the Institute of Policy Studies blog—http://www.ips-dc.org/inequality). In 2007 one half of Americans owned only 2.5 percent of the country's wealth while the top 1 percent owned 1/3 (33.8 percent). While in 2000 of this wealth only 15 percent was in the form of financial assets (stocks and bonds, etc.) in 2007 over 40 percent of it was. And needless to say, financial assets are particularly maldistributed—the bottom 50 percent owning less than 0.5 percent while the top 1 percent own 50.9 percent. The share of the top 1 percent in capital income went up from 36 percent in 1980 to 58 percent in 2003—and climbing (Shapiro and Friedman, 2006). The average hourly earnings for

The Global Crisis: The Loss of Legitimacy

The critics of untrammeled free market capitalism ("neoliberalism" as per the Washington Consensus), especially in the financial press, have conceived of a "legitimacy crisis of capitalism," citing polls showing substantial majorities questioning the injustice and damaging effects of the capitalist system, the vast and growing inequalities, and the rigged rules by which banks exploit their size ("too big to fail") to raid the Treasury at the expense of social programs. In short the advocates of the thesis of the "global crisis of capitalism" make a strong case, demonstrating the profound and pervasive destructive effects of the capitalist system on the lives and livelihoods of the great majority of people—"humanity."

The problem is that a presumed "crisis of humanity" (more specifically a crisis of labor—of salaried and wage workers) or a "human disaster" is not the same as a crisis of the capitalist system. In fact as we shall argue below growing social adversity, declining income and employment, have been major factors in facilitating the rapid and massive recovery of the profit margins of many large-scale corporations in the wake of the "global financial crisis." Moreover, the thesis of a "global" crisis of capitalism amalgamates disparate economies, countries, and classes with sharply divergent experiences at different historical moments.

A Global Crisis or Uneven and Unequal Development?

It is incorrect and somewhat foolish to argue for a "global crisis" when several of the major economies in the world economy did not suffer a major downturn and others recovered and expanded rapidly. China and India did not suffer even a recession. Even during the worst years of the Euro-US decline (2008–09), the economies and emerging markets of the Asian giants grew on average about 8 percent a year. Latin America's economies, especially those of the major agro-mineral export countries (Argentina, Brazil, Peru, Chile ...) with diversified markets that respond to the growing demand for natural resource-

US workers fell from $20.06 in 1972 to $18.5 in 2008 while the remuneration of CEOs rose by almost 300 percent (Executive Excess, 2006); Bureau of Labor Statistics, *Current Employment Statistics*, "Average Hourly Earnings in 2008 dollars"). In 1950 the ratio of the average executive's pay, only a part of total remuneration, to the average worker's pay was 30 to 1. Since 2000 it has exploded to between 300 and 500 to one. And the recession has erased eight million private sector jobs in the US alone, and 40 million Americans are now on food stamps. According to a Pew Research center study approximately 37 percent of Americans between the ages 18 and 29 have been either unemployed or underemployed during the recession.

based commodities in China and India, paused briefly (in 2009) before resuming moderate to rapid rates of growth (3 to 7 percent from 2010 to 2012).[7]

By aggregating economic data from the Euro-zone as a whole the advocates of global crisis, overlooked the enormous disparities in performance within the zone. While Southern Europe wallows in a deep sustained depression from 2008 into the foreseeable future, German exports in 2011 set a record of a trillion euros; Germany's trade surplus reached 158 billion euros, after a 155 billion euro surplus in 2010 (BBC News, February 8, 2012).

While aggregate Eurozone unemployment has reached 10.4 percent, internal differences defy any notion of a "general crisis." Unemployment in Holland is 4.9 percent, Austria 4.1 percent and Germany 5.5 percent, with employer claims of widespread skilled labor shortages in key growth sectors. On the other hand in Southern Europe, on the margins of European capitalism, unemployment runs to depression levels: Greece 21 percent, Spain 22.9 percent, and Portugal 13.6 percent (*Financial Times*, January 19, 2012, 7). In other words, "the crisis" does not adversely affect some economies, which in fact profit from their market dominance and techno-financial strength over dependent, indebted and more backward economies. Thus to conceive of a "global crisis" obscures the fundamental and dominant exploitative relations that facilitate "recovery" and growth of some advanced capitalist economies over and against their competitors and client states. In addition, global crisis theorists mistakenly amalgamate crisis-ridden, financial-speculative economies (US, UK) with dynamic productive export economies (Germany, China).

Another problem with the thesis of a "global crisis" is that it overlooks profound internal differences in age_cohorts. In several European countries youth unemployment (16–25) hovers from between 30 to 50 percent (Spain 48.7 percent, Greece 47.2 percent, Slovakia 35.6 percent, Italy 31 percent, Portugal 30.8 percent and Ireland 29 percent) while in Germany, Austria and Holland youth unemployment runs to 7.8 percent, 8.2 percent and 8.6 percent respectively (*Financial Times*, February 1, 2012, 2). These differences underlie the reason why there is no "global youth movement" of the "indignant" and "occupiers." A fivefold difference in the rate of youth unemployment is not conducive to "international" solidarity. The concentration of high youth unemployment explains the uneven development of mass street protests and its concentration in Southern Europe. It also explains why the northern Euro-American "anti-globalization" movement is largely a lifeless forum which attracts academic pontification on the "global capitalist crisis" and why the "social forums" in the anti-globalization movement are unable to attract the millions of unemployed youth in Southern Europe.

Given rates of youth unemployment averaging 20 to 30 percent, and reaching 60 percent in some countries, and given the unresponsiveness of European state

7 On these developments, and the associated reconfiguration of economic power, see Petras and Veltmeyer (2011).

officials to the demand for change in their austerity policies (in thrall as they are to the dictates of capital) these youth are more attracted or given to direct action. In this regard, globalists and globalization theorists (for example, Antonio Negri, in his celebrated but rather useless intellectual intervention with his notion of "multitudes") overlook the specific way in which the multitude of unemployed young workers are exploited in their dependent debt-ridden countries. They ignore the specific way they are ruled and repressed by center-left and rightist capitalist parties. The contrast was evident in the winter of 2012 when Greek workers were pressured to accept a 20 percent wage cut while workers in Germany were demanding a 6 percent increase. Since then workers all over Europe, and most particularly in Spain and Portugal, but also Italy, have been pressured to accept a serious cutback in wages and benefits, and an even deeper cut in the social wage via austerity measures mandated by the guardians and officials of the European capitalist state system. In March 2012, 24 EU heads of state signed a "fiscal pact" to make neoliberal austerity policies binding on all governments. The "Treaty on Stability, Coordination and Governance in the Economic and Monetary Union," as the European Fiscal Pact is officially called, is more than the result of unrealistic plotting by neoliberal economists and politicians. Further waves of privatization, destruction of jobs, restriction of public services, social degradation, and wage reduction, are pre-programed across the whole of Europe; and all to protect the profits of a small group of rich capitalists. The destructive policies, pushed ahead mainly by Germany and France, have been accepted and put into practice by nearly all EU governments, because in every state there is a wealthy clique who profit from the increasing pressure on the wage-earning population.

If the "crisis" of capitalism is manifest in specific regions, so too does it unevenly affect different age and racial segments of the waged and salaried working classes—and there is likely a gender dimension to these differences as well (although for some unknown reason(s) there are no studies of this issue in the most recent context of capitalist development in conditions of crisis). The unemployment rates among youth and older workers varies enormously: in Italy the ratio is 3.5/1, Greece 2.5/1, Portugal 2.3/1, Spain 2.1/1, Belgium 2.9/1 while in Germany it is 15/1 (*Financial Times*, February 1, 2012). In other words, because of the higher levels of unemployment among youth they have a greater propensity for direct action "against the system"; meanwhile older workers with higher levels of employment (and unemployment benefits) have shown a greater propensity to rely on the ballot box and engage in limited strikes over job and pay related issues.

The concentration of unemployment among young workers means that they form the main agency and "available core" for sustained direct action, but it also means that they can only achieve limited unity of action with the older working class that are experiencing single digit unemployment. But, it is also true that the great mass of the unemployed youth provides a formidable weapon in the hands of employers with which to threaten to replace employed older workers. As Marx might have predicted, capitalists not infrequently today resort to unemployment as a lever of capital accumulation, using the unemployed to lower wages and benefits, and to intensify the rate of exploitation (= "increase productivity") and thus increase profit margins. Far from being simply an indicator of "capitalist crisis," high levels of unemployment continues to serve as a mechanism for increasing the rate of profit and for capitalists to make money. Thus, as the capacity of the working class for material consumption declines—viewed by some sociologists and economists as evidence of a "disappearing middle class" (hollowing out of middle strata in the income distribution)—the consumption of luxury goods for the capitalist class is on the increase: for example, the sales of luxury cars and watches is booming.

A Labor Crisis: The Counter-Thesis

Contrary to the "global capitalist crisis" thesis, a substantial amount of available data refutes its assumptions. For example, a recent study reports that "US corporate profits are higher as a share of gross domestic product than at any time since 1950" (*Financial Times*, January 30, 2012). US companies' cash balances have never been greater, thanks to an intensified exploitation of workers, and a multi-tiered wage system in which newly hired workers work for a fraction of what older workers receive (thanks in part to agreements signed by "doormat" labor bosses).

These and other data on a "recovery" of the rate of profit in the wake of the global crisis not only reflects an increase in the rate and dominant forms of labor exploitation—as well as an expansion of imperialist exploitation (see the discussion below)—but they point towards a major consequence of the class war launched by the capitalist class against workers in the early 1970s: a steady and continuing decline in the share of labor in the social product, and a weakening of the organizational and political capacity of the working class.[8] These changes in the capital-labor relation can be traced back to the crisis that brought to an end the "the golden age of capitalism" in the early 1970s,[9] but they also implicate the more recent and perhaps current systemic crisis, which is unique in that it is the

8 On these changes in the capital-labor relation—which was extended by the agency of imperialist exploitation into a north-south development divide within the 'new world order' of neoliberal globalization—see, inter alia, Berberoglu (2010); Davis (1980); Crouch and Pizzorno (1978); Petras and Veltmeyer (2001); and Veltmeyer and Petras (1997, 2000).

9 Representing the most serious involution in the system of global capitalist production since the Great Depression, the systemic crisis of the early 1970s has been explained both in Marxist terms (as a fall in the average rate of profit, overproduction, underconsumption, etc.) and by French Regulationists (Lipietz, 1987) as a crisis in the Fordist form of global production. In these terms, the crisis is essentially "structural"—rooted in the structure of the system, which is defined in the one case by a particular combination of productive forces and corresponding social relations, and in the other by the articulation of a certain "regime of accumulation" and a corresponding "mode of regulation." Others, however (e.g., Marglin and Schor, 1990), saw the cause of the crisis not so much in the structural limits of capitalist production as in its political limits—in the "profit crunch" deriving

first capitalist crisis in history triggered by banks lending to workers for them to buy houses, so providing them a short-lived (and illusory) buy into the "American dream" (and thereby an ideology of possessive individualism and striving to accumulate).[10]

Although most analysts and critics on the center-left have focused on the distribution of household income—on the concentration of income within the top 1 percent of income earners or households, the disappearance of the middle strata in this distribution, and the immiseration of households at the bottom end—arguably a more critical variable of the capitalist development process is the share of labor (and capital) in the distribution of national (and global) income. In this regard there are no hard data but all the indications are that the decline in the relative participation of labor (in the form of wages and salaries) and capital (income available for investment) in the national (and global) income distribution has increased in recent years. Statistics that indicate this include a persistent decline in the remuneration of labor and the value of wages, a pattern accentuated by recent post-crisis developments, and a corresponding incline in the returns to capital and remuneration of services to capital—for example, the income and benefits that accrue to the CEOs of major capitalist enterprises. Of even greater import is the return to invested capital in key economic sectors (for example, the natural resources extraction industry) in the most recent conjuncture of post-crisis capitalist development.[11]

On the other side of the ledger many European and American workers can no longer find or have lost their jobs, millions of US workers have lost their homes or have been forced to take on an unaffordable level of personal debt, masses of migrant workers all over the capitalist world are subjected to conditions of superexploitation in the informal sector, and millions have been impoverished or

---

from the power of organized labor to demand concessions from capital under conditions of depressed capital accumulation.

10 The basic question addressed in the crisis literature (Konings, 2010) is: How could small losses on subprime housing loans in the United States, estimated at about $100 million in early 2007, lead to a global financial and economic crisis? Worldwide stock markets plunged and housing values declined sharply during 2007–08; and the IMF has projected that output losses are likely to be about $4.7 trillion between 2008 and 2015. Most experts were blindsided by the magnitude and speed with which this financial crisis, which originated in the US, spread to the rest of the world. Large investment banks, big corporations, millions of jobs, and about $1 trillion of private capital flows to developing countries evaporated within days of the Lehman Brothers collapse on September 12, 2008. Some argue that if Lehman had been bailed out, the US financial system would not have melted down and, consequently, a global recession could have been avoided. Others, such as Kenneth Rogoff (*The Economist*, September 12, 2009), argue that even if Lehman had been saved it would still have had to be sacrificed later, along with other investment banks, because the system had exceeded sustainable levels: trillions of dollars had been borrowed against an asset bubble in stock and house prices.

11 On this see Veltmeyer and Petras (2012).

pushed into crime, drugs and suicide. In Greece suicides increased 40 percent between 2009 and 2012. In conditions of US and European capitalism these and other such problems have reached crisis proportions, but they are to some extent mitigated by what remains of the welfare state. Even so, under current conditions, by all appearances and the few available accounts, the situation of many workers continue to deteriorate. What we have is a system in crisis—but a crisis from which a few profit and many suffer.

The "crisis of capitalism" theorists have failed to examine the financial reports of the major US corporations. According to General Motors 2011 report to its stockholders, they celebrated the greatest profit ever, turning a profit of $7.6 billion, surpassing the previous record of $6.7 billion in 1997. And General Motors is no exception. In the booming extractive sector of multinational corporations (in energy, mining and the export sales of fossil fuels) and commodity traders profits are particularly large. For example, the *Financial Times* (April 15, 2013) calculates that "[t]he world's top commodities traders have pocketed nearly $250 billion over the last decade, making the individuals and families that control the largely privately-owned sector big beneficiaries of the rise of China and other emerging countries." In 2000 the companies and traders in the sector made $2.1 billion in profits but in 2012 $33.5 billion. And while some traders enjoyed returns in excess of 50–60 percent in the mid-2000s today, in the aftermath of a "global financial crisis" and a downturn in some commodity prices, they are still averaging returns of 20–30 percent, huge by any business standard. In the aftermath of the 2008–09 financial crisis, and in the vortex of a subsequent and continuing production crisis, these commodity traders have made more money than industrial giants such as Toyota, Volkswagen, Ford Motor, BMW and Renault combined, and their net income have surpassed that of the mighty Wall Street banks—Goldman Sachs, JPMorgan Chase and Morgan Stanley.

Some of these profits derive from resource rents and super-profits extracted from the booming industry of large-scale investments in land and natural resources. However a large part results from the squeezing of labor, wage cutbacks, austerity measures affecting the social wage, freezing of underfunded pension funds, and super-exploitation—increasing the productivity of labor by harder work and longer work hours at lower rates of pay to fewer workers. In other words, intensified exploitation by means of cutting hourly wages of new hires by as much as one half (*Earthlink News*, February 16, 2012).

There is also a North-South dimension to the issue of labor exploitation and the growing class divide. The increasing importance of imperialist exploitation is evident as the share of US corporate profits extracted overseas keeps rising at the expense of employee income growth. In 2011, the US economy grew by 1.7 percent, but median wages fell by 2.7 percent. According to the financial press "the profit margins of the S & P 500 leapt from 6% to 9% of the GDP in the past three years, a share last achieved three generations ago. At roughly a third, the foreign share of these profits has more than doubled since 2000" (*Financial Times*, February 13, 2012: 9). If this is a "capitalist crisis" then who needs a capitalist boom?

Surveys of top corporations reveal that US companies are holding 1.73 trillion in cash—"the fruits of record high profit margins" (*Financial Times*, January 30, 2012: 6). These record profit margins result from mass firings, which have led to intensifying exploitation of the remaining workers. Also negligible federal interest rates and easy access to credit allow capitalists to exploit vast differentials between borrowing and lending and investing. Lower taxes and cuts in social programs result in a growing cash pile for corporations. Within the corporate structure, income is concentrated at the top where senior executives pay themselves huge benefits and bonuses. Among the leading S & P 500 corporations the proportion of income that goes to dividends for stockholders is the lowest since 1900 (*Financial Times*, January 30, 2012: 6). A real capitalist crisis would adversely affect profit margins, gross earnings and the accumulation of "cash piles." Rising profits are being hoarded because as capitalists profit from intense exploitation the capacity for mass consumption stagnates.

Crisis theorists also tend to confuse what is clearly the degrading of labor, the savaging of living and working conditions and even the stagnation of the economy, with a "crisis" of capital: when the capitalist class increases its profit margins, hoards trillions, it is not in crisis. The point is that the "crisis of labor" is a major stimulus for the recovery of capitalist profits. But we cannot generalize from one to the other. No doubt there was a moment if not a cycle of capitalist crisis (2008–09), but thanks to the agency of capitalist state in an unprecedented massive transfer of wealth from the public treasury to the capitalist class—Wall Street banks in the first instance but then the corporate sector—recovered. Meanwhile the working class and the rest of the economy remained in crisis in conditions of bankruptcy, mortgage foreclosures, reduced income and high unemployment.

The Revolving Door: From Wall Street to the Treasury and Back

Effectively the relation between Wall Street and Treasury has become a "revolving door": from Wall Street to the Treasury Department to Wall Street. Private bankers take appointments in Treasury (or are recruited) to ensure that all resources and policies Wall Street needs are granted with maximum effort, with the least hindrance from citizens, workers or taxpayers. Wall Streeters in Treasury give highest priority to Wall Street survival, recovery and expansion of profits. They block any regulations or restrictions on bonuses or a repeat of past swindles.

Wall Streeters "make a reputation" in Treasury and then return to the private sector in higher positions, as senior advisers and partners. A Treasury appointment is a ladder up the Wall Street hierarchy. Treasury is a filling station to the Wall Street Limousine: ex- Wall Streeters fill up the tank, check the oil and then jump in the front seat and zoom to a lucrative job and let the filling station (public) pay the bill. Approximately 774 officials (and counting) departed from Treasury between January 2009 and August 2011 (*Financial Times*, February 6, 2012: 7).

All provided lucrative "services" to their future Wall Street bosses finding it a great way to re-enter private finance at a higher more lucrative position.

A report in the *Financial Times* (February 6, 2012: 7) entitled appropriately "Manhattan Transfer" provides typical illustrations of the Treasury-Wall Street revolving door. *Ron Bloom* went from a junior banker at Lazard to Treasury, helping to engineer the trillion dollar bailout of Wall Street and returned to Lazard as a senior adviser. *Jake Siewert* went from Wall Street to becoming a top aide to Treasury Secretary Tim Geithner and then graduated to Goldman Sachs, having served to undercut any cap on Wall Street bonuses. *Michael Mundaca*, the most senior tax official in the Obama regime came from the Street and then went on to a highly lucrative post in Ernst and Young a corporate accounting firm, having help write down corporate taxes during his stint in "public office." *Eric Solomon*, a senior tax official in the infamous corporate tax-free Bush Administration made the same switch. *Jeffrey Goldstein*, who Obama put in charge of financial regulation and succeeded in undercutting popular demands, returned to his previous employer Hellman and Friedman with the appropriate promotion for services rendered. *Stuart Levey*, who ran AIPAC sanctions against Iran policies out if Treasury's so-called "anti- terrorist agency" was hired as general counsel by HSBC to defend it from investigations for money laundering (*Financial Times*, February 6, 2012: 7). In this case Levey moved from promoting Israel's war aims to defending an international bank accused of laundering billions in Mexican cartel money. Levey spent so much time pursuing Israel's Iran agenda that he totally ignored the Mexican drug cartels' billion dollar money laundering cross-border operations for the better part of a decade. *Lew Alexander*, a senior advisor to Geithner in designing the trillion-dollar bailout is now a senior official in Nomura, the Japanese bank. *Lee Sachs* went from Treasury to Bank Alliance (his own "lending platform"). *James Millstein* went from Lazard to Treasury bailed out AIG insurance run into the ground by Greenberg and then established his own private investment firm taking a cluster of well-connected Treasury officials with him.

The Goldman-Sachs-Treasury revolving door continues today. In addition to past and current Treasury heads, Paulson and Geithner, former Goldman partner *Mark Patterson* was recently appointed Geithner's Chief of Staff. *Tim Bowler*, former Goldman managing director was appointed by Obama to head up the capital markets division.

It is abundantly clear that elections, parties and the billion dollar electoral campaigns have little to do with "democracy" and more to do with selecting the President and legislators who will appoint non-elected Wall Streeters to make all the strategic economic decisions for the 99 percent of Americans. The policy results of the Wall Street-Treasury revolving door are clear and provide us with a framework for understanding why the "profit crisis" has vanished and the crisis of labor has deepened.

The Wall Street-Treasury Consortium (WSTC) has performed a Herculean task for finance and corporate capital. In the face of universal condemnation of

Wall Street by the vast majority of the public for its swindles, bankruptcies, job losses and mortgage foreclosures, the WSTC publically backed the swindlers with a trillion dollar bailout. A daring move on the face of it; that is if majorities and elections counted for anything. Equally important the WSTC dumped the entire "free market" doctrine that justified capitalist profits based on its "risks," by imposing the new dogma of "too big to fail" in which the state treasury guarantees profits even when capitalists face bankruptcy, providing they are billion dollar firms. The WSTC dumped the capitalist principle of "fiscal responsibility" in favor of hundreds of billions of dollars in tax cuts for the corporate-financial ruling class, running up record peace time budget deficits and then having the audacity to blame the social programs that are supported by popular majorities. (Is it any wonder these ex-Treasury officials get such lucrative offers in the private sector when they leave public office?) Thirdly, Treasury and the Central Bank (Federal Reserve) provide near zero percent interest loans that guarantees big profits to private financial institutions which borrow low from the Fed and lend high (including back to the Government!), especially in purchasing overseas Government and corporate bonds. They receive anywhere from four to ten times the interest rates they pay. In other words the taxpayers provide a monstrous subsidy for Wall Street speculation. With the added proviso, that today these speculative activities are now insured by the Federal government, under the "too big to fail" doctrine.

With the ideology of "regaining competitiveness" the Obama economic team (from Treasury, the Federal Reserve, Commerce, Labor) has encouraged employers to engage in the most aggressive shedding of workers in modern history. Increased productivity and profitability is not the result of "innovation" as Obama, Geithner and Bernanke claim. It is a product of a state labor policy that deepens inequality by holding down wages and raising profit margins. Fewer workers producing more commodities. Cheap credit and bailouts for the billion dollar banks and no refinancing for households and small and medium size firms leading to bankruptcies, buyouts and "consolidation"—namely, greater concentration of ownership. As a result, the mass market stagnates but corporate and bank profits reach record levels. According to financial experts under the WSTC "new order" "bankers are a protected class who enjoy bonuses regardless of performance, while relying on the taxpayer to socialize their losses" (*Financial Times*, January 9, 2012, 5). In contrast, under Obama's economic team, labor faces the greatest insecurity and most threatening situation in recent history: "in what is unquestionably novel is the ferocity with which US business has shed labor, now that executive pay and incentive schemes are linked to short-term performance targets" (*Financial Times*, January 9, 2012: 5).

From Exploitation to Pillage: Dynamics of Extractive Capitalism

Crisis is endemic to capitalism, but we need to distinguish between financial crises, i.e. crises rooted in the overfinancialization of production or the malfunctioning of financial institutions, and the more fundamental production crises that result from the incapacity of the system to expand production under existing class relations. If, as in the case of the latest outbreak of financial crisis (and a production crisis triggered by this crisis), the propensity towards crisis persists despite the efforts made to rebalance the relation between capital and production it is a sure sign that the problem lies deeper than a financial malfunctioning. Thus it is possible to conceive of the current crisis as having multiple dimensions—ecological (with production exceeding the limits of the underlying eco-system), energy (the growing demand exceeding the limited supply), food (the incapacity of people to meet their basic need for food under the existing global food regime), and systemic (the inability to extract surplus value and realize profit at a rate needed for the reproduction of capital). Under these conditions, as well as a disconnect between the circuits of financial capital and the capitalist development process,[12] productive capital was restructured not by means of technological advance—the revolutionary pathway of capitalist development, according to Marx—but by shifting capital away from industry and the exploitation of labor towards natural resource extraction, a more straightforward pillage of wealth.

We do not have the time or space in this chapter to analyze or discuss the dynamics of this latest phase in the capitalist development of the forces of production—extractivist imperialism, as we term it, with reference to the "inclusionary activism" of the state in advancing the operations of extractive capital (Veltmeyer and Petras, 2014). Suffice it to note that "large-scale investments in the acquisition of land"—"landgrabbing," in the parlance of critical agrarian studies (Borras et al., 2011)—and the extraction of natural resources (minerals, and metals, fossil and bio-fuels and other sources of energy, agrofood products for the "global middle class") have come a long way towards reactivating the capital accumulation process on a global scale. Given the destructive impact of extractive capital on both the environment and the communities in the environs of this capital, and given also the yawning and growing gap between the beneficiaries of this capital and those who are forced to bear its exceedingly high environmental and social costs, the capitalist system once again is sowing the seeds of its own destruction. By a number of accounts (see the various case studies in Veltmeyer and Petras, 2014) these seeds have

12 It is estimated that in the 1970s the international flows of financial resources or capital were related to and functional for the expansion of production and the forces of capitalist development. However, already in the 1990s some establishment economists estimated that less than 5 percent of global capital flows had any productive function whatsoever, leading to a disconnect that was only exaggerated by the ventures of Wall Street and other speculators. At the height of the global financial crisis, the total value of financial transactions on just one capital market, the London-based market on currency exchange rates, exceeded (it was estimated) the value of world trade by a factor of 20.

already begun to germinate and are taking form as a social movement organized not just to resist the assault of extractive capital on society and nature, on livelihoods and the environment, but in rejection of capitalism as a system.

Features of extractive capitalism and the resulting post-neoliberal rentier state,[13] conditions for which can be found primarily in the global south on the periphery of the world system, include an increase in the concentration of capital, the use of very little labor in the production process, and an extremely unequal distribution of wealth and income. Under these conditions the working class, it is estimated, receives less than 10 percent of the social product in the mining sector—for example, only 6 percent in the case of Argentina and Chile (Solanas, 2007: 2).[14] This contrasts markedly with the capitalism of the post-war years under the developmental state (from the 1950s to the 70s), which was based not so much on the extraction of natural resources as the exploitation of the "unlimited supplies of [agricultural surplus] labor" generated in the capitalist development process. It is evident that this type of capitalism, notwithstanding its contradictions, had much broader development implications than extractive capitalism, providing or allowing labor a much greater share of the national income—up to 60 percent in the case of the European welfare state. What this means, among other things, is that the social base of support for capitalism on the global periphery is rather narrow and shallow. It also means that if or when the resistance to extractive capital and extractivist imperialism on the periphery of the system were to combine or unite their forces with the victims of financial capital and the neoliberal state and its austerity measures at the center then capitalism will be forced to confront its political limits in the formation of a new revolutionary proletariat.

13 On the formation of this state in South America, where the conditions of its formation are most evident, see Grugel and Riggirozzi (2012) and Macdonald and Ruckert (2009).

14 Moreover, in spite of the commodities boom, workers in Latin America have received little in terms of wage increases. An index of real average wages in the formal sector of the labor market in Argentina, Bolivia, Brazil, Chile, Colombia, Mexico, Peru, Uruguay and Venezuela shows some discouraging results. Using 2000 as the base year, ECLAC data yield a cumulative increase in average wages of just 0.46 percent by 2006 (ECLAC, 2007, Table A-28). Studies undertaken by Petras and Veltmeyer (2009) in Brazil, as well as in Bolivia and Ecuador, point toward similar discouraging results. Notwithstanding the reduction in the incidence of poverty among income earners (down from 40 to 20 percent in these countries from 2003 to 2008), and the inclusion of the income poor in the government's social programs (health, education and minimal welfare), to date there is scant to no evidence of improvement in the social condition of the people in the populous sector of society—the landless and semi-proletarianized rural workers and the urban proletariat of informal workers (Veltmeyer and Tetreault, 2013).

From Financial Crisis to the Recovery of Profits: 2008 to 2013

The "recovery" of corporate profits had little to do with the business cycle and everything to do with Wall Street's large-scale takeover and pillage of the US Treasury. Between 2009 and 2012 hundreds of former Wall Street executives, managers and investment advisers seized all the major decision-making positions in the Treasury Department and channeled trillions of dollars into leading financial and corporate coffers. They intervened financially troubled corporations, like General Motors, imposing major wage cuts and dismissals of thousands of workers.

Wall Streeters in Treasury elaborated the doctrine of "too big to fail" to justify the massive transfer of wealth. The entire speculative edifice built in part by a 234-fold rise in foreign exchange trading volume between 1977 and 2010 was restored (*Financial Times*, January 10, 2012: 7). The new doctrine argued that the state's first and principal priority is to return the financial system to profitability at any and all cost to society, citizens, taxpayers and workers. "Too big to fail" is a complete repudiation of the most basic principle of "free market" capitalism: the idea that those capitalists who lose have to bear the consequences; that each investor or CEO is responsible for their action. Financial capitalists no longer need to justify their activity in terms of any contribution to the growth of the economy or "social utility." According to the current rulers Wall Street must be saved because it is Wall Street, even if the rest of the economy and people sink (*Financial Times*, January 20, 2012: 11). State bailouts and financing are complemented by hundreds of billions in tax concessions, leading to unprecedented fiscal deficits and the growth of massive social inequalities. The pay of CEOs as a multiple of the average worker went from 24 to 1 in 1965 to 325 to 1 in 2010 (*Financial Times*, January 9, 2012: 5).

The ruling class flaunts their wealth and power aided and abetted by the White House and Treasury. In the face of popular hostility to Wall Street pillage of Treasury, Obama went through the sham of asking Treasury to impose a cap on the multi-million dollar bonuses that the CEOs running bailed out banks awarded themselves. Wall Streeters in Treasury refused to enforce the executive order, the CEOs got billions in bonuses in 2011. President Obama went along, thinking he conned the US public with his phony gesture, while he reaped millions in campaign funds from Wall Street!

The reason Treasury has been taken over by Wall Street is that in the 1990s and 2000s, banks became a leading force in Western economies. Their share of the GDP rose sharply "from 2% in the 1950s to 8% in 2010" (*Financial Times*, January 10, 2012: 7). Today it is "normal operating procedure" for Presidents to appoint Wall Streeters to all key economic positions; and it is "normal" for these same officials to pursue policies that maximize Wall Street profits and eliminate any risk of failure no matter how risky and corrupt their practitioners.

The European Working Class in the Wake of the Global Financial Crisis

In the 1990s a series of financial crises, with a devastating effect on productive sectors, hit various economies on the periphery of world capitalism—Mexico in 1995, Asia in 1997, Russia and Brazil in 1998, and Argentina in 1999. However, unlike this cycle of financial crisis, the "global financial crisis" triggered by the US sub-prime debacle hit the center of the system rather than the periphery—and it almost entirely missed the economies not fully integrated into the neoliberal world order, or those that like Brazil (also India, Russia, and China) were big enough to convert themselves into alternative centers of capital accumulation and engines of economic growth.

The epicenter of the production crisis precipitated by the 2008–09 financial crisis is in Europe. Indeed Europe is experiencing the deepest crisis of capitalism since the Great Depression of the 1930s, even deeper than the system-wide production crisis of the early 1970s. One reason for the apparent intractability of the crisis in Europe is that normally a crisis is "resolved" via a restructuring of the capital-labor relation—restructuring the system on the backs of workers and their families. It is no different in Europe, but because of the multinational structure of the system in Europe the capital-labor relation has materialized as a relation between core of relatively stronger economies and a number of weaker or more vulnerable economies on the southern periphery of the EU. Because of the integration into the Eurozone these governments are unable to resolve the crisis by normal means, i.e. by restructuring their international relations. Thus the governments on the southern periphery of the EU are forced to accept the dictates of the more powerful members of the Union, Germany in particular, as regards austerity measures designed to reduce the level of consumption, which is like pouring oil on the fires of European capitalism! From the very beginning, some governments in the union have prevented a solidarity-based solution to the crisis in Europe and are significantly responsible for its exacerbation. This refers particularly to Germany, which, in August 2008, blocked a substantial economic stimulus package for the EU. Hardly had the recession reached its lowest point in Germany (in 2009) when the German government preached the neoliberal ideology of the need for hard austerity policies.

The austerity measures taken in various EU states to reduce the debt affected above all wage earners, pensioners, the unemployed and the self-employed, while the wealthy, the banks and the corporations were spared. This is in line with the notion that capitalists have a greater propensity to invest their savings than workers, who will simply increase their consumption. Thus, in order to activate the economic growth process while reducing the weight of debt on the economy labor has to be disciplined while capital has to be spared and even given additional resources to invest. In the spring of 2010 the German government blocked aid for Greece, causing a steep rise in the yields of Greek government bonds and thus an increase in the national debt, making a solution of the crisis even more difficult and more expensive, forcing the Greek working and middle classes to bear the brunt of the needed "adjustment."

Needless to say, the loan agreements with Greece and other countries in crisis and their ridiculous austerity demands only made the crisis worse. For example, the reduction in the Greek minimum wage does not contribute to an increase in "competitiveness," as the country's current account deficit is as much due to the mercantile policies of the core Eurozone countries as to the role of deregulated finance. Instead, the reduction of the minimum wage has further destroyed the internal market and with it needed forces of production. This example makes clear that the current crisis politics redistributes wealth from wage earners to those who possess capital, regardless of the macro-economic and societal consequences. Greek wages have already been forcibly reduced by 20–30 percent, hundreds of thousands have lost their jobs, over 10,000 schools are closed, hospitals are running out of medication, and children are starving. And Greece is not alone. Similar developments are also looming or omnipresent in Portugal and Spain, where unemployment is well over 20 percent—from 40 to 60 percent among youth and the most productive sectors of the labor force.[15] Needless to say, these conditions are a breeding ground for forces of resistance that can be turned not only against the government of the day but against the system itself.

Conclusion: Wall Street Takes Off while the Crisis of Labor Deepens

On July 16, 2013, Goldman Sachs, the fifth largest US bank by assets announced that its second quarter profits doubled those of the previous year to $1.93 billion. J.P. Morgan Chase, the country's largest bank, made $6.1 billion in the second quarter up, 32 percent over the year before and expects to make $25 billion in profits in 2013. Wells Fargo, the fourth largest bank, reaped $5.27 billion, up 20 percent. Citigroup's profits topped $4.18 billion, up 42 percent over the previous year.

The pay of the highest functionaries of the ruling elite, the financial CEOs, is soaring: John Stumpf of Wells Fargo received $19.3 million in 2012; Jamie Dimon of J.P. Morgan Chase pocketed $18.7 million and Lloyd Blankfein of Goldman Sachs took in $13.3 million.

15 According to a recent ILO report (ILO 2013: 58), "The number of unemployed worldwide rose by 4.2 million in 2012 to over 197 million." And the report goes on to warn that global unemployment could increase even further in 2013. Global youth unemployment, meanwhile, remains particularly dire. According to the report, nearly 74 million people between the ages of 15 and 24 worldwide are unemployed. "Some 35 percent of unemployed youth in advanced economies have been out of a job for six months or longer," the report continues. "As a consequence, increasing numbers of young people are getting discouraged and leaving the labor market." And for those currently languishing in the global reserve army of labor, the forecasts for meager growth offer little hope for a reprieve.

The Bush-Obama Wall Street bailout has resulted in the deepening financialization of the US economy: Finance has displaced the technology industry as the profitable sector of the US economy. While the US economy stagnates and the European Union wallows in recession and with over 50 million unemployed, US financial corporations in the Standard and Poor 500 index earned aggregate profits of $49 billion in the second quarter of 2013, while the tech sector reported $41.5 billion. For 2013, Wall Street is projected to earn $198.5 billion in profits, while tech companies are expected to earn $183.1 billion. Within the financial sector the most "speculative sectors," investment banks and brokerage houses, are dominant and dynamic, growing 40 percent in 2013. Over 20 percent of the S&P 500 corporate profits are concentrated in the financial sector.

The financial crash of 2008–09 and the Obama bailout reinforced the dominance of Wall Street over the US economy. The result is that the parasitic financial sector is extracting enormous rents and profits from the economy and depriving the productive industries of capital and earnings. The recovery and boom of corporate profits since the crises turns out to be concentrated in the same financial sector that provoked the crash a few years back.

The new speculative bubble of 2012–13 is a product of the central bank's (the Federal Reserve in the United States) low (virtually zero) interest policies that allows Wall Street to borrow cheaply and speculate, activities which puff up stock prices but do not add value or generate employment, depress industry and further polarize society.

The Obama regime's promotion of financial profits is accompanied by its policies reducing living standards for waged and salaried workers. The White House and Congress have slashed public spending on health, education and social services. They have cut funds for food stamp programs, day care centers, unemployment benefits, social security inflation adjustments, Medicare and Medicare programs. As a result, the gap between the top 10 percent and the bottom 90 percent have widened. Wages and salaries have declined in relative and absolute terms, as employers take advantage of high unemployment (7.8 percent official) underemployment (15 percent) and precarious employment.

In 2013 capitalist profits, especially in the financial sector are booming, while the crises of labor persists, deepens and provokes political alienation. Outside of North America, especially in the European periphery, mass unemployment and declining living standards has led to mass protests and repeated general strikes.

In the first half of 2013 Greek workers organized four general strikes protesting the massive firing of public sector workers; in Portugal two general strikes have led to calls for the resignation of the Prime Minister and new elections. In Spain corruption at the highest level, fiscal austerity leading to 25 percent unemployment and repression have led to intensifying street fighting and calls for the regime to resign.

The bi-polar world of rich bankers in the North racking up record profits and workers everywhere receiving a shrinking share of national income spells out the class bases of "recovery" and "depression": prosperity for the few and immiseration for the many. By the end of 2013, the imbalances between finance and production foretell a new cycle of boom and bust. Emblematic of the demise of the "productive economy" is the city of Detroit's declaration of bankruptcy: with 79,000 vacant homes, stores and factories the city resembles Bagdad after a US bombing attack. The Wall Street devastated city, has debts totaling $20 billion, as the big three auto companies relocate overseas and in non-union states and bankers "restructure" the economy, breaking unions, lowering wages, reneging on pensions and ruling by administrative decree.

To conclude, the deep financial crisis of 2008–09 has provoked a serious questioning of capitalism as a system in crisis. We hope that our reflections on the crisis will be of some use in advancing the forces of resistance to capitalism in the current conjuncture. This remains the most important challenge of our troubled times.

References

Bárcena, A. 2009. *Preliminary Overview of the Economies of Latin America and the Caribbean*. Santiago: ECLAC.

Bello, W. 2009. "The Global Collapse: A Non-Orthodox View," *Z Net* (February 22).

Berberoglu, B. (ed.) 2010. *Globalization in the 21st Century: Labor, Capital, and the State on a World Scale*. New York: Palgrave Macmillan.

Berberoglu, B. 2012. *Beyond the Global Capitalist Crisis: The World Economy in Transition*. Farnham: Ashgate Publishing.

Borras, S., J. Franco, C. Kay and M. Spoor. 2011. "Landgrabbing in Latin America and the Caribbean Viewed from Broader International Perspectives," Paper presented at the Latin America and Caribbean seminar: "Dinámicas en el mercado de la tierra en América Latina y el Caribe," 14–15 November, FAO Regional Office, Santiago, Chile.

Bustillo, I. and H. Helloso. 2009. *The Global Financial Crisis: What Happened and What's Next*. Washington, DC: ECLAC, Washington Office, February.

Crouch, C. and A. Pizzorno. 1978. *Resurgence of Class Conflict in Western Europe since 1968*. London: Holmes & Meier.

Foster, J.B. and F. Magdoff. 2008. "Financial Implosion and Stagnation: Back to the Real Economy," *Monthly Review*, 60(6), 1–10.

Foster, J.B. and F. Magdoff. 2009. *The Great Financial Crisis: Causes and Consequences*. New York: Monthly Review Press.

Gills, B. (ed.) 2011. *Globalization in Crisis*. London and New York: Routledge.

Grugel, J. and P. Riggirozzi. 2012. "Post Neoliberalism: Rebuilding and Reclaiming the State in Latin America," *Development and Change*, 43(1).

ILO (International labour Organization). 2013. *Global Employment Trends*. Geneva: ILO.

Konings, M. (ed.) 2010. *Beyond the Subprime Headlines: Critical Perspectives on the Financial Crisis*. London: Verso.

Landler, M. 2009. "IMF Puts Bank Losses from Global Financial Crisis at $4.1 Trillion," *The New York Times* (April 21).

Levine, R. 2009. "Growing Out of Crisis," Development Outreach, World Bank Institute (December).

Lipietz, A. 1987. *Mirages and Miracles: The Crisis in Global Fordism*. London: Verso.

Macdonald, L. and A. Ruckert. 2009. *Post-Neoliberalism in the Americas*. Basingstoke: Palgrave Macmillan.

Marglin, S. and J. Schor. 1990. *The Golden Age of Capitalism: Reinterpreting the Post-War Experience*. Oxford: Clarendon Press.

Petras, J. and H. Veltmeyer. 2011. *Social Movements in Latin America: Neoliberalism and Popular Resistance.* New York: Palgrave Macmillan.

Petras, J. and H. Veltmeyer. 2012. *Beyond Neoliberalism*. Williston, VT: Ashgate.

Sherman, H.J. 2011. "The Great Recession and the Financial Crisis in the United States, the Epicenter of the Global Capitalist Crisis," pp. 35–64 in Berberoglu, B. (ed.). *Beyond the Global Capitalist Crisis: The World Economy in Transition*. Williston, VT: Ashgate.

Solanas, F. 2007. "El despojo de los metales argentinos (Parte IV)," Rebelión (July 31), 1–9. http://www.rebelion.org/seccion.php?id=9.

Spector, A. 2011. "The Origins and Development of the Global Capitalist Economy and Capitalist Crises," pp. 17–34 in Berberoglu, B. (ed.). *Beyond the Global Capitalist Crisis: The World Economy in Transition*. Williston, VT: Ashgate.

Veltmeyer, H. (ed.). 2010. *Imperialism, Crisis and Class Struggle: The Verities of Capitalism*. Leiden: Brill Publishers.

Veltmeyer, H. 2011. *Socialism of the 21st Century: Possibilities and Prospects*. Halifax: Fernwood Publications.

Veltmeyer, H. and D. Tetreault. 2013. *Poverty in Latin America: Public Policies and Development Pathways*. Kumarian Press.

Veltmeyer, H. and J. Petras. 2012. "The Natural Resource Dynamics of Post-Neoliberalism in Latin America: New Developmentalism or Canadian Extractivist Imperialism?" Paper prepared for ACAS, Universidad Nacional Autónoma de Honduras, Tegucigalpa, 27 al 31 de agosto.

Veltmeyer, H. and J. Petras. 2014. *The New Extractivism in Latin America*. London: Zed Books.

Veltmeyer, H. and M. Rushton. 2011. *The Cuban Revolution as Socialist Human Development*. Leiden: Brill.

Zoelick, R. 2009. "After the crisis," *Development Outreach*, World Bank Institute (December), 1–3.

Chapter 5
The Global Capitalist Crisis and the 2008 Financial Meltdown in the United States

Levin Welch

Introduction

The 2008 US financial meltdown and the subsequent Great Recession were not so much the result of a massive housing bubble bursting as they were the consequences of the contradictions of the global capitalist system unfolding over the past four decades.

This chapter provides an analysis of the inherent contradictions of the global capitalist system, its neoliberal policies, and the resultant financial meltdown that led to some of the worst economic and social conditions seen in the United States since the Great Depression. Those who occupy the top echelons of economic and political power have developed the most advanced economic system to extract and accumulate wealth through the exploitation of labor and the environment for private gain. Since the 1970s, the United States has undergone major economic changes such as the outsourcing of production, the deregulation of the banking and financial sector, and an increasing reliance on consumer debt as a way to maintain purchasing power in an era of declining wages. Wall Street has been on the forefront of this economic restructuring and has reasserted itself as the paramount institution in American business. However, their practices, guided by neoliberal economic ideology and policies, accelerated and expanded the contradictions of capitalism as they transformed the overall economy into a casino, leading to the wholesale gambling of US workers' future. This chapter shows that the present economic system, built upon unequal property relations, exploitation of labor, colonialism, and imperialist plunder, along with its periodic crisis of recessions and depressions, has become far worse for many more people as capitalism reaches its "invisible hand" further into the pockets of working people across the globe. The havoc experienced after the 2008 financial meltdown was the result of corrupt and self-serving activities that have led to the near-collapse of the entire global capitalist system. The paper concludes by arguing that given the reality of contemporary global capitalism, real change can only come through the organized will of working people poised to build a new and just political and economic system that serves the interest of *all* the people.

Origins of the Crisis

As the global marketplace opened for business in the 1970s, the US working-class was no longer favored by the owners of industry who moved their production to etc. low-wage sweatshops in free-trade and export-processing zones overseas. An investment made overseas to make a quick dollar is money that could be invested in the domestic economy for long-term growth and expansion; however, profits are much higher abroad than in the United States. The problem became then to keep the American consumer spending while living on lower wages. To keep order during this major economic restructuring and increasing inequality, economic and political elites encouraged the accumulation of debt as a way to falsely maintain a "middle class" standard of living (Callari, 2010; Mizruchi, 2010; Perelman, 2008). Those who created the policies of unsustainable illusionary capital played into their own game by creating bubbles to extract incredible amounts of wealth from consumer debt, real estate, and "exotic" insurance and trading schemes.

The decline in home values starting in 2006, and culminating in 2008 with a financial crisis, a housing bust, and a downturn in the global economy created a level of economic distress not seen since the Great Depression. In 2008 alone the US economy lost 2.6 million jobs (Sherman, 2010: 23). Consumer spending slowed and began to decline. Decline in spending is correlated to mass job loss and overall reduction in family income. As commodity sales slumped prices began to fall and profits began to decline, leading to downsizing. By August, 2010 some 7.6 million jobs had evaporated (Bivens, 2011: 17). This is how trickle-down economics really works; when money is lost at the top the losses are trickled down for the taxpayer to redress.

While the recent capitalist crisis is an outcome of the downturn in the capitalist business cycle, from which big business has recovered through massive state intervention and tax benefits, it is the working people who are continuing to suffer the consequences of the conditions created by the owning class. One of capitalism's historical strengths is its ability to rebuild itself by moving money and by manipulating governments and public opinion in times of economic downturns. The *business cycle*, that is, capitalism's pattern of boom and bust (expansion and contraction), is an inherent and effective way to redistribute wealth from the bottom to the top layers of society (Bivens, 2011; Mizruchi, 2010; Sherman, 2010; Yates, 2003). Volscho and Kelly (2012) clearly and comprehensively illustrate how segments of the owning class profited tremendously and concentrated their power as a result of the Great Recession. For example, in the case of a stock market collapse, those with ample funds buy up stock at pennies to the dollar and sit back to watch their fortunes grow as the economy begins to recover. As illustrated in figures 5.1 and 5.2, stock markets and the owners of large corporations are fairly quick to recover from a recession.

Figure 5.1 Stock market activity of Dow Jones Industrial Average (DJIA), March 2007–March 2014

Source: Dow Jones Industrial Average (DJIA) History, http://www.fedprimerate.com/dow-jones-industrial-average-history-djia.htm (2013). Retrieved March 3, 2014.

In looking at stock market movements between 2006 and 2014, we see that at the height of the boom in late 2007, the Dow Jones peaked at over 14,000, the NASDAQ topped 2,800, and the S&P 500 surpassed 1,500—all of which were historical highs. Just after this peak of the 2001–07 expansion, led by the housing boom, the stock markets quickly deflated and within less than two years each index had lost over half their value: the Dow Jones fell down to just over 6,600, the NASDAQ to 1,200, and the S&P 500 to 680. In June, 2009, the Great Recession had officially ended, yet, to call it the end was a misnomer as it was only the stock markets (and, therefore, the owners of giant corporations and banks) that had begun to recover. Working people, on the other hand, were still experiencing increasing unemployment, foreclosures, and poverty rates, all of which are still above pre-recession levels (Bivens, 2011; Petras and Veltmeyer, 2012; Sherman 2010). In the years following the so-called "recovery," business became as profitable as ever as the Dow Jones reached over 16,300, the NASDAQ passed 4,300 (well above its pre-recession level), and the S&P 500 surpassed 1,800 by March 2014 (see figures 5.1 and 5.2).

Between 1948 and 2001 there were ten minor recessions (Sherman, 2010: 5). The pattern was bad enough when the economy was largely contained within the borders of a nation; yet, as economies grow larger and larger across national borders, so do the corporations, the profits, and the booms and busts. Since the 1980s the global economy has been subjected to the increasingly devastating

Figure 5.2 Stock market activity of Standard & Poor's 500 (S&P 500) and the National Association of Securities Dealers Automated Quotation (NASDAQ), March 2007–March 2014

Note: The Great Recession ended in June, 2009[1] for top US corporations. The DJIA, NASDAQ, and S&P 500 have surpassed their 2007 prerecession highs by more than 2,400 points, 680 points, and 110 points respectfully. This is counter to "Main Street's" reality as unemployment,[2] foreclosure,[3] and poverty rates[4] are still well above their prerecession levels. The data is for March of each year.

Note sources:

[1] CNN Money. "Recession Officially Ended in June 2009." http://money.cnn.com/2010/09/20/news/economy/recession_over/index.htm (2012). Retrieved July 27, 2012.

[2] Bureau of Labor Statistics, "Labor Force Statistics from the Current Population Survey." http://data.bls.gov/timeseries/LNS14000000 (2013). Retrieved July 9, 2013.

[3] US Census Bureau, "Mortgage Originations and Delinquency and Foreclosure Rates." http://www.census.gov/compendia/statab/2012/tables/12s1194.pdf (2012). Retrieved July 9, 2012.

[4] US Census Bureau. "Income, Poverty, and Health Insurance Coverage in the United States, 2011." http://www.census.gov/prod/2012pubs/p60-243.pdf (2012). Retrieved July 5, 2013.

Figure sources: NASDAQ Composite, http://www.fedprimerate.com/nasdaq-composite-history.htm (2014). Retrieved March 3, 2014; Standard & Poor's 500 Index History, http://www.fedprimerate.com/s-and-p-500-history.htm (2014). Retrieved March 3, 2014.

business cycles of capitalism (Berberoglu, 2012). The severity of these cycles translating into crisis of global proportions is only now becoming apparent under conditions of capitalist globalization.

Accumulation and Exploitation

The United States economy was not always characterized by the capitalist business cycle. During the nineteenth century, the capitalist market in the United States was largely nonexistent as most families were small farmers who relied more upon subsistence farming than selling food in a marketplace. The lack of market was complemented with virtually no unemployment. The only real market was that of the slave economy, but even this economic system did not involve unemployment. The capitalist class of the US had seized control of the state from the slave owning class after the Civil War, and by the 1900s the Industrial Revolution had transformed the American economy into a capitalist market dependent on the sale of mass produced commodities (Berberoglu, 2009; Sherman, 2010; Parenti, 2011). This gave birth to the phenomenon of unemployment, as any given job was dependent on the sale of the goods labor produced. Selling one's labor for subsistence quickly became the norm as did the purchase of labor power to accumulate profits (Sherman, 2010: 15). As both rely upon the production of goods in a market, the first necessary "precondition for a business cycle" is production for the market (Sherman, 2010: 16).

Money is the second necessary precondition of a business cycle, as it is the basis for any economic transaction under capitalism. During periods marked by patterns of heavy spending, those who are participants in the economy will benefit, if even moderately. On the other hand, the absolute "reliance on money allows economies [and the many people involved] to suffer from a lack of spending" (Sherman, 2010: 16). Money is the standard by which all market transactions occur, be it purchasing or selling a product, contracts for construction or loans, the net worth of a family or individual, and the overall health of a local, regional, or national economy.

The institutionalization of money markets in America also gave rise to stock market trading, evolving into what many would later call "casino capitalism" (Ho, 2009; Bivens, 2010; Campbell, 2010; Financial Crisis Inquiry Commission, 2011; Frontline, 2012; Lansley, 2010; Sherman, 2011; Yates, 2003). After the stock market crash of 1929 and the Great Depression that followed—events which resulted in part from highly unregulated trading and betting in the markets—it took nearly 40 years after the Second World War for corporate America to begin accepting stock markets as legitimate indicators of corporate success. These post-War US corporations (for the most part) formally adopted a philosophy of "corporate social responsibility" and viewed stocks as arbitrary indicators (Ho, 2009: 125). The corporate elite of this era were moderate Keynesians, who in many respects were "constrained" by New Deal policies—a federal response to the Great Depression—and organized labor—a consequence of America's militant labor movements of the early twentieth century—and, thus encouraged some social spending programs and bargaining with unions (Mizruchi, 2010: 125). Social spending (as opposed to contemporary avocation of austerity or "sequestration") was to keep the poor and disadvantaged content enough not to revolt. Bargaining with labor (as opposed to flagrant union busting as witnessed in 2011 in Wisconsin) was to keep the militant elements pacified within the unions. In other words, social responsibility was first and foremost a survival strategy of the capitalist class, forced upon them by the people (Mizruchi, 2010).

This "corporate social responsibility" was also a long-term profit strategy, put in place largely as a response to US social movements that demanded the reform of certain corporate practices. As the workforce of US corporations was mostly living within the borders of the United States, corporations had to take care of their workers, because healthy and happy employees will be more innovative and productive than sick and miserable ones—that is, until the political, social and military conditions in certain parts of the world allowed for the opening of the *new global markets.* This gave rise to the transnational corporation (TNC) as billions of people were added to the labor pool, in turn making corporate social responsibility null and void, as the health and wellbeing of employees simply did not matter because workers became easier to replace (Berberoglu, 2009; Bivens, 2011; Callari, 2008; Harris and Sarewitz, 2012; Ho, 2009; Mizruchi, 2010; Spector, 2005; So, 2005; Sherman, 2010; Parenti, 2011).

A major opportunity appeared for Wall Street as the foreign policy of Washington had successfully completed many goals, including the subordination of the southern hemisphere of the American continent by the iron fist of their northern neighbor—the United States (Berberoglu, 2009: 64; also see Blum, 2005; Chomsky, 1994; Klein, 2008; Pilger et al., 2007), the destruction of popular communist movements in Vietnam, Laos and Cambodia (Blum, 2005; Chomsky, 1994), and the continued genocide of indigenous people who possessed the basic blueprints for sustainable living on this planet in places like North America, Latin America, and East Timor (Blum, 2005; Chomsky, 1994; Zinn, 2003). Along with the domestic deregulation that allowed pension and social security funds to be siphoned off from the US workforce, the bankers and financiers of Wall Street soon discovered a whole new trough of resources (raw and human) to be made into liquid assets for their "shareholders."

Contradictions of Neoliberalism

A central tenet of the prevailing Western conservative economic theory, neoliberalism, is that state regulation hinders the "efficient" nature of market "self-regulation" in "free market" capitalism (Friedman, 1962). However, it has become clear and is well documented that the state, even after a thorough process of deregulation starting in the 1970s, has continually played a critical role in the expansion, reproduction, and maintenance of markets that are "free" to be manipulated by those who control them, whether in Latin America, the Middle East, Europe, Canada or the United States (Dorn, 2011; Harris and Sarewitz, 2012; Financial Crisis Inquiry Commission, 2011; Klein, 2008; Konings, 2010 Mizruchi, 2010; Volscho and Kelly, 2012). By deregulation, or making some economic action "legal" or "accepted," the state has been playing a major role in the market. Moreover, any economic system whose foundation is based on unequal property (power) relationships, the state has acted to maintain it.

For example, the post-Second World War world witnessed governments (most notably the US) becoming major contributors to research and development, whether it be agriculture, medicine, energy, media, nuclear engineering, transportation, military, and so-on (Parenti, 2011: 39). More than that, corporate monopolies, from "blue chip" to finance, have come to expect state intervention when their companies fail. This point can be further illustrated by the bank bailouts of 2008:

> In the sense that the state was poised to intervene as the lender of last resort when the financial markets got into serious trouble these *markets were never free markets at all* ... [Also], a variety of regulatory moves by the state affected how they [the banks] were organized and how they performed in the first place. Much of this had the effect of aligning incentives among market actors so as to reinforce what we now know to have been excessive risk taking. (Campbell, 2010: 70–71, emphasis added)

Monopolies have not developed on their own. The US government has played a clear role in the development of big business—AT&T, Wal-Mart, US Steel, and textile, tobacco, iron, and airline industries, for example, have all received heavy subsidies and tax benefits to help them "compete" (Parenti, 2011: 62).

The state has also played its part in creating explosive speculative bubbles:

> The market for subprime mortgages soared in part after 2004 because the two government-backed mortgage giants, Fannie Mae and Freddie Mac, began buying up huge swaths of subprime mortgages. They did so in response to political pressure from Washington where politicians wanted to expand the financing for housing for the middle class. Fannie and Freddie's move to buy subprime mortgages institutionalized the congressional will to help people buy homes. And it created incentives for mortgage lenders to make subprime loans because they knew that they could turn around and sell the mortgages to Fannie and Freddie. In effect, then, Fannie and Freddie began to regulate albeit informally how much money was available in the mortgage market. This in combination with the Fed's low interest rates and speculative building contributed to a booming housing market, rising property values and a housing bubble that finally burst in 2006. (Campbell, 2010: 73)

The capitalist state is a critical actor when a business cycle comes to a head, as it will rush in to fix the problems caused by the private sector. Many of those involved in the creation of the housing bubble that burst in 2006, "anticipated not only a crash, but also an *eventual bailout*, on the grounds that Wall Street investment banks were 'too big to fail,'" despite their extremely risky behavior (Ho, 2009: 291, emphasis in original) (see Appendix A for US bailout history). More than that, the social conditions of extreme inequality in the United States provided the groundwork for the rise of finance, which is the institution most responsible for the most recent increases in economic and social inequality (Board of Governors of the Federal Reserve System, 2012; Financial Crisis Inquiry Commission, 2011; Perelman, 2008).

The Reemergence of Finance and Casino Capitalism

The Great Depression had inflicted tremendous blows to the reputation of Wall Street and the legitimacy of the stock market, changing the career courses of most Ivy League graduates from banking and finance to industry and public service (Ho, 2009; Perelman, 2008). For Wall Street, the first step in the post-Depression era was to re-legitimate itself by an alliance with American Ivy League universities, namely Harvard, Princeton and Yale. As described by ethnographer Karen Ho (2009), this reputation has succeeded in justifying power and influence, in both the public and private sector, as Ivy League graduates are seen as the "smartest people" around. Wall Street has exploited these national and global reputations of "smartness" and constructed how "excellence" is understood by extracting workers from these historically white, male, and upper-middle-class-dominated institutions.

An economic system that has the power to disenfranchise millions by the actions of a few can remain intact only if it can be justified by the latter to the former. The majority of those who created the 2008 financial meltdown are Ivy League graduates and seen as the only ones in a position to fix the problems.

> Smartness leads to market [and social and political] dominance, not only because of explicit assumptions about talent and credibility, but also through the premise that smartness is spatial, that it should rightly spread, colonize, and necessarily manifest as the natural determinate and arbiter of global market leadership. (Ho, 2009: 69)

Running parallel with Manifest Destiny's justification for imperialist expansion, neoliberal views of the world, rooted in Western culture's assumed superiority, have justified the spreading of not only Wall Street's, but global capitalism's cultural domination.

These institutionalized assumptions of superiority also provided justification for the deindustrialization, downsizing, and outsourcing of corporate America. In the name of progress, or, more specifically, "*shareholder value*," Wall Street has internalized a "moral superiority," viewing "complacent, less capable workers out in 'the real world' [as those who need] to be restructured to more efficient use" (Ho, 2009: 104; also see Zajac and Westphal, 2004). In other words, the people who lose their jobs are merely casualties of "progress." Appendix B shows the top 50 US corporations in terms of employee layoffs in relation to the pay of their CEO and is a clear illustration of who wins and who loses in times of economic hardship. The ideology of shareholder value that Wall Street holds in the highest regard is simply another variation of the capitalist mindset. Shareholder value is the justification for workers to produce surplus value for the owners at the expense of the worker, consumer, and environment. To illustrate, consider the following statement from a former Vice President of High Yield Bonds at Bankers Trust:

> Investment bankers are a qualitatively 'different' kind of people than 'nine to five' workers. They possess a particular combination of intelligence, ambition, and hard work, which they view as the driving and legitimating forces behind their dominant position in the financial markets. (Ho, 2009: 103)

After re-establishing the legitimacy of Wall Street as an institution through academia, the second phase was to put shareholder value theory into practice by intimately connecting the financial world of stock markets with the wider corporate community. Furthermore, when considering the decline of industry in the US and the rise of mutual and money market funds (replacing savings accounts and, thus reducing the capital accessible to commercial banks), financing and investment banking became an attractive option for corporate America (Mizruchi, 2010: 122). The 1980s mark this transition from social responsibility to shareholder value (also known as a period of "hostile takeovers"). The timing couldn't have been better as technology was becoming increasingly available, cheap, and fast. There had been a landslide victory among free-market champions and their ideology of shareholder value in academia, business and politics. The unions' power had been weakening, social service spending had been declining, and almost every major industry—from media, food, energy, weapons, construction, to resource extraction—had been monopolized. Financial institutions like the World Bank, IMF, and the WTO had guaranteed TNCs access to *cheap oil* (the essential ingredient for global trade, food production, and warfare) via military support and the *opening of global labor and raw material surpluses* via "free-trade" agreements and military coercion (Ahmed, 2010; Berberoglu, 2009; Blum, 2005; Chomsky, 1994; Parenti, 2011; Zinn, 2003).

Wall Street has publically conceptualized its ultimate goal as producing profits for all their shareholders—which, by convention would include anyone who owns stocks. However, the real goal of Wall Street is to generate profits for the owners of large corporations. Profits have become the main rationale for corporate restructuring whereas, of course, it is the owners who reap the profits every quarter, and, as the logic of capitalism goes, demand more growth in profits the next quarter. The workers, or "stakeholders," on the other hand, are the ones who create the value of a corporation and are intimately involved with its operations, and are those most easily cast aside as their role in the corporation is to produce as much value (profits) for the owners as possible, even if that means losing their job all together. A corporation's stock has a tendency to rise when layoffs occur (in the short term) and the stock market is how capitalists make most of their money.

Since the 1929 stock market crash, stocks had been seen as arbitrary business indicators that had historically been the catalyst for owners of private corporations to accumulate massive profits at the expense of investments in commodity production (Ho, 2009). Be that as it may, the conservative ideologues of free-market capitalism—namely Milton Friedman (1962) and Ayn Rand (1962)—had already championed shareholder value theory and were working with policy makers and mass producing propaganda to implement their plans for 'free markets' (Klein, 2008). Their first targets were regulatory institutions, many of which had been installed in direct response to the 1929 crash. When the teeth began to be pulled from regulatory agencies (the EPA or SEC, for example), it was in-step with the beginnings of Wall Street's 'hostile takeover' of US firms. The takeover mania of the 1980s solidified the conception that stock prices equaled efficiency, which, in turn, resulted in higher profits. Corporations that had been acquired by larger firms immediately went through a process known as "trimming the fat," which is another way of saying corporate downsizing. This creates short term profits and is how Wall Street understands growth and progress. This is also reflective of US capitalism's shift from dependence on a productive and high-consuming working class to accumulate profits to a service sector economy greased by finance and credit (Callari, 2010).

The first obstacle to hostile takeovers (or mergers and acquisitions) was anti-monopoly laws, stating that the merging of companies in the same field is illegal. However, a clever way around this was for a corporation to buy completely unrelated companies. The price of stock of the purchasing company increases in the case of bankruptcy of the bought company (which is the usual case) as the corporate takeover provides the medium to transfer the property of the bought out company to the buyer's portfolio. The adverse effects of the massive corporate profits of the 1980s and 1990s created by hostile takeovers were experienced by the average worker in terms of increased unemployment, debt, and poverty.

The implications of neoliberal ideology dictating major structural shifts in the US economy can be illustrated in the following ways: The weakening of labor unions and their collective bargaining power; advancement of technology which quickly replaces workers and lowers overall wages; outsourcing of jobs to create greater profit revenues; severe increases in inequality; incredible rise is consumer debt to accommodate for four decades of stagnating wages; dangerously unsustainable reliance on fossil fuels and imported goods; massive cuts to social spending; asset-bubbles that give rise to boom and bust; and a reliance on taxpayer

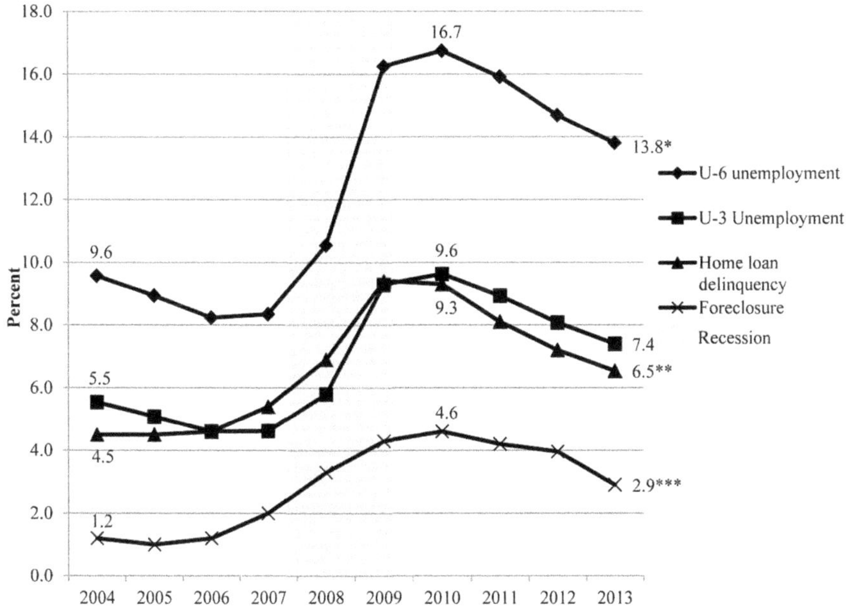

Figure 5.3 Annual unemployment, foreclosure, and home loan delinquency rates, 2004–13

Note: * The most commonly used official US government unemployment statistics are known as U-3 and qualify an individual as unemployed if they are jobless and formerly working full-time, are looking for work, and stay available for work. People who could not find work by the time their benefits run out are no longer considered unemployed. Furthermore, anyone who is underemployed (part-time), institutionalized (prisoners or students), or has quit looking for work (discouraged) is not considered to be unemployed as they are no longer in the "labor force."[1] The U-6 alternative unemployment includes all previously mentioned persons excluded in the U-3 measurements.[2] Furthermore, despite analysis predicting growth and recovery provided by mainstream economists, the global economy is experiencing growth slowdowns.[3] The International Monetary Fund (IMF) has documented world output (global GDP growth) is down from 5.2 percent in 2010 to 3 percent in 2013.[3] The US GDP growth is down from 2.8 percent in 2012 to 1.9 percent in 2013.[3] ** According to a study conducted by the Federal Reserve Board of New York and New York University, the US Federal Housing Administration, the bureau in charge of official statistics on home-loan delinquency rates, have grossly underestimated risk as they have "[counted] refinanced mortgages as successful loan terminations, even though the same borrowers are refinancing into new mortgages backed by the government insurer."[4] *** As of December 31, 2013 there have been approximately 4.8 million foreclosures completed since the financial collapse in 2008.[5] 620,111 foreclosures were completed in 2013, down 146,000 from 2012.[5] In December 2013 around 837,000 homes were in some stage of foreclosure, down from 1.2 million in December 2012.[5] 45,000 homes were foreclosed, down from 52,000 in December of 2012, yet substantially higher than the national monthly average of 21,000 between the years 2000 and 2006.[5] Nonetheless, if the current trends continue, anywhere between 8 and 13 million foreclosures may come as a result of the GFC.[6]

Note sources:

[1] Bureau of Labor Statistics, "How the Government Measures Unemployment." http://www.bls.gov/cps/cps_htgm.htm (2012). Retrieved July 9, 2012.

[2] Bureau of Labor Statistics, "Alternative Measures of Labor Underutilization." http://www.bls.gov/news.release/empsit.t15.htm (2012). Retrieved July 9, 2012.

[3] International Monetary Fund. (2013). "World Economic Outlook (WEO)." http://www.imf.org/external/pubs/ft/weo/2013/01/ (various years). Retrieved February 15, 2014.

[4] Bloomberg, "FHA Underestimates Mortgage Delinquency Rates, Study Says." http://www.bloomberg.com/news/2012-06-28/fha-underestimates-mortgage-delinquency-rates-study-says.html (2012). Retrieved July 11, 2012.

[5] National Forecast Report: December 2013." http://www.corelogic.com/research/foreclosure-report/national-foreclosure-report-december-2013.pdf (2013). Retrieved February 14, 2013.

[6] Financial Crisis Inquiry Commission. (2011). *The Financial Crisis Inquiry Report*. Washington, DC: US Government Printing Office.

Figure sources: Data for the unemployment rate for 2004–2013: Bureau of Labor Statistics, "Labor Force Statistics from the Current Population Survey." http://data.bls.gov/timeseries/LNS14000000 (2013). Retrieved February 15, 2014; Foreclosure and delinquency data for 2004–2010: US Census Bureau, "Mortgage Originations and Delinquency and Foreclosure Rates." http://www.census.gov/compendia/statab/2012/tables/12s1194.pdf (2011). Retrieved February 15, 2014; Foreclosure and delinquency data for 2011–2013: Lender Processing Services, "LPS' Mortgage Monitor" (various months). http://www.lpsvcs.com/LPSCorporateInformation/CommunicationCenter/DataReports/Pages/Mortgage-Monitor.aspx. Retrieved February 15, 2014.

money to bail out corporations—also known as corporate socialism—when they go underwater (Ahmed, 2010; Bivens, 2011; Campbell, 2010; Carruthers, 2012; Kotz, 2009; Parenti, 2011; Petras and Veltmeyer, 2012; Sherman, 2010; Volscho and Kelly, 2012).

The championing of short-term profits has led to the systematic liquidation of the global economy. Corporate bankruptcy, foreclosures, repossessions, credit failure, job loss, rampant outsourcing, a national rise in hunger and child poverty, and increases in the number of homeless have been accompanied by a very small number of people accumulating unimaginable amounts of wealth (Bivens, 2011; Campbell, 2010; Dorn, 2011; Fasenfest, 2010; Ghotge, 2009; Konings, 2010; Lansley, 2010; Parenti, 2011; Petras and Veltmeyer, 2012; Treas, 2010; Volscho and Kelly, 2012). As Figure 5.3 (above) shows, rising unemployment over the course of the crisis has helped contribute to a rise in home loan delinquency rates and mortgage rates and foreclosures.

Deregulation and Profits

Maximizing profits in newly accessible markets in the global economy meant that the domestic markets needed to become deregulated so that the US could stay "competitive," because, according to neoliberal doctrine, the only thing that state regulation does is hamper the "efficiency" of the "free market." Following the Great Depression, concessions had been made to the US labor movement in the form of regulating financial markets, pensions, unemployment insurance, and social security, which created huge swaths of wealth, that were off limits to the bankers and financiers of Wall Street. Thus a process of deregulation, as a way to extract this wealth, began in the 1970s and has been accelerating ever since.

John Campbell (2010) provides in detail the changes in regulation that directly contributed to the harsh consequences of the crash of 2008. One of the first was in 1978 where the state of Maine passed the first state law that allowed out-of-state banks to operate within their borders. This was a clear step in the dismantling of the philosophy of corporate responsibility to the local economy as banks could now take funds out of a local economy and funnel them to headquarters in some other state. Prior to the 1970s and the rise of finance capital, commercial banks had played the role of moderator between corporations as the banks represented "the interests of business as a whole" including social welfare for labor (Mizruchi, 2010: 118). However, as social welfare was now being dismantled and the biggest of the big corporations (particularly manufacturing) were losing revenue, the banks turned to new sources of profit and updated their justifications for business. The trend became popular among states, and by 1994 the "federal government passed the Interstate Banking and Branching Efficiency Act, which mandated interstate banking by 1997 unless a state explicitly chose to opt out, which only two did" (Campbell, 2010: 76).

Next, the Alternative Mortgage Transactions Parity Act of 1982 was passed and allowed "nonfederally chartered mortgage companies to write adjustable mortgages, such as those with interest-only payment and balloon payment schemes that were sold to subprime customers" (Campbell, 2010: 75). A "subprime" customer is one who is considered "high risk," because of low income or poor credit. This encouraged lenders to loan "asset-backed securities" to risky borrowers which would leave the original lender, who would sell these toxic debts to other companies who were unaware of the risk, free of risk if the borrower defaulted as they could take out an insurance policy against that same loan. In 1986 the Tax Reform Act stopped deductions for interest paid on consumer debt but still allowed people to write off the interest on mortgages for their first and second homes. These second mortgages created additional incentives for homeowners as they were now able to finance the lifestyles they wanted while still benefiting from an interest deduction. The Office of the Comptroller of the Currency (OCC) also "passed rules by which federally regulated lenders were exempted from state regulations, which were often stricter than federal regulations" (Campbell,

2010: 75). Formally illegal practices such as "mortgage prepayment penalties" and "balloon payment schemes," both of which raise default rates, were now acceptable—and increasingly popular—under the guise of the OCC and could not be regulated by individual states.

Other notable re-regulations include: Depository Institutions Deregulation and Monetary Control Act of 1980, Gramm-Leach-Bliley Financial Services Modernization Act, which overturned the Glass-Steagall Act of 1933, and the Commodity Futures Modernization Act. In short, what these deregulations did was to legally allow monopolization in the banking and financial sectors of the US economy. These firms were now allowed to operate anywhere they pleased and to buy up other corporations. There is a direct connection between deregulation and the development and proliferation of trading in "asset-backed securities," or "derivatives" (Dorn, 2011; Ghotge, 2009; Ho, 2009; Konings, 2010; Kotz, 2009).

Asset-backed securities are also known as "financial derivatives," which is a financial instrument whose value is derived from the value of something else. These derivatives prompted the rise of credit default swaps. The main goal here was to manage or eliminate risk from corporate credit. The same method that had traditionally been used in commodities trading was now being applied to loans. Farmers have long used derivatives to protect them against dramatic price falls or crop failure, but now financial institutions were using them to protect themselves against loan failure.

Credit default swaps are also known as collateralized debt obligations or synthetic CDO's and have created their own market where risk could be bundled together, traded and betted on—either for or against, regardless of if the bank owned that debt or not. It is a private market (unlike commodities trading) that was completely unregulated. The fundamental flaw here was that those involved in this new profit scheme assumed that one could simply eliminate risk. On the contrary, the risk was simply moved around from one party to another and ended up creating a toxic situation where "$33 trillion of debt [was] being traded" (Frontline, 2012). More striking is the "toxic" debt for all parties involved. As of 2009, the amount of debt accumulated from derivatives by the private sector was US$473 trillion; in the same year, the average economic output was US$12 trillion and the average savings was US$2.4 trillion (Ghotge, 2009: 85–6) (see Figure 5.4).

The rise of unregulated synthetic CDO trading created an environment where conflicts of interest became common. For example, credit rating agencies like Moody's or S&P were being paid by those they rate, and of course, the higher the rating of a CDO the easier it was to sell it to a client (Campbell, 2010; Dorn, 2011; Ho, 2009; Konings, 2010; Kotz, 2009). Furthermore, "investment banks [were selling] products to public authorities 'either with the aim of flattering their balance sheets or [promising] high returns'" (Dorn, 2011: 434; also see the Financial Crisis Inquiry Commission, 2011).

> After 2000 the deregulated financial sector found ways to make huge profits from making mortgage loans to a broad swath of the population including those

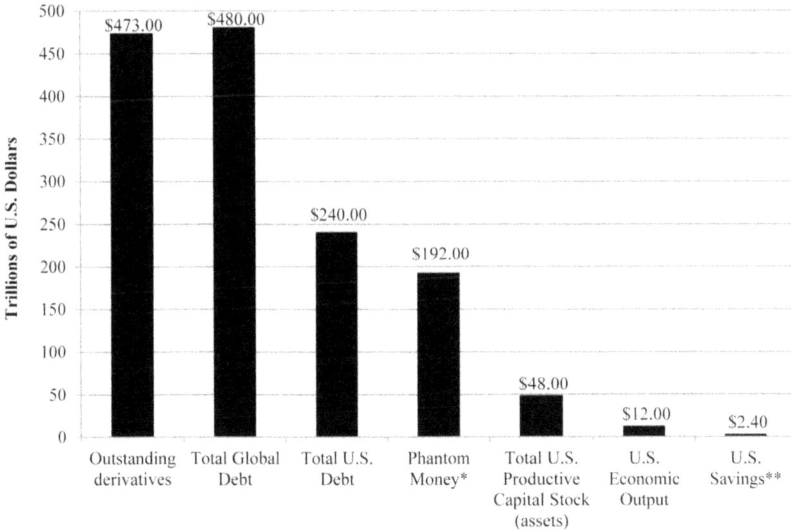

Figure 5.4 Toxic debt (private), global debt, and US debt vs US economic output and savings in 2009 (in trillions of US dollars)

Note: * Phantom money is the total US debt ($240 trillion) minus US assets ($48 trillion) and is manufactured credit that is put against assets and used to buy real resources like land and fuels. Because of the way derivatives were packaged and the size and scope of the financial crisis, it has become increasingly difficult to distinguish between real and phantom money. ** US saving estimate is extremely conservative as it includes individual corporate and local government with individual household savings.

Source: Figure constructed from data provided in Sanjeev Ghotge "Financial Meltdown: An Intriguing Silence at the Core." *Capitalism, Nature, Socialism* (December 2009) 20(4), 85–88.

> with moderate or low incomes, through subprime mortgages, alt-A mortgages, and other new types of mortgages. Any undue risk was transferred by the issuers onto others through securitization of mortgages, with compliant security rating agencies often giving undeserved AAA ratings to such securities. Furthermore, such loans seemed safe as long as housing prices kept rising, since foreclosure would bring the creditor institution an asset that was appreciating in value. As always happens during large-scale asset bubbles, many actors became persuaded that the rising asset prices would continue indefinitely. (Kotz, 2009: 312–313)

This lack of regulation prompted prospective customers to buy products they most likely would not have bought otherwise. These new, unregulated markets had created trillions of dollars by selling, trading, and betting on "risky mortgage-backed securities, derivatives, and other types of securities," proved to be extremely lucrative for some (Kotz, 2009: 311). For context, the profits of financial

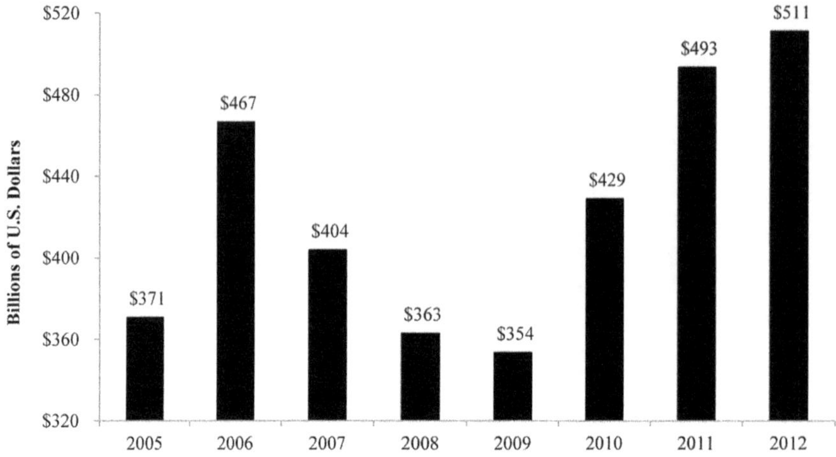

Figure 5.5 Profits of top 50 fortune 500 corporations, 2005–12 (in billions of US dollars)

Note: In 2012 the Fortune 500 accumulated $824 billion in total profits, smashing the 2006 record of $785 billion.[1] [[1] Yahoo Finance. "Fortune 500 Top 20." http://finance.yahoo.com/news/fortune-500-top-20.html?page=all (2013). Retrieved July 9, 2013.]

Source: CNN Money. "Fortune 500 Annual Rankings of America's Largest Corporations: Top Companies by Profits." http://money.cnn.com/magazines/fortune/fortune500/performers/companies/profits/. Retrieved July 9, 2013.

institutions compared to total profits increased from 21.1 percent in 1979 to 41.2 percent in 2002. These profit margins slumped back down to 37.2 percent by 2006 (Kotz, 2009: 311). As for the top 50 Fortune 500 corporations, total profits spiked in 2006 to an incredible $467 billion, fell dramatically in 2007 ($404 billion), 2008 ($363 billion), and 2009 ($353 billion) only to rise again in 2010 ($429 billion), 2011 ($493 billion), and 2012 ($511 billion), surpassing the profit levels reached in 2006—prior to the onset of the crisis in 2007–08—displaying that all sectors of the economy were affected by the actions of financial institutions and banks, yet were quick to bounce back (see Figure 5.5). Table 5.1 shows the total profits of the top five Fortune 500 companies, during this period, which include primarily oil companies and banks.

This type of behavior was the foundation for the expansion period between November 2001 and December 2007 and was characterized by a wave of predatory lending that had become rampant and largely undetected (Bivens, 2011; Campbell, 2010; Kotz, 2009; Ghotge, 2009; Financial Crisis Inquiry Commission, 2011; Frontline, 2012). People were receiving loans for more than the worth of the purchased home. Even people who had no jobs were given mortgages. Predatory lending helped to artificially inflate home prices–and therefore the overall performance of the economy—which in-turn "justified" Wall Street's behavior (Ho, 2009: 299).

Table 5.1 Profits of top five Fortune 500 corporations, 2005–2012 (in billions of US dollars)

2005		2006		2007		2008		2009		2010		2011		2012	
Exxon Mobil	$36.13	Exxon Mobil	$39.50	Exxon Mobil	$40.61	Exxon Mobil	$45.22	Exxon Mobil	$19.28	Exxon Mobil	$30.50	Exxon Mobil	$41.10	Exxon Mobil	$44.88
Citigroup	$24.59	UAL	$22.88	General Electric	$22.21	Chevron	$23.93	Microsoft	$14.57	AT&T	$19.90	Chevron	$26.10	Apple	$41.73
Bank of America	$16.47	Citigroup	$21.54	Chevron	$18.69	Microsoft	$17.68	Wal-Mart Stores	$14.34	Chevron	$19.02	Apple	$25.92	Chevron	$26.18
General Electric	$16.35	Bank of America	$21.13	JPMorgan Chase	$15.37	General Electric	$17.41	Procter & Gamble	$13.44	Microsoft	$18.80	Microsoft	$23.20	JPMorgan Chase	$21.28
Chevron	$14.10	General Electric	$20.83	Bank of America	$14.98	Wal-Mart Stores	$13.40	International Business Machines	$13.43	JPMorgan Chase	$17.40	Ford Motor	$20.21	Wells Fargo	$18.89

Source: CNN Money. "Fortune 500 Annual Rankings of America's Largest Corporations: Top Companies by Profits." http://money.cnn.com/magazines/fortune/fortune500/performers/companies/profits/. Retrieved February 14, 2014.

Growth and Inequality

To call the period between November 2001 and December 2007 an economic expansion would be only partly correct—it was a period of incredible growth and prosperity for a few while the majority experienced an illusion of those things with borrowed money they were encouraged to take (Bivens, 2011; Callari, 2008; Sherman, 2010; Parenti, 2011; Volscho and Kelly, 2012; Yates, 2003). The expansion of 2001 to 2007 can be illustrated in the following way:

> the economy grew more slowly than in the previous five expansions; wages and salaries grew slower than in the last five cycles, but corporate profits grew with amazing speed; jobs declined in the first two years of the expansion, then grew slowly; credit grew and grew far faster than in most previous expansions; and, housing grew rapidly, but with mortgages that many people had no chance of paying. (Sherman, 2010: 22)

Significant to our understanding as to why this recession is the worst since the Great Depression, we must recognize the trends of stagnating wages and increased worker productivity since the 1970s. Many of the things big business, mainstream media and our national leaders tell us are necessities of the good life and that we deserve, have become increasingly out of reach for many people with the wages they had been earning. So when Alan Greenspan said on the news that homeowners should borrow against their own home with mortgage refinancing—the fast way to get the things that all Americans should have—people obviously could not resist (Bivens, 2011: 15).

To further illustrate this, for US workers "the economic expansion from 2001 to 2007 was among the weakest on record [regarding] growth in overall gross domestic product (GDP), workers' salaries and benefits, investment, and employment ... since World War II" (Bivens, 2011: 13). Americans were also forced to cope with rising costs of necessities such as health care (Treas, 2010), gas, and food (Ahmed, 2010). Instead of investing taxpayer money directly into job and wage growth, policy makers focused their time on providing large corporations with tax cuts and other forms of corporate welfare, all at the expense of social wellbeing (Lansley, 2010; Parenti, 2011; Spector, 2005; Sherman, 2010; Yates, 2003). Obviously, wage growth would have only threatened corporate profit which was the only above average economic trend of the 2000s. The growth of the 2001–07 expansion was largely contained within the financial sector cashing in on the housing bubble that burst in 2008.

One reason the consequences of the housing bubble burst became so severe so quickly was US workers' desire to increase their living standards by accumulating debt—by borrowing against the equity of one's home and by purchasing goods with credit cards—as the economy as a whole was not affording them the opportunities to do so with the wages being brought home. In fact, at the height of the boom, Americans' home equity borrowing equaled about 8 percent of personal

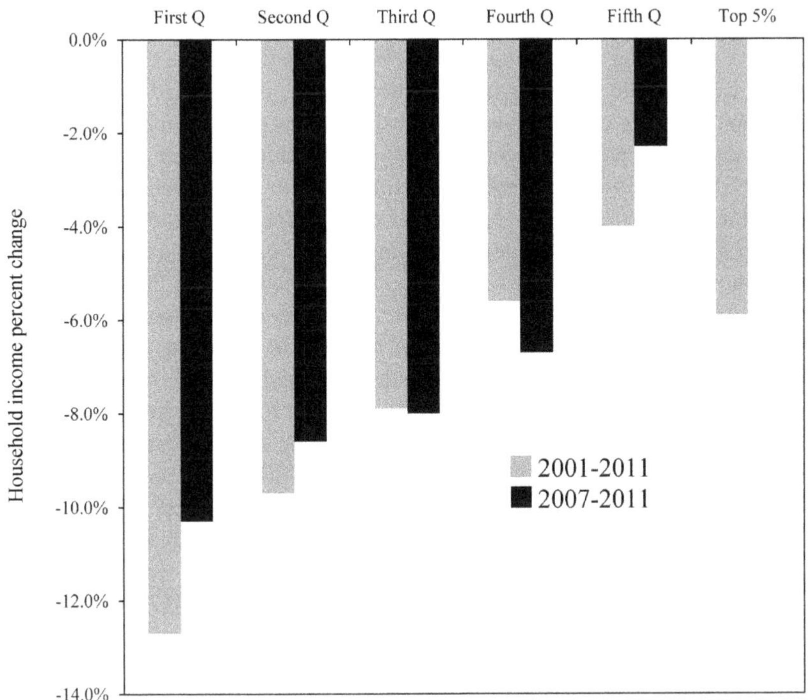

	Average household income for each income quintile and top 5 percent of income earners (adjusted to 2011 US dollars)					
	Lowest fifth	Second fifth	Third fifth	Fourth fifth	Highest fifth	Top 5 percent
2001 average income	$12,877	$32,354	$54,155	$84,911	$185,438	$330,889
2011 average income	$11,239	$29,204	$49,842	$80,080	$178,020	$311,444
Percentage change (2001–11)	**-12.7%**	**-9.7%**	**-7.9%**	**-5.6%**	**-4.0%**	**-5.9%**
2007 average income	$ 12,530	$31,937	$54,202	$85,814	$182,203	$311,542
Percentage change (2007–11)	**-10.3%**	**-8.6%**	**-8.0%**	**-6.7%**	**-2.3%**	**-0.0%**

Figure 5.6 Changes in average household income, by quintile and top 5 percent, 2001–11 and 2007–11 (percent)

Note: Capital gains, overseas investments, and inheritance are not included in income statistics. These sources of capital skews data as the money gained can range into the billions of dollars. Income is a paycheck earned from work as defined by the IRS. This loss in income represents gains for many who are wealthy yet have no income (Parenti, 2011; Petras and Veltmeyer, 2012; Sherman, 2010; Volscho and Kelly, 2012).

Source: US Census Bureau. "Mean Household Income Received by Each Fifth and Top 5 Percent, All Races: 1967 to 2011." http://www.census.gov/hhes/www/income/data/historical/household/index.html. Retrieved July 6, 2012.

disposable income. In other words, "*Americans were using the housing bubble to give themselves the 8% raise that the job market ... was not generating for them*" (Bivens, 2011: 14, emphasis in the original). Increasing home values meant that homeowners could refinance their homes through secondary mortgages to generate additional cash to increase their consumption. And when the housing market stopped growing, there was no more debt to extract and the consequences of living off of borrowed as opposed to earned money became quickly apparent. Figure 5.6 (above) and the accompanying table illustrates the decline in average household income by quintile and the top 5 percent during 2001–11 (including the expansion period of 2001–07) quite well. The decline has been more harsh for the lower three quintiles than that of the top two, revealing the unequal nature of the income loss. The top 5 percent of income earning households (which excludes capital gains, inheritance, assets, or other forms of capital predominantly controlled by the owning class and super-rich) are the only group to not suffer a relative loss of income between 2007 and 2011. This figure does not account for the dramatic (and steady) rise of wealth controlled by the top 1 percent, who, as a group, gained much more from the financial collapse than what was lost (see Volscho and Kelly, 2012, for an expanded discussion).

This trend is counter to expansion experiences from 1947 through 1973, as growth rates across income brackets were equally distributed. The poorest 20 percent of families were on par with growth experienced by the richest 20 percent. The same was true for those in other brackets (Bivens, 2011: 65). However, the rates from 1974 to 1995 saw the bottom quintiles of the American people's income begin to stagnate, while the highest segments of society continued to enjoy a steady increase in their income. Between 1996 and 2001, during the internet bubble, this trend shifted but was short lived, and as soon as the bubble burst the trend between 1974 and 1995 resumed.

Put differently,

> Neoliberal capitalism not only brought profits that rose rapidly relative to wages but also rapidly rising inequality in the distribution of income among households. From 1979–2004 the share of the top 5 percent of households rose from 15.3 percent to 20.9 percent while that of the poorest 20 percent fell from 5.5 percent to 4.0 percent (Economic Policy Institute 2007). Toward the end of the neoliberal period to date, income growth has been particularly concentrated at the very top. In 2000 and again in 2005 the richest hundredth of one percent (0.01 percent) of families in the United States received 5 percent of total income, a level that had not been reached previously since 1929. (Kotz, 2009: 310)

Adding injury to insult, over the past 30 years worker productivity has increased significantly by 75 percent (advancements in technology must be acknowledged), yet wages in 2009 were lower than they were in 1973 when adjusting for inflation (Parenti, 2011: 38). To illustrate this, in 1968 the minimum wage (in 2009 dollars) was $8.54 per hour. In 2006, the minimum wage had fallen to $5.48 per hour. In

2007, that number had risen up to $7.25 per hour, yet it was still lower than in 1968, despite increased productivity from workers across the board (Parenti, 2011: 38). This is why Americans were borrowing so much. The financial sector did not see any increases in productivity during that time, yet experienced the greatest growth in terms of salaries and profits (Bivens, 2011: 56; also see Sakamoto and Kim, 2010).

With direct correlation to trends of increased worker productivity and stagnating wages fostered by significant regulatory reform measures taken since the 1970s and 1980s discussed earlier is the decline of the labor unions. In 1973 about 27 percent of American workers were union members or covered by union contract, while in 2007 that number had dropped to about 14 percent (Bivens, 2011: 60; also see Jacobs and Dixon, 2011; Sherman, 2010; So, 2005; Spector, 2005). Some of this decline was in part the result of the manufacturing sector having come to a standstill due to outsourcing of jobs and advancing technology, but much had to do with the outright assault on unions by corporations and the state (Jacobs and Dixon, 2011; Sherman, 2010; Parenti, 2011). The justification of such attacks was, and is, to accommodate global markets with a US workforce that could be "competitive" and "efficient." Of course, these types of strategies have done nothing more than crush the earning (and therefore spending) power of US workers as the wages and working conditions they are "competing" with are sweatshop and plantation labor across the globe (Bivens, 2011: 56).

> Deregulation of previously regulated sectors such as transportation, communication, and power led to sharp reductions in wages in those sectors. Deregulation in the international arena facilitated capital flight and intensified import competition from low-wage countries. Privatization of state services often, although not always, has shifted the work to low-wage employees in private contractor firms. Giving up fiscal policy aimed at low unemployment led to a higher average level of unemployment, *reducing workers' bargaining power*. Reduction in social programs lowered the 'social wage' which had previously reinforced workers' bargaining power. Reduction in taxes on business and the rich increased after-tax inequality. Perhaps most obviously, the attack on trade unions undermined workers' wage bargaining power. The shift to temporary and part-time workers replaced high-wage jobs with low-wage jobs. Unrestrained competition among large corporations put downward pressure on wages. Finally, the market in CEOs caused executive salaries to skyrocket, rising from 42 times the pay of an average worker in 1982 to 411 times in 2005. (Campbell, 2010: 307, emphasis added)

Outsourcing jobs is also part of larger neoliberal policies promoting continuous profit growth at the expense of workers, both domestic and foreign. Domestically, this practice has played a significant role in increased unemployment, the decline of social services, and the stagnation of wages. Foreign laborers, on the other hand, are subjected to slave-like conditions to produce commodities that will be exported

(Berberoglu, 2009; Bivens, 2011; Parenti, 2011; Pilger, et al. 2007; Sherman, 2010; Yates, 2003). The policy of shipping jobs overseas leads to greater unemployment and under-employment, which lowers the purchasing power of workers in United States (the world's foremost consumers) which would, ironically, in the long run, lead to a significant decline in corporate profits.

The three significant ways in which American families coped with stagnating wages were by working more, saving less and acquiring more debt. Working more hours works but only up to a point. Taking on more debt is a temporary fix since borrowing money depends on willing lenders. Saving less allows for more spending, but only until the savings accounts run dry. This is exacerbated by the fact that any gains in net worth that families made in the 2000s were largely driven by the booming housing market and erased when the boom turned bust.

When the Great Recession hit in 2008, families began to save much more, which is good for the long-term. However, it has been hurting the recovery, as consumer spending is the fastest way to climb out of such a hole. Both the internet and housing bubbles made it possible for American families to save less while not having to worry about retirement and college funds as the bubbles artificially increased net wealth across the board. But when the bubbles burst, most of the wealth was dissolved and redistributed to the top income earners (Kotz, 2010; Petras and Veltmeyer, 2012; Sherman, 2010; Volscho and Kelly, 2012).

Besides stagnating wages and increasing unemployment, we must recognize that those covered by substantial health insurance and any sort of retirement plan have also been declining (US Bureau of the Census, 2011). Of course, the most disadvantaged segments of society have been hardest hit by this and past recessions as the inequalities within these populations have been more pronounced historically (see Hernandez, 2009 for details concerning predatory lending and foreclosures in historically redlined urban neighborhoods).

Technology has certainly played its role in the decline of the unions, increases of worker productivity, stagnation of wages, the outsourcing of jobs, and the accelerating pace of globalization. It is critical to understand that technology creates

> completely new modes of generating wealth, along with cultural shifts and new social relations. And while most societies have come to view the cumulative impact of these waves of change as the underlying dynamo of modern progress—each wave leading to a new level of productivity, wealth creation, and material benefit—this view conceals the reality that tens of millions of people will pay a high cost for such progress. (Harris and Sarewitz, 2012: 30)

Last, but certainly not least, "globalization, especially globalization governed by rules that protect the interests of the corporate class while making no attempt to shield vulnerable American workers, has also constituted a powerful drag on American wages in recent decades" (Bivens, 2011: 83). Globalization also creates larger problems that affect more people in more countries, as markets are intimately connected by both trade and financial channels. This interconnectedness (and sometimes lack thereof) can easily produce a domino effect, as when one nation's economy fails, so go the others (Perelman, 2008).

Impact of the Crisis

The expansion period between November 2001 and December 2007 was one that provided great wealth for a few who took clear and unprecedented advantage of millions of working people. However, the extent to which poor and working people were preyed upon was not put on full display until the entire financial system came crashing down. When the crisis began, starting with the bankruptcy of Lehman Brothers, people across the world were given a clear example of the inherent contradictions of capitalism, though, it is arguable, that few understood the crisis in those terms. In fact, that lack of understanding is a fundamental aspect of why no one responsible for the calamity has gone to prison (see Ho, 2009). More than that, many are still occupying their positions of power!

The bankruptcy of Iceland (who had invested heavily in CDOs) was the first domino to fall. As thousands of banks across the world—most notably IKB in Germany—had placed heavy bets on these "toxic assets," no one wanted to lend money to anyone. This led to the bankruptcy of Lehman Brothers, which, in turn, completely froze the capital markets and inoculated the entire economy with panic and a loss of trust for regulators and big business. It was publically acknowledged by government officials that Lehman was allowed to fail as a way to defend against "moral hazard"—the notion that if people are not held accountable for their actions any incentive for behavioral change is lost. The Lehman bankruptcy caused all on Wall Street (and therefore, the larger economy) to panic and halt spending.

The results after the fall of Lehman appear to be the sum of the inadequate understanding, foresight, and therefore preparedness, of those "regulating" markets, guiding and ratifying legislation, and carrying out orders on behalf of big business. The situation was out of control, as commercial paper, an essential in almost every business sector, could no longer be bought as the credit lines for many corporations had run dry (Campbell, 2010; Kotz, 2010). Next, as CDOs and subprime mortgages were failing in an extraordinary way, they were putting insurance companies (namely AIG) on the hook to pay out claims for these toxic assets (Campbell, 2010; Financial Crisis Inquiry Commission, 2011; Sherman, 2011). This caused US financiers and politicians to panic and demand the largest bailout that the world had ever seen.

These bank bailouts that were rushed through the Congress—despite an outcry by the public not to do so—did nothing but rebuild the house of cards, as those who were responsible were given enormous sums of money with almost *no regulatory oversight*, *obligations to change practices*, *or lower salaries*

(Frontline, 2012; Financial Crisis Inquiry Commission, 2011; Hogg, 2013). What is known as "systemic risk"—the interconnection of financial institutions, banks, and other corporations—had created "moral hazard." It was clear governmental intervention in the marketplace that effectively rewarded those who burned their corporations and the US economy at large to the ground. Meanwhile, millions of ordinary people who had no part in the deregulation of finance, the development of CDOs, or the proliferation of their trading and gambling, were tossed out onto the streets, drawn down into poverty, lost their health insurance, and their pensions had disappeared.

Many small businesses had credit lines cut and were hard pressed to find any available loans while the Federal Reserve secretly pumped *$16.1 trillion* in bailout funds to large domestic and foreign banks, insurance companies, financial firms, and industrial giants (US Government Accountability Office, 2011). This $16.1 trillion was in addition to the $787 billion bailout passed by Congress in 2008. However, this did not stop many political and social commentators in the United States from squawking to the drum beat of "blame the victim," pointing the fingers at the workers instead of the corporations that had "let them go" (Treas, 2010).

One example is what happened after General Motors and Chrysler went bankrupt, causing thousands to lose their jobs, when Senator Phil Gramm (who holds a PhD in economics) stated that the US had "become a nation of whiners" and that the recent economic downturn was merely a "mental recession" (Sherman, 2010: 7). In 2011, Herman Cain, GOP presidential hopeful, was quoted by MSNBC as saying: "Don't blame Wall Street, don't blame the big banks. If you don't have a job and you're not rich, blame yourself! It is not a person's fault because they succeeded; it is a person's fault if they failed" (MSNBC, 2011). However, a recent report by the Board of Governors of the Federal Reserve System (2012) paints a much different picture of how structure is much more important than agency in the case of an economic recession: median net worth for all families dropped 38.8 percent and the average fell by 14.7 percent between 2007 and 2010 to which most of this decline can be attributed to the housing bubble burst (Board of Governors of the Federal Reserve System, 2012: 4).

To make matters worse, conservative think tanks attributed rising unemployment to high corporate taxes, not because corporations were firing people (Sherman, 2010: 7). Again, the opposite is true. Consider the following example of General Electric (GE): In 2009 GE received $24.9 million in loans from the $787-billion TARP fund, simultaneously cutting 18,000 US-based jobs. Furthermore, in 2010, GE made $14.2 billion in profits and paid no federal income taxes—in fact, they received a $3.2 billion tax benefit from the federal government (McIntyre et al., 2011: 18). (See Appendix C for a list of the lowest corporate tax rates in 2008, 2009, and 2010.) GE's total foreign employment in 2010 was 154,000, down from 172,000 in 2007, but substantially higher than 84,000 in 1996 (Kaptur, 2011). The logic of conservative economics is pervasive, providing justification for inequality, and is used as a cornerstone for much of US economic and foreign policy (Perelman, 2008).

Conclusion

Nothing has been done to reign in the power and influence of the financial sector. Just four years after the stock market crash of 2008, JPMorgan Chase, one of the few banks to come out of the calamity with minimal losses, lost $4 billion in speculative bets. In June 2012 CEO Jamie Dimon—"Obama's favorite banker" (Sorkin, 2010: 546)—was called in by the Senate Banking Committee (SBC) to explain. He was scorned by several protestors (who were quickly removed) yet warmly praised and welcomed by the Committee. Senator Jim Demint (R-SC) commented that "it is important that we talk about things happening in the industry. It will, I think, advise us, help us and—as we look forward, and hopefully it will contribute to best practice scenario in the industry, and I appreciate your emphasis on a continuous quality improvement. We can hardly sit in judgment of your losing $2 billion" (DemocracyNow! 2012). Furthermore, the conversation concluded by a consensus that regulation of any sort imposed onto the "free markets" would impede efficiency and progress. It should be of no surprise as JPMorgan Chase spent $7.6 million in 2011 for lobbying and many on the SBC (committee chair, Democrats and Republicans alike) were recipients of those funds. One of the current staffers on the SBC, too, is a former JPMorgan Chase lobbyist (DemocracyNow! 2012).

This example reflects an even more disturbing reality that despite the overwhelming evidence of widespread fraud and other criminal activities (directly contributing to the financial collapse of 2008) going up to the highest levels of business, the Department of Justice has failed to prosecute even one single person of a crime (Financial Crisis Inquiry Commission, 2011; Frontline, 2013; Hogg, 2013; O'Connor, 2013). Hundreds of traders, executives, hedge fund managers, board members, and the like, each deserve to be locked behind bars as according to state and federal law. But, just as the bankers at HSBC who laundered billions of dollars for international drug cartels and terrorist organizations received no judicial penalty (the bank was fined $1.9 billion by the DoJ, or, roughly five weeks of revenue) while the victims of their crimes (drug users, murder victims) continue to be punished severely at astonishing rates (Stevenson, 2011; Tabbi, 2012; Wacquant, 2007; US Senate Committee on Homeland Security and Governmental Affairs, 2012), those who robbed millions of Americans' jobs, homes, and futures walk with impunity, the victims suffer the consequences. It is also worth mentioning that the man in charge of how the federal government handled both HSBC and Wall Street firms in connection with the financial collapse, Lanny Breuer, Assistant Attorney General for the Criminal Division of the DoJ, returned to a lucrative position with the international corporate law firm Covington & Burling (*Washington Post*, 2013).

Regulation of the financial markets most likely would not have stopped the housing bubble from expanding and imploding, but it certainly would have made the injuries that were suffered much less severe. There is also no question that without the bank bailouts the entire economy would have collapsed, creating a second Great Depression. The problem lies in the question brought about by moral hazard: if you bail someone out of a problem they themselves caused, what incentive will they have the next time to avoid causing the same problem? The answer, of course, is no incentive. So if the bailouts keep credit markets afloat but create "moral hazard," what is there to do? Provide a bailout, but break up the institutions, replace management, prosecute those who were engaged in criminal behavior, and provide a bailout to the people who were adversely affected by the financial collapse.

There are those who would say that all that is needed is reform of business and political practices, arguing that this would prevent the occurrence of future economic crisis (Allen and Carletti, 2010; Perelman, 2008). These same arguments have transpired from a lens where the core problem is structural integrity as opposed to the structure itself. In an economic and social system that is founded on unequal property relationships, reform is no more than pablum for the people. The problems we face are, in fact, *structural and systemic*, and require a *complete transformation of the prevailing economic system*—a task that can only be accomplished through collective social action by those who have most adversely been affected by the system, i.e., working people across the globe.

Appendix A

Timeline of US corporate bailouts, 1970–2008

Industry/ corporation	Year	Scenario*	Total in 2008 $US
Penn Central Railroad	1970	May 1970, Penn Central Railroad, then on the verge of bankruptcy, appealed to the Federal Reserve for aid on the grounds that it provided crucial national defense transportation services. The Nixon administration and the Federal Reserve supported providing financial assistance to Penn Central, but Congress refused to adopt the measure. Penn Central declared bankruptcy on June 21, 1970, which freed the corporation from its commercial paper obligations. To counteract the devastating ripple effects to the money market, the Federal Reserve Board told commercial banks it would provide the reserves needed to allow them to meet the credit needs of their customers.	$3.2 billion
Lockheed	1971	In August 1971, Congress passed the Emergency Loan Guarantee Act, which could provide funds to any major business enterprise in crisis. Lockheed was the first recipient.	$1.4 billion
Franklin National Bank	1974	In the first five months of 1974 the bank lost $63.6 million. The Federal Reserve stepped in with a loan of $1.75 billion.	$7.8 billion
New York City	1975	During the 1970s, New York City became over-extended and entered a period of financial crisis. In 1975 President Ford signed the New York City Seasonal Financing Act, which released $2.3 billion in loans to the city.	$9.4 billion
Chrysler	1980	In 1979 Chrysler suffered a loss of $1.1 billion. That year the corporation requested aid from the government. In 1980 the Chrysler Loan Guarantee Act was passed, which provided $1.5 billion in loans to rescue Chrysler from insolvency. In addition, the government's aid was to be matched by US and foreign banks.	$9.5 billion
Continental Illinois National Bank and Trust Company	1984	Then the nation's eighth largest bank, Continental Illinois had suffered significant losses after purchasing $1 billion in energy loans from the failed Penn Square Bank of Oklahoma. The FDIC and Federal Reserve devised a plan to rescue the bank that included replacing the bank's top executives.	$9.5 billion
Savings & Loan	1989	After the widespread failure of savings and loan institutions, President George H.W. Bush signed and Congress enacted the Financial Institutions Reform Recovery and Enforcement Act in 1989.	$293.3 billion
Citicorp	1991	Citicorp was secretly overtaken by regulators at the Federal Reserve Bank of New York (FRBNY) amidst fears of a global run on the banks. Shortly after, the FRBNY provided $3.4 billion in loans to "one or more money centered banks" (it is speculated, yet unconfirmed, that most of those loans went directly to Citicorp). Under their direct control, FRBNY forced Citicorp to sell assets and reduce shareholder dividends. Furthermore, Saudi Prince al-Waleed bin Talal infused $590 million into Citicorp by purchasing preferred stock, and another $600 million came from various Middle-Eastern and US institutions. 11,000 bank employees lost their jobs.	$3.4 billion

Goldman Sachs	1995	After a decade of speculative bond trading and selling national assets (i.e., forests, industry, farmland) to foreign investors, Mexico entered into a major economic recession when the investment bubble burst as a result of NAFTA and the deflation of the peso. The US provided $20 billion in loans and guarantees for short-term Mexican bonds, where most of that money was funneled through Mexican state banks to Goldman Sachs as they were heavily invested in those same bonds.	$20 billion
Long-Term Capital Management	1998	The Federal Reserve Bank of New York organized a private bailout of Long-Term Capital Management (LTMC) after they lost 50 percent of their capital investments. Fifteen private banks pooled $3.6 billion to save LTCM, although Warren Buffet had previously offered to pay off the shareholders with $250 million.	$3.6 billion
Airline Industry	2001	The terrorist attacks of September 11 crippled an already financially troubled industry. To bail out the airlines, President Bush signed into law the Air Transportation Safety and Stabilization Act, which compensated airlines for the mandatory grounding of aircraft after the attacks. The act released $5 billion in compensation and an additional $10 billion in loan guarantees or other federal credit instruments.	$18.6 billion
Bear Stearns	2008	JPMorgan Chase and the federal government bailed out Bear Stearns when the financial giant neared collapse. JPMorgan purchased Bear Stearns for $236 million; the Federal Reserve provided a $30 billion credit line to ensure the sale could move forward.	$30 billion
Fannie Mae/ Freddie Mac	2008	On September 7, 2008, Fannie and Freddie were essentially nationalized: placed under the conservatorship of the Federal Housing Finance Agency. Under the terms of the rescue, the Treasury has invested billions to cover the companies' losses. Initially, Treasury Secretary Hank Paulson put a ceiling of $100 billion for investments in each company. In February, Tim Geithner raised it to $200 billion. The money was authorized by the Housing and Economic Recovery Act of 2008.	$400 billion
American International Group (AIG)	2008	On four separate occasions, the government has offered aid to AIG to keep it from collapsing, rising from an initial $85 billion credit line from the Federal Reserve to a combined $180 billion effort between the Treasury ($70 billion) and Fed ($110 billion). ($40 billion of the Treasury's commitment is also included in the TARP total.)	$180 billion
Auto Industry	2008	In late September 2008, Congress approved a more than $630 billion spending bill, which included a measure for $25 billion in loans to the auto industry. These low-interest loans are intended to aid the industry in its push to build more fuel-efficient, environmentally-friendly vehicles. The Detroit 3—General Motors, Ford and Chrysler—will be the primary beneficiaries.	$25 billion
Troubled Asset Relief Program	2008	In October 2008, Congress passed the Emergency Economic Stabilization Act, which authorized the Treasury Department to spend $700 billion to combat the financial crisis. Treasury has been doling out the money via an alphabet soup of different programs.	$700 billion

Citigroup	2008	Citigroup received a $25 billion investment through the TARP in October and another $20 billion in November. (That $45 billion is also included in the TARP total.) Additional aid has come in the form of government guarantees to limit losses from a $301 billion pool of toxic assets. In addition to the Treasury's $5 billion commitment, the FDIC has committed $10 billion and the Federal Reserve up to about $220 billion.	$280 billion
Bank of America	2009	Bank of America has received $45 billion through the TARP, which includes $10 billion originally meant for Merrill Lynch. (That $45 billion is also included in the TARP total.) In addition, the government has made guarantees to limit losses from a $118 billion pool of troubled assets. In addition to the Treasury's $7.5 billion commitment, the FDIC has committed $2.5 billion and the Federal Reserve up to $87.2 billion.	$142.2 billion
Total**:	$2.13 trillion		

Note: * The net return from the bailouts between 1970 and 2001 to the Treasury Department is approximately $10.1 billion. The net return from the 2008 bailout to the Treasury Department is $642 billion (see www.propublica.org); ** Total bailout does not include the $3.6 billion private bailout of Long-Term Capital Management nor does it include the $16.1 trillion provided to big business by the Federal Reserve (see US Government Accountability Office 2011).

Sources for 1970–89 and 2001–09: Nankin, Jesse, Eric Umansky, Krista Kjellman, and Scott Klein. "History of U.S. Government Bailouts." *Pro Publica*, http://www.propublica.org/special/government-bailouts#aig Retrieved April 28, 2012; Sources for 1991: EIR Economics Staff. (1991). "Citicorp Loses Billions, Suspends Dividend Payments." *Executive Intelligence Review*, 18(42), 4–5; Hoefle, John. (1993). "Citicorp Bailout Leaves Debt as Unpayable as Ever." *Executive Intelligence Review*, 20(21), 4–5.

Sources for 1995: Brown, Ellwn. (2008). *Web of Debt: The Shocking Truth About Our Money System and How We Can Break Free*. Baton Rouge, LA: Third Millennium Press; Ahmad, Eqbal. (1995). "The Reconquest of Mexico," tni.org (March 1995). Retrieved June 1, 2014.

Sources for 1998: Freeman, Richard. (2007). "Bear Stearns Funds' Failure Opens the Door to Credit Crash." *Executive Intelligence Review*, 34(27), 62–63; Haubrich, Joesph. (2007). "Some Lessons on the Rescue of Long-Term Capital Management." *Federal Reserve Bank of Cleveland*, Policy Discussion Paper (No. 9), 1–12.

Appendix B

TOP 50 CORPORATE LAYOFF LEADERS AND RESPECTIVE CEO TOTAL COMPENSATION IN 2009

	Corporation	2009 CEO	2009 CEO total compensation*	Total announced layoffs (11/1/08–4/1/10)
1	General Motors	Frederick Henderson [a]	$5,445,000	75,733
2	Citigroup	Vikram S. Pandit [b]	$128,751	52,175
3	Bank of America	Kenneth D. Lewis [c]	$32,171	35,000
4	Caterpillar	James W. Owens	$6,764,531	27,499
5	Verizon	Ivan G. Seidenberg	$17,485,796	21,308
6	Pfizer	Jeffrey B. Kindler	$13,659,266	19,872
7	Emerson Electric	David Farr	$6,899,987	14,200
8	JPMorgan Chase	James Dimon [d]	$1,265,708	14,000
9	Alcoa	Klaus Kleinfeld	$11,214,266	13,985
10	Wal-Mart Stores	Michael T. Duke	$19,234,269	13,350
11	United Technologies	Louis Chenevert	$17,897,666	13,290
12	AT&T	Randall Stephenson	$20,244,312	12,300
13	Las Vegas Sands	Sheldon Adelson	$5,575,149	11,500
14	Boeing	W. James McNerney	$13,705,435	11,304
15	Sprint Nextel	Dan Hesse	$12,334,096	10,250
16	Johnson & Johnson	William C. Weldon	$25,569,844	8,900
17	Schering-Plough	Fred Hassan [e]	$49,653,063	8,000
18	Merck	Richard Clark [f]	$11,892,903	8,000
19	Home Depot	Francis S. Blake	$9,927,573	8,000
20	IBM	Samuel J. Palmisano	$21,159,289	7,800
21	Dow Chemical	Andrew N. Liveris	$15,676,522	7,500
22	Macy's	Terry Lundgren	$12,848,407	7,000
23	U.S. Steel	John P. Surma	$1,507,042	6,705
24	Starbucks	Howard Schultz	$14,970,792	6,700
25	Hewlett-Packard	Mark V. Hurd	$24,201,448	6,400
26	Textron	Scott C. Donnelly	$8,902,401	6,315
27	Sun Microsystems	Jonathan I. Schwartz	$6,983,421	6,000
28	PNC Financial Services	James E. Rohr	$14,801,880	5,800
29	Microsoft	Steven Ballmer	$1,276,627	5,800
30	Eaton	Alexander M. Cutler	$6,809,616	5,609
31	Eli Lilly & Co.	John C. Lechleiter	$16,374,524	5,500
32	Intel	Paul S. Otellini	$14,407,900	5,000
33	Goodyear	Robert J. Keegan	$14,014,167	5,000
34	Terex	Ronald M. DeFeo	$3,417,736	5,000
35	Ford	Alan Mulally	$17,916,654	4,700
36	Eastman Kodak	Antonio Perez	$10,157,273	4,500
37	El du Pont de Nemours	E.J. Kullman	$8,343,305	4,500
38	American Express	Kenneth I. Chenault	$16,796,132	4,000

39	Hertz Global Holdings	Mark P. Frissora	$9,019,690	4,000
40	Wyndham Worldwide	Stephen Holmes	$6,095,801	4,000
41	Motorola	Gregory Q. Brown	$3,774,885	4,000
42	Bristol-Myers Squib	James M. Cornelius	$17,002,765	3,813
43	3M	George W. Buckley	$13,992,628	3,700
44	General Electric	Jeffrey R. Immelt	$5,585,322	3,568
45	Walt Disney	Robert A. Iger	$21,578,471	3,400
46	Texas Instruments	Richard K. Templeton	$9,816,091	3,400
47	Danaher	H. Lawrence Cult, Jr.	$11,047,304	3,300
48	Algilent Technologies	William Sullivan	$6,472,033	3,300
49	Avon Products	Andrea Jung	$7,091,871	3,242
50	Omnicom Group	John D. Wren	$7,884,598	3,145
	Average		$11,977,128	10,627
	Median		$11,130,785	6,358
	Total		$598,856,381	531,363

Note: * Despite many high-profile cuts in executive compensation on Wall Street, other employee bonuses have increased by 17 percent on average. For Goldman Sachs, Morgan Stanley and JPMorgan Chase, employee compensation grew by 31 percent in 2009 from 2008.[1] *Total Compensation* refers to "salary, bonuses, perks, above-market interest on deferred compensation and the value of stock and option awards."[2] a = Frederick Henderson resigned on December 1, 2009.[2] b = Citigroup CEO Vikram S. Pandit is the first of the two anomalies expressed in the appendix (i.e., one of the two CEOs that did not receive $1 million or more in compensation). In the calamity transpiring from the financial meltdown, some corporate boards and top executives attempted to avoid increasingly hostile public sentiment towards big banks by cutting salaries—especially if that company received bailout money (Citigroup received $45 billion in TARP funds). In 2010, Pandit took home $1 in compensation, turning down a lucrative offer made by the board of directors in order to save face.[3] However, in 2011, Pandit received $1.8 million in salary and was awarded $23.2 million retention package comprised of $16.5 million in stock options and $6.7 million in a "profit-sharing program."[5] He is still the CEO of Citigroup. c = Bank of America's CEO, Kennith D. Lewis is the second anomaly expressed in the appendix, and for the same reasons (Bank of America received $45 billion in TARP funds). Lewis was relieved of his duties as CEO at the end of 2009, yet left with an $83 million retirement package including "pension and insurance benefits, stock and other compensation."[6] In 2010, Bank of America's new CEO, Brian T. Moynihan, received $9.05 million in bonuses and $950,000 for his salary, totaling $10 million.[7] In 2011, Moynihan's compensation was $8.1 million.[8] Moynihan is still CEO of Bank of America. d = In 2009, Jamie Dimon received $6,858,692 in options that are not included in his total compensation.[2] e = Merck merged with Schering-Plough on Nov. 3, 2009, under the Merck name. Hassan resigned and Clark assumed responsibilities of CEO. The new Merck announced 16,000 layoffs, 8,000 for each firm.[2]

Note sources:

[1] *Los Angeles Times*. "Wall Street bonuses soar 17% in 2009, even as banks reduce pay for top executives." http://articles.latimes.com/2010/feb/23/business/la-fi-wall-street-jobs24-2010feb24 (2010). Retrieved July 10, 2012.

[2] Anderson, Sarah, Chuck Collins, Sam Pizzigati, & Kevin Shih. "CEO Pay and the Great Recession." *Institute for Policy Studies: 17th Annual Executive Compensation Survey* (2010). pp. 26–27.

[3] *The New York Times*. "Citigroup's Pandit Takes $1 in Compensation for 2010." http://www.nytimes.com/2010/09/25/business/25citi.html (2010). Retrieved July 10, 2012.

[4] *The Wall Street Journal*. "Citigroup Restores Vikram Pandit's Salary to $1.75 Million." http://blogs.wsj.com/deals/2011/01/21/citigroup-restores-vikram-pandits-salary-to-175-million/ (2011). Retrieved July 10, 2012.

[5] *The New York Times*. "As Citi Revives, Pandit Wins Big Pay Package." http://dealbook.nytimes.com/2011/05/18/pandits-take-of-citigroups-profits/?scp=1&sq=citigroup%20pandit%20&st=Search (2011). Retrieved July 11, 2012.

[6] *The Wall Street Journal*. "Retirement Benefits for BofA's Lewis: $83 Million." http://online.wsj.com/article/SB10001424052748704625004575089742035330432.html (2010). Retrieved July 10, 2012.

[7] *The Washington Post*. "Bank of America CEO gets $9.05 million bonus." http://www.washingtonpost.com/wp-dyn/content/article/2011/01/31/AR2011013105314.html (2011). Retrieved July 10, 2012.

[8] *The Huffington Post*. "Bank of America CEO Brian Moynihan's Compensation Quadrupled In 2011." http://www.huffingtonpost.com/2012/03/28/bank-of-america-ceo-made-n1385435.html (2012). Retrieved July 10, 2012.

Appendix source: Anderson, Sarah, Chuck Collins, Sam Pizzigati, and Kevin Shih. 2010. "CEO Pay and the Great Recession." *Institute for Policy Studies: 17th Annual Executive Compensation Survey*, pp. 26–27.

Appendix C: Corporate Tax Rates of 0% and Below and Layoffs†‡, 2008–10

37 corporations tax rate 0% and below in 2010 (in millions of US dollars)			
Corporation	**US profits**	**Tax**	**Tax rate**
State Street Corp. * †	$ 731	$ -885	-121.1%
Pepco Holdings	$ 229	$ -270	-117.9%
Con-way	$ 46	$ -53	115.4%
International Paper †	$ 217	$ -249	-114.7%
General Electric †	$ 4,248	$ -3,253	-76.6%
Omnicare	$ 18	$ -14	-76.1%
SPX	$ 90	$ -36	-40.4%
Reinsurance Group of America	$ 543	$ -216	-39.8%
Honeywell International	$ 1,243	$ -482	-38.7%
Dean Foods	$ 126	$ -49	-38.4%
Integrys Energy Group	$ 353	$ -84	-23.7%
Atmos Energy	$ 328	$ -74	-22.5%
Navistar International †	$ 162	$ -30	-18.5%
DTE Energy	$ 950	$ -172	-18.1%
NiSource	$ 433	$ -62	-14.3%
Pantry	$ 29	$ -4	-12.7%
Capital One Financial *	$ 1,259	$ -152	-12.1%
DuPont †‡	$ 949	$ -109	-11.5%
Yahoo †	$ 855	$ -82	-9.6%
Consolidated Edison	$ 1,528	$ -144	-9.4%
Scana	$ 533	$ -47	-8.8%
American Electric Power †	$ 1,869	$ -134	-7.2%
Verizon Communications †‡	$ 11,963	$ -705	-5.9%
PNC Financial Services Group*	$ 3,584	$ -208	-5.8%
PPL	$ 935	$ -51	-5.5%
Casey's General Stores	$ 150	$ -7	-4.5%
Chesapeake Energy	$ 2,806	$ -120	-4.3%
Domtar	$ 162	$ -6	-3.8%
CMS Energy	$ 561	$ -21	-3.7%
Progress Energy	$ 1,419	$ -46	-3.2%
Rockwell Automation	$ 148	$ -4	-2.4%
FirstEnergy	$ 1,207	$ -23	-1.9%
PG&E Corp.	$ 1,530	$ -12	-0.8%
El Paso Corp.	$ 1,231	$ -4	-0.3%
Duke Energy	$ 2,150	$ -5	-0.2%
Boeing †	$ 4,450	$ -3	-0.1%
Corning	$ 974	–	–
Total	*$50,009*	*$ -7,816*	*-15.6%*

49 corporations tax rate 0% and below in 2009 (in millions of US dollars)			
Corporation	**US Profits**	**Tax**	**Tax Rate**
Paccar	$ 83	$ -108	-130.7%
General Electric †	$ 1,574	$ -833	-52.9%
Holly	$ 46	$ -24	-52.1%
NiSource	$ 412	$ -197	-47.9%
NYSE Euronext	$ 67	$ -31	-46.3%
Pepco Holdings	$ 359	$ -160	-44.6%
PG&E Corp. †	$ 1,735	$ -747	-43.1%
Marathon Oil	$ 571	$ -232	-40.7%
Eastman Chemical	$ 204	$ -82	-40.2%
Cliffs Natural Resources	$ 128	$ -49	-38.4%
Exxon Mobil	$ 2,490	$ -954	-38.4%
Ryder System	$ 126	$ -45	-36.0%
Interpublic Group	$ 148	$ -48	-32.7%
Insight Enterprises	$ 15	$ -5	-32.3%
PPL	$ 234	$ -72	-30.8%
Apache	$ 439	$ -130	-29.7%
American Electric Power	$ 2,014	$ -575	-28.6%
Tenet Healthcare	$ 194	$ -53	-27.3%
Yum Brands	$ 294	$ -70	-23.7%
Entergy	$ 1,992	$ -433	-21.7%
CenterPoint Energy	$ 538	$ -103	-19.1%
Wells Fargo* †	$ 21,797	$ -3,967	-18.2%
FirstEnergy	$ 1,191	$ -183	-15.4%
Duke Energy	$ 1,768	$ -271	-15.3%
Southwest Airlines	$ 165	$ -24	-14.5%
Ingram Micro	$ 14	$ -2	-13.4%
Atmos Energy	$ 283	$ -37	-13.1%
Boeing †‡	$ 1,494	$ -136	-9.1%
Ameren	$ 953	$ -73	-7.7%
Reliance Steel & Aluminum	$ 197	$ -15	-7.5%
Mattel	$ 356	$ -21	-5.9%
Halliburton †	$ 565	$ -30	-5.3%
H.J. Heinz	$ 500	$ -26	-5.3%
Verizon Communications ‡	$ 12,261	$ -611	-5.0%
Wisconsin Energy	$ 543	$ -26	-4.8%
CMS Energy	$ 307	$ -12	-3.9%
Xcel Energy	$ 1,048	$ -40	-3.8%
Hewlett-Packard ‡	$ 2,424	$ -87	-3.6%
Health Management Associate	$ 244	$ -7	-3.0%
Baxter International	$ 466	$ -12	-2.7%
PNC Financial Services Group * ‡	$ 4,398	$ -110	-2.5%
Honeywell International	$ 1,723	$ -28	-1.6%
NextEra Energy	$ 1,865	$ -18	-1.0%

Merck	$ 5,766	$ -55	-1.0%
Corning †	$ 202	$ -8	-0.4%
Peabody Energy	$ 280	$ -1	-0.3%
Occidental Petroleum	$ 2,068	$ -4	-0.2%
Deere & Co. †	$ 907	$ -1	-0.1%
El Paso Corp.	$ 1,205	$ -1	-0.1%
Total	*$ 78,652*	*$ -10,758*	*-13.7%*

22 corporations tax rate 0% and below in 2008 (in millions of US dollars)

Corporation	US Profits	Tax	Tax Rate
Eli Lilly	$ 202	$ -208	-102.9%
Computer Sciences	$ 626	$ -397	-63.4%
Baxter International	$ 279	$ -93	-33.2%
CenterPoint Energy	$ 712	$ -221	-31.0%
Paccar	$ 105	$ -28	-26.6%
Pepco Holdings	$ 294	$ -78	-26.5%
Wisconsin Energy	$ 529	$ -131	-24.7%
PG&E Corp.	$ 1,590	$ -268	-16.9%
Goldman Sachs * †	$ 4,909	$ -786	-16.0%
General Electric †	$ 4,638	$ -651	-14.0%
R.R. Donnelley & Sons	$ 561	$ -49	-8.8%
NextEra Energy	$ 2,060	$ -132	-6.1%
Integrys Energy Group	$ 172	$ -11	-6.1%
Time Warner	$ 2,031	$ -74	-3.7%
FedEx	$ 1,208	$ -38	-3.2%
El Paso Corp.	$ 1,669	$ -36	-2.2%
Tenet Healthcare	$ 63	$ -1	-1.6%
Ryder System †	$ 349	$ -4	-1.2%
Boeing †	$ 3,791	$ -39	-1.0%
Sempra Energy	$ 1,171	$ -10	-0.9%
FMC Technologies	$ 67	--	-0.2%
Peabody Energy	$ 185	--	--
Total	*$ 27,211*	*$ -3,254*	*-12.0%*

	US Profits	Tax	Tax Rate
Grand totals (2008–2010)	*$ 155,872*	*$ 21,826*	*-13.80%*

Note: † Between 500 and 5,000 layoffs by the end of the year; ‡ Between 5,001 and 10,000 layoffs by the end of the year; †‡ 10,001 layoffs or more by the end of the year; * Received TARP bailout funds. Source for profit, tax, and tax rate data: McIntyre, Robert, Matthew Gardner, Rebecca Wilkins, and Richard Phillips. (2011). Corporate Taxpayers and Corporate Tax Dodgers: 2008–10. *A Joint Project of Citizens for Tax Justice and the Institute on Taxation and Economic Policy*, November 2011; Only US profits are listed as profits made overseas are often untaxed.[1] Seven corporations—Capital One, NiSource, Insight Ent., Cliffs Natural Resources, First Energy, Ingram Micro, and El Paso Corp.—cut between 200 and 499 jobs at least once between 2008 and 2010.[2] 2010 layoffs: State Street

Corp. (1,400);[3] International Paper (2,200);[4] Navistar Intl. (800),[5] DuPont (17,000);[6] Verizon (30,000);[6] Boeing (3,700);[6] Yahoo (600);[7] American Electric Power (2,200).[8] 2008–2009 layoffs: PG&E (500),[9] Halliburton (2,000),[9] Wells Fargo (936),[9] Boeing (10,800),[9] Verizon (8,188),[9] Hewlett-Packard (6,200),[9] PNC Financial (5,800),[9] Corning Inc. (3,500),[9] Deere & Co. (1,700),[9] Goldman Sachs (3,200),[9] Ryder System (3,100),[9] General Electric (18,000).[10] TARP bailout recipients: State Street Corp. ($2 billion),[11] Capital One ($3.5 billion),[11] PNC Financial ($7.6 billion),[11] Wells Fargo ($25 billion),[11] and Goldman Sachs ($10 billion).[11]

Note sources:

[1] McIntyre, Robert, Matthew Gardner, Rebecca Wilkins, and Richard Phillips. (2011). Corporate Taxpayers and Corporate Tax Dodgers: 2008–10. A Joint Project of Citizens for Tax Justice and the Institute on Taxation and Economic Policy, November 2011.

[2] Portal Seven. "Layoffs." http://portalseven.com/employment/ (2010). Retrieved July 20, 2013.

[3] Boston Globe. "State Street begins layoffs in Boston." http://www.boston.com/business/articles/2010/12/02/state_street_begins_layoffs_in_boston/ (2010). Retrieved July 20, 2013.

[4] Daily Press. "International Paper Shutdown is Complete." http://articles.dailypress.com/2010-06-30/news/dp-nws-ip-closure-20100630_1_international-paper-displaced-workers (2010). Retrieved July 20, 2013. World Socialist Web Site. "International Paper Shuts Three Mills, Laying Off 1,600 Workers." http://www.wsws.org/en/articles/2009/11/intp-n28.html (2009). Retrieved July 20, 2013.

[5] CoStar Group. "Closures & Layoffs (April 25–May 1), Navistar, Sysco Make Cuts." http://www.costar.com/News/Article/Closures-Layoffs-Apr-25-May-1-Navistar-Sysco-Make-Cuts/119809 (2010). Retrieved July 20, 2013. The Dispatch. "Navistar Plant in West Point Announces Layoffs." http://www.cdispatch.com/news/article.asp?aid=7141&TRID=1&TID= (2010). Retrieved July 20, 2013. Springfield News-Sun. "Navistar Issues Layoff Notices." http://www.springfieldnewssun.com/news/news/local/navistar-issues-layoff-notices/nNxdW/ (2010). Retrieved July 20, 2013.

[6] Daily Finance. "The Layoff Kings: The 25 Companies Responsible for 700,000 Lost Jobs." http://www.dailyfinance.com/2010/08/18/the-layoff-kings-the-25-companies-responsible-for-700-000-lost/ (2010). Retrieved July 20, 2013.

[7] Huffington Post. "Yahoo Layoffs: 600 to 700 Workers Mark Fourth Mass Cuts in 3 Years." http://www.huffingtonpost.com/2010/12/14/yahoo-layoffs-600-to-700-_n_796295.html (2010). Retrieved July 20, 2013.

[8] Recareered. "Who's Firing—Layoffs Week Ended 4-16-10." http://www.recareered.com/blog/2010/04/18/whos-firing-layoffs-week-ended-4-16-10/ (2010). Retrieved July 20, 2013.

[9] Portal Seven. "Layoffs." http://portalseven.com/employment/ (2010). Retrieved July 20, 2013.

[10] ABC. "General Electric Paid No Federal Taxes in 2010." http://abcnews.go.com/Politics/general-electric-paid-federal-taxes-2010/story?id=13224558 (2011). Retrieved July 20, 2013. Portal Seven. Layoffs. http://portalseven.com/employment/ (2010). Retrieved July 20, 2013.

[11] NY Times. "Tracking the $700 Billion Bailout." http://www.nytimes.com/packages/html/national/200904_CREDITCRISIS/recipients.html (2013). Retrieved July 19, 2013.

References

Ahmed, Nafeez. 2010. *A User's Guide to the Crisis of Civilization: And How to Save It*. London: Pluto Press.

Allen, Franklin and Elena Carletti. 2010. "An Overview of the Crisis: Causes, Consequences, and Solutions." *International Review of Finance*, 10(1), 1–26.

Berberoglu, Berch. 2009. *Class and Class Conflict in the Age of Globalization*. Lanham, MD: Lexington Books.

Berberoglu, Berch. 2012. *Beyond the Global Capitalist Crisis: The World Economy in Transition*. Farnham: Ashgate Publishing.

Bivens, Josh. 2011. *Failure by Design: The Story Behind America's Broken Economy*. Ithaca, NY: ILR Press, an imprint of Cornell University Press.

Blum, William. 2005. *Rouge State: A Guide to the World's Only Superpower*. Monroe, ME: Common Courage Press.

Board of Governors of the Federal Reserve System. 2012. *Changes in U.S. Family Finances from 2007 to 2010: Evidence from the Survey of Consumer Finances*. Federal Reserve Bulletin, 98(2).

Callari, Antonio. 2010. "2008: A New Chapter for U.S. Imperialism." *Rethinking Marxism: A Journal of Economics, Culture & Society*, 22(2), 210–218.

Campbell, John L. 2010. "Neoliberalism in Crisis: Regulatory Roots of the U.S. Financial Meltdown." *Research in the Sociology of Organizations*, 30(B), 65–101.

Carruthers, Bruce. 2012. What's Haute in the Sociology of Finance? *Contemporary Sociology*, 41(6), 739–746.

Chomsky, Noam. 1994. *What Uncle Sam Really Wants*. Berkeley, CA: Odonian Press.

DemocracyNow! 2012. JPMorgan Chase CEO gets warm hill welcome from senators flooded with millions in Wall St. donations. Pacificia Media. http://www.democracynow.org/shows/2012/6/14. Retrieved June 14, 2012.

Dorn, Nicholas. 2011. Regulatory Sloth and Activism in the Effervescence of Financial Crisis. *Law & Policy*, 33(3), 428–448.

Fasenfest, David. 2010. Global Economy, Local Calamity. *Critical Sociology*, 36(2), 195–200.

Friedman, Milton. 1962. *Capitalism and Freedom*. Chicago, IL: The University of Chicago Press.

Financial Crisis Inquiry Commission. 2011. *The Financial Crisis Inquiry Report*. Washington, DC: US Government Printing Office.

Frontline. 2012. *Money, Power & Wall Street*. New York, NY: PBS Productions. http://www.pbs.org/wgbh/pages/frontline/money-power-wall-street/. Retrieved April 24, 2012.

Frontline. 2013. *The Untouchables*. New York, NY: PBS Productions. http://www.pbs.org/wgbh/pages/frontline/untouchables/. Retrieved August 3, 2013.

Ghotge, Sanjeev. 2009. "Financial Meltdown: An Intriguing Silence at the Core." *Capitalism, Nature, Socialism*, 20(4), 85–88.

Harris, Paul and Daniel Sarewitz. 2012. "Destructive creation and the New World Disorder." *Current History; Science Global Trends*, 2012(January), 29–33.

Hernandez, Jesus. 2009. "Redlining Revisited: Mortgage Lending Patterns in Sacramento 1930–2004." *International Journal of Urban and Regional Research*, 33(2), 291–313.

Ho, Karen. 2009. *Liquidated; An Ethnography of Wall Street*. London: Duke University Press.

Hogg, Russell. 2013. "Populism, Law and Order and the Crimes of the 1%." *International Journal for Crime and Justice*, 2(1), 113–131.

Jacobs, David and Marc Dixon. 2010. "Political Partisanship, Race, and Union Strength from 1970 to 2000: A Pooled Time-Series Analysis." *Social Science Research*, 39, 1059–1072.

Kaptur, Marcy. 2011. "Rep. Marcy Kaptur says G.E. pays no taxes and creates no jobs but makes record profits." *Politico*, CNS. http://www.politifact.com/ohio/statements/2011/apr/20/marcy-kaptur/rep-marcy-kaptur-says-ge-pays-no-taxes-and-creates/. Retrieved April 1, 2012.

Klein, Naomi. 2008. *Shock Doctrine: The Rise of Disaster Capitalism*. New York, NY: Metropolitan Books/Henry Holt.

Konings, Martijn. 2010. "Neoliberalism and the American State." *Critical Sociology*, 36(5), 741–765.

Kotz, David M. 2009. "Systemic Crisis of Neoliberal Capitalism." *Review of Radial Political Economics*, 41(3), 305–317.

Lansley, Stewart. 2010. How soaring inequality contributed to the crash. Soundings on Read Periodicals. http://readperiodicals.com/201004/2061446041.html. Received on April 1, 2012.

McIntyre, Robert, Matthew Gardner, Rebecca Wilkins, and Richard Phillips. 2011. "Corporate Taxpayers and Corporate Tax Dodgers: 2008–10." *A Joint Project of Citizens for Tax Justice and the Institute on Taxation and Economic Policy* (November).

Mizruchi, Mark. 2010. The American Corporate Elite and the Historical Roots of the Financial Crisis of 2008. In *Markets on Trial: Pt. B: The Economic Sociology of the U.S. Financial Crisis.* Lounsbury, Michael and Paul Hirsch (eds), pp. 103–139. Bingley: Emerald Group Publishing Ltd.

MSNBC. 2011. Video: No job? Cain says "blame yourself." NBC Universal. http://thelastword.msnbc.msn.com/_news/2011/10/05/8172530-no-job-cain-says-blame-yourself. Retrieved April 26, 2012.

O'Connor, Tyler. 2013. "Prosecuting Executives for Financial Fraud: The Responsible Corporate Officer Doctrine as an Alternative Means of Criminal Liability." *Social Science Research Network*. http://ssrn.com/abstract=2243124. Retrieved August 9, 2013.

Parenti, Michael. 2011. *Democracy for the Few*, 9th Edition. Boston, MA: Wadsworth, Cengage Learning.

Perelman, Michael. 2008. "The Corrosive Qualities of Inequality: The Roots of the Current Meltdown." *Challenge*, 51(5), 40–64.

Petras, James and Henry Veltmeyer. 2012. "The Global Capitalist Crisis: Whose Crisis, Who Profits?" *International Review of Modern Sociology*, 38(2), 199–219.

Pilger, John, Christopher Martin, and Wayne Young. 2007. *The War on Democracy*. Granada, UK: Youngheart Entertainment.

Sakamoto, Arthur and Changhwan Kim. 2010. Is Rising Earnings Inequality Associated with Increased Exploitation? Evidence for U.S. Manufacturing Industries, 1971–1996. *Sociological Perspectives*, 53(1), 19–43.

Sherman, Howard J. 2010. *The Roller Coaster Economy: Financial Crisis, Great Recession, and the Public Opinion*. Armonk, NY: ME Sharpe, Inc.

So, Alvin. 2005. "Class Structure and Class Conflict in Advanced Capitalist Society." In *Globalization and Change: The Transformation of Global Capitalism*. Berch Berberoglu (ed.). pp. 23–34. Lanham, MD: Lexington Books.

Sorkin, Andrew. 2010. *Too Big To Fail*. London: Penguin Books, Ltd.

Spector, Alan J. 2005. "Class Polarization and Class Struggle Under Advanced Capitalism." In *Globalization and Change: The Transformation of Global Capitalism*. Berch Berberoglu (ed.). pp. 35–45. Lanham, MD: Lexington Books.

Stevenson, Bryan. 2011. "Drug Policy, Criminal Justice and Mass Imprisonment." *The Global Commission on Drug Policies*, Geneva, 24–25 January 2011.

Taibbi, Matt. 2012. "Outragrous HABC Settlement Proves the Drug War is a Joke." *Rolling Stone*, http://www.rollingstone.com/politics/blogs/taibblog/outrageous-hsbc-settlement-proves-the-drug-war-is-a-joke-20121213. Retrieved August 1, 2013.

Treas, Judith. 2010. "The Great American Recession: Sociological Insights on Palme and Pain." *Sociological Perspectives*, 53(1), 3–17.

US Census Bureau. 2011. *Income, Poverty, and Health Insurance Coverage in the United States, 2010*. Washington, DC: US Census Bureau.

US Government Accountability Office. 2011. *Federal Reserve System: Opportunities Exist to Strengthen Policies and Processes for Managing Emergency Assistance*. Washington, DC: US Government Accountability Office.

US Senate Committee on Homeland Security & Governmental Affairs. 2012. *HSBC Exposed U.S. Financial System to Money Laundering, Drug, Terrorist Financing Risks*. Washington, DC: The Permanent Subcommittee on Investigations.

Volscho, Thomas and Nathan Kelly. 2012. "The Rise of the Super-Rich: Power Resources, Taxes, Financial Markets, and the Dynamics of the Top 1 Percent, 1949 to 2008." *American Sociological Review*, 77(5), 679–699.

Wacquant, Loïc. 2007. "The Place of the Prison in the New Government of Poverty." Excerpted from *Prisons of Poverty*, Minneapolis, MN: University of Minnesota Press.

Washington Post. 2013. Lanny Breuer, chief of DOJ's criminal division, returns to Covington & Burling. *The Washington Post*. http://www.washingtonpost.com/blogs/capital-business/post/lanny-breuer-chief-of-dojs-criminal-division-returns-to-covington-and-burling/2013/03/27/3b27d7a6-9703-11e2-b68f-dc5c4b47e519_blog.html. Retrieved August 9, 2013.

Yates, Michael D. 2003. *Naming the System: Inequality and Work in the Global Economy*. New York, NY: Monthly Review Press.

Zajac, Edward and James Westphal. 2004. The Social Construction of Market Value: Institutionalization and Learning Perspectives on Stock Market Reactions. *American Sociological Review*, 69(1), 433–457.

Zinn, Howard. 2003. *A Peoples History of the United States: 1492–Present*. New York, NY: HarperCollins Publishers.

Chapter 6

The Impact of the Global Capitalist Crisis on the Eurozone

David L. Elliott

> … the euro zone is now essentially an economic prison, with Germany as the jailer and the common currency as the bars. No matter what happens they face a future of stagnation—as aging societies with expensive welfare states whose young people will sit idle for years, unable to find work, build capital or start families. (Douthat 2013)

A hundred years ago, coal miners would take caged canaries into mines because canaries were more sensitive to the effects of carbon monoxide (CO) than humans, and when a canary showed distress or died, the miners would leave the mine. If the miners had been scientists possessing the instrumentation to measure the CO, there would have been no need for the canaries. In 2008, the tiny nation of Iceland suffered a financial crash that should have served as the canary for the capitalist system; one economic scientist had used his own instruments and saw it coming and raised the alarm. But his advice was shelved and probably never even read by those with authority. The Icelandic crash accompanied financial crisis in the United States and was followed in rapid succession by heightened crisis in the European Union, especially the eurozone countries that adopted the euro as official currency. Outside Europe and the United States, the impact was more transient though appearing in almost every other country, giving China the opportunity to invest in building its own infrastructure (Harvey, 2011).

Recurring crises have characterized capitalism throughout its history. Each succeeding crisis to a greater or lesser extent saw the enhanced concentration of capital in the hands of the capitalists vis-à-vis the working classes and peasantry, and a reconfiguration of sectors within the ruling capitalist class. The Great Depression of the 1930s was an extended crisis that started on Wall Street in 1929 but spread across the capitalist world over the next decade while its recovery coincided with the Second World War and *the war's* end and recovery. This chapter explores the continuing European crisis and explains why it differs from that of the United States (at least as of this moment) and what its impact has been upon the working and middle classes of Europe. Analyzing why the crisis occurred, how and why the European manifestation was unique, and what the prospects are for the future of the eurozone are the main goals of this chapter. The chapter argues that the leading economic policies of each capitalist state impact the rate and nature of its crisis recovery with the important exception of nations within the eurozone. In the eurozone, the policy leadership resides in the largest national economy, Germany, and this is realized by actions of the European Central Bank (ECB). The concentrated economic power across the eurozone means that monetary policy exercised by the ECB is often in conflict with the fiscal policies of the more seriously crisis-impacted nations: Portugal, Italy, Ireland, Greece, Spain, and Cyprus.

The recovery from the Great Depression, followed by a lengthy period of robust capital growth, was occasioned at least in part by economic policies advocated by John Maynard Keynes who published *The General Theory of Employment, Interest and Money* (Keynes, 1936), a work that suggested "Keynesian" counter-cyclical pressures—monetary and fiscal—that helped to stabilize the growing capitalist economy for several generations. Beyond Keynes, traditional economists have generally failed to provide an explanation for the repeated crises that, though smaller, continue to confront the capitalist system. While many, such as Schumpeter (1939), have traced the economic indicators and identified a number of apparently concurrent cycles of boom and bust, persuasive systemic theoretical explanation is lacking. Schumpeter was willing to let crises continue in the process that he called "creative destruction"—a process that is superficially apparent today as the ruling class has concentrated and reconfigured ownership of the means of production. However, economists following delusional ideologies that include creative destruction, invisible hands, or free and efficient markets are self-precluded from analytical thinking and they usually reduce each recurring crisis to isolated idiographic episodes, each with its own largely unique explanation.

The Recurring Crises of the Capitalist System

Critics of the capitalist system, however, since the time of Marx, have identified an elegantly simple explanation that provides for critique of the contradictions of capitalism as a system and for its recurring crises. The foundation for this explanation is the labor theory of value: all economic value is produced by human labor power. This is not to say that there are no other manifestations of value.

The defining contradiction of capitalism is the purchase (by capitalists) of the labor power of the worker and collectively paying workers less in wages than the total value of the goods and products that they produce. The profit realized allows the capitalist class to accumulate capital for its own purposes at the expense of the working class. What does a capitalist do with the accumulated profits? If it is spent on conspicuous consumption, this removes it as a key factor in the capitalist system. In capitalism the accumulated profits are reinvested in additional wage labor and the materials of production to produce yet more goods and products. The contradiction here is that, sooner or later, more goods that are produced by the working class are placed for sale than the working class as a whole has the wages to purchase. There are temporary solutions that may appear "creative":

bankruptcy of some merchants or industrialists, extension of credit to workers, globalized commerce and production, etc.; however, eventually the system enters a crisis of overproduction (or under consumption) that often results in cut-backs in production, rise in unemployment, and it may take months or years for the system to recover. Japan is only now recovering from its crisis of the 1990s.

While this analysis is based on a more simple system of the nineteenth century, in essence, it remains valid today. Of course, today's world is more complicated. In addition to the economic spheres of production and consumption that were most salient during most of the nineteenth century, the spheres of distribution and exchange have in many respects become the key elements of globalization in the twenty-first century. A century or more ago, Lenin identified the emergence of finance capital as the defining element of imperialism and published his famous treatise, *Imperialism, the Highest Stage of Capitalism* in 1917. He argued that no longer were goods, alone, exported for sale abroad; capital was exported to support capitalist production in the periphery (Lenin, 1975). The accumulation process was thus extended to other parts of the world and the crisis of overproduction was forestalled as some profits made at home were invested for production and sale abroad, rather than for the home market.

This development signaled the emergence of imperialism and today's heightened importance of the spheres of distribution and exchange vis-à-vis production and consumption. Computers and electronic communications in the Internet Age have contributed significantly to neoliberal capital accumulation as goods and products may now be produced, marketed, and distributed to consumers across the world much more quickly and with fewer workers involved in the process. This contributes to capital accumulation at the expense of the workers employed in the distributive industries. But of greater interest here is financialization, a moment in the sphere of exchange. Finance capital has provided credit for workers, consumers, and students. It has also provided leverage for firms to buy out others for expansion through monopoly, as well as for research and development. No longer is direct extraction of surplus value in the process of production the sole, or necessarily the main, means of capital accumulation. Now, extraction of surplus value from the working class via interest on debts, especially consumer credit, car loans, and home mortgages, has appeared. This contributed to the dot-com, real estate, and other speculative economic bubbles that disproportionately impact working individuals negatively, as opposed to corporations, even corporations that invest at high risk, sometimes unknowingly. Corporations, however, have access to derivatives that offer insurance against major investment losses.

While world production and commerce have changed markedly in the past century, finance capital still plays a key role within the capitalist system. But today, the cause of the crisis may be traced directly back to the role that finance and growing debt have played in the accumulation process of neoliberal globalization. It is here that we turn our attention to analyze the current crisis, particularly in Europe. A key factor that makes the European crisis experience unique was the evolution of the European Community (EU) and the single currency, the euro. The euro is used in the eurozone, comprised of many (not all) EU member states. The EU has emerged as a politically weak, policy-setting body for sovereign states as members of the Community alongside the eurozone's relatively strong, semi-independent central bank, the ECB.

By the 1980s and 1990s, Keynesian policies had fallen from use in favor of neoliberal policies—deregulation, financialization, and other economic practices of the ruling class—largely due to the efforts of followers of economist Milton Friedman and politicians Ronald Reagan and Margaret Thatcher. Whereas Keynesianism was designed to stabilize the capitalist *system as a whole*, neoliberal ideology is more firmly rooted in classical economic thought dating back to Adam Smith and is designed effectively to *enrich the individual capitalists and the class, itself*, vis-à-vis the system as a whole, and especially the system that includes the working class. Indeed, the last three decades have seen the massive shift in the ownership of social wealth toward a smaller number of wealthy families and individuals owning an increasingly larger proportion of society's wealth. And this time period also saw the increased accumulation of concentrated wealth for most capitalist countries (Germany excepted) that measured in terms of nation-based accounting data now looks more like the extremes of global inequality, as seen in the nineteenth century (Piketty and Zucman, 2013).

The current crisis, first manifested in 2007–08, is second in severity only to the Great Depression. It, too, has spread beyond the north Atlantic rim largely through financialization, with varying degrees of intensity, landing early-on in Europe where it continues with its own recurring episodes that seem to repeatedly throw the political and economic institutions of the European Union and the eurozone into turmoil (Lapavitsas, 2012). By spring 2013, capitalists in the US and Europe had largely recovered and enhanced their profitability when financial crisis in Cyprus erupted, throwing the eurozone into turmoil far beyond what one might have expected given Cyprus's heretofore modest role within the capitalist system of Europe. The European manifestation of the crisis thus appears to continue with little sign of systemic recovery.

The epicenter of the crisis was the United States; its financialization had bled into the economies of most of Europe. The key financial activities in the United States that precipitated the crisis were debt-centered and included:

- fraudulent and other questionable acts related to securities
- home loans to persons with insufficient resources that caused a real estate bubble along with improper or illegal foreclosures that helped burst the bubble
- massive mismanagement of debt and consolidation of risky toxic assets
- inept or fraudulent assessments of debt risk, etc.

Many of the tainted debt packages were marketed internationally such that financial institutions abroad were placed at high risk when they purchased toxic US financial products, or engaged in similar activities of their own. But the US is not the only country that suffers from fraud and mismanagement; we see similar practices across the capitalist world, and this contributed to the crisis of the entire system.

Iceland, 2008: Prelude to the Eurozone Crisis

For most of its more than one millennium of human habitation, Iceland has depended upon the sea for its economic base, indeed even well into the twenty-first century. For most of this time, Iceland was associated with the Nordic countries—often ruled (sometimes nominally) by Norway or Denmark—though its annual parliament, the Althing, first met in the tenth century. In the twentieth century, Iceland was occupied by the Nazis, but after the Second World War, once freed from German occupation, Iceland began to emerge as a modern democratic country, notwithstanding disputes with its neighbors as it extended its claims for fishing rights out to 320 kilometers, and with the International Whaling Commission over whale hunting (Macheda, 2012).

By the last decade of the twentieth century, class conflict had emerged as Iceland developed a robust trade union sector that challenged management and had a record of work stoppages that rivaled other capitalist economies. However, as Iceland's three major banks adapted to the neoliberal, deregulated international system of financialization, profitability rose thus advantaging shareholders and depositors. Iceland emerged as an international financier, purchasing toxic US assets with funds earning high interest rates deposited by Europeans and by Icelandic union pension funds. After the crash, British and Dutch bank depositors, through their respective states, kept intense pressure on Iceland until the bank deposits were finally honored, though the Icelandic labor movement increasingly collaborated with capital and quickly lost its progressive nature (Macheda 2012). Macheda identifies the five characteristics of financialization in Iceland: 1) Deregulated financial sector; 2) Increased profits outside the productive sector; 3) Shareholder profit-making became more salient; 4) Household credit driven increasingly by consumption; and 5) Finance capital penetrated workers' own social and economic reproduction. These characteristics and others reappeared across Europe in various configurations as the crisis spread.

Meanwhile, as the US economy stumbled in late 2007 and the first half of 2008, Congress and the Federal Reserve began to execute a series of extraordinary measures to save the capitalist system. This action was the key difference between the US and the EU response to the crisis: the US used Keynesian fiscal tools while the EU/ECB largely restricted themselves to monetary tools. For the US, this included authorizing hundreds of billions of dollars in currency swap lines with Britain, Sweden, Norway, Canada, Switzerland, Japan, Australia, and the European Central Bank. More importantly, the US Treasury made available in excess of $800 billion to subsidize financial and manufacturing companies. Iceland, with far fewer resources and clout in the world, and with overexposure to the toxic

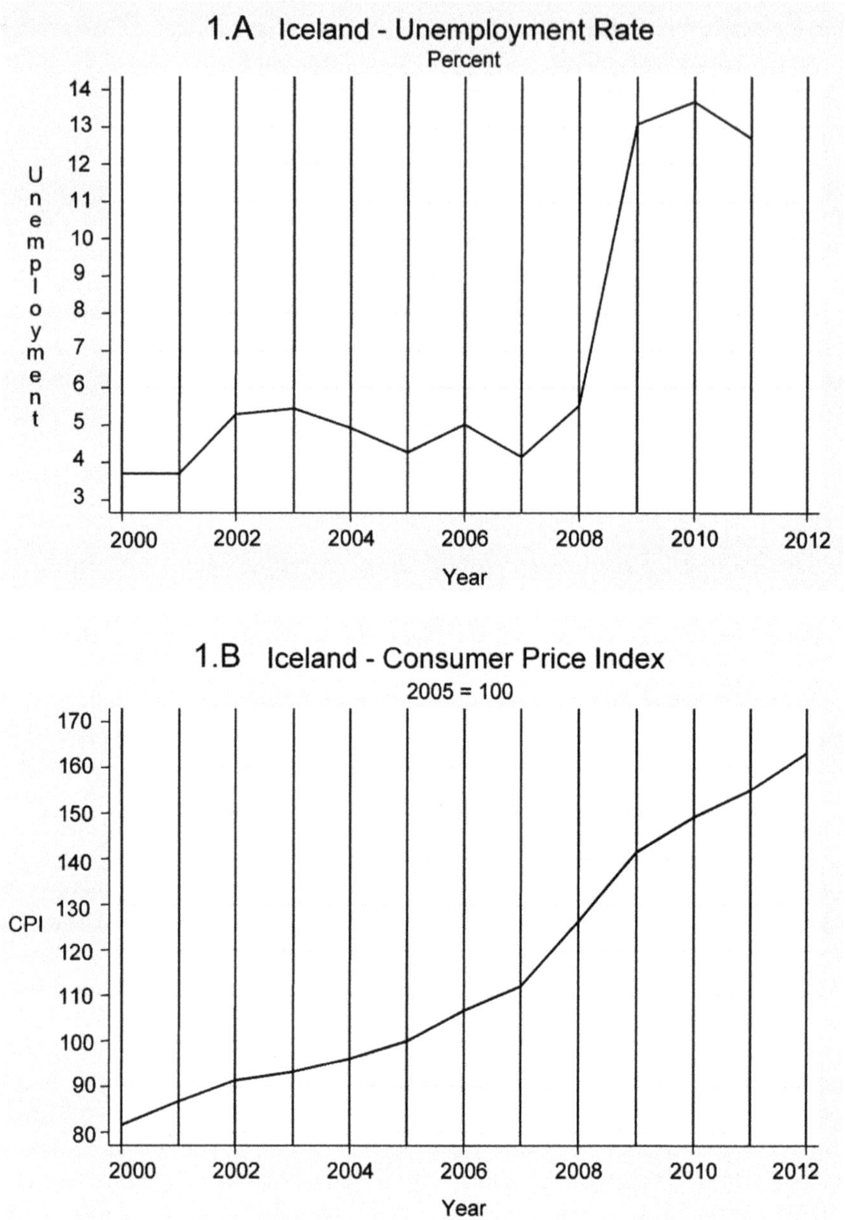

Figure 6.1 Iceland: A = Unemployment rate and B = Consumer price index, 2000–2012

Source: Federal Reserve Bank of St Louis. Created 26 July 2013, https://research.stlouisfed.org/fred2/.

financial products from the US, saw its three major banks collapse in October 2008, and in November it received IMF approval for a $2 billion loan. This should have come as no surprise to the bankers: Joseph Stiglitz was the economist who authored a working paper for the Central Bank of Iceland in 2001 cautioning them about the financial risks of crisis for small economies, specifically Iceland's, in the midst of growing global financial instability (Stiglitz 2001).

Iceland's center-right government fell after the October 2008 crash but it was the workers that paid the price. Pension funds were reduced in value and used to prop up the nationalized (later re-privatized) banking system. Each Icelander effectively was expected to pay $8000 to restore the economy. By 2010, unemployment had shot up to over 10 percent (see Figure 6.1). And during this time, since 2008, trade unions have continued their collaborationist relationship with the bankers and other capitalists responsible for Iceland's economic crisis, paid for by the workers. By 2013, the crisis had resulted in significant hardship for the working and middle classes with the state still deep in debt (see Figure 6.1a and 6.1b).

European Union and the Eurozone

What made the crisis experience of the eurozone countries unique? In the year 2000, European Union countries seemed to be strong economically—but Belgium, Italy, and Greece had debts greater than their GDPs. By 2005, on the cusp of the crisis, Belgium's debt had fallen somewhat, but Portugal, France, Germany, and Austria had each accumulated debt that exceeded 60 percent of their GDPs, the maximum mandated by the 1992 Treaty of Maastricht and subsequent amendments (European Commission 2010). By 2011, Portugal and Ireland were added to Greece and Italy as having debt over 100 percent of GDP, and France, Britain, and Germany had each seen their debt rise above 75 percent of the GDP. Spain's debt level remained below 50 percent in the years leading to the crisis (less than Germany's) but rose to the 60s in 2010–11 and then jumped to 84 percent in 2012. Ireland's debt was likewise less than 50 percent before the crisis but then rose sharply to 117 percent in 2012. The corpus of this debt was the result of financial speculation and manipulations including rampant extension of credit to those who could not repay the inflated prices of the goods (especially housing) when the bubbles burst. High government debt, above the 60 percent of GDP cap as established by the Maastricht Treaty, was a sign of concern but government debt, alone, did not define the most troubled economies, especially prior to the crisis (see Figure 6.2a and 6.2b).

It might seem at first important to identify those countries that suffered most (Portugal, Ireland, Italy, Greece, Spain, and Cyprus) and name the factors that led these countries to their present situations, noting the negative implications for workers and consumers. However, the eurozone is an inclusive system in itself within the EU, with its own central bank playing a key role that must be examined.

A

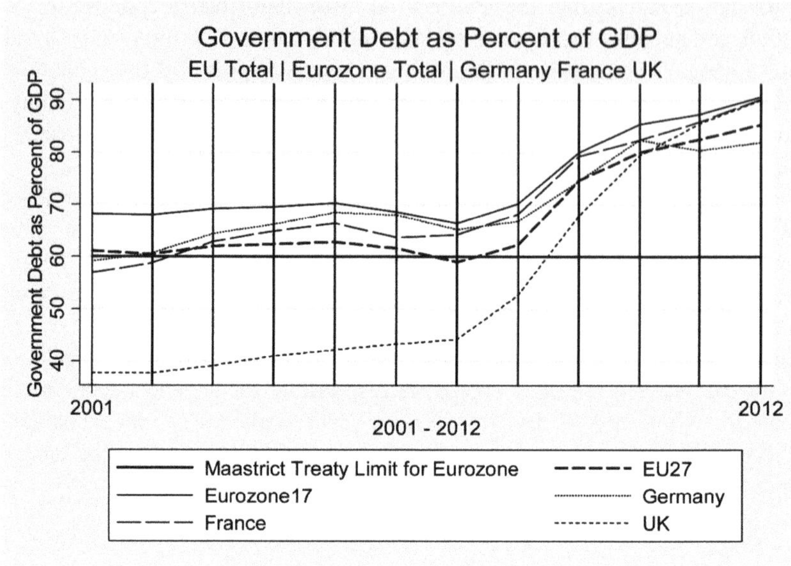

B

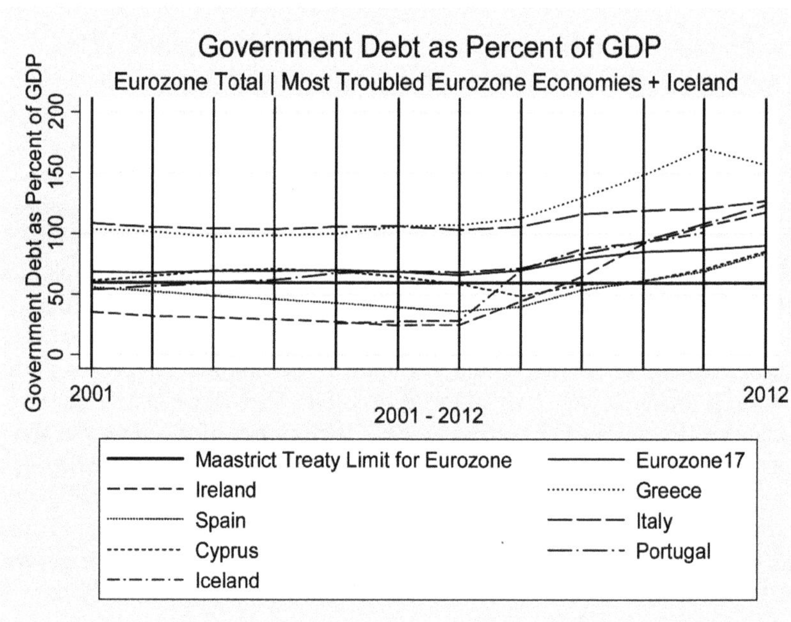

Figure 6.2 Select European and Icelandic government debt as a percent of GDP, 2001–12

Source: Eurostat. Last Update: 26.06.13. Extracted: 24.07.13, http://epp.eurostat.ec.europa.eu/portal/page/portal/eurostat/home/.

A nation's central bank (for example, the Bank of England or the US Federal Reserve Bank [the Fed]) traditionally sets the monetary policy related primarily to inflation and interest rates. The capitalist ideological environment of the late twentieth and early twenty-first centuries advocated using interest rates as a tool for keeping inflation low. All states may exercise fiscal policy (taxes and spending) and that is part of the Keynesian tool box for regulating the overall economy. However, the rightist, neoliberal ideology rooted in Milton Friedman's monetarist perspective was the one that held sway with the ECB. In addition, the ECB wanted the euro to replace the dollar to become a new global currency—irrespective of the implications for individual nations that were members of the eurozone, as a system. The eurozone, as a whole, thus lacked the authority to exercise fiscal policy as this was the responsibility of each state. The result is that important fiscal resources—such as in the United States, the $840 billion in fiscal tools that had been used as of June 2012—were not directly available to the ECB, even if it had wanted them. The European Union, however, did agree to a 200 billion euro stimulus plan in late 2008.

Fiscal policy relating to taxes and state expenditures has rarely been used explicitly to regulate the economy by most countries in the neoliberal period; capitalists have been loath to employ the counter-cyclical pressures advocated by Keynes for those purposes. Taxes and expenditures have generally been employed to reinforce the ideological goals of nations' ruling parties, including making the rich, richer. In the United States, for example, Democratic administrations of Obama and Clinton have tended to spend more than Republicans for social purposes, but even so, the overall shift in ownership of wealth has been toward the rich—the capitalist class. The biggest exception, the Obama administration's use of national debt to bail out corporations in 2008 and later, has been excoriated by the right-wing Tea Party ideological advocates of balanced budgets. In today's neoliberal world, ruling parties have generally only resorted to Keynesian tactics when confronted with imminent collapse, and not always then. In many cases, when the state can no longer increase its debt, increase the money supply, and chooses not to default, it turns to the International Monetary Fund (IMF) that follows a neoliberal path often including severe austerity measures that disproportionately impact the workers. The IMF essentially dictates the fiscal measures a nation must take to receive the bailout funding.

The Central Role of Germany in the Eurozone Crisis

In Europe, Britain and especially Germany have been most strident in opposing fiscal policy for counter-cyclical purposes. Britain and Germany have also been most successful in oppressing their working classes (Lapavitsas, 2012), with Germany extracting sufficient surplus value to minimize economic crisis—other than the cost of ongoing economic stagnation. The German situation was fairly unique as the Federal Republic struggled to incorporate many workers from the

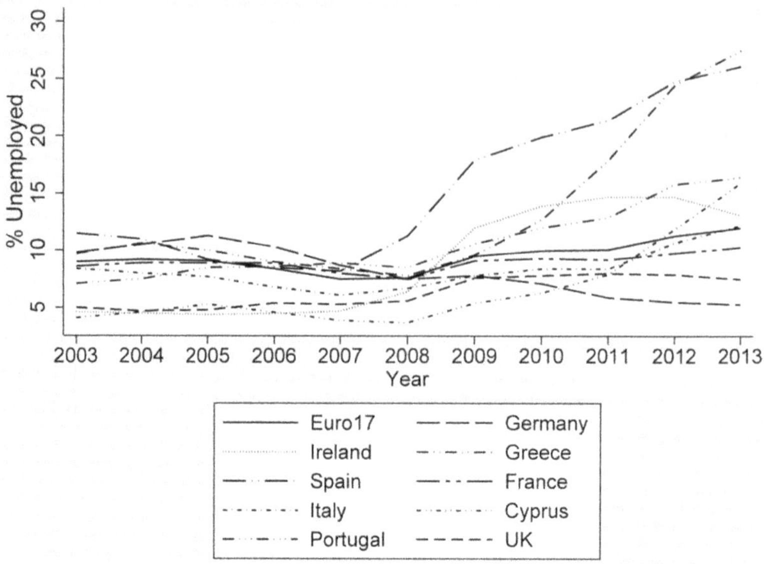

Figure 6.3 European unemployment rate, selected countries, 2003–13
Source: Eurostat. Last update: 30.06.14. Extracted: 30.06.14, http://appsso.eurostat.ec.europa.eu/nui/show.do?dataset=une_rt_a&lang=en.

former East Germany into the labor market. Many of these workers lacked the experience needed for the high-tech capitalist economy of the west and various means were attempted to integrate them into the work force. While bureaucratic solutions with respect to employment search, etc., may have helped in some regard, in the final analysis, it appears that reductions in the benefits for the unemployed and introduction of more low-wage job helped to raise the employment rate (Bonin, 2012) (see Figure 6.3), and certainly the profit rate of corporations now with access to more low-wage labor. How long this will remain effective is questionable but the "success" of this hard line would seem to have emboldened the German state to force other nations to apply austere measures to their workers and consumers to resolve the crises brought by the neoliberal capitalist system.

Moreover, as the largest economy in the eurozone, Germany was able to play a heavy-handed role within the EU, as well with its own workforce. In the early years of transitioning to the euro, 1999–2002, Germany's current accounts balance vis-à-vis Portugal, Italy, Greece, and Spain went steadily down from 2003 until 2008, meaning that Germany exported increasingly more than it imported with respect to these countries. In addition, Germany's overall current accounts balance as a percentage of its GDP went from a slight negative in 1999–2000 up to 6–7 percent in 2007–10. Clearly something was happening here, and Rosenthal

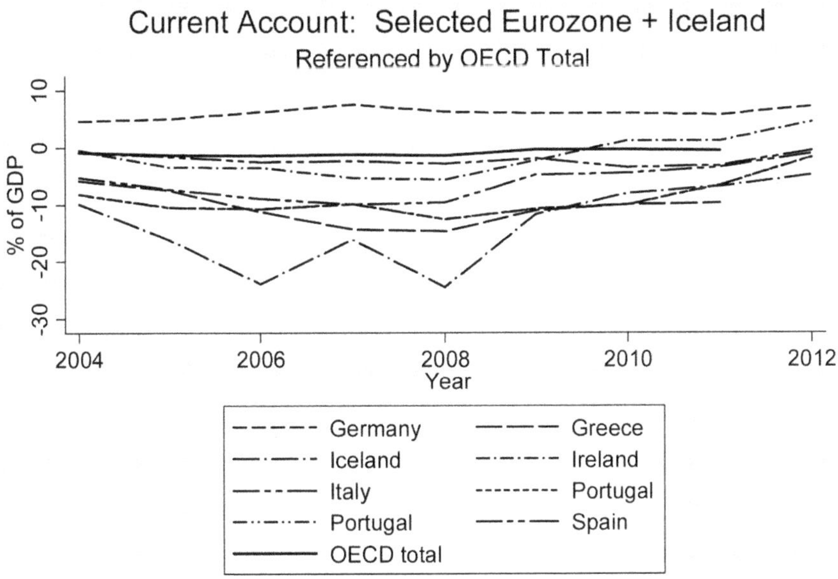

Figure 6.4 Eurozone current account, 2004–12
Source: OECD. Current account balance of payments 2012, http://stats.oecd.org/.

argues that currency speculation and manipulation was in Germany's favor as the individual currencies were finding their value with respect to the euro before the euro actually became a fact (Rosenthal 2012) (see Figure 6.4).

Germany began to experience the effects of the crisis in 2007–08, especially with respect to its tainted US investments. The Christian Democrat dominated government (with Social Democrats) did not move rapidly when the scope of the problem became obvious, and refused to carry out the Keynesian counter-cyclical policies advocated by the Social Democrats. The Christian Democrats did all they could to avoid any apparent nationalization (unlike the US approach that took partial ownership of some companies) and focused primarily on lowering taxes to stimulate the economy. Even though France in 2008 recommended a common eurozone bailout fund, Germany opposed it. France and Germany have the two largest economies in the eurozone. When they are in agreement, their view generally guides eurozone policy. But when they disagree, eurozone policy and eurozone action effectively reverts to the positions of the ECB and the IMF, which are largely monetarist. By 2009, in German internal politics, the governing coalition fell and the election brought back the Christian Democrats with the Social Democrats suffering heavy losses (Zohlnhöfer, 2011b), an election that seemed to provide evidence of public support for Angela Merkel's hardline, rightist approach.

The Eurozone's Troubled Periphery

Elsewhere in Europe, the crisis that already hit Iceland and the US had not manifested itself fully, if at all. The ultimately hardest hit countries--Portugal, Italy, Ireland, Greece, Spain, and finally Cyprus—were occupied with national and intra-European issues. In Portugal, increased fuel prices caused demonstrations by fishermen. Ireland was more preoccupied with remaining political issues related to Northern Ireland vis-à-vis the Republic. Italian electoral politics drifted to the right with Berlusconi once again the Prime Minister, and the right taking on the mayor's office in Rome. Greece was feeling the impact of pervasive fraud in the pension system and, unlike the more compliant Icelanders, Greek workers protested repeatedly against plans to reduce benefits and add years to the retirement dates of some workers, primarily women (who could retire at earlier ages than men). Of greater significance, by the end of 2008, Spain had the highest unemployment rate in the EU and was moving to pay for the repatriation of immigrant workers whose unemployment rate was 17 percent.

The most troubled eurozone members of the European Union, however, faced a more complex situation; since monetary policy was centralized and not necessarily designed for the good of any specific country most member nations had little control over their monetary environment. Moreover, the way the euro was established and each country's currency linked to it favored the largest and strongest economy, Germany. One result was that German exports of machinery, expensive automobiles, etc. could sell at high prices since during this period there was little competition abroad; however, Portugal and Spain were in competition with low-wage areas such as China, and their exports suffered. In fact, in the years leading up to the crisis, even the value of internal eurozone trade increasingly favored Germany over the countries in the Mediterranean region—Greece, Italy, Spain, and Portugal. In addition to the European Central Bank that sets monetary policy for the 17 member nations out of 27 members of the EU, there are other institutions including a parliament and a European Commission of national leaders. Since technically the EU is an international organization built upon a patchwork of treaties, it has no internal police powers to hold states to their treaty agreements and obligations. However, the European Commission does exercise some power over the ECB and exercises influence within the 27 members of the Union. The chair of the European Commission rotates annually among the membership of the Union, not a source of strength.

Sarkozy of France had tried and failed to orchestrate a change in EU rules to appoint a permanent European Commission chairperson (presumably himself), but instead the new member of the EU, the Czech Republic, took on the rotating chair responsibilities. This caused both personal and structural fissures in the EU and decreased its already weak political influence. As a consequence, monetary policy executed through the ECB remained the primary means by which the EU and the eurozone addressed the growing crisis. The political weakness of the EU was further illustrated by European Commission Chairman Topolanek of the Czech

Republic openly and publicly criticizing Obama's bailout of US corporations and banks, much to the consternation of many EU nations. Exercising national fiscal measures (raising taxes and cutting expenditures) was politically risky without significant external pressure and without leadership from the European Commission. The external pressure was primarily the threat of IMF demands if a loan were offered, as European Union treaties alone were not generally effective in implementing the drastic measures seen by many as needed to save the system.

European parliamentary elections were held in early June of 2009 with a low turnout (43 percent), but significant indications of dissatisfaction with contemporary political and economic issues. A small number of ultra-right candidates were elected that generally signaled a shift to the center-right across Europe.

In 2009, the impact of the ECB ideology was felt by the eurozone's second largest economy, France:

> … the head of the European Central Bank, Jean-Claude Trichet, warned European governments against accumulating more debt. 'There is a moment where you cannot spend more and accumulate more debts. We are at that moment,' Mr Trichet said during an interview on French radio Europe 1.
>
> Further stimulus spending would present a serious problem for future generations to deal with he said, adding that the current packages were 'completely extraordinary' and also 'sufficient' to deal with the downturn. (Willis, 2009)

At the time, France's budget deficit (tax receipts minus spending) was expected to exceed 7 percent and her overall debt remained well over the Maastricht Treaty's limit of 60 percent of the GDP. The strong arm of the ECB thus reflected the ideology of externally-designed monetary policy that placed pressure on a nation's own fiscal policy, an act that was followed three years later by President Sarkozy's loss to socialist François Hollande in a bid for re-election. But the French government was not the only eurozone state on the line in 2009.

By the end of 2009, after a year of strikes, demonstrations, and other violent protests, Greece began to face ECB pressure as deputy finance minister Philippos Sachinidis announced that debt had reached 300 billion euros, 113 percent of the GDP (BBC News, 2009). This was just the beginning of a continuing public debacle that pitted rival ideologies against one another (right vs. populist) as well as geopolitics (in eurozone terms: core vs. periphery or north vs. south). Greece was still basking in the glory of the debt-funded, over-budget 2004 XXVIII Olympiad games (Harvey, 2011) and civil servants were provided with enviable benefits. But as the eurozone would soon learn from a 2010 Eurostat report (European Commission, 2010), Greek national accounts suffered from both methodological and governance issues that called into question the quality of reports that Greece had issued (with known inconsistencies) in its attempt to respond to the growing crisis. As Greece slid toward default at the end of 2009, the EU and IMF pledged a three-year, 110 billion euro bail-out package in exchange for Greece's austerity agreement that would raise taxes and cut the income of public sector workers and retirees.

Greece was not alone in facing the looming crisis in 2009; Spain began the year with the bursting of a housing bubble. For decades Spain's warm weather and cheap prices had attracted northern Europeans for vacation and as long-time residents, thus driving up real estate prices during the boom years that ended in 2008. Unemployment rose, and prices that had risen during the boom years dropped precipitously until by April they had become deflationary. As Paul Krugman remarked in his blog at the end of the year, Spain

> needs to become more competitive—but it can't have a devaluation, because it's a euro country. So the only alternative is wage cuts, which are desperately hard to achieve (and create big problems for debtors).
>
> Contrary to what everyone seemed to be saying even a few weeks ago, being a member of the eurozone doesn't immunize countries against crisis. In Spain's case (and Italy's, and Ireland's, and Greece's) the euro may well be making things worse. (Krugman, 2009)

At the end of 2009, Ireland was similarly afflicted: still recovering from the decades of rebellion in Northern Ireland, the housing bubble that had been encouraged by banks prior to 2007 had burst sending housing prices in a freefall (26 percent drop since 2007) and unemployment rose to over 12 percent. By 2010, most European Union members were in technical violation of the Maastricht treaty that expected nations to maintain public debt below 60 percent of the GDP (see Figure 6.2a and 6.2b).

In Greece the crisis was most acute. Not only did Greece have the highest debt as a percentage of its GDP, but the Greeks continued to struggle against the austerity measures prescribed by Germany and the ECB. Greek workers and civil servants protested vigorously and the first bailout of 2009 had not fixed the debt problem. The continued pressure on the Greek government by ECB to enhance fiscal austerity measures met by mass mobilizations against these measures winter and spring (Psimitis, 2011) continued through 2010 as did the EU/IMF loan promises.

As of 2010, Ireland (to be followed by Portugal, Spain, and Italy) had embarked on a similar path toward default as Greece. And two long years after the crisis erupted, the eurozone and the IMF (minimally under the circumstances) propped up their economies:

- to the tune of 85 billion euros for Ireland;
- a permanent eurozone bailout fund of 500 billion euros was created;
- 78 billion euros went to Portugal;

- the ECB purchased Spanish and Italian bonds;
- Italian debt rating was cut;

and the crisis was spreading to Britain, Belgium, and France. Meanwhile, austerity spread across the hard-pressed eurozone members with heightened alarms sounding for the entire eurozone experiment.

During the next year, 2011, Greece continued to flirt with default, and deal with repeated rounds of austerity and protests as eurozone leaders added an additional 109 billion euros of support—in light of the 90 billion euros owed to Germany and France, alone. In October, eurozone leaders offered a 50 percent debt write-off, conditional upon yet another round of austerity measures which Prime Minister Papendreau offered up as a referendum for the public. Next month after intense criticism of the referendum plan, Papendreau resigned. By the end of 2011, Greece had been granted another 8 billion euros in loans, and banks agreed to another 21 percent loss on loans to Greece. But the banks had little say in swallowing the losses on the Greek bonds. Cyprus would emerge a year and a half later with its own crisis rooted, in part, on the severe impact of the Greek bailout upon its own banks that had invested heavily in presumably safe Greek bonds. Ironically, in a report issued in spring 2013, the IMF admitted to the ineffectiveness of some austerity measures it had extracted from Greece (Executive Board of the International Monetary Fund, 2013).

The following year, 2012, started in January with the downgrading of both French debt and the eurozone bailout fund, itself. The next month, Greece executed severe austerity measures that resulted in an additional 130 billion euro bailout, but the measures once again sparked violent protests. Greek electoral politics went into a tailspin with the conservative New Democracy party winning the election in June, but it took until year's end to renegotiate loans and facilitate the next bailout. Meanwhile, the eurozone economy as a whole began to shrink and eurozone unemployment grew to a record of 10.7 percent across the board for January, with 19 million people out of work. Spain was hardest hit with an unemployment rate of 23 percent (see Figure 6.3).

The same year, 2012, saw the most recent eurozone country, Cyprus, approach the ECB for assistance. The losses Cypriot banks realized on the loans to Greece enormous: they amounted to about 22 percent of the nation's GDP in 2011 (Higgens, 2013). And only four to five years after joining the eurozone in 2008, national politics were on the rocks and the Russians (whose money of questionable origins was deposited in the Cyprus banks, and lost) refused to bail the Cypriots out. In March 2013, the latest of the heavy-handed ECB actions brought the Cypriots to their knees as well.

By the end of 2013, the worst crisis episodes were past and Europe settled into a new stasis of German hegemony in the eurozone and what may prove to be high and prolonged levels of unemployment in the European Union, especially the eurozone (see Figure 6.5, Euro area EA17 and EU28 unemployment rates as published by Eurostat in January 2014).

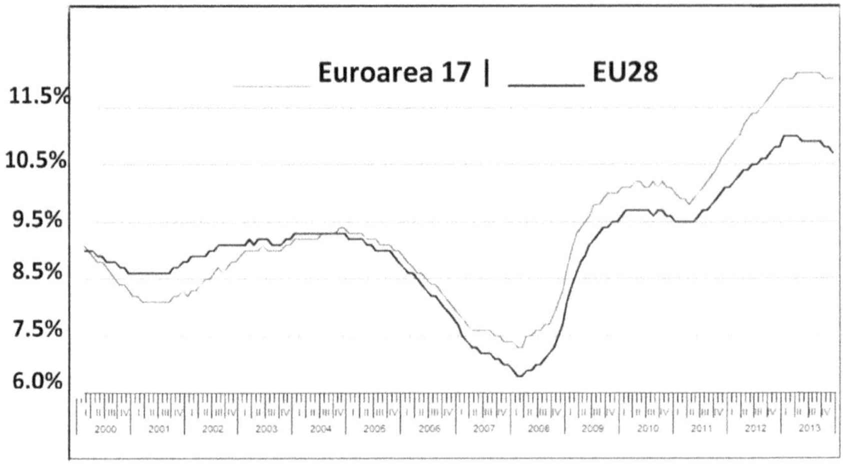

Figure 6.5 Euro area EA17 and EU28 unemployment rates, 2000–2014
Source: Eurostat Newsrelease: Euroindicators, 17/2014–31 January 2014. Eurostat news releases on the internet: http://ec.europa.eu/eurostat.

The Future: Stalemate?

Both the working/middle classes and the ruling capitalist class are plagued with national and other divisions that have, on the one hand, prevented the workers of Europe from effectively uniting to confront capital. On the other hand, the divisions prevented the ruling class from more effectively exploiting the workers, peasants, and middle classes across the world as they continue to compete with one another within the framework of imperialism inherited from the nineteenth century. At the same time, EU leading perspectives were characterized by the use of national units of analysis or points of view rather than, for example, the eurozone as a transnational system. Thus the European Community including the eurozone is trapped in a stalemate: a web of nationalist, neoliberal, monetarist economic policy spun by Germany, the IMF, the ECB, and supported by Britain and other non-euro members of the EU versus the fragmented workers and middle classes.

If the workers and middle classes continue to fail to see their shared interest to unite across national lines, and if the capitalists retain their unholy marriage between centralized euro-monetarism and decentralized political nationalism, this crisis is likely to continue indefinitely. Japan has stagnated for nearly two decades of monetarism and only recently, under Prime Minister Shinzo Abe's pro-fiscal approach, is Japan beginning to see its way out of its late twentieth-century crisis. Will Japan's experiences over the next few years serve for Europe as a roadmap out of the stalemate the eurozone is in? And till then, what will happen to Portugal, Ireland, Italy, Greece, Spain, and Cyprus? According to Eurostat (2014) as this book went to press, their unemployment rates in December 2013 ranged from 12.1 percent in Ireland to 25.8 percent in Spain, with the latest rate for Greece 27.8 percent in October 2013. By contrast, Iceland's unemployment rate had fallen to 5.2 percent and the US rate to 6.7 percent at the end of 2013.

Conclusion

The focus of this chapter was an analysis of the divisions that have stalemated European capitalist development; the European ruling class is unable to effect a full and viable capitalist auto-recovery with the people of Europe unable to unite and take advantage of the contradictions of today's capitalism to finally end its reign once and for all.

The historic eurozone experiment in financialization—European Central Bank monetary policy concentrated within the EU but decentralized tax and spending fiscal policy in nations across the EU—has worked poorly for both the ruling classes and the working classes. It has essentially subjected each nation's fiscal policy to international law through treaty obligations and placed the ECB beyond the bounds of national law and leadership.

The eurozone experience stands in striking contrast to the immediate EU response to the crisis in the Ukraine that began to unfold as this book went to press. While the ECB and IMF forced severely debilitating monetary measures upon Greece (especially) and Portugal, Cyprus, Spain, Italy, and Ireland leading to the fall of many governments, the EU offered $15 billion in aid to the Ukraine, much of it designed to support the rebel government and to soften the harsh terms they expected the IMF to impose. Once again, we saw the hegemonic posture in the euro crisis by the German-French powers that undermined the southern European periphery, but this time it appears as anti-Russian and directly from the European Commission, itself. The balance of fiscal-monetary measures was reversed for the Ukraine to better serve the immediate political and ultimate economic goals of the EU to maintain a power imbalance within the EU with an eye toward Ukraine's eventual joining the EU.

This is the outcome of an ideology of weak, laissez-faire political control over a rigid, centralized financial structure. European civilization is deep-rooted and the accompanying national/ethnic antagonisms and prejudices go back centuries; but, it would be a mistake to read too much into these beliefs. The failure of the eurozone experiment is nothing if it is not the ultimate failure of an economic ideology rooted in the Enlightenment but now moribund, and slipping relentlessly toward the next cataclysm that may eventually lead to the final collapse of global capitalism.

References

Adejumobi, Said. 2013. "Europe: The Failure of Structural Adjustment?" *New African*, 58–60.

Altman, Roger C. 2013. "The Fall and Rise of the West." *Foreign Affairs*, 92: 8–13.

BBC News. 2009. "Greece's Debt Reaches 300 Billion Euros."

BBC News Business. 2012. "Eurozone Unemployment Continues to Rise."

Bergsten, C. Fred. 2012. "Why the Euro Will Survive." *Foreign Affairs*, 91: 16–22.

Birnbaum, Norman. 2010. "The Economic Crisis, US Progressivism, and West European Socialism and Social Democracy." *Social Europe: The Journal of the European Left*, 5: 5–10.

Bofinger, Peter, Jürgen Habermas, and Julian Nida-Rümelin. 2012. "The Case for a Change of Course in European Policy." *Social Europe: The Journal of the European Left*, 7: 5–8.

Bonin, Holger. 2012. "The Two German Labour Market Miracles: Blueprints for Tackling the Unemployment Crisis?" *Comparative Economic Studies*, 54: 787–807.

Broome, Andre. 2010. "The International Monetary Fund, Crisis Management and the Credit Crunch." *Australian Journal of International Affairs*, 64: 37–54.

Callaghan, Helen. 2010. "Beyond Methodological Nationalism: How Multilevel Governance Affects the Clash of Capitalisms," pp. 564–580 in *Journal of European Public Policy*, vol. 17. Routledge: http://www.mpifg.de/people/hc/Publications/documents/2009_JEPP_%20Multilevel%20governance.pdf.

Douthat, Ross. 2013. "Prisoners of the Euro," in *New York Times*. New York: The New York Times Publishing Co.

European Commission. 2010. "Report on Greek Government Deficit and Debt Statistics." Eurostat.

Eurostat. 2014. Newsrelease: Euroindicators. Euro area unemployment rate at 12.0%: EU28 at 10.7%. January.

Executive Board of the International Monetary Fund. 2013. "IMF Executive Board Concludes 2013 Article IV Consultation, Completes Third Review of the Extended Fund Facility (EFF), and Discusses Ex Post Evaluation of 2010 Stand-By Arrangement (SBA) with Greece." International Monetary Fund.

Habermas, Jürgen. 2012. *The Crisis of the European Union : A Response*. Trans by Cronin Ciaran. Cambridge, UK: Polity.

Harvey, David. 2011. "Roepke Lecture in Economic Geography-Crises, Geographic Disruptions and the Uneven Development of Political Responses." *Economic Geography*, 87: 1–22.

Harvey, David. 2012. *The Enigma of Capital and the Crises of Capitalism*. London: Profile Publishers.

Higgens, Andrew and Liz Alderman. 2013. "Europeans Planted Seeds of Crisis in Cyprus," in *The New York Times*. New York: The New York Times Publishing Co.

International Monitary Fund. 2013. *World Economic Outlook* (WEO) database. Washington, DC: International Monitary Fund.

Jones, Alun, Julian Clark, and Angus Cameron. 2010. "The Global Economic Crisis and the Cohesion of Europe." *Eurasian Geography & Economics*, 51: 35–51.

Krugman, Paul. 2009. "Pain in Spain," in *The Conscience of a Liberal*, Vol. 2013. New York: The New York Times Publishing Co.

Kundnani, Hans. 2011. "Germany as a Geo-economic Power." *Washington Quarterly*, 34: 31–45.

Lapavitsas, Costas et al. 2012. *Crisis in the Eurozone*. London/New York: Verso.

Lenin, Vladimir Ilich. 1975. *Imperialism: The Highest Stage of Capitalism*. Peking: Foreign Languages Press.

Loftsdóttir, Kristín. 2010. "The Loss of Innocence: The Icelandic Financial Crisis and Colonial Past." *Anthropology Today*, 26: 9–13.

Macheda, Francesco. 2012. "The Role of Pension Funds in the Financialisation of the Icelandic Economy." *Capital & Class*, 36: 433–473.

Medrano, Juan Díez. 2012. "The Limits of European Integration." *Journal of European Integration*, 34: 191–204.

Momigliano, Anna. 2011. "European Economic Crisis: Why Italy is Seen as Too Big to Bail Out." *Christian Science Monitor*.

Piketty, Thomas and Gabriel Zucman. 2013. "Capital is Back: Wealth-Income Ratios in Rich Countries 1700–2010." *Paris School of Economics*.

Psimitis, Michalis. 2011. "The Protest Cycle of Spring 2010 in Greece." *Social Movement Studies*, 10: 191–197.

Puetter, Uwe. 2012. "Europe's Deliberative Intergovernmentalism: The Role of the Council and European Council in EU Economic Governance." *Journal of European Public Policy*, 19: 161–178.

Rose, Richard. 2011. "Micro-economic Responses to a Macro-economic Crisis: A Pan-European Perspective." *Journal of Communist Studies & Transition Politics*, 27: 364–384.

Rosenthal, John. 2012. "Germany and the Euro Crisis." *World Affairs*, 175: 53–61.

Sanfey, Peter. 2011. "South-Eastern Europe: Lessons Learned from the Global Economic Crisis in 2008–10." *Journal of Southeast European & Black Sea Studies*, 11: 97–115.

Schumpeter, Joseph A. 1939. *Business Cycles; A Theoretical, Historical, and Statistical Analysis of the Capitalist Process*. New York/London: McGraw-Hill Book Company, Inc.

Shore, Cris. 2012. "The Euro Crisis and European Citizenship: The Euro 2001–2012—Celebration or Commemoration?"*Anthropology Today*, 28: 5–9.

Stiglitz, Joseph. 2001. "Monetary and Exchange Rate Policies in Small Open Economies: The Case of Iceland."

Stiglitz, Joseph. 2010. *The Stiglitz Report: Reforming the International Monetary and Financial Systems in the Wake of the Global Crisis*. New York: The New Press.

Stiglitz, Joseph. 2011. *Freefall: America, Free Markets, and the Sinking of the World Economy*. New York: Norton.

Thorhallsson, Baldur. 2010. "The Corporatist Model and its Value in Understanding Small European States in the Neo-Liberal World of the Twenty-First Century: The Case of Iceland." *European Political Science*, 9: 375–386.

Trilling, Daniel. 2012. "A Warning from Athens." *New Statesman*, 141: 22–29.

Willis, Andrew. 2009. "France's Budget Deficit to Top 7 Percent," in euobserver.com/. Belgium: EUobserver.

Wolf, Martin. 2012. "Confronting the Eurozone Crisis." *Brown Journal of World Affairs*, 18: 11–16.

Xinbo, Wu. 2010. "Understanding the Geopolitical Implications of the Global Financial Crisis." *Washington Quarterly*, 33: 155–163.

Zohlnhöfer, Reimut. 2011a. "Between a Rock and a Hard Place: The Grand Coalition's Response to the Economic Crisis." *German Politics*, 20: 227–242.

Zohlnhöfer, Reimut. 2011b. "The 2009 Federal Election and the Economic Crisis." *German Politics*, 20: 12–27.

Chapter 7
Japan's Long Stagnation and the Global Capitalist Crisis: The Onset of Inter-State Rivalry?

Bill Lucarelli

Introduction

Japan has now been mired in economic stagnation, punctuated by recurrent recessions, for the past two decades. What are the causes of this longstanding malaise? Is it merely the natural consequence of financial retrenchment and the onset of a pervasive "liquidity trap" after the collapse of the "bubble" economy in the early 1990s, or does the present slump signify a more profound historical phase of structural decline? The aim of this chapter is to provide several tentative answers. In the first section, some of the possible causes of this phase of prolonged stagnation will be examined. Section 2 evaluates whether the historical evidence lends credence to the debt-deflation theory of depressions. Section 3 examines the possible international repercussions of Japan's recent resort to competitive devaluations in order to engineer an export-led recovery in the wake of the global financial crisis. More specifically, what is the likelihood of the outbreak of currency and trade wars as a result of the Japanese state pursuing aggressive monetary easing in order to induce a sharp devaluation of the yen in the aftermath of the current continuing global capitalist crisis?

The Rise and Fall of Japan's Euphoric Bubble

Japan's current economic malaise has its roots in the chain of events that led to the expansionary monetary policies enacted after the September 1985 Plaza accords. A new economic strategy was inaugurated by the Reagan administration in which a more orthodox monetarist strategy was adopted to resolve the incessant problem of stagflation. The essential aim of the Volcker "shock" was to impose a highly restrictive set of monetary policies in order to dampen the inflationary forces generated by the second oil price shock in 1979. A strong dollar was therefore pursued by the Reagan administration, which was driven by a sharp upsurge in interest rates. The vertiginous rise in the US dollar, however, was neither induced by a substantial improvement in the American trade deficit, nor by a recovery of its industrial export competitiveness. Instead, the massive inflow of capital was governed almost entirely by the inducement of high nominal interest rates. In retrospect, the contradictory US strategy of tight monetary policies accompanied by expansionary fiscal policies, which were partly driven by increased military expenditure, could not be sustained as long as the US continued to accumulate a burgeoning balance of payments deficit.

The strong dollar policy in the first term of the Reagan administration generated two contradictory outcomes. Although the strong dollar and high nominal interest rates contributed to a curtailment of domestic inflation, it also had a negative impact on US export competitiveness, which was reflected in the deterioration of the balance of payments. The US trade deficit had increased from an average of $US27 billion in 1978–80 to $US148 billion in 1985, while the current account deficit had blown out from $US4 billion to about $US128 billion over the same period (Parboni, 1986). By March 1985, the dollar was estimated to have appreciated by more than 30 percent on a trade weighted average since the beginning of 1981. International pressure began to mount for a series of sustained dollar depreciations, especially after the realization that the US economy had become a net debtor for the first time since the turn of the century. This was accompanied by a growing protectionist sentiment in the US Congress. The Reagan administration could either succumb to these protectionist demands or divert them through dollar depreciations. With the onset of a severe international recession in the early 1980s, caused to some extent by the highly restrictive, anti-inflationary policies enacted by most OECD countries, the Reagan administration propounded the "locomotive theory" in which they attempted to persuade the major surplus countries of Japan and Germany to pump prime their economies, arguing that a concerted fiscal stimulus would redress the widening trade imbalances and generate a sustained recovery. Both the German and Japanese authorities, however, were quite reluctant to pursue more expansionary policies because of the inflationary risks involved.

In light of these events, a more interventionist policy emerged in contrast to the prevailing policy of "benign neglect" that had informed US exchange rate policies. With the breakdown of macroeconomic policy co-ordination between the major industrial countries (the G-5), the central bankers of these countries launched a series of concerted interventions in order to avert a crash landing of the US dollar. An estimated $US12 billion was mobilized in March 1985 to engineer a soft landing. Within a year, the dollar had depreciated by 35 percent on a trade-weighted average; the dollar/mark rate had fallen from 3.47 to 2.25 and its yen value from 260 to 175. After the Plaza Accords of September 1985, another concerted central bank intervention was orchestrated to counter the cascading, speculative frenzy in global currency markets. The failure of Germany and Japan to stimulate their economies as the US had requested during the Plaza Summit only provoked US officials to "talk down" the dollar in what soon developed into a dangerous game of monetary brinkmanship (Funabashi, 1986). Although this American strategy eventually persuaded the Japanese to pursue a more expansionary policy after the stock market crash of October 1987, the German authorities remained intransigent.

As the dollar rapidly fell from 1985 onwards, a vicious circle developed with the emergence of inter-state rivalries over markets and investment outlets (Parboni, 1986). It was in this volatile environment that international summits were convened to engineer a "soft landing" of the US dollar and to co-ordinate macroeconomic policies. Given the high reliance of Japanese exports destined to the US market, the Japanese monetary authorities succumbed to US pressure and the Bank of Japan (BoJ) accommodated a dollar depreciation through quite substantial open market operations. But the sharp appreciation of the Japanese yen failed to restore the balance of payments equilibrium with the US. The period of *endaka*, or the skyrocketing increase in the value of the yen, soon began to undermine the profitability of Japan's exports. Japanese investors incurred huge foreign exchange losses as a result of the depreciation of the US dollar from 240 yen in 1985 to 80 yen in 1995. By shifting a substantial proportion of their labor-intensive manufacturing offshore to the cheap labor zones of South East Asia, Japanese transnational corporations were, to some extent, able to temporarily restore their export competitiveness. In order to mitigate the effects of an appreciating yen, the Japanese government embarked upon a program of monetary accommodation by reducing interest rates. Yet by pursuing relatively loose monetary policies, the government set in motion an unprecedented expansion of excess liquidity in the financial markets, most of which was channeled into what became known as *zaitech* operations, or speculative financial engineering (Yoshikawa, 2001). As a result, a financial mania was triggered in the real estate and equity markets.[1] The boom became self-fulfilling. As asset prices rose sharply, further borrowing only served to fuel the asset price spiral in a self-reinforcing dynamic. As Johnson quite succinctly argues:

> The result of the US pursuing an exchange-rate approach to the problem of trade with Japan was profound. They made no difference to the trade imbalance, but they stimulated Japan to undertake countermeasures to the high yen, which led to Japan's bubble economy, then to the collapse of the bubble economy, then to Japan's export of its bubble economy to South East Asia, and finally to the economic meltdown that confronts us today. (Johnson, 1998: 656)

These events set in train the biggest build-up of excess liquidity in modern Japanese history. In 1989–90, the BoJ increased interest rates from 3.8 percent to 8.2 percent, which triggered the bursting of the financial bubble. Stock market prices

1 During the 1980s, the price of real estate rose by a factor of 5. At their respective peaks, the total estimated value of Japanese land was 60 percent of world property values, while Japanese equities accounted for almost 40 percent of world stock market values (Linge, 1997: 62).

tumbled by more than 60 percent from their peaks (Halevi and Lucarelli, 2002). The Japanese economy was effectively caught in a liquidity trap from which it has yet to recover. At the very core of this problem was the lack of effective demand. The structural propensity to build-up productive capacity while experiencing a concomitant and relative diminution of effective demand has led a generalized crisis of over-accumulation. Indeed, the only components of effective demand keeping the Japanese economy afloat are government spending and net exports. In the absence of a recovery of domestic consumption, both of these components will ultimately reach their economic and political limits.

The large *keiretsu* who had invested in extra capacity to meet the demand by the 1980s boom soon found that they were burdened with massive excess capacity and escalating debt/equity ratios (Itoh, 2000). Problems of excess capacity emerged since investment in fixed capital was dependent upon long-term rates of return, which could not be validated in the short run as borrowing costs rose quite precipitously. Under these circumstances, it was very difficult to reactivate the process of capital accumulation, even at very low rates of interest since the accumulated investment or the "sunk costs" in fixed capital tended to depreciate very slowly over a long period of time (Lucarelli, 2011: 42). Excess capacity and depressed profitability therefore set in train the dynamics of stagnation. By the late 1980s, most of the large *keiretsu* began to generate internal funds for investment and curtailed their traditional reliance on BoJ and the big banks. In the early 1970s the large oligopolies relied on about 40 percent of their loans from the big banks. By the late 1980s, after the "big bang" reforms which led to the deregulation and liberalization of capital markets, this dependence had fallen to only 6 percent (Yoshikawa, 2001: 57). Deprived of their traditional sources of investment, the banks began to engage in reckless speculation in real estate and the stock market. Japan's financial institutions injected about $US220 billion in new loans to the property sector alone between 1985 and 1990 (Whittaker and Kurosawa, 1998).[2] A protracted phase of deleveraging was now set in motion as the corporate sector sought desperately to restore their respective balance sheets. By the mid-1990s most of the banking system was technically insolvent. "Zombie banks" were put on life-support through enormous state bail-outs.

It can be argued, with considerable justification, that Japan had generated a speculative mania in the East Asian region after the collapse of its own asset price bubble in 1991–92. This claim can be supported by the fact that Japan's commercial loans to the region had increased from only $US40 billion in 1984 to over $US265 billion in 1996 (Yoshikawa, 2001: 9). The sharp fall in the volume of exports from East Asia just before the East Asian financial crisis had triggered a

2 To quote from Hoshi and Kashyap (2004: 6), "According to the land price indices compiled by the Japan Real Estate Institute, land prices for all uses roughly doubled from 1980 to their peak in 1991, but by 2003 land prices had fallen back almost to their 1980s level. As of 2003, land prices were still falling and on average were about 45 percent below their peak value."

series of balance of payments deficits, which were financed by short-term capital inflows, predominantly from Japan. At the same time, the collapse of Japan's speculative bubble led to a curtailment of their foreign direct investment (FDI) in the region from 1995 onwards. This process of retrenchment was also amplified by the sharp depreciation of the yen at about the same time. Between June 1995 and June 1997, Japanese claims in the Asian NICs fell from $US301 billion to $US180 billion (Hughes, 2000: 229). Hence, the crisis of over-accumulation in Japan was regionalized before the onset of the East Asian financial meltdown of 1997–98 (Lucarelli, 2002). As soon as the East Asian countries encountered balance of payments deficits, spurred by problems of overcapacity, Japanese FDI was sharply curtailed and then acted as one of the catalysts for the ensuing currency crises in 1997–98.

By the early 1990s, the Japanese economy was engulfed in a debilitating crisis of over-accumulation. The rate of capacity utilization in Japanese manufacturing in 1993 had declined by 17 percent from its peak of 1990, and it fell again after a tepid recovery in 1994. As Itoh notes:

> Continuing excess capacity certainly depresses investment in plant and equipment (27) … With huge excess productive capacity, Japanese firms sharpened their competitive pressure in the market. Thus a vicious circle leading to a spiral of depression set in the Japanese economy, comprising falling prices of shares and land, falls in workers' income, and depressant prices in the markets for products and services. (Itoh, 2000: 91)

To be sure, increases in productivity had outstripped wages growth by a large margin. The lack of effective demand in the domestic market only further encouraged outflows of capital, mostly destined to the East Asian region. By the early 1990s, East Asia had been transformed into a formidable export zone. Whereas in 1985, East Asia (excluding China) had only accounted for 12 percent of world exports, by 1993 this figure was 19 percent and reached as high as 23 percent before the outbreak of the financial crisis in 1997 (Hatch and Yamamura, 1996: 189). The high yen made Japanese wages simultaneously too high and too low. In terms of costs, wages were too high to compete against East Asian exports and sustain previous levels of manufacturing employment. From the standpoint of effective demand, however, wages were too low to absorb the excess capacity. Consequently, Japanese corporations accelerated their export strategies in order to resolve their problem of domestic surplus capacity and counteract a falling profitability. The high yen after 1985 therefore had a perverse effect in that capital could appropriate higher profits through a strategy of exporting capital to East Asia in order to export goods from these production zones to Europe and the United States. The domestic market could not act as the engine of growth as long as wage repression was remorselessly imposed by capital in order to increase the rate of profitability. FDI provided low cost production sites in East Asia that enabled Japanese corporations to export to the high wage markets in Europe and the United

States (Steven, 1991: 59). In essence, Japan sought "to maintain its export-led growth by 'regionalizing' it" (Gilpin, 2000: 270).

Japan's Phase of Debt-deflation

By the mid-1990s, Japan had acquired the dubious distinction of sliding into a prolonged phase of debt-deflation; a chronic condition that has not been witnessed since the Great Depression of the 1930s (Fisher, 1933; Minsky, 1980). The crisis of over-accumulation was also characterized by a pervasive "liquidity trap" (Krugman, 1999). In its original exposition by Keynes in the *General Theory*, a liquidity trap was designated as the "paradox of thrift."[3] According to Wray:

> This is the idea of the paradox of thrift: investment determines saving so that given low investment by firms when households are excessively thrifty, income falls until the aggregate of saving decisions (as determined by the marginal propensity to save) is consistent with the aggregate of investment decisions. Alternatively, aggregate saving cannot be increased by trying to have more, but only by investing more—which raises income and thus saving. (Wray, 1998: 82)

In other words, under the conditions of radical uncertainty, money reverts to its intrinsic role as a store of value. Confronted by an avalanche of non-performing loans, an increase in the liquidity preferences of banks themselves ultimately led to a sudden curtailment of lending. Japanese corporations also engaged in a process of prolonged deleveraging. Despite near zero short-term interest rates, Japanese corporations not only curtailed their demand for credit but accelerated their repayment of existing loans in order to restore their respective balance sheets. By 2002–03, net debt repayment in the corporate sector increased to over ¥30 trillion per year on average (Koo, 2008: 18). In the context of saturated markets and an intensification of competition, the restoration of profitability was engineered not only through the repression of wages but also by a long, protracted strategy of deleveraging. Consequently, the level of aggregate demand was depressed by both a fall in the rate of investment and by the propensity of households to increase their rate of saving at the expense of private consumption.[4]

This vicious circle witnessed the destruction of asset values as a result of falling prices, estimated at over 3 years of national output (Koo, 2008: 27). Indeed, the cost

---

3 An excellent account of Japan's liquidity trap is elaborated by Boltho and Corbett (2000: 5), "The Japan of the last decade could be a living example of Keynes's "paradox of thrift"—a country in which desired (or ex ante) savings exceed planned (or ex ante) investment by the private sector."

4 According to Boltho and Corbett (2000: 6), "The existence of a gap between actual and potential output, at some 3.5 percent of GDP, is the single, strongest signal that aggregate demand is falling well short of productive potential."

to Japanese taxpayers' bail-out of the major financial and insurance corporations was estimated at around 4 percent of GDP (¥20 trillion). At the same time, the cumulative loan losses incurred between 1990 and 2004 have been estimated at ¥91.5 trillion (18 percent of Japan's 2004 GDP) (Hoshi and Kashyap, 2004: 12). The only redeeming feature of Japan's banking crisis is that it has not (as yet?) experienced a classic run by depositors (Krugman et al., 1998: 175). Depositors and holders of Japanese government bonds (JGBs) continue to finance Japan's burgeoning public debt despite near zero interest rates. The interest rate of the 5-year JGB (Japan's benchmark rate) has experienced a long-term decline from 4 percent in 1994 to a mere 0.2 percent in 2012.

Despite successive rounds of fiscal stimulus, the Japanese economy remains mired in stagnation. It would be plausible to contend that in the absence of a sustained recovery in investment and output, expansionary fiscal and monetary policies have prevented a full-scale descent into a deflationary spiral. As Koo quite correctly claims: "Government spending played a critical role in supporting the economy, and only through these annual stimulus packages was the government able to prevent deflationary gap from emerging" (Koo, 2008: 25). In other words, Japan continues to enjoy the luxury of financing its public debt from private savings, while the vast majority (94 percent) of this debt is denominated in its own currency.[5] With the official interest rate at close to zero, the financing of this public debt does not pose any real risks to the solvency of the government's sovereign debt (Taggart-Murphy, 2009: 3). There are essentially two reasons for Japan's escalating public debt to GDP ratio. First, the primary deficit or the difference between government spending and tax revenues has risen quite sharply because of the collapse in tax revenues as a result of the slump in nominal GDP. Government spending has also increased to finance increased social security with rising unemployment and an aging population. In other words, the automatic stabilizers have been activated and have prevented the economy from lurching into a depressive spiral. Second, the interest rate gap, or the difference between government interest costs (the yield on government debt) and the rate of nominal GDP, has been positive. As a result, the very low rates of nominal GDP have tended to increase the debt-to-GDP ratio despite very low rates of interest.

Japan's secular stagnation has therefore imparted a burgeoning public debt burden, growing from 15 percent of GDP in 1990 to nearly 140 percent in 2012. If the total debt that has been incurred by Japan's government agencies, including the Post Office, is included, the public debt ratio was estimated at 220 percent of GDP in 2012. Indeed, much of this sharp increase in Japan's public debt occurred after 1997 and in the wake of the global financial crisis of 2007–08. It can be surmised that Japan's rather incoherent fiscal stimulus programs have not been sufficient to revive economic growth but have played a crucial role in stabilizing

5 More than 50 percent of Japan's ¥1,400 trillion of financial assets in 2008 were held in cash and deposits and a large proportion was invested in JGBs via the banking system (*Economist*, 2010).

the economy and averting a descent into a full-scale depression.[6] The successive rounds of fiscal stimulus were never applied consistently enough to counter the onset of a deflationary gap. The multiplier effects of each round of fiscal stimulus have thus diminished over time as the public debt burden has inexorably risen in the absence of a sustained recovery in economic growth.

This argument in favor of a more concerted expansionary fiscal policy can be supported by the quite disastrous policies of fiscal retrenchment implemented by the Hashimoto government in 1997–98. In retrospect, the Hashimoto reforms represented a serious reversal in Japan's Keynesian policies of fiscal and monetary stimulus; the deleterious consequences of which reverberated over the next decade. The Hashimoto administration had embarked on a program of fiscal consolidation and attempted to reduce Japan's fiscal deficit by ¥15 trillion. At the same time, the consumption tax was increased from 3 percent to 5 percent, which had quite a severe contractionary impact on the level of aggregate demand and led to a year-long economic slump. The ensuing credit crunch and collapse in tax revenue caused the fiscal deficit to increase sharply by ¥16 trillion by 1999. The traumatic experience of Hashimoto's brief embrace of austerity was eventually abandoned by the Koizumi administration in 2002–03. Fiscal policy resumed acting as an automatic stabilizer and a mild recovery was temporarily engineered.

At the very epicenter of Japan's descent into stagnation has been the longstanding fall in nominal wages. Wages growth has consistently lagged behind productivity growth. To be sure, unit labor costs (ULC) (or compensation per head divided by GDP per capita) have been falling since the mid-1990s as Figure 7.1 demonstrates. The effects of deflation and rising unemployment have generated considerable uncertainty and discouraged private consumption from acting as an engine of growth. Both households and corporations have engaged in a self-reinforcing process of deleveraging, which continues to have a depressive impact on Japan's potential rate of growth. Indeed, it is precisely this cumulative output gap, estimated as high as 5 percent of GDP per annum that prevents a sustained recovery and compels successive governments to run budget deficits in order to compensate for the lack of effective demand (Krugman, 2000). The other mechanism by which effective demand can be augmented is the promotion of balance of payments surpluses.

Japan continues to suffer from a structural excess of saving in the private sector. This endemic problem is reflected in what Koo describes as a "balance sheet recession" in which solvent but highly leveraged corporations are reluctant to invest in new productive capacity but are obliged, if not forced, to deleverage in order to restore profitability. [7] As household saving began to decline as a result of an aging population, the high rate of domestic saving was increasingly driven

6 In 2003, for example, it was estimated that Japan required a budget deficit of 7 percent of GDP merely to achieve a steady state GDP growth rate of zero (Koo, 2008: 145).

7 It has been estimated that the sum total of depreciation and retained earnings of Japan's corporate sector was equivalent to 29.5 percent of GDP in 2011 (Wolf, 2013).

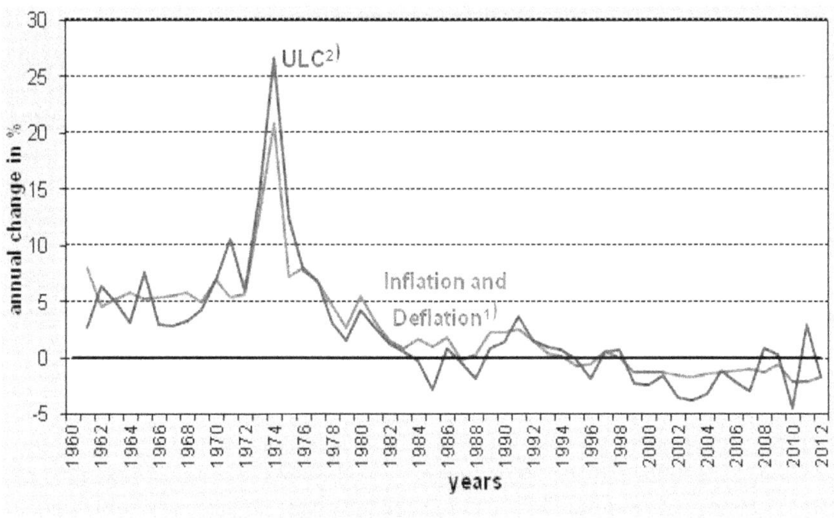

Figure 7.1 Japan: ULC and inflation, evidence for 50 years, 1960–2012

Note: [1] GDP deflator; [2] Compensation of employee per head divided by real GDP per head. Source: AMECO Database (November 2012); my calculations.

Source: Flassbeck Economics blog: 11/2/2013: http://www.flassbeck.de/wordpress/tag/heiner-flassbeck/.

by the accumulation of retained earnings from the corporate sector (Tyers, 2012: 522–523). As has already been alluded, after the collapse of the bubble economy, investment opportunities for the private sector evaporated. In the absence of potential new investment outlets, the process of deleveraging in the corporate sector has been accompanied by their willingness to invest in government bonds, even at very low interest rates.

In order to break out of the decade-long liquidity trap, the BoJ engaged in a sustained program of quantitative easing (QE) between March 2001 and March 2006 in which it injected ¥25 trillion of reserves or equivalent to 5 times the required reserves of the banking system.[8] The money supply increased by about the same amount to cover government borrowings over the same period. According to Koo: "The increased availability of reserves was totally irrelevant to growth in money supply because the banking system was awash in excess reserves long before quantitative easing began" (Koo, 2011: 73–74). This first attempt at QE proved to be quite ineffectual. In the wake of the global financial crisis (GFC) in 2007–08, the Liberal Democratic Party (LDP), which had ruled for most of the past 55 years, was defeated by the Democratic Party of Japan (DP). However, the

8 QE is a euphemism for fiat money creation in order to lower the cost of borrowing in the credit markets. As soon as the official interest rate is at zero percent, QE is the only other monetary instrument available to central banks to stimulate private investment.

failure of the DP to orchestrate a recovery witnessed the election of a new LDP government, led by Abe in December 2012. The impact of the GFC on Japan's economy was quite devastating. By February 2009, the volume of exports had fallen by almost 50 percent from their peak a year earlier. Indeed, by the first quarter of 2009, Japan's GDP had collapsed by 8.4 percent on an annualized basis. Aggregate profits also fell by two thirds over the same period, while manufacturing profits had disappeared altogether, recording a net loss for the first time on record (Turner, 2009: 125–127).

In response to the most severe recession since the Great Depression, the BoJ announced a program of "quantitative and qualitative easing." The aim has been to double the monetary base and more than double the average maturity of Japanese government bonds (JGBs) that it purchases. Under the Abe administration, an inflation target of 2 percent has been set by 2014 (Tabuchi, 2013: 4). At the same time, the government launched another fiscal stimulus package of ¥10 trillion (or about $US100bn) in the 2013 budget. Whether this ambitious monetary and fiscal strategy will eventually overcome the powerful deflationary headwinds—which have been entrenched for almost two decades—remains to be seen. The two possible channels through which this strategy might reverse Japan's secular stagnation are: 1) a sustained yen depreciation, which improves Japan's export competitiveness and increases their ability to export excess savings through a rise in the current account surplus; and 2) by inducing negative real interest rates, which could stimulate investment (Wolf, 2013). An inflationary upsurge would also have the effect of monetizing the public debt.

The Onset of Trade and Currency Wars?

In the continuing current global economic crisis the export-led strategies pursued by Japan will encounter their limits. Sooner or later, Japan could be forced to curtail their massive central bank interventions to mitigate the effects of exchange rate appreciation and their support for the US dollar will begin to wane. An effective exchange rate depreciation in the US appears to be consistent with the view that growing and cumulative US current account deficits will become more difficult to finance as investors diversify their holdings of US dollar assets into other key currencies in order to hedge their exposure to exchange rate risk. In other words, if yields and spreads are no longer attractive relative to other key currencies, US dollar denominated assets could be liquidated (Dooley, et al., 2003: 5). In this context, the US continues to act as the issuer of the most important international reserve asset, while its financial markets intermediate the allocation of global savings from the surplus countries/regions to the deficit countries/regions. The excess saving of Japan and the other major surplus countries (i.e., the OPEC member states, Germany and the BRIC countries) therefore acts as a channel through which monetary stimulus and credit growth becomes increasingly global. In the wake of international financial deregulation, the "contagion effect" of financial instability has been transmitted through the greater ease by which highly liquid, short term funds are able to cross national borders and engage in speculative trading. These destabilizing flows of capital are also amplified by increased exchange rate exposure and international interest rate arbitrage and speculation, which are capable of setting in train self-fulfilling speculative manias and cross-border contagion (Wolfson, 2002: 397).

Even though the US is a net creditor in relation to foreign direct investment and the ownership of equities abroad, this is more than offset by its net liability position in the more interest-sensitive debt markets. The bias towards the holding of debt and interest bearing assets by foreigners, most notably China and Japan, reinforces the seigniorage privileges enjoyed by US financial markets and the pre-eminent role performed by the US dollar as both a store of international value and means of payments. A fall in the effective US exchange rate therefore tends to have a beneficial effect on US net investment income by increasing the dollar value of its overseas earnings. At the same time, the value of its stock of net foreign debt will diminish via the "valuation effect" of a dollar depreciation. In short, unlike the rest of the capitalist world, the US is capable of borrowing abroad in its own currency. The risk of a sustained dollar depreciation is incurred almost entirely by the foreign holders of US dollar denominated assets, most notably by the central banks of Japan and China. In other words, by accumulating substantial balance of payments surpluses, Japan has financed successive US current account deficits either directly by purchasing US bonds and securities, or indirectly by denominating its trade and overseas claims in the US dollar rather than the yen. As long as Japan continues to have access to the US domestic market for its exports, the BoJ has been willing to recycle their burgeoning foreign exchange reserves by purchasing US bonds and securities.

Consequently, the US has so far been able to finance these trade deficits without experiencing a major sell-off of US bonds and securities. Since almost all US foreign liabilities are denominated in its own currency and about 70 percent of US foreign assets are in foreign currencies, a sustained dollar depreciation represents a net transfer of wealth from the rest of the world. The extent to which the US can continue to enjoy these "exorbitant" privileges of dollar seigniorage will ultimately depend upon the willingness of its global capitalist rivals to continue to finance the US current account deficits and the burgeoning foreign debt in the event of a major collapse of the US dollar (Eichengreen, 2011). The received wisdom is that foreign holders of US dollar assets cannot continue to finance US external deficits indefinitely. Sooner or later, the United States will be compelled to make a painful structural adjustment by curtailing its domestic consumption spending on imports (Davidson, 2006: 479).

This adjustment will inevitably impart a depressive impulse on those countries in East Asia, most notably Japan and China, which have relied too much on an export-led strategy of growth and to which the American domestic market continues to act as a market of last resort. The impact of a prolonged US recession could lead to a dampening of the level of effective demand and falling profitability in those sectors in Japan most exposed to exports as an engine of growth. In the event of a sudden and quite severe dollar depreciation, the foreign holders of US dollar-denominated assets, most notably the BoJ, will incur enormous losses. The appreciation of the yen against the US dollar could induce a deflationary adjustment domestically as was witnessed in the aftermath of the 1985 Plaza accords and set in motion yet another deep recession (a depressive spiral of falling profitability and income).

The real danger of Japan's implementation of QE (quantitative easing) is the possibility of igniting trade and currency wars with their rivals. This very real likelihood, especially in the context of sluggish global demand, is even greater because the US Federal Reserve is also pursuing a similar strategy in order to encourage a recovery of investment in the wake of the global financial crisis.[9] By running a current account surplus, the BoJ has intervened in the foreign exchange markets by creating domestic currency in order to buy other currencies, especially US dollars. The build-up of foreign exchange reserves, mostly denominated in US dollars, allows the BoJ to intervene at a greater scale and by so doing, prevents the yen from appreciating. Indeed, in the last six months of 2012, the yen had devalued by 20 percent on a trade weighted basis. The Nikkei stock market index surged by a staggering 55 percent since the election of the Abe administration until May 2013 (*Economist*, 2013). Some analysts have warned of the risks of yet another equity bubble engineered by the BoJ (Duncan, 2013).

At the same time, the combined QE policies of Japan and the US have played a major role in the upsurge in the prices of commodities, equities and bonds. In the long run, the quite dramatic upsurge in commodity prices, most notably in food and energy, could generate a phase of cost-push inflation, which could eventually spill-over into bond markets as fears of a resurgence of inflation put upward pressure on interest rates (McKinnon, 2011). Moreover, higher interest rates could also provoke a stock market sell-off (Duncan, 2013: 168). The quite extraordinary creation of fiat money by the US Fed, the BoJ, the Bank of England and more recently, by the European Central Bank has created a "carry trade" in which a torrent of "hot money" has flooded into the higher growth, higher yielding

9 The recent resort to "quantitative easing" by the US Federal Reserve represents a more perilous continuation of these US predatory, "beggar-thy-neighbor" type policies. Since the onset of the global credit crunch in 2008–09, the US Federal Reserve has injected enormous amounts of liquidity into the banking system. In the context of near-zero official short-term interest rates and the looming threat of pervasive liquidity trap, the US Fed has injected over $US2 trillion during 2009–10 and has injected another US$1 trillion in 2011–12. It is assumed that these expansionary monetary policies will revive bank lending, restore the housing market, and stimulate consumer spending. However, instead of lending domestically, the US banks and hedge funds have engaged in speculative operations in foreign exchange and commodity markets. The flood of cheap dollars has destabilized international currency markets as US dollars are recycled back into low-yielding US Treasury securities by central bankers. Beyond a certain threshold, these enormous injections of liquidity could ultimately undermine confidence in the US dollar as an international reserve asset.

bond markets of the emerging markets and commodity exporters, setting off a commodity boom. The imminent collapse of this most recent commodity bubble could act as a powerful brake in the rather tentative recovery recently experienced in Japan and the US. In short, there is a very real possibility of the outbreak of currency wars as each country or region attempts to stimulate an export-led recovery through competitive devaluations.

Concluding Remarks

Japan's prolonged descent into a seemingly irreversible phase of debt-deflation over the past two decades is quite portentous. It could be the harbinger of a more profound global crisis that has already engulfed the peripheral states of Europe and appears to be threatening a sustained recovery in the US and the UK as interest rates are approaching close to zero. Despite the implementation of expansionary fiscal and monetary policies, albeit in a rather inconsistent manner, the Japanese economy has so far been unable to overcome these powerful and entrenched deflationary undercurrents. Moreover, the excessive level of corporate savings and the protracted process of deleveraging prevent a substantial increase in investment despite interest rates at near zero. It might be more accurate to declare that the banking crisis is symptomatic of a much deeper structural distortion. Severe excess capacity has been built up over the past decades regardless of profitability. Domestic private consumption has been neglected over the decades because of a deliberate strategy to accumulate capital by investing in the capital goods sector. While this strategy of rapid industrialization and export-led growth has been successful in terms of a "late-starter" in its efforts to catch-up with their western competitors, the downside has been a neglect of the development of the wage-goods sector. Quite simply, the long term increase in the profit share of national income has caused chronic problems of excess productive capacity in the absence of a concomitant increase in real wages. As long as real wages lagged behind productivity growth, the problem of a severe lack of effective demand persisted and has become more endemic.

In this context, the problem is one of "surplus absorption." In the absence of domestic outlets for profitable investment, Japan becomes more reliant on an export-led strategy of growth and the export of capital. The temptation of the Japanese authorities to embark upon an aggressive export-led strategy of growth through a sustained yen depreciation, carries with it quite serious risks. Despite the domestic problems of deflation and a liquidity trap, Japan continues to accumulate a current account surplus, most notably in relation to the United States. A large proportion of this trade surplus has been accomplished by falling imports as a result of the stagnation of domestic demand. The problem of excess capacity will compel Japanese corporations to expand their exports in order to counteract a falling profitability on the domestic market. The burgeoning trade deficit in the US, however, could provoke retaliatory trade and currency wars that may well emerge in the aftermath of the global capitalist crisis. The conditions are therefore quite favorable for the outbreak of a classical Keynesian trade war as each country pursues "a desperate expedient to maintain employment at home by forcing sales on foreign markets and restricting purchases, which, if successful, will merely shift the problem of unemployment to the neighbour" (Keynes, 1936: 382–383). In the final analysis, Japan's plan-rational and state-led developmental model appears to have reached its historical limits, especially in this most recent context of emerging rivalries in the global economy in crisis.

References

Boltho, A. and J. Corbett. 2000. "The Assessment: Japan's Stagnation—Can Policy Revive the Economy?" *Oxford Review of Economic Policy*, Vol. 16, No. 2, pp. 1–17.

Davidson, P. 2006. "The Declining Dollar, Global Economic Growth and Macro Stability." *Journal of Post Keynesian Economics*, Vol. 28, No. 3, Spring, pp. 473–488.

Dooley, M.P., D.F. Landau and P. Garber. 2003. "An Essay on the Revived Bretton Woods System." National Bureau of Economic Research (NBER), *Working Paper*, No. 9971, September, Cambridge, MA.

Duncan, R. 2012. *The New Depression.* John Wiley & Sons: Singapore.

Economist. 2010. "Crisis in Slow Motion" (April 8).

Economist. 2013. "Abe's Master Plan" (May 18).

Eichengreen, B. 2011. *Exorbitant Privilege.* Oxford University Press: Oxford.

Fisher, I. 1933. "The Debt-Deflation Theory of Great Depressions." *Econometrica*, October, Vol. 1, No. 3, pp. 337–357.

Funabashi, Y. 1988. *Managing the Dollar: From the Plaza to the Louvre.* Institute for International Economics: Washington.

Glipin, R. 2000. *The Challenge of Global Capitalism.* Princeton University Press: New York.

Halevi, J. and B. Lucarelli. 2002. "Japan's Stagnationist Crisis." *Monthly Review*, Vol. 53, No. 9, pp. 24–36.

Hatch, W. and K. Yamamura. 1996. *Asia in Japan's Embrace: Building a Regional Production Alliance.* Cambridge University Press, Cambridge.

Hoshi, T. and A. Kashyap. 2004. "Japan's Financial Crisis and Economic Stagnation." *Journal of Economic Perspectives*, Vol. 18, No. 1, pp. 3–26.

Hughes, C.H. 2000. "Japanese Policy and the East Asian Currency Crises: Abject Defeat or Quiet Victory?" *Review of International Political Economy*, Vol. 7, No. 2, pp. 219–253.

Itoh, M. 2000. *The Japanese Economy Reconsidered.* Palgrave: New York.

Johnson, C. 1998. "Economic Crisis in East Asia: The Clash of Capitalisms." *Cambridge Journal of Economics*, Vol. 22, No. 6, pp. 653–661.

Keynes, J.M. 1936. *The General Theory of Employment, Interest and Money.* Macmillan & Co: London.

Krugman, P. 1999. *The Return of Depression Economics.* Penguin: London.

Krugman, P. 2000. "The Japan Syndrome." *New York Times* (9/2).

Krugman, P., K.M. Dominquez and K. Rogoff. 1998. "It's Baaack!: Japan's Slump and the Return of the Liquidity Trap." *Brookings Papers on Economic Activity*, Vol. 2, pp. 137–205.

Koo, R.C. 2008. *The Holy Grail of Macroeconomics: Lessons from Japan's Great Recession.* Wiley & Sons (Asia): Singapore.

Koo, R.C. 2011. "The World in Balance Sheet Recession: Causes, Cures and Politics." *Real World Economics Review*, Vol. 58, pp. 19–37.

Linge, C. 1998. *The Rise and Decline of the Asian Century.* Macmillan: Melbourne.

Lucarelli, B. 2002. "The East Asian Financial Meltdown." *Journal of Contemporary Asia*, Vol. 32, No. 4, pp. 500–516.

Lucarelli, B. 2011. *The Economics of Financial Turbulence.* Edward Elgar: Cheltenham, UK.

McKinnon, R.I. 2011. "Beggar-Thy-Neighbour Interest Rate Policies." *Journal of Policy Modelling*, Vol. 33, pp. 759–775.

Minsky, H.P. 1980. "Money, Financial Markets and the Coherence of a Market Economy." *Journal of Post Keynesian Economics*, Vol. 3, No. 1, pp. 21–33.

Morris, J. (ed.) 1991. *Japan and the Global Economy.* Routledge: New York.

Parboni, R. 1986. "The Dollar Weapon from Nixon to Reagan." *New Left Review*, Vol. 158, pp. 5–18.

Robins, B. 2013. "Abenomics Turns Japan Upside Down." *Sydney Morning Herald* (May 25–26).

Steven, R. 1991. "Structural Origins of Japan's FDI" in Morris J. (ed.). *Japan and the Global Economy.* Routledge: New York, pp. 53–71.

Tabuchi, H. 2013. "Japan's Economy Growing at 3.5% Annualised." *New York Times* (15/5).

Taggart-Murphy, R. 2000. "Japan's Economic Crisis." *New Left Review*, Vol. 1 (second series), January/February, pp. 25–52.

Taggart-Murphy, R. 2009. "Is Japan Heading for a Fiscal Doomsday?" *The Asia-Pacific Journal*, Vol. 46, No. 4, pp. 1–4.

Turner, G. 2009. *No Way to Run an Economy.* Pluto Press: London & New York.

Tyers, R. 2012. "Japanese Economic Stagnation: Causes and Global Implications." *Economic Record*, Vol. 88, No. 283, pp. 517–536.

Whittaker, D.H. and Y. Kurosawa. 1998. "Japan's Crisis: Evolution & Implications," *Cambridge Journal of Economics*, Vol. 22, No. 7, pp. 761–771.

Wolf, M. 2013. "Japan's Unfinished Policy Revolution." *Financial Times* (9/4).

Wolfson, M.H. 2002. "Minsky's Theory of Financial Crises in a Global Context." *Journal of Economic Issues*, Vol. 36, No. 2, June, pp. 393–399.

Wray, Randall L. 1998. *Understanding Modern Money.* Edward Elgar Publishing: Cheltenham, UK and Lyme, NH, USA.

Yoshikawa, H. 2001. *Japan's Lost Decade.* International House of Japan: Tokyo.

Chapter 8
The Continuing Global Capitalist Crisis and the Transition to State-Neoliberalism in China

Alvin Y. So

As we enter the sixth year of the continuing global capitalist crisis that began with the September 2008 financial meltdown on Wall Street, Berberoglu (2012) remarked that the prospects for a rapid recovery of the economies of the United States and Europe appear to be dim.

In mid-2013, even though the United States is growing at "encouraging rates," the Organization for Economic Cooperation and Development (OECD) reported that a sustainable recovery is not yet firmly established and important tasks remain, among them the 17-nation euro zone's continuing vulnerability to renewed financial, banking and sovereign debt crises. Unemployment, currently at high levels across the developed world, could become entrenched. The OCED pointed out that as long-term joblessness become structural unemployment, high-level unemployment could remain even as the recovery takes hold (Jolly, 2013).

Furthermore, the global capitalist crisis has spread from the developed countries to the so-called "emerging markets," including the BRICS (Brazil, Russia, India, China, and South Africa). Paul Krugman (2013) observed in mid-2013 that "India's rupee and Brazil's real are plunging, along with Indonesia's rupiah, the South African rand, the Turkish lira, and more." Although India was poised to take its place alongside China as one of the dominant economic strategic powerhouses of Asia before the 2008 global capitalist crisis, analysts now fear that a falling rupee, higher inflation, softening growth, crippling budget deficits, and waning investor confidence in mid-2013 could spin India into a vicious cycle that will be difficult to contain (Harris and Wassener, 2013; Subramanian, 2013). Sharma (2012) also reports that India's annual growth rate has dropped from nine to six percent since 2008.

If the continuing global capitalist crisis has led to a downward trend in India, would it have the same impact on China? Has China experienced the same decelerating path as India?

At the beginning of the global capitalist crisis in 2009, I optimistically argued that its impact on China is highly positive, with China emerging from in the crisis considerably strengthened. Indeed, I further argued that the crisis not only provides an opportunity for China to strengthen its model of "*state-developmentalism*," but also the chance to expand its power in the inter-state system. The crisis has increased the probability of the rise of China as a global power as well as the shift in the center of global capital accumulation from the West to the East in the twenty-first century (So, 2012b).

I wrote the above article in 2009, when the global capitalist crisis had just started unfolding. The situation has been quite different with the deepening of the continuing crisis since 2012. In this chapter I will first explain why I made such an optimistic statement on China's development at the beginning of the crisis. I will then argue that the deepening of the global capitalist crisis since 2012 has led to the worsening of the Chinese economy and has led China to rethink its model of "*state-developmentalism*." Following this, I will discuss why I believe China since 2012 is moving towards a new model of "*State-Neoliberalism*" in order to revitalize the Chinese economy. Finally, I will discuss the future prospects for the "state-neoliberalism" model in the conclusion.

The Global Capitalist Crisis and China's "State-developmentalist" Model

Over the past few decades, China has pursued a path which can be called "*State-Developmentalism*." China's path of development is actually more similar to that of the East Asian developmental state than to the neoliberal state in the West. China's state-developmentalist path has the following distinctive features.

First, the Chinese state put economic growth as its highest priority. It set up a series of five-year plans and GNP growth targets; it single-handedly focused on development to meet GNP growth targets, despite the fact that these targets could only be met at the expense of other important goals, such as social equality, democracy, and environmental protection.

For example, once the party leaders set up a target GNP growth rate of say 10 percent, the recruitment, promotion, and merit increase of local (city, provincial, and national) state officials are judged on whether their regions could attain this target 10 percent growth rate. This explains why the local officials are so eager to initiate new development projects in their territories; such projects would not only bring revenue and jobs to their region, but they themselves would get handsome merit increases and advancement in the state bureaucracy.

As a result of the excessive focus on development, economic growth in China over the past few decades was nothing but spectacular. The average growth rate of real gross domestic product was in double-digit figures, with China rapidly transformed from a poor, backward third world country to an economic powerhouse of the world (So, 2012a).

Second, the Chinese state has actively intervened in the economy; it has become the engine powering capital accumulation. China's pattern of development was said to be investment-driven because the Chinese state carried out many mega infrastructure projects like building high-speed railways, a national freeway system, many new cities, airports, subways, and harbors. In addition, it also developed plans for strategic development, decreed prices, regulated the movement of capital, shared risks and underwrote research and development.

Third, the state has adopted authoritarian policies to pacify civil society, discipline labor, and suppress dissent in order to maintain political stability to attract foreign and domestic investment. It seems that authoritarianism is unavoidable in export-led industrialization because labor subordination is an important means to cheapen labor and to make the working class docile. Otherwise, Chinese exports would not be so competitive in the world economy, and transnational corporations would not relocate their labor-intensive production to China. It is ironic that China, with its tightly-organized state machinery, has proven to be very effective in co-opting labor activists, dividing the working class, and silencing labor protests.

Fourth, although the transnationals have dominated China's export sector (e.g., foreign-owned global corporations account for 60 percent of Chinese exports to the US) (Roach, 2006), China has also built up a strong capital-intensive sector to capture the huge domestic market. China is able to produce for the domestic market and for the global economy because imports and exports are performed by a dual economic structure of state and non-state sectors. On the one hand, small and medium-scale companies have propped up the export-oriented economy; capital investment in these companies has been supplied from the informal market rather than from state banks. On the other hand, large companies in the state sector have specialized in upstream sectors that had been developed by import substitution industrialization. The financing of these large state enterprises have completely depended on state banks, thus achieving economies of scale (Baek, 2005). In China, the export sector and the import-substitution sector coexist side by side. After 30 years of development, China's domestic corporations in the strategic sectors (such as telecommunications, steel, and automobile), which are closed to foreign capital, can produce to meet the demands of the domestic market and to compete with foreign corporations.

Fifth, in China, as in other East Asian developmental states, the basis of legitimacy of the regime was mainly derived from growth and nationalism. The claim was that Chinese citizens should support the state because their income had greatly improved, their living standards were much better than that of an earlier generation, and they should unite behind the state in order to create a rich and powerful nation free of domination by foreign capital.

In short, China's path of "*state-developmentalism*" is characterized by economic growth, which has become the highest priority of the state's agenda -- intervention in the economy, a set of authoritarian policies to pacify civil society and discipline labor, a large state sector which favors the state enterprises over the non-state enterprises, rapid growth, and nationalism.

At the onset of the global capitalist crisis, this state-developmentalist model is further consolidated by China's response to the crisis. In late 2008, China set up a massive stimulus package budgeted at 4 trillion yuan (US$586 billion). While no pubic breakdown of funds exists, most experts say the bulk of the stimulus package that China pumped out for new highways, railroads, and other big projects went to state-owned companies. Thus, there was a huge expansion of the state sector at the expense of the private sector, aptly expressed in the catchphrase "*guo jin, min tui*" or "the state advances, the private sector retreats." During 2008–09, investment by state-controlled companies skyrocketed, driven by hundreds of billions of dollars of government spending and state bank lending to combat the global financial crisis (So, 2012b).

Since China quickly restored its remarkable growth rate in 2009 and 2010, it was widely believed at the time that the state-developmentalist model served China well, and China would continue to grow at 9–10 percent a year for the next decade or longer (Pettis 2013).

Deepening of the Global Economic Crisis and the Signs of Distress in China

As the global capitalist crisis deepened, however, the Chinese economy began to show signs of distress in 2012 and 2013.

China's remarkable economic growth was propelled by throwing tons of resources into its economy—mountains of cash to build factories, roads and bridges, apartment towers and shopping malls, and millions of peasant migrants into making iPads, mobile phones, blue jeans, shoes, and cars. Under China's state-developmentalism, the state often directed the cash into massive infrastructure projects or targeted industries. Nevertheless, this investment-driven growth engine is clearly not sustainable and cannot continue indefinitely. By 2013, researchers began to worry about whether China's state-developmentalist model had reached its limit and outlived its usefulness (Pei, 2013; Schuman, 2013).

Facing declining demands in the global market, China suddenly realized that its manufacturing industries have *massive excess capacity*. Excess capacity is plaguing major manufacturing industries—including steel, cement, automobile, solar panel, and wind turbines—and destroying profitability in sector after sector (Pei, 2013). Take the case of green industry. In a mad-cap quest to dominate green energy, China's banks pumped billions into solar-panel manufacturing, creating hundreds of factories and vaulting China into the world's largest producer. Now the solar sector has become the victim of its own success: Chinese companies are failing, symbolized by the recent bankruptcy of market leader Suntech Power.

Chinese steel companies, too, continue to invest in new capacity even though debt is rising and losses are mounting. Each steel mill is backed by local officials eager to create jobs but dismissive of the larger costs. New investment projects prop up GNP to make China look good in development indicators, but only at the expense of the health of the overall economy. Inefficient, heavily subsidized state-owned enterprises gobble up credit while more nimble private firms starve.

With urban housing prices rising at around 10 percent monthly in early 2010, analysts are warning of the formation of a *residential property bubble*, which could lead to serious political consequences. There was massive overcapacity in housing, with one Chinese electric company reporting 60 million units connected and not using any electricity, so presumably empty. If another 20 to 30 million units under construction are added, China's excess capacity could house the entire US population (Dapice, 2010). A public opinion poll showed that housing affordability is rated to be a top domestic problem in China. Rising housing prices would exclude low-income urban residents and rural migrant workers from the housing market, making China more polarized and divided (Yao and Luo, 2010).

Much of China's recovery has been fueled by aggressive lending and soaring property prices. Lending by state-run banks was one of China's most aggressive forms of stimulus in 2009, but analysts constantly warned that banks could face the risk from overbuilding, overcapacity, and nonperforming loans (Barboza, 2010).

Indeed, the massive 4 trillion yuan (US$586 billion) stimulus package not only has left a legacy of murky accounting, off-balance-sheet transactions and dodgy lending, it also has ended up as non-performing loans of the state enterprises and the mounting debts of the local governments.

Pei (2013) reports that the biggest short-term risk for China is *financial over-leveraging*. Thanks to its decade-long credit boom, the Chinese economy as a whole is far more leveraged (indebted) than any of the major emerging market economies. Net domestic credit as a share of GDP is close to 140 percent in China, compared to 90 percent in Brazil and 75 percent in India. To make the matter worse, most of the debt is owed by state-owned enterprises, real estate developers, and local governments that are known for making risky, hasty decisions on their investments.

Bad loans hidden in Chinese banks vary, due to the opacity of the Chinese financial system. The most conservative estimates suggest that they are around 10 to 15 percent of China's GDP. If this is true, the Chinese banking system is technically insolvent.

Schuman (2013) points out that the most frightening thing is the *speed* of the rise of the debt. Rating agency Fitch says credit relative to GDP reached 198 percent at the end of 2012, a startling increase from 125 percent in 2008. Local government debt has escalated in recent years after the global financial crisis, to an estimated $2 trillion or 25 percent of China's GDP.

The risks have been heightened by the emergence of "shadow banking"—mysterious, unconventional sources of lending often kept off the bank's balance sheets—which George Soros recently warned could be as risky as the toxic subprime mortgage securities that tanked Wall Street.

Thus, in 2012 the Chinese economy began to show the following signs of distress: massive excessive capacity, residential property bubble, financial overleveraging, nonperforming loans, the rapid rise of debt, and financial instability. China's GNP growth rate also has fallen to an annual pace of about 7.5 percent, down from a peak of more than 14 percent in 2007, before the global capitalist crisis (Lowrey, 2013).

In mid-2013, it is reported that the Chinese economy has lost much of its previous vigor. Exports fell 3.1 percent from a year earlier, and imports declined 0.7 percent (Wassener, 2013). Both figures were far below the expectations of analysts, who had projected a 4 percent rise in exports and 8 percent climb in imports, leading to a loss of confidence in the outlook for China's economic growth rate (Schuman, 2013).

Since these signs of economic distress and falling growth rate happened at the same time as the once-a-decade leadership transition was taking place in the communist party (with incoming President Xi Jinping and Premier Li Keqiang replacing the outgoing President Hu Jintao and Premier Wen Jiabao), this distressing state of the economy had led the new leaders to rethink whether they have to adopt new policies to face the challenge of the global capitalist crisis (Summers, 2013).

Departure from the State-developmentalist Model

Since taking office in mid-March 2012, Premier Li Keqiang and his state council have taken a different policy path from his predecessor. Yiping Huang (2013) labels Li's economic policy framework as "*Likonomics*," which has the following features.

The first feature is that Li *no longer insists that China needs to have a double digit growth rate* to sustain its economy. It seems that the days of 10 percent annual growth rate are over in China. Growth potential is now projected around 6–7 percent. The minimum growth rate has also shifted downwards. It is predicted that China would probably fall to just 3 percent for this decade. In other words, China no longer sees economic growth as its highest priority in development or a high growth rate at any cost (Parker, 2013).

The second feature is *no more stimulus package* to upstart the Chinese economy. Li (2013) said "We can no longer afford to continue with the old model of ... high investment." Li believes that relying on state-led investment for economic growth is not only difficult to sustain but also creates new problems and risks. The 4 trillion yuan (US$586) stimulus package in 2008 is said to be causing overcapacity in certain areas of infrastructure, significant fiscal risks due to reckless local government borrowing, asset bubbles, and the threat of bad debt following the huge credit expansion.

The third feature is *deleveraging*. The state bank moved to curtail the credit bubble in the interbank market underlines Li's desire to deleverage and reduce future financial risks. Li wants to strengthen market discipline as a preparatory step towards interest rate and capital account liberalization. This implies that deleveraging is likely to continue and some of the smaller and weaker financial institutions may fail in the near future.

In mid-2013, the central bank, People's Bank of China, eager to rein in soaring lending growth and financial risk, initially refrained from intervening as bank-to-bank interest rates suddenly soared from around 3 percent in 2012 to a record high of 13.44 percent in June 2013, making banks and other financial institutions afraid of lending to one another and create *a credit squeeze*. Those in need of short-term cash, or liquidity, must pay dearly; failure to do so raises the possibility of defaults. Rumors of defaults swirled in late June 2013 and some foreign commentators even suggested that China's financial system was on the verge of a Lehman Brothers-like crash.

The state is holding off the credit for a reason: it is trying to restructure the economy, curb excesses in shadow banking and property sectors, engineering a shift from investment-driven growth to consumption-driven growth, and weed out the weaker banks and enterprises (Gough and Barboza, 2013). The credit squeeze is getting the banks to adopt more cautious lending practices and Beijing is prepared to tolerate a degree of pain in its pursuit of financial overhaul.

The fourth feature is *structural reforms*. Current policy discussion indicates reforms in the areas of financial liberalization, the fiscal system, land use, administrative controls, monopolies, and the household registration system—many of which could be formally approved by the state over the next few years.

Li wants to open important sectors of the economy (finance, energy, railways, and telecommunication) to private businesses and market forces; foreign investors will be given more opportunities to invest in finance, logistics, health care and other sectors. At the Davos Forum in Dalian in 2013, Li said that he "will continue to support the Doha round of World Trade Organization talks, work for the signing of bilateral free trade agreements, upgrade the China-Asean Free Trade Area, establish a Shanghai free trade zone, and provide a level playing field and a better legal environment for foreign investors" (Li, 2013).

In addition, Li also wants to reduce the state's role in the market and allow more competition among businesses. In the Davos Forum, Li said "he will continue to streamline government and delegate power, press ahead with structural changes and grow economic sectors under diverse ownership. Government will leave to the market and society what they can do well while concentrating on those matters within its purview" (Li, 2013; see also the report on Davos Forum in Zakaria, 2013; Barboza and Buckley, 2013).

Since 2012, the Chinese state has shown traces of market liberalization and opened up the state sector to foreign investment. It also has taken a less active role in economic intervention, as shown by the no stimulus and the deleveraging policies. As such, is China moving in the direction of Neoliberalism?

China's Transition to State-neoliberalism?

Since Likonomics just started in mid-2012, it is too early to tell whether its pro-market policies get institutionalized and China moves towards the neoliberal model. What is certain, however, is the Chinese path of development from 1978 to the present has been cyclical—usually taking two steps forward and one step back backward, or one step forward and two steps backward—but it has never moved in a straight line. Thus, the final product is usually the uneasy and unstable combination of contradictory elements, a hybrid which defies any conventional labeling.

As such, the pro-market policies in Likonomics should not be taken as the triumph of neoliberal forces in China. Instead, it is more appropriate to treat the new policies as a balancing act of the Chinese state. Market forces were brought back in China during the global capitalist crisis in order to facilitate the party to stay in power.

This situation is different from the "*neoliberal state*" in the West as discussed by David Harvey (2005: 7), who uses the term "neoliberal state" to refer to "a state apparatus whose fundamental mission was to facilitate conditions for profitable capital accumulation on the part of both domestic and foreign capital." Whereas the Western neoliberal state is induced to serve the interests of the capitalist class, market reforms in China in 2012 are selectively adopted to preserve the domination of the communist party-state over the economy and society when the state is threatened by the deepening of the global capitalist crisis. I call this mode of operation in China "*State-neoliberalism*" so as to highlight its difference with the neoliberal state in the West.

In China's state-neoliberalism, the party-state is further strengthened, not weakened, through the control over state officials, over the domestic market forces, over foreign transnationals, and over the rising "middle class."

First of all, in order to strengthen the state, the new President Xi Jinping quickly kicked off the Mass Line Education campaign, which is set to last a year and is intended in part to purge the party of formalism, bureaucratism, hedonism, and extravagance. The mass line campaign is aimed to enforce party authority that goes beyond its periodic calls for discipline.

Second, President Xi launched a campaign on the ideological front. On the one hand, Xi 's "mass line" campaign signaled a shift to a more leftist stance to defend the legacy of Mao Zedong, which included a publicized visit to a historic site where Mao undertook one of his own attempts to remake the Chinese communist party in the 1950s. Xi also said Mao Zedong's era of revolutionary socialism should not be dismissed as a failure. On the other hand, Xi has vehemently denounced Western constitutional democracy as an attempt to negate the party's leadership and a tool of Western subversion to weaken the communist states. The new leaders, therefore, have no intention of carrying out any bourgeois democratic reforms, despite the fact that they had opted for the introduction of more market forces into the Chinese economy (Buckley, 2013).

Third, President Xi has called for the purification of state officials. State cadres should adhere to the "mass line" and develop close ties with the people. They should be critical and self-critical in the spirit of rectifying their work styles. The mass line campaigns should focus on self-purification, self-perfection, self-renewal and self-progression. The party should adopt more comprehensive criteria for assessing the performance of its officials. In promoting officials, the party should consider integrity as a priority and then capability; and the *party should never judge a cadre simply by the growth of gross domestic product (GDP)*. In this respect, Xi has silently discarded the model of state-developmentalism whose most important principle was to promote economic growth at whatever cost.

Fourth, although foreign corporations hope that under *Likonomics*, market liberalization would give them more opportunities to do business in the excluded state sectors, they are bound to be disappointed. In mid-2013, a landmark ruling in the Supreme People's Court in China ruled that contracts used by non-Chinese citizens to gain access to sectors of the Chinese economy that are protected from foreign investment were invalid (Wong, 2013).

In the past, sectors the Chinese government considers sensitive, like finance, media, technology, the internet and education, have long been off-limits to foreign investment. To get around that, some of the biggest companies in China, founded by Chinese people, including the Internet giants Baidu, Alibaba, Tencent, and Sina, have created variable interest entities, or *V.I.E.'s*, that give overseas investors de facto control over companies technically owned by their Chinese partners. V.I.E's account for differing proportions of these companies' income and assets, ranging from several percent to as much as 100 percent.

Problems arise if the Chinese partners decide they don't want to follow the V.I.E. contracts any longer because, for example, they already have the money and know-how they were seeking. When that happens, the foreign party most likely has no legal recourse once the above landmark ruling has passed in mid-2013 and they remained excluded from the strategic sectors.

Fifth, a strong state also means that foreign corporations and foreigners could not impose their wishes on their Chinese workers. New York Times reported that foreigners are relatively helpless when their foreign business owners are embroiled in legal disputes in China. A strong state also means that it can go after the transnationals if the Chinese government finds their business practices problematic. For example, in mid-2013, Chinese officials investigated the Swiss food packaging giant Tetra Pak for abusing its market dominance in China. Tetra Pak is suspected of price-fixing and anti-competitive behavior. Analysts say that it is not unusual for the government to investigate the pricing practices of Chinese and international companies. Although most prices in China are set by market forces, the government maintains control over large part of the economy, including energy and telecommunication prices. In response to the government investigation, several international brands, including Nestle and Danone, have announced price cuts—as much as 20 percent—on infant milk formula sold in China (Barboza, 2013a).

In September 2013, Peter Humphrey and Yu Yingzheng—two well-known figures in the foreign business world in China—were charged of illegally acquiring private personal information. Humphrey and Yu own a business consulting firm and their company sell services that are considered essential for doing business in China, including background checks, fraud investigations, and trademark protection. In the capitalist world, such work is fairly mundane. But in China, where public records are limited and corruption is rampant, it can be tricky and dangerous.

Humphrey's case, together with the bribery investigation against GlaxoSmithKline which put increasing pressure on American car companies to lower their prices in China, and the not-so-veiled threats against American technology companies to subcontract to Chinese companies, the state appears to be throwing new obstacles in the way of foreign companies doing business in China (Perlez, 2013).

China Central Television also severely criticized Apple's warranty practices and accused Apple of discriminating against Chinese iPhone owners by offering shorter guarantees than in other countries, using refurbished rather than new parts and shirking after-sale obligations. Gordon Chang remarks that the Apple accusation appears to be the beginning of a long-term campaign against foreign brands: in 2013 the state targeted Apple and Volkswagen; in 2012 it went after McDonald's and Yum Brands; and Google has been the object of a multi-year effort to undermine its operations in China.

Officials of transnational corporations operating in China have complained in mid-2013 that "the Chinese government is using law enforcement to weaken international competitors in commercial sectors where Chinese companies are not strong or have spent very little money to develop their own products" (Barboza, 2013b). Thus, Gordon Chang (2013) concludes that Chinese state officials, determined to protect domestic firms, started to take on foreign brands one by one. Under state-neoliberalism, the state will do its best to cripple foreign companies and to exclude them from the strategic sectors in order to nurture domestic companies into national companions to compete in the global market.

Sixth, whereas there is a retreat of the state in the Western neoliberal states as market forces play a more important role in the economy, the communist party-controlled state views a pure market economy as excessively volatile and it shows no sign of relinquishing its role of planning for the Chinese economy. Indeed, Premier Li Keqiang has made urbanization the centerpiece of his economic policies (*China Daily*, 2013), and China is going to build many new cities, many new housing complexes, many new freeways, and many new subways. According to Li's urbanization scheme, the state can resolve the problem of wasted investment by pushing for the engine of urbanization, i.e., it can engage in a massive investment program related to the need to build infrastructure for all the newly urbanized areas. It is estimated that China will have 300 million people—equivalent to the entire population of the United States—migrating from the countryside to the cities over the next couple of decades. Since city-dwellers earn more and spend more than their rural cousins, urbanization will create a vast body of consumers, boost consumer demand, accelerate China's economic rebalancing, and ultimately propel China to pass the US as the world's biggest economy.

Sixth, the state has further heightened its nationalist credentials. In numerous comments since the start of his tenure, President Xi has highlighted his goal to "rejuvenate the Chinese nation" and to make China prosperous and strong (*fuqiang*), tapping into deep-seated desires in the modern Chinese psyche (Summers, 2013). Thus, President Xi is known to be a tough nationalist who will go further than his predecessors in asserting China's territorial claims. He is willing to back the Chinese military in its attempts to assert primacy in the South China Sea over Vietnam and the Philippines and East China Seas over Japan. China's aggressive approach to maritime dispute in the South China Sea, to a certain extent, is a response to Obama's reorientation of US strategic policy toward the Asia-Pacific region.

Finally, despite the great pressure from the liberal faction of the Chinese Communist Party to embark on political reform, Xi's position is a firm "no" to the liberal proposals.

Conclusion

The global capitalist crisis is a period of turbulence, upheaval, political vacuums, and prolonged conflict; it is a period where states, classes, and ethnic groups try to re-define their relationship, to re-align their configuration, to re-think their development models, and to re-set the rules governing their access to key resources in the global economy.

As such, we have argued that when China's hyper-growth economy eventually slowed down in 2012 during the deepening global capitalist crisis, the state silently discarded its *Developmentalist* model. Thus, it no longer provided a massive stimulus package to jumpstart the economy like it did in 2008. Instead, the new leaders opted for the tightening of credit, the strengthening of market discipline, market liberalization, streamlining the state bureaucracy, and the opening of the state sector for foreign investment.

Despite adopting a more pro-market policy, however, China is not moving in the direction of neoliberalism. Instead, it is moving along a new path that can be called "*state-neoliberalism*." This state-neoliberalist model in China is different from the *neoliberal state* in the West in the following ways. First, whereas the neoliberal state in the West is aimed to serve the interests of the capitalist class, state-neoliberalism in China is aimed to enhance the domination of the communist state when it was threatened by the deepening global capitalist crisis.

Second, whereas the Western neoliberal state has shown signs of retreat from the economy, the Chinese state continues to intervene into the Chinese economy (through long-term planning and the urbanization project).

Third, whereas the Western neoliberal state is weakened by public management reforms to downsize the state bureaucracy, the Chinese state is strengthened, not weakened, through its mass-line education and anti-corruption campaigns since 2012.

Finally, whereas the Western neoliberal state advocates globalization and the opening of the domestic economy to the transnationals, the Chinese state has taken an aggressive stand to protect its strategic sectors from the assault of the transnationals and to heighten its national credentials in territorial disputes in the South China Sea and the East China Sea. Although transnationals are now allowed to enter the strategic sectors, the Chinese state also wants to upgrade and strengthen Chinese companies so they can compete with foreign capital in both the Chinese market and the world-economy.

If the Chinese developmental experience is characterized by trial and error, mid-course corrections, and reversals of policies, what is the future trajectory of state-neoliberalism in China? There seems to be the following scenarios: return to state-developmentalism, move to neoliberalism, and the consolidation of state-neoliberalism.

First, given the fact that China has a remarkable growth rate over the past three decades, the Chinese would hope that this hyper-growth state-developmentalist model will continue and China could serve as a growth engine to pull the world out of the global capitalist crisis. However, it seems highly unlikely that China could ever put up a double-digit growth rate for a long period of time again because of the maturation of the economy, the aging of the Chinese population, and the growing turbulence of the capitalist world-economy. Thus, China has reached the limit of the hyper-growth model and it is unlikely that it will return to the path of state-developmentalism.

Another scenario is the move to neoliberalism. The major beneficiaries of state-neoliberalism are those Chinese capitalists who have little connection with the state and have difficulties in getting the state to grant them license, the banks to grant them loans, and to protect them from corrupt state officials. Thus, those Chinese capitalists who have few links to the state and foreign interests (the transnationals, the World Bank, etc.) would like the state to further liberalize the market, to de-regulate the bureaucracy, and to discipline the state enterprises. However, given the strength of the party, the size of the state sector, and the dominance of the cadre-capitalist class (So, 2003), full-scale market liberalization is going to meet strong resistance from the vested interest in the state bureaucracy and the state enterprises. Unless the state is much weakened by domestic turmoil (e.g., by labor or peasant protests) and by the global capitalist crisis, it seems unlikely that China will turn to the path of neoliberalism.

The most likely scenario is the consolidation of state-neoliberalism. This chapter has argued that state-neoliberalism is the product of the deepening of the global capitalist crisis over the past few years: Selected market forces are introduced into the Chinese economy in order to solve excessive credit creation and misallocation of resources by state enterprises and local governments. In late 2013, it was reported that although India's economy has kept falling with declining growth rate and depreciation of the rupee, the market has rebound in China with factory orders expanding, trade surplus rising, and borrowing by local government and shadow banking under control, showing the state's resolve to keep things on track (Bishop, 2013; Bloomberg, 2013; The Editorial Board, 2013). Since the state still has enormous foreign exchange reserves and has successfully dealt with the Asian financial crisis before, there is reason for optimism that China will be able to pull out of the global capitalist crisis unscathed.

If China does continue to move along the path of state-neoliberalism, it could end up in a position that Silver and Arrighi (2000: 69) had envisioned two decades ago: "China appears to be emerging as the only poor country that has any chance in the foreseeable future of subverting the Western-dominated global hierarchy of wealth." Whether China succeeds in achieving this will depend on, to a large extent, how global capitalism is able to deal with the unfolding worldwide economic and financial crisis that is now threatening the very survival of the global capitalist system.

References

Barboza, David. 2010. "Report Warns of Risks to China's Bank System." *The New York Times*, July 14, 2010.

Barboza, David. 2013a. "Tetra Pak Comes Under Scrutiny in China." *The New York Times*, July 5, 2013.

Barboza, David. 2013b. "China Arrests British Adviser Hired by GlaxoSmithKline." *The New York Times*, August 21, 2013.

Barboza, David and Chris Buckley. 2013. "Beijing Plans to Reduce the State's Role in the Economy." *The New York Times*, May 24, 2013.

Baek, S.W. 2005. "Does China follow the East Asian Development Model? *Journal of Contemporary Asia*, 35(4), pp. 485–498.

Berberoglu, Berch. 2012. "Introduction: The Global Capitalist Crisis and its Impact on a World Scale." *International Review of Modern Sociology*, 38(2), pp. 163–168.

Bishop, Bill. 2013. "Market Rebound in China Shows Beijing's Resolve." *The New York Times Dealb%k*, September 9, 2013.

Bloomberg. 2013. "China Local Debt may Top Estimates, Former Minister Says." *Bloomberg News*, April 7, 2013.

Buckley, Chris. 2013. "China Takes Aim at Western Ideas." *The New York Times*, August 19, 2013.

Chang, Gordon. 2013. "Did China Just Declare War on Apple? Sure Looks Like it." *Forbes*, March 24, 2013.

China Daily. 2013. "Premier Calls for New Urbanization Strategies." *China Daily USA*, September 10, 2013.

Dapice, David. 2010. "Once a Winner, China Sees Globalization's Downsize—Part II." *Yale Global Online*, October 11, 2010.

Gough Neil and David Barboza. 2013. "China Facing Cash Squeeze as Rising Rate Crimp Lending." *The New York Times*, June 20, 2013.

Harris, Gardiner and Bettina Wassener. 2013. "A Summer of Trouble Saps India's Sense of Confidence." *The New York Times*, August 18, 2013.

Harvey, David. 2005. *A Brief History of Neoliberalism*. New York: Oxford University Press.

Hua, Yu. 2013. "Misrule in Law." *The New York Times*, August 18, 2013.

Huang, Yiping. 2013. "Likonomics' Policies in China." *East Asia Forum*, July 7, 2013.

Jolly, David. 2013. "World Economy Growing Unevenly, O.C.E.D. Says" *The New York Times*, September 3, 2013.

Johnson, Ian. 2012. "Relatives of Dissidents Said to Face Harassment." *The New York Times*, May 10, 2012.

Krugman, Paul. 2013. "This Age of Bubbles." *The New York Times*, August 22, 2013.

Li, Keqiang. 2013. "China Will Stay the Course of Sustainable Growth." *Financial Time*, September 6, 2013.

Levin, Dan. 2013. "Standoff in China Drags on for U.S. Man Held by Workers." *The New York Times*, June 25, 2013.

Lowrey, Annie. 2013. "I.M.F. Tells China of Urgent Need for Economic Change." *The New York Times*, July 17, 2013.

Parker, James. 2013. "Is the World Ready for a Great Rebalancing?" *The Diplomat*, February 14, 2013.

Pei, Minxin. 2013. "China on Verge of Worst Economic Crisis in Decades." *CNN World*, September 4, 2013.

Perlez, Jane. 2013. "In China, the Dangers of Due Diligence." *The New York Times*, September 13, 2013.

Pettis, Michael. 2013. "The Changing Debate over China's Economy." *Credit Expansion, Predictions*, August 7, 2013.

Roach, Stephen S. 2006. "Doha Doesn't Matter Any More: Despite Stiff Resistance to the Doha Agenda for Five Years, There Have Been Powerful Gains in World Trade in the Same Period." *Business Times Singapore*, August 8, 2006.

Schuman, Michael. 2013. "The Real Reason to Worry About China." *Time*, September 28, 2013.

Sharma, Ruchir. 2012. "Broken BRICs." *Foreign Affairs*, November/December 2012.

Silver, Beverly J. and Giovanni Arrighi 2000. "Workers North and South." pp. 53–76 in *2001 Socialist Register: Working Classes, Global Realities*, edited by Leo Panitch and Colin Leys. New York: Monthly Review Press.

So, Alvin Y. 2003. "The Making of a Cadre-Capitalist Class in China," in Joseph Cheng (ed.). *China Challenges in the Twenty-First Century*. Hong Kong: City University of Hong Kong Press.

So, Alvin Y. 2012a. "Development Models." pp. 1–23 in *Handbook of Contemporary China*, edited by William S. Tay and Alvin Y. So. Singapore: World Scientific.

So, Alvin Y. 2012b. "The Global Capitalist Crisis and the Rise of China to the World Scene." pp. 123–144 in *Beyond the Global Capitalist Crisis: The World Economy in Transition*, edited by Berch Berberoglu. Farnham: Ashgate.

Subramanian, Arvind. 2013. "Why India's Economy is Stumbling" *The New York Times*, August 30, 2013.

Summers, Tim. 2013. "China's New Leadership: Approaches to International Affairs." *Briefing Paper.* Chatham House.

The Editorial Board. 2013. "India in Reverse." *The New York Times*, September 8, 2013.

Wassener, Bettina. 2013. "China's Trade Data is Significantly Weaker than Forecast." *The New York Times*, July 10, 2013.

Wong, Sue-Lin. 2013. "China Court Ruling Could Threaten Foreign Investment in Country." *International Herald Tribune (IHT) Rendezv US*, June 17, 2013.

Yao Shujie and Dan Luo. 2010. "Chinese Economy 2009: Leading the World Economy out of Crisis." The University of Nottingham, China Policy Institute, Briefing Series—Issue 59.

Zakaria, Fareed. 2013. "Can China Change its Economic Course?" *The Washington Post*, July 18, 2013.

Chapter 9
Russia and the Global Capitalist Crisis

David M. Kotz

The global financial and economic crisis that broke out in 2008 emerged from the United States and quickly spread to most of the rest of the world. It has affected some countries more than others. Russia (the informal name for the Russian Federation) is among the countries that were significantly affected by the outbreak of the global crisis.

To understand how the crisis has affected Russia, it is necessary to consider the main features of its socio-economic system. This chapter first examines the political economy of post-Soviet Russia, including the manner of its insertion into the global capitalist system, in the period prior to the start of the recent global capitalist crisis. Then it considers the impact of the crisis on Russia including the likely long-term effects of the continuing global crisis of capitalism over the coming years.

Background

Kotz and Weir (2007) provide a detailed account of Russia's transition to capitalism following the demise of the Soviet Union at the end of 1991. They examine in detail the evolution of the post-Soviet political economy in Russia during this transition through two important periods under the succeeding regimes of Boris Yeltsin (1992–99) and Vladimir Putin (2000–present). This section draws upon that analysis.

The Yeltsin Regime

Under post-Soviet Russia's first president, Boris Yeltsin, Russia followed the neoliberal transition strategy, which called for rapid liberalization and privatization combined with tight monetary policy and large reductions in public spending. The state, rather than seeking to actively guide the transition to capitalism, adopted a hands-off approach that limited the state role in the transition to dismantling central planning and the price controls associated with it and privatizing the previously state-owned enterprises and banks. Showing its dedication to free-market theory, for the first six months of 1992 Russia was one of the few countries in the world with no import tariffs at all.

This transition strategy led to a process of economic retrogression through 1998, with the following features:[1]

1. A hyperinflation, unleashed by the sudden lifting of price controls in the face of large liquid savings of households, immediately impoverished the majority of the population as wages, salaries, and pensions increased far more slowly than prices, while the real value of the accumulated household savings of most people fell to near zero.[2]
2. Within a few years the previously state-owned enterprises and banks fell into the hands of one of four types of new owner: former Communist Party and state officials, the former top manager of the enterprise, organized criminal groups, or members of a new class of fleet-footed wheeler-dealers. The latter group was made up of speculators who got rich in the economic and political chaos of the early 1990s and then used their financial wealth to gain control of large enterprises. By 1996 a new class referred to as "oligarchs" had emerged in control of the most valuable enterprises and banks, coming mainly from the speculators who made up the fourth group listed above but also including some individuals from the other three groups.
3. Most of the new owners proved to have as their aim short-run profit from such activities as the export of mineral products to the world market or various forms of looting of the assets of the enterprise.
4. The economy entered a long and deep depression unprecedented for any major country in peace-time, lasting from 1990 when the Soviet economy first began to contract until 1998. By the latter year Russian GDP had fallen by 51 percent compared to its 1990 level.[3] This depression resulted mainly from three factors: 1) the economic disorder caused by the sudden transformation of the economic system including its property relations; 2) the demonetization of the economy due to super-tight monetary policy which led to barter substantially replacing money-based exchange; and 3) the rapid decline in aggregate demand resulting from falling consumer spending by impoverished households, declining state spending in line with the neoliberal program, and collapsing fixed investment as the state

1 Unless otherwise cited, the source for the account of Russia's economic trajectory during 1992 to 1998 in the text is Kotz and Weir (2007, chs 10–14).

2 Those with means and financial savvy were able to find ways to convert their savings from bank deposits into real property in Russia or foreign hard currency assets.

3 The sources for the 51 percent decline in Russia's GDP are International Monetary Fund 1992 and 1993 and Federal State Statistics Service, 2002. The World Bank also produced a GDP growth rate series for Russia, available at http://data.worldbank.org/datacatalog/worlddevelopmentindicators. The World Bank GDP growth series shows a significantly smaller GDP decline in the early post-Soviet years than the IMF and Russian state statistical agency series. According to the World Bank series, Russia's GDP declined by 43 percent from 1990 to 1998.

pulled back from investment and the new enterprise owners sought only short-run profits.

5. The sectoral structure of the economy changed rapidly, as deindustrialization took hold. All sectors of the Russian economy contracted, but oil and gas production declined by much less. By 1998 oil extraction had fallen by 32 percent and natural gas output by 15 percent, while chemical and petrochemical production had declined by 57 percent, machine-building by 65 percent, building materials by 71 percent, and light industry (primarily textiles, leather goods, and clothing) by 89 percent. Real gross investment fell by an astonishing 84.1 percent by 1998 compared to its 1990 level (Kotz and Weir, 2007, 240, 241).
6. Public order broke down as the state became impoverished and withdrew from an active role. Organized criminal groups fought gun battles for control over turf on the streets of Moscow in the early 1990s. Every enterprise had to make protection payments to a "roof," that is, an organized criminal group or in some cases a state agency such as the armed forces of the Interior Ministry. By the mid 1990s the new oligarchs, each of whom built a military-like enforcement organization, established some order, pushing the smaller criminal groups to the margins of society, although assassinations remained commonplace in disputes over control of property and markets.
7. A public health disaster emerged, as the death rate climbed and the birth rate dropped. This lead to a natural rate of population decrease that rose to over 6 per thousand in the early 2000s. Not until 2012 did the birth rate climb slightly above the death rate (Federal State Statistics Service, various years).

In 1998 a severe financial crisis broke out in Russia. While the immediate cause was contagion from the Asian financial crisis of the previous year, underlying conditions in the Russian economy had set it up for a financial collapse (Kotz and Weir, 2007, 242–244). As the major banks failed and Russia defaulted on its foreign debt, the legitimacy of the Yeltsin regime was threatened. A newly assertive opposition majority in the state duma, led by the Communist Party of the Russian Federation, was able to force President Yeltsin to name an opposition prime minister, Yevgeny Primakov, and a cabinet with some Communist ministers. However, as the economy began to finally recover from the long depression in 1999, Yeltsin reasserted the power that resides in the office of the president and dismissed the new government. On New Year's Eve 1999, Yeltsin resigned and named his recently appointed prime minister, Vladimir Putin, as Acting President.

The Putin Regime

Vladimir Putin has remained the top leader since 2000, despite four years during which his aide Dmitry Medvedev served officially as President. The Putin regime has differed from the Yeltsin regime in significant ways. Power was centralized in the federal state and in the President's office. In the Yeltsin period the free and fair elections that had been introduced at the end of the Soviet period gave way to increasingly fixed elections, particularly for the all-powerful office of president. In 1996 President Yeltsin had won re-election over the Communist Party candidate Gennady Zyuganov by various unsavory methods including vote-rigging (Kotz and Weir, 2007: 260–264). However, other elections in the Yeltsin era, for duma seats, regional governorships, and mayoral offices remained relatively clean, as evidenced by the frequent victories of opposition candidates. This changed under President Putin. While the presidential elections became even more obviously fixed, now that came to characterize elections for other offices as well. Putin abolished the election of regional governors and took control over the outcome of mayoral elections in the major cities, while hardball tactics gained a majority in the duma for supporters of the regime.

As the central government's power grew, the chronic disorder of the Yeltsin era gave way to at least a semblance of normalcy. President Putin asserted control over the oligarchs, imprisoning one, Mikhail Khodorkovsky, and forcing a few others into exile. Foreign policy evolved from the deference shown to the United States by the Yeltsin regime to a more independent assertion of Russia's perceived national interests under Putin. This helped to create a significant popular base of support for the regime which had been lacking in the Yeltsin era.

The Putin regime has been widely misunderstood outside of Russia. Observers have taken note of the concentration of political power in the central government and the nationalization of a few oil and gas companies such as Gazprom, the giant natural gas monopoly, and Yukos Oil, the big oil company previously controlled by Khodorkovsky. This has led some to conclude that the neoliberal strategy of the Yeltsin era gave way to state capitalism in the Putin era. To understand the effects of the global capitalist crisis on Russia, as well as to explain its economic trajectory before and after the onset of the crisis, some clarity is needed about Russia's socio-economic model in the Putin era.

The term "state capitalism" has been used in various senses. Some analysts regard the former Soviet system, not as a form of socialism or as a new type of class system, but as a form of capitalism referred to as state capitalism (Bettelheim, 1976; Resnick and Wolff, 2002). A second meaning of state capitalism refers to countries in which the state engineered the transformation of a pre-capitalist feudal/agrarian society into a capitalist system, such as the case of Japan in the nineteenth century. A third meaning involves a state in a less developed capitalist country that actively guides the development of the economy aiming to achieve a high-income, technologically advanced capitalist economy. Another name for this third form of state capitalism is the developmental state, which usually involves such measures as industrial policy, direction of credit to key sectors, large state investments in infrastructure, education, and technology, and temporary protection of domestic producers. An example of this would be South Korea since the 1950s.

Of the above three meanings of state capitalism, only the third could possibly apply to the Putin regime. We will consider whether Russia under Putin has followed a developmental state path. In class terms, in a developmental state at first the capitalist class is either non-existent (nineteenth century Japan) or underdeveloped (South Korea). Some group controls the state and exercises significant control of the developing capitalist class, compelling it to adhere to a national development plan rather than simply pursuing short-run profits. The ruling group in developmental states in the past has included a section of the feudal ruling class in late nineteenth century Japan or the military in twentieth century Turkey and South Korea. In China the Communist Party has held onto power while running what can be considered a developmental state.

It is obvious that Putin's Russia has not returned to the Soviet model, despite the suggestion from some unreconstructed Western Cold Warriors that such a development has occurred. About the only feature of Soviet life that the Putin regime has brought back is the revival of an old Soviet anthem, but there is no central planning and the overwhelming majority of industry is privately owned. Putin's Russia does not fit the second meaning of state capitalism, since Russia was not pre-capitalist in 2000 but rather had established a capitalist economy by that year, albeit one with significant distortions and retrograde features.

By the year 2000, the neoliberal transition strategy had underdeveloped Russia, and a shift to a state capitalist road to rebuild Russian industry appeared at the time to be a promising path for the new president to follow. The power of the state has indeed grown in the Putin era. While Yeltsin had occasionally persecuted an oligarch, such as in the case of the oligarch Vladimir Gusinsky, Putin brought the group as a whole to heel. As political power has shifted from the regions to the central government, the latter's bureaucracy has grown rapidly. The state asserted control over all the major mass media. Opposition political parties have been marginalized. The state has asserted control over some key sectors of the economy: oil, gas, and aircraft manufacturing.

However, there has been no abandonment of the neoliberal strategy. Despite the growing size and strength of the state, the government has not sought to direct the development of the economy. As growing oil and gas revenues flowed into Russia after the early 2000s, the state used some of them to finally repair the crumbling transportation infrastructure. In 2008 spending on transportation reached 2.2 percent of GDP, from under 0.5 percent in 2000 (Federal State Statistics Service, 2001, 2009).[4] However, there is no industrial policy and no subsidized credit for Russian industry. The government has focused monetary policy on combating inflation by keeping interest rates high, forcing domestic enterprises to borrow heavily abroad. There has been no protection of domestic industry. While potential foreign investors face many obstacles in Russia, these result from bribe-taking,

4 The figure cited for the 2000 budget was for the combined category of "transportation, road service, communication, and information science." In later years the statistical agency published separate budget data for transportation and road service.

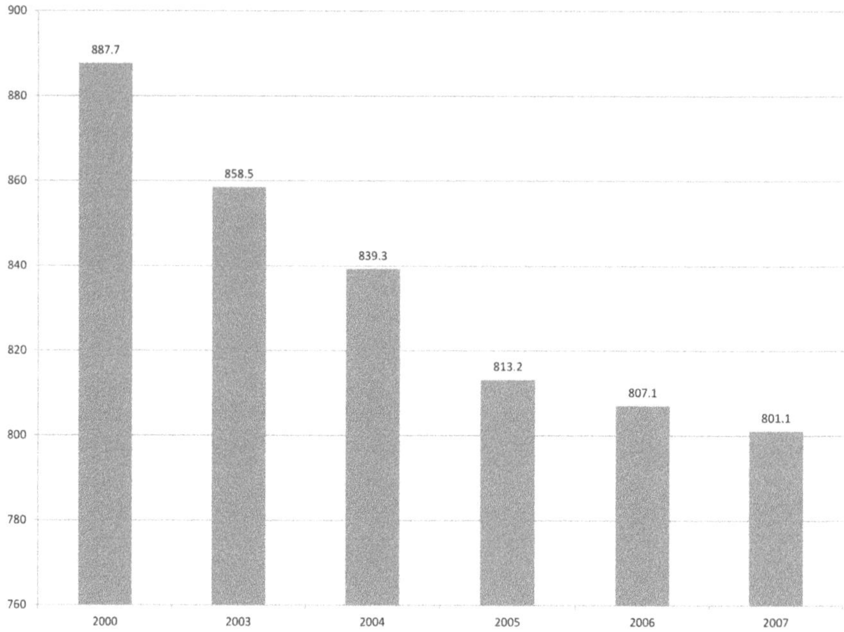

Figure 9.1 Personnel employed in research and development, 2000–2007 (thousands at year end)

Note: Data not available for 2001–02.

Source: Federal State Statistics Service, 2009, table 22.2, p. 354.

bureaucracy, and occasional theft of assets, rather than any effort by the state to direct inward foreign investment in ways that would benefit Russia's development. Figure 9.1 shows the number of personnel employed in research and development. The number declined over the Putin era, and by 2007, the last year for which this series was available, the number had fallen by 47 percent compared to 1992.

Lacking a developmental state, Russia's economy has been shaped by its "comparative advantage" in the global economy. The previously diversified industrialized economy of Russia at the end of the Soviet era rapidly evolved into an economy centered around the production and export of oil, gas, and other natural resources along with some development of the first stage of processing natural resources, such as steel manufacturing.

Figure 9.2 shows the share of natural resources in Russia's exports. Mineral products, which are made up mainly of oil and gas, rose from 42.5 percent of exports in 1995 to 53.8 percent in 2000. In the Putin era the dependence on mineral exports has increased further, to 65 percent to 70 percent.[5] The share of metals and

5 Oil and gas exports alone made up 61 percent to 66 percent of exports in 2005–08 (World Bank, 2013).

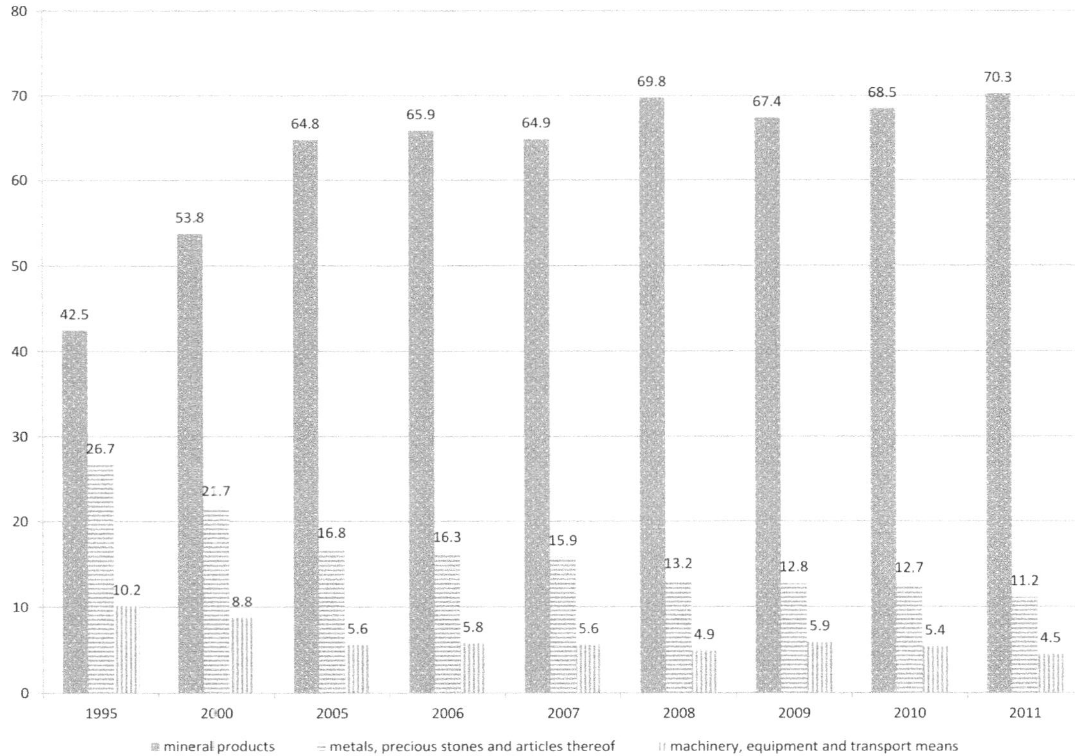

Figure 9.2 Commodity structure of exports of Russia, 1995–2011 (percentage of total exports)

Source: Federal State Statistics Service, 2011, 2012.

precious stones has fallen, but combined with minerals the two categories now make up about 80 percent of exports. The share of machinery and equipment fell over the whole period from 10.2 percent to 4.5 percent of exports.

The share of GDP accounted for by oil and gas production is understated in official statistics. Russia's official national income accounts indicate that oil and gas production account for about 8 percent of GDP. However, much of Russia's oil and gas exports are sold through transfer pricing schemes, in which the Russian producer sells to an affiliated trading company at a low price, followed by resale by the trading company at the world market price. Such schemes serve several purposes, including minimizing taxes, avoiding hard currency return regulations, enabling capital flight, and/or facilitating the theft of company revenues by insiders. A World Bank study in 2005 estimated, taking account only of technically legal transfer pricing, that oil and gas production actually account for 20 percent of GDP rather than 8 percent (World Bank, 2005: 8). Thus, the approximately 1 percent of the workforce employed in oil and gas production account for at least 20 percent of GDP. The majority of the Russian population is peripheral to the main source of revenue in the economy, a condition that underlies many of the pathologies that afflict states whose economy centers on energy exports.

Economic Recovery in Russia

In 1998 the eight-year-long depression finally hit bottom, and the economy began to expand in the following year. Figure 9.3 shows Russia's GDP growth rate starting with the first year following the dissolution of the USSR. From 1998 to 2007 Russia's GDP grew at the relatively high average rate of 7.1 percent per year. This led commentators to include Russia among the so-called "BRICs" along with Brazil, India, and China as a "newly emerging economy." However, Russia's growth has been dependent on rising oil and gas exports, making Russia more similar to Saudi Arabia than to China—that is, a larger Saudi Arabia with a big military capability and a permanent seat on the UN Security Council. A top economist in the Russian Ministry of Industry estimated that in 2003 the direct and indirect effects of the volume and price changes for oil and gas contributed between 58 percent and 63 percent of Russia's 7.3 percent GDP growth rate that year.[6]

Figure 9.4 shows the price of crude oil since 1990. After remaining at about $20 per barrel in the 1990s, in about 2000 the price of oil began a long upward climb. From 2000 to 2005 it tripled to $60 per barrel. Then it stabilized until mid 2007, when it began a steep rise to over $130 per barrel in mid 2008. The financial crisis sent oil prices plummeting to the low $40s until March 2009 when oil prices began a gradual rise to over $100 per barrel in March 2011. Since then there has been no further trend up or down through mid 2013.

Russia's GDP growth rate has followed oil prices up and down since 1999. One study found that the sales of the top 100 Russian companies outside the oil

6 Interview with Andrei Klepach, Moscow, June 14, 2004.

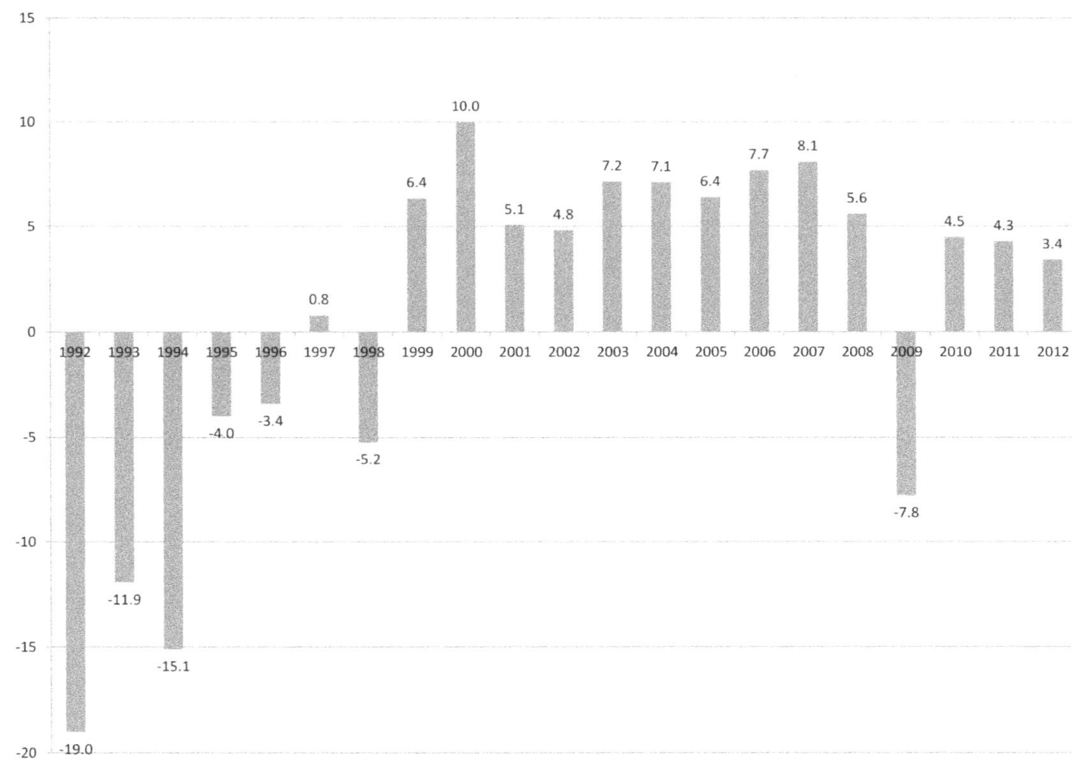

Figure 9.3 Annual growth rate of GDP for Russia, 1992–2012
Source: International Monetary Fund, 1992, 1993; Federal State Statistical Service, various years.

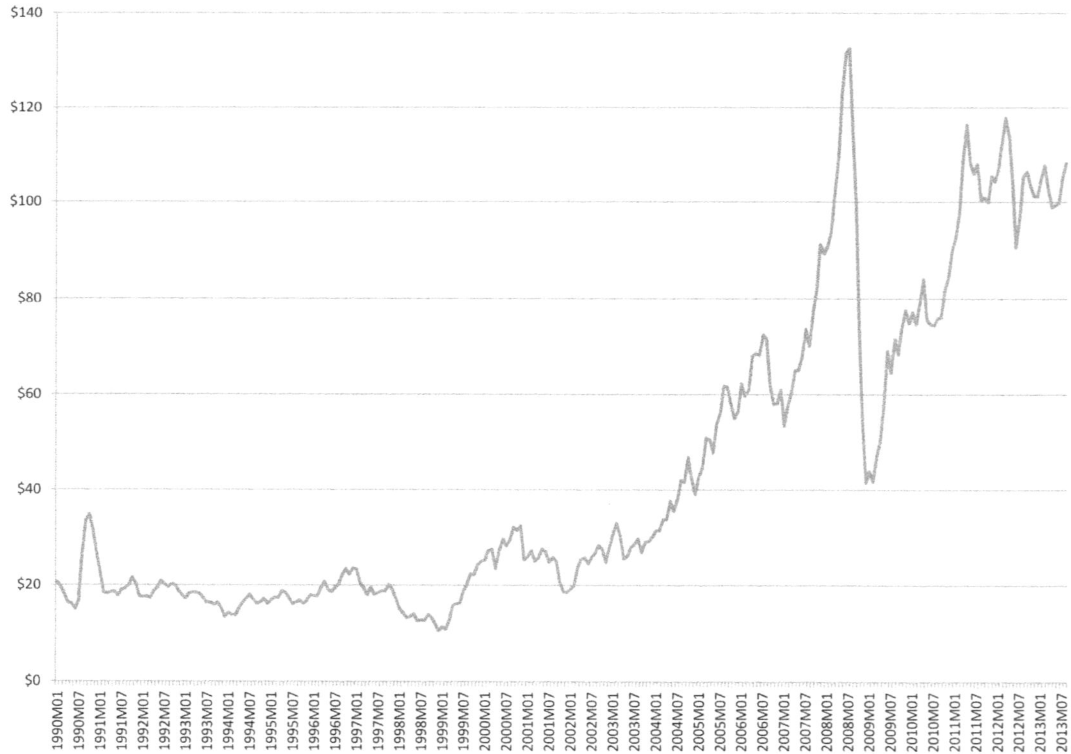

Figure 9.4 Monthly crude petroleum price, 1990–2013 (in US dollars)

Source: International Monetary Fund website: http://imf.org/external/np/res/commod/index.aspx.

and gas sector almost exactly mirrored the movements in oil prices from 2002 to 2009 (Gaddy and Ickes, 2010: 285, figure 3). Gaddy and Ickes (2010) also found that household income and retail sales followed oil prices in that period.

Thus, before the global crisis erupted in 2008, Russia had emerged from the long transition depression to become a petrostate, dependent on the price and quantity of oil it could sell to the world market. Russia received rapidly growing revenue from the long rise in oil prices prior to 2008. Russia's political system had stabilized in the form of an authoritarian regime that rules by a combination of repression along with support from a significant section of the population. The oligarchs continue to dominate the economy and expand their fortunes, free of state repression as long as they do not in any way challenge the regime. President Putin and his circle function like the top oligarch, enriching themselves while maintaining order in the economy and society through their position in charge of the state. In class terms, the Putin era state represents the interests of the new big bourgeoisie in Russia, whose members continue to effectively enrich themselves under the neoliberal regime maintained by the state without bringing any economic progress to Russia.

The Global Capitalist Crisis and its Impact on Russia

The 1998 financial crisis in Russia was a searing experience for the Russian state, almost causing a collapse of the Yeltsin regime. The Putin regime was determined to insulate itself from any future economic crisis that might originate from abroad. Figure 9.5 shows Russia's net exports as a percentage of GDP, a percentage that was very high and grew steadily from 2002 to 2005. Maintaining such a high ratio of net exports to GDP means that Russia sells much more to the world market than it buys from it. The large export surplus brought in a large amount of hard currency each year. As the growing oil and gas revenues flowed in starting in the early 2000s, the government used part of the hard currency earnings first to pay off its foreign debt, then to build a large stabilization fund.[7] By the eve of the crisis, it had accumulated a hard currency reserve fund of $590 billion, the third largest such fund in the world after China and Japan (Connolly, 2009: 2–3).

When the global capitalist crisis broke out in 2008, it hit Russia's exports hard. By December 2008 the price of oil had fallen by 68 percent from its peak monthly value reached in June of that year. As Figure 9.6 shows, in 2009 Russia's exports fell sharply, by just over one-third. At the same time, the large capital

7 The large export surplus also facilitated capital flight, as rich Russians sent their wealth to safe havens abroad to avoid taxation and as a safeguard against the danger to their wealth from a possible collapse of the economy or the regime. The continuing very high ratio of net exports to GDP after the global economic crisis means that Russia still does not receive on aggregate the full value it produces each year in the form of individual consumption, government services, or additions to the country's productive capacity.

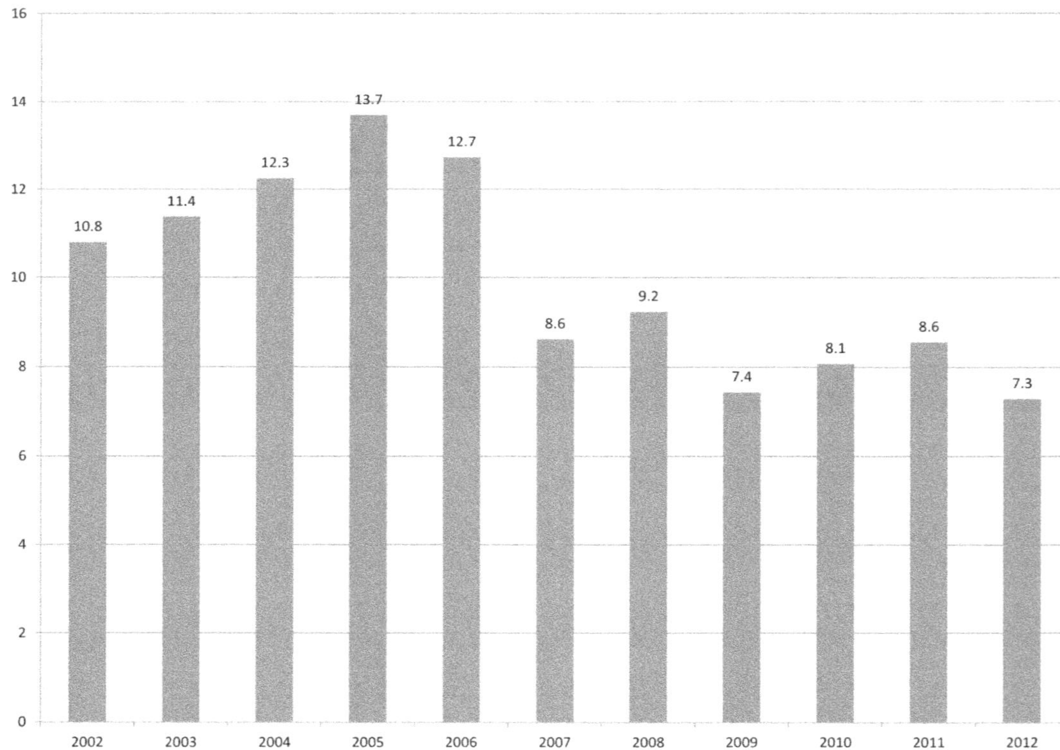

Figure 9.5 Net exports of goods and services as a percentage of GDP for Russia, 2002–12
Source: World Bank, 2013.

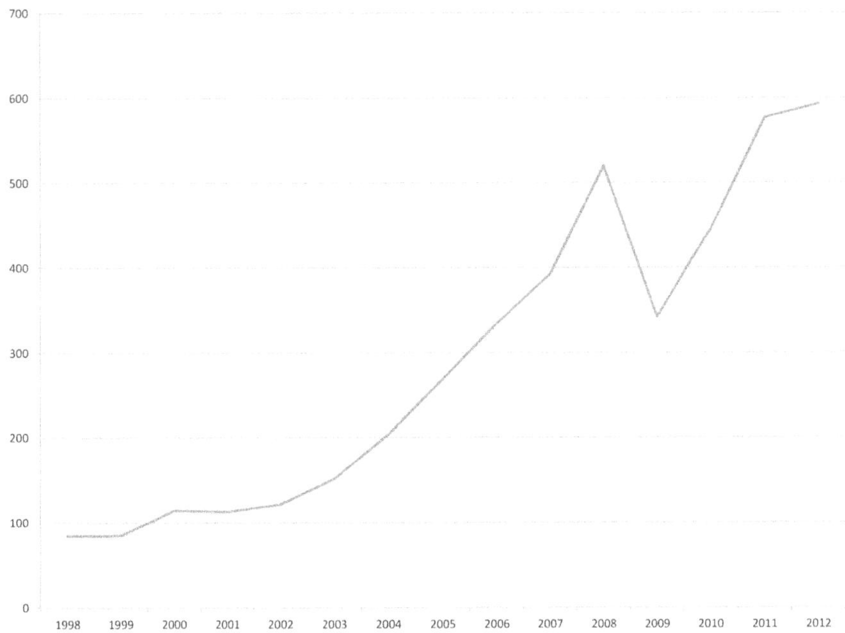

Figure 9.6 Russia's exports of goods and services, 1998–2012 (in billions of US dollars)

Source: World Bank, 2013.

inflow of $81.2 billion in 2007, attracted by Russia's rapid energy-export-driven growth in the years before the crisis, turned into a capital outflow of $148 billion in 2009 (Sutela, 2010: 5). From 2007 to 2009 Russia's government budget went from a surplus of 5.5 percent of GDP to a deficit of 5.9 percent of GDP (Sutela, 2010: 4). Russia had the largest percentage GDP decline of the major countries in 2009, of 7.8 percent, a greater decline even than that of Iceland whose oversized banking system collapsed (International Monetary Fund World Economic Outlook Database, 2013).[8] Russia's official unemployment rate rose from 6.4 percent to 8.4 percent from 2008 to 2009 (International Monetary Fund World Economic Outlook Database, 2013).

The government used its huge stabilization fund to finance a bailout of big companies and banks, a bailout estimated at about 13 percent of GDP (Desai, 2010: 143). While the government had no significant foreign debt, Russia's big companies and banks had borrowed heavily from abroad, with their debt reaching about $307 billion in June 2008, equal to 25 percent of GDP (Connolly, 2009: 4). The big companies controlled by the oligarchs received cash infusions of as much as $50 billion total to prevent them from falling under the control of European

8 However, Iceland's decline continued in 2010 while Russia recovered in that year.

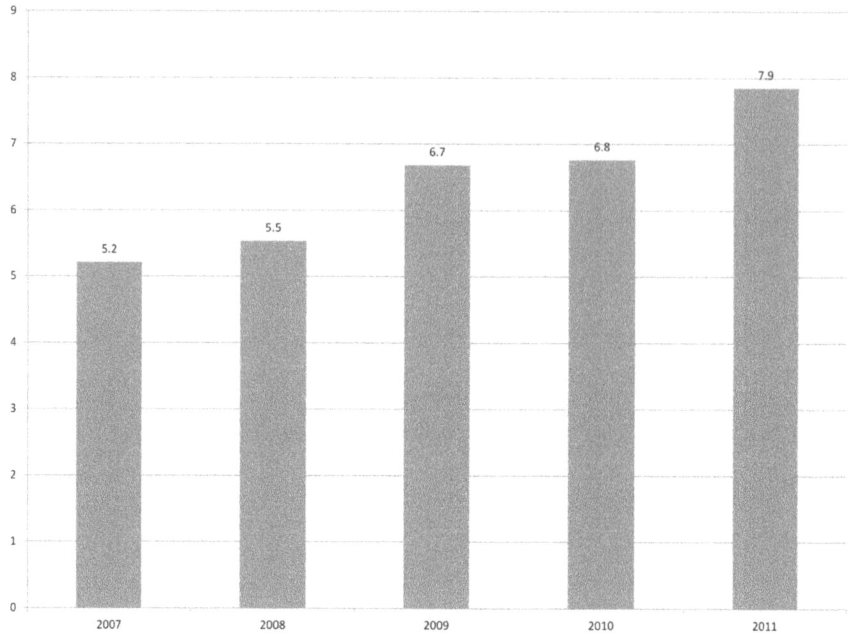

Figure 9.7 Russian exports to countries in East Asia and the Pacific as a percentage of total Russian merchandise exports, 2007–11
Source: World Bank, 2013.

bank creditors (Desai, 2010: 144). The big Russian banks were bailed out although small ones were allowed to fail (Connolly, 2009: 4). By August 2009 Russia's hard currency reserves had fallen from $590 billion to about $400 billion as a result of both the bailouts of companies with big foreign debts and actions taken to defend the value of the ruble (Connolly, 2009: 2). While the big banks were bailed out, the Russian working class suffered big layoffs as indicated by the sharp rise in the official unemployment rate cited above.

In late 2009 the price of oil resumed its rise, going above $100 per barrel in March 2011, which by one estimate was the oil price required for the government budget to be balanced (Sutela, 2010: 8).[9] As mineral exports returned to growth after 2009, Russia's economy began to expand again. However, despite the recovery of the price of oil, GDP growth since 2009 has been far below the 7.5 percent annual growth rate in the five years preceding 2007. As Figure 9.3 shows, GDP growth has been in the range of 3.4 percent to 4.5 percent since 2010, with a declining trend. While rapid growth in China helped to sustain Russia's energy export growth, it has been slowed by the sluggish economic recovery in Europe

9 The estimate by Sutela (2010) that an oil price of $100 per barrel would bring budget balance was for the year 2010. Such estimates vary somewhat from year to year.

and the United States, which has been partly due to the turn to austerity policy but also has been a consequence of the continuing structural problems of global capitalism.[10] Figure 9.7 shows that the share of Russia's exports going to East Asia and the Pacific rose significantly from 2007 to 2011, which reflects the contrast between rapid growth in raw-materials-hungry China and slow growth in Europe and the United States.

Future Prospects

As long as the current regime remains in power in Russia, we can expect that Russia will remain a petrostate, with all of the pathologies that are associated with such a political economy. State officials talk about the need to diversify the economy and build technologically advanced industry, and some industrial managers have asked for state action to revive Russian industry. In March 2013 Konstantin Babkin, the owner of a big farm machinery enterprise, sponsored an international forum in Moscow that focused on the problem of Russia's distorted economy. Babkin's enterprise is able to sell only about 450 tractors per year in Russia but owns a subsidiary in Canada that produces farm equipment and has healthy sales throughout the Americas. The forum attracted government officials as well as academics and foreign guests. However, the government officials insisted that current policies were already diversifying Russia's economy and strengthening industry, although no sign of this can be found in the data.[11]

Official talk about rebuilding Russian industry dates to December 1992 when President Yeltsin named Viktor Chernomyrdin, the head of the natural gas monopoly Gazprom, as Prime Minister, replacing the neoliberal economist Yegor T. Gaidar who had been Acting Prime Minister. Although Chernomyrdin came from the natural resource sector, his appointment was supported by the centrist Civic Union organization that called for measures to strengthen Russian industry. Chernomyrdin stated that "No reform will work if we destroy industry completely ... We should ... pay serious attention to production" (*The New York Times*, December 15, 1992: A16).

However, despite the talk, no policy changes to assist the development of Russian industry occurred under Chernomyrdin. This set a pattern of leadership calls for rebuilding industry followed by no action to carry it out that has characterized every post-Soviet Russian administration, with the exception of the very brief government of Prime Minister Yevgeny Primakov after the Russian financial crisis of 1998. It appears that the dominant sector of Russia's post-Soviet capitalist class is unwilling to give up the enormous riches that the neoliberal model has brought them. The export of minerals, and to a lesser extent steel and

10 See Kotz (2015) for an analysis of the roles of austerity policy and the underlying structural crisis of capitalism in the continuing stagnation since 2009.

11 The author attended the March 2013 forum in Moscow.

other metals, brings a huge flow of wealth. Those capitalists who ended up with manufacturing enterprises have found ways to extract wealth even from money-losing companies through various strategies, without fear that the neoliberal state will crack down on such practices (Kotz and Weir, 2007: 198, 284). Occasionally a maverick industrialist such as Babkin raises a complaint, and some academics are critical of the existing system, but so far the regime has had a secure power base in the capitalist class for continuing the neoliberal strategy that consigns Russia to a future of energy export dependence.

A shift to a developmental state would entail constraints on the capitalist class. They would be expected to devote profits to long-run investments, not siphon off revenues from their enterprise. Energy export revenues would be devoted to rebuilding Russian industry rather than enrichment of those who control the energy sector. Over time more of Russia's oil would go into domestic uses rather than export. State agencies would direct credit based on long-run development needs rather than market criteria or political influence. A shift in that direction has little support in the Russian state or its main base of support among the oligarchs and lesser capitalists.

The economic devastation resulting from the neoliberal model in Russia has fallen primarily on the Russian working class. Public opinion surveys in Russia have consistently shown that a large majority of the population believes they were better off under the Soviet system, despite its well-known defects. One defect of the Soviet system was that it depoliticized the Soviet working class. While working people received significant material benefits including a high degree of economic security under the Soviet system, they were turned into passive recipients of those benefits. The very class that in 1917 had overthrown one of the world's great autocracies was itself demobilized and depoliticized by the system that arose in the wake of the revolution. When the Soviet system was dismantled and replaced by a harsh form of capitalism after 1991, the Russian working class was unable to mount any effective protest at the loss of their social and economic rights.

The likelihood of major change in the future will depend partly on the price of oil. Long-run forecasts of the price of oil show a continuing rise for at least several decades, as oil usage is projected to grow and the sources of new oil become increasingly expensive to extract. If the price of oil does continue to rise, Russia's petrostate economy is likely to continue to grow and remain immune to a challenge from below, although growth is not likely to resume at the rapid rate of the mid 2000s. Such continuing growth is predicated on significant investment in the oil sector to at least maintain production levels. Figure 9.8 shows the output of energy-producing materials, mainly oil and gas. Output has increased since 1995, but since 2005 the rate of increase has been quite low.

However, the long-run forecasts of the price of oil assume a normal trajectory of growth for the global capitalist system, but the global crisis is likely to continue for some time. That means that global economic output is likely to stagnate in the coming years. An even worse possibility would be a second economic downturn. In addition, there is no guarantee that China will continue to grow rapidly, particularly

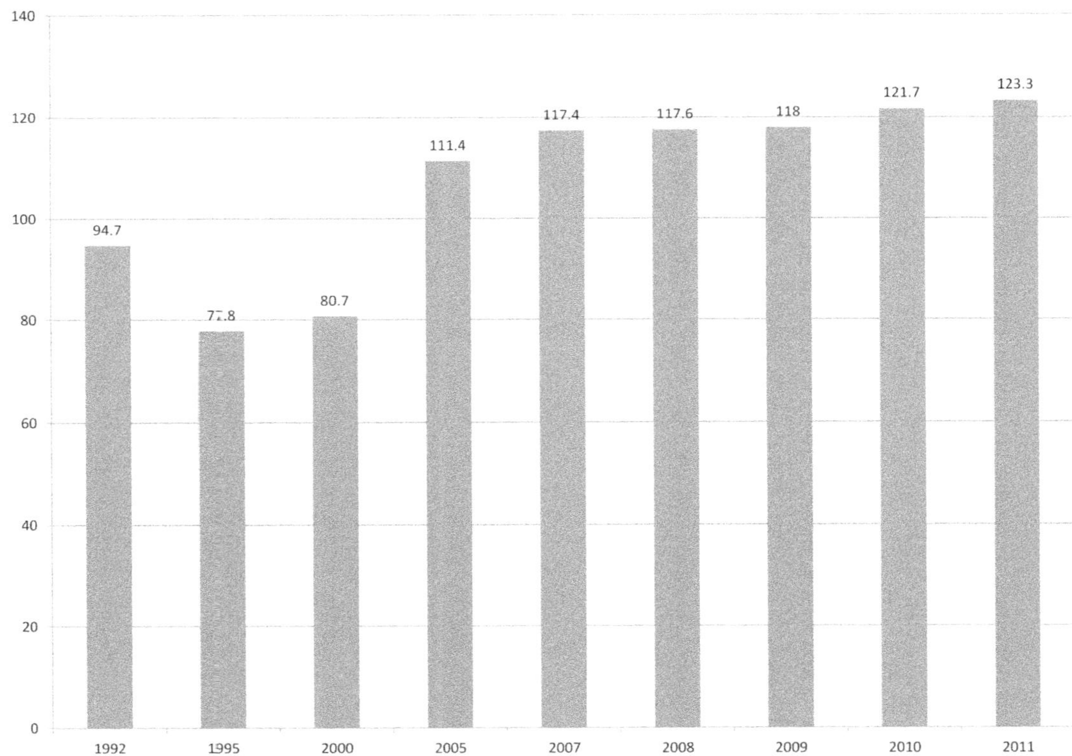

Figure 9.8 Production index for mining of energy producing materials, 1992–2011 (1991 = 100)
Source: Federal State Statistical Service, 2012.

if the increasingly powerful advocates of full neoliberal transformation in China achieve their goal. If China shifts from its current state-guided development model to a fully neoliberal model, its rapid growth would come to an abrupt end (Kotz, 2013). Such developments would worsen the stagnation in global capitalism. If a period of stagnation in global capitalism lies ahead, global oil demand would also stagnate, and both the price of oil and the volume of Russia's oil exports would stagnate.

If Russia's petro-state is unable to deliver increasing export revenues and GDP growth in the years ahead, the regime might face serious challenges. In the absence of rising energy export revenues, the current regime, which is based on distribution of those revenues among the oligarchs with some going to sections of the population, would become unstable. The order established among the oligarchs under the Putin regime might collapse if they were forced to fight against one another to maintain a growing flow of wealth in the face of stagnation or decline in the total inflow. That would likely unleash a struggle among various groups and classes in Russia. Such a development might enable the Russian working class, which has so far been unable to affect the course Russia's post-Soviet development, to again step onto the stage of history as an active force in determining Russia's future.

References

Bettelheim, Charles. 1976. *Class Struggles in the USSR*, volumes 1 and 2. New York: Monthly Review Press.

Connolly, Richard. 2009. "Financial Vulnerabilities in Russia." *Russian Analytical Digest*, No. 65, October 6, 2–6.

Desai, Padma. 2010. "Russia's Financial Crisis: Economic Setbacks and Policy Responses." *Journal of International Affairs*, 63(2), Spring–Summer, 141–151.

Federal State Statistics Service. Various years. *Russia in Figures: Statistical Handbook.* Moscow, Federal State Statistics Service. Recent years available at http://www.gks.ru/wps/wcm/connect/rosstat_main/rosstat/en/main/.

Gaddy, Clifford G. and Barry W. Ickes. 2010. "Russia after the Global Financial Crisis." *Eurasian Geography and Economics*, 51(3), 281–311.

International Monetary Fund. Various years. *Economic Review: Russian Federation.* Washington, DC: The International Monetary Fund.

International Monetary Fund World Economic Outlook Database. 2013. Available at http://www.imf.org/external/pubs/ft/weo/2013/01/weodata/index.aspx.

Kotz, David M. 2013. "Can China's Rise Continue?" *China Policy Review*, in Chinese, November. (An English language version is available from the author on request.)

Kotz, David M. 2015. *The Rise and Fall of Free-Market Capitalism.* Cambridge, MA: Harvard University Press.

Kotz, David M. and Fred Weir. 2007. *Russia's Path from Gorbachev to Putin: The Demise of the Soviet System and the New Russia.* London and New York: Routledge.

Resnick, Stephen A. and Richard D. Wolff. 2002. *Class Theory and History: Capitalism and Communism in the USSR.* New York and London: Routledge.

Sutela, Pekka. 2010. Russia's Response to the Global Financial Crisis. *Carnegie Endowment for International Peace Policy Outlook*, July 29, available at http://carnegieendowment.org/files/russia_crisis.pdf.

World Bank. 2005. *From Transition to Development: A Country Economic Memorandum for the Russian Federation.* March, Washington, DC: The World Bank.

World Bank. 2013. "World Development Indicators." Available at http://data.worldbank.org/datacatalog/worlddevelopmentindicators.

Zhu, Andong and David M. Kotz. 2011. "The Dependence of China's Economic Growth on Exports and Investment," *Review of Radical Political Economics.* Special Issue on "China and Global Capital Accumulation," 43(1), Winter, 9–32.

Chapter 10
Latin America and the Epochal Crisis of Capitalism

Luis Arizmendi and Gordon Welty

Introduction

This chapter examines the impact of globalization and the global capitalist crisis on Latin America. Globalization and neoliberalism proved a potent force from the 1970s to 2008. Together they were the watchwords of global capital around the world. They will prove crucial to our discussion of their impact on Latin America. Because of space considerations we are limited here to focus our attention on five countries in Latin America—Bolivia, Brazil, Ecuador, Mexico and Venezuela. We will present a model of post-neoliberal society and state in Latin America that suggests that there are four types or trends in these societies and states in terms of their response to neoliberalism, and thereby their response to globalization and the global capitalist crisis. Three of these four trends are what we call the *post-neoliberal trend*, which is characterized by anti-imperialist ideologies and practices: the *specific post-neoliberal trend*, where the societies and states act in a contradictory but promisingly counter-hegemonic anti-imperialist and anti-capitalist way; the *circumscribed or moderate post-neoliberal trend*, which seeks substantial state intervention but not the complete rejection of neoliberalism; and the *ambiguous post-neoliberal trend*, which is characterized by a deep and ongoing struggle between anti-neoliberal tendencies and neoliberal tendencies. Finally, confronting the previous three trends, there is a *neo-authoritarian trend*, which is actively opposed to post-neoliberalism and develops a capitalist configuration that is increasingly violent.In our focus on countries of Latin America, we argue that Mexico, for example, illustrates the neo-authoritarian trend. Moreover, we argue that Brazil, for another example, illustrates the circumscribed or moderate post-neoliberal trend. Finally, we argue that Bolivia, Ecuador, and Venezuela, for further examples, illustrate the specific post-neoliberal trend.

The Epochal Crisis of Capitalism and Latin America

Governments emerged in Latin America in the late 1990s whose programs questioned, with more or less scope, the neoliberal State. These governments included those led by Hugo Chavez in Venezuela (1998), followed by Lula in

Brazil (2003), Nestor Kirchner in Argentina (2003), Vazquez in Uruguay (2005), Evo Morales in Bolivia (2006), Manuel Zelaya in Honduras (2006), Rafael Correa in Ecuador (2007), Fernando Lugo in Paraguay (2008), Mauricio Funes in El Salvador (2009) and Ollanta Humala in Peru (2011). Cristina Fernández, José Mujica and Dilma Rousseff, respectively, continued governments already initiated in Argentina, Uruguay and Brazil.

Thus, Latin America became the first region of the world where cynical capitalism—a historical formation of increasingly violent anti-liberal capitalism (see Bourdieu, 1998; Hinkelammert, 1998; also Douzinas, 2013) –had once been established. Two and a half decades later, this also became the first region to try to explore the construction of an interstate alliance, the Union of South American Nations (UNASUR), to define the historical identity of Latin America according to anti-imperialism that nurtured the *rapport de forces* against the "neoliberal" state. States that can arguably be characterized as specifically post-neoliberal include Ecuador, Venezuela and Bolivia (since they manifest both genuinely anti-imperialist state initiatives and a certain post-capitalist potentiality), while Brazil, Argentina and Uruguay can be characterized as states that display a circumscribed or limited post-neoliberalism (if this term is understood as suggesting certain state interventions to confront the destructive dynamics of capital accumulation, which, however, either do not fully reject "neoliberalism" but limit it); leaving Guatemala, El Salvador and Nicaragua in a situation of ambiguous post-neoliberal states (where an anti-neoliberal trend and another neoliberal trend are struggling with one another without either able to define the outcome).

Tearing through Latin America, due to the hegemonic domination the US seeks to maintain in the region, a neoauthoritarian trend confronts and opposes the post-neoliberal trend. It moves in exactly the opposite direction, striving to take more and more aggressive steps that lead the violence of global capitalism beyond that which has produced the historical cynicism. Finally, Colombia, Honduras, and above all Mexico are the three states that manifest the neoauthoritarian trend in response to the epochal crisis of capitalism in Latin America. These differentiating trends cannot be identified with one another, despite having some points of convergence in the post-neoliberal dynamic. It can be argued that two intersections—two pairs of crossroads—are juxtaposed that characterize the complex situation in Latin America in the early twenty-first century.

First, the liberal trend and neoauthoritarian trend collide at a crossroads while disputing the redefinition of contemporary capitalism. The liberal trend—a trend imparting new forms of liberalism—recognizes that the offensive launched by cynical capitalism has gone too far and, with the aim of strategically containing the class struggle, strives to build, at least to some extent, a "liberal state" of the twenty-first century. The neoauthoritarian trend will not relinquish the enormous wealth and surplus value gained for capitalist domination through its historical cynicism. (Arizmendi, 2011a, 2011b) This trend opposes the twenty-first century liberalism and escalates, even radicalizes, through the exercise of destructive political violence, the capitalist offensive in the class struggle and with the power of the authoritarian state. (Echeverria, 1998: 94–106; Horkheimer, 2006) Second, at this juncture, these trends are facing each other striving to reconfigure modern capitalism with competing conceptions of the state itself: the authoritarian state and the "liberal state" as a historical response, opposite one to the other, that can manage and traverse the contemporary global crisis of capital. No region synthesizes like Latin America the complexity of this pair of crossroads as it manifests itself in the epochal crisis of capitalist globalization in the twenty-first century.

Mexico: Global Subordination as a New Form of Center/ Periphery Subordination

Global subordination—a new historical configuration of the center/periphery subordination—constitutes a form of domination established to counter the economic crisis of advanced capitalism. (Boltvinik and Arizmendi, 2007: 49–50; Arizmendi, 2012a) And, all the more, this constitutes the historical outcome which the *secular trend* of advanced capitalism has sought: defeat the protective barriers of peripheral capitalism in favor of capitals that stand at the vanguard of the technological revolutions taking place in the world economy. By the second decade of the twenty-first century, Mexico has become the prototype of the new form of global center/periphery subordination.

The classic configuration center/periphery subordination makes up a power relationship wherein a struggle unfolds. Confronted by, and opposed to the technological might of metropolitan capitalism, the capitalism of the periphery instituted a pair of protective monopolies advanced on its exceptionally rich strategic natural resources and its exceptionally cheap labor power, on behalf of their nation states. These protective monopolies sought to defend public goods in the peripheral state—factors in the national interest rather than in merely privatized interests—against imperialist incursions. However, advanced capitalism has imposed its economic dominion—derived from its monopoly on technology—to snatch away, again and again, huge transfers of wealth and surplus value from the periphery. *Technological rent* is the term that best describes the systematic imposition of tribute that peripheral nations must pay to the capitalism of the center, due to the technological supremacy that the latter holds in the world economy.

One of the international financial arrangements that best represents the attempt to achieve the ultimate victory of technological rent is the Brady Plan—named after Nicholas Brady, the US Secretary of the Treasury. Based on it, during the last decade of the twentieth century, advanced capitalism attacked the peripheral nations of the former Third World as well as those of the former Second World.

In Latin America, in principle, Argentina, Brazil, Ecuador, Mexico, Panama, Peru, Uruguay and Venezuela were the states subjected to the offensive that sought to bring the secular trend of technological rent to its ultimate conclusion. But economic history is not destiny. So, depending on the historical responses of these states, responses that were very different and even conflicting, highly contrasting results were generated.

As a result of the debt cycle of the seventies and early eighties, the most indebted states restructured their external debts through the International Monetary Fund (IMF) between 1990 and 1996, turning the debts into bonds that were placed in international capital markets. Banks got rid of their bad debts with the birth of a bond market where, rather than having high returns, the external debt was restructured by implementing aggressive programs of pro-market reforms and privatization of strategic public enterprises. In other words, precisely the historical function of the Brady Plan with so-called "emerging markets" was to start the process of establishing the foundation of global subordination of the periphery to the center.

As can be seen in Table 10.1, the Brady Plan focused on about 175 billions of dollars; no region received more capital than Latin America, and, within it, only Brazil was above Mexico, which was the first country to sign. A real feedback mechanism developed, as the cycle of debt triggered the genesis of global subordination, but the global subordination, far from overcoming the debt cycle, actually exacerbated the cycle of indebtedness. Its functionality carried the global subordination farther and farther—if in 1990 Mexico received 20 percent of the financial capital of the Brady Plan, in 2008, Mexico was one of three countries, along with Colombia and Poland, that exceptionally were granted an IMF loan for an amount equivalent to a thousand times the quota from that organization.

The peculiarity of the new form of global subordination of the periphery to the center is that with it emerges an internal domination over the core of strategic sectors of the national economy, an internal domination that aims to integrate the structure for long-term subordination.

Regarding the strategic cores of the productive sector, it is obvious that Mexico, which has never excelled in production technology, has brought the capital goods industry to the worst crisis in its history through the privatization of strategic state enterprises that, precisely, had operated as a driving force for the development of the capital goods industry. The horizontal technological dismantling of the Mexican economy through its vertical technological articulation with transnational accumulation was the first expression of economic restructuring imposed by the "neoliberal" regime in Mexico. This resulted in the formation of an *unchecked strategic technological dependence*, namely, the emergence of a state that had abandoned any attempt at self-determination over national technological development.

The global subordination of the strategic core of production has radically reversed the historically protective monopoly over strategic oil and gas in Mexico. In the early twenty-first century, it has become clear that Mexico has one of the most important reserves of both oil and gas in the world. The global subordination of Mexican energy supplies becomes palpably functional for the new form of subordination of periphery to the center: through it, US capitalism is assured

Table 10.1 The Brady Plan: Countries that issued bonds in debt swap with commercial banks

Country	Year	Nominal value of bonds (billions of dollars)	Percentage of total
Brazil	1994	51.3	29
Mexico	1990	35.6	20
Argentina	1993	24.8	14
Venezuela	1990	15.8	9
Ecuador	1995	6.3	4
Peru	1996	4.2	2
Panama	1996	2.9	2
Uruguay	1991	1.1	1
Costa Rica	1990	0.6	0
Dominican Republic	1994	0.5	0
Latin America		143.1	82
Poland	1994	7.1	4
Russia	1993	6.4	4
Bulgaria	1994	4.6	3
Philippines	1990	3.9	2
Morocco	1990	2.8	2
Nigeria	1992	2.1	1
Ivory Coast	1997	2.0	1
Croatia	1996	1.5	1
Jordan	1993	0.7	0
Vietnam	1997	0.5	0
Slovenia	1996	0.2	0
Others		31.8	18
Total		174.9	100

Source: Database from *Global Development Finance*, elaborated by Mario Rapoport and Noemí Brenta, *Las grandes crisis del capitalismo contemporáneo* (ed.). Capital Intellectual, Argentina, 2010, p. 76.

dominion over and direct exploitation of strategic energy deposits in Mexico, but the workings of the anti-crisis mechanism of the US economy is also transferred to and exacerbates the effects of the crisis in Mexico.

Since the presidency of Carlos Salinas (1988–94), the emergence of Mexico as a prototype of the global subordination has imposed an aggressive strategic deindustrialization of Pemex as the basis of a colossal transfer of petroleum rents from Mexico to the US. Integrating a grotesque circuit of accumulation unilaterally favorable to the US, Mexico is the only oil country in the world that imports gasoline. Intentionally Pemex does not invest in petrochemicals (simply because the US state does not allow it), and exports cheap oil to the US. Therefore Mexico is embedded in a vicious cycle that leads to an unending importation of expensive gasoline from the US. Among the oil countries, Venezuela has 24 refineries, Japan has 31, Russia has 41, China has 51, USA has 131, while Mexico, as a result of the strategic deindustrialization of Pemex, *has only 6*.

Along with the enormous transfer of petroleum rents to private capital due to strategic deindustrialization, Pemex transfers huge masses of spurious extraordinary profits to private capital based on a process of absolutely unnecessary and artificial indebtedness. Pemex is one of the most profitable companies in the world economy but it has been indebted for an amount equivalent to 96 percent of its assets in order to leverage and ensure, structurally, colossal transfers of petroleum rents to private capital. No company in the history of the world economy has been an object of such inordinate indebtedness as Pemex.

In early 2014, the Coalition of Petroleum Workers reported that even before the adoption of the structural reform of the energy industry in Mexico in late 2013, the comprehensive service contracts for the exploration, development and production of hydrocarbons, signed by PEMEX, gave total control over the operation of wells to private companies. With the fast track approval of energy (counter) reform in 2013, the illegal exploitation of natural gas fields by transnational private capitalism, concealed by the Multiple Service Contracts, has mushroomed. (Saxe Fernandez, 2002: 227–376) It has opened the door wide for the entry of transnational capital, above all the US corporations, to directly access one of the most important strategic reserves of both petroleum and natural gas in the world. In 2013, Pemex announced the discovery of a deepwater mega oil field in the Gulf of Mexico, 180 km from the eastern coast of Tamaulipas, with a potential of 4 to 10 million barrels of crude oil. The Gulf of Mexico is becoming recognized as one of the largest reserves of oil in the world. At the same time, the Secretary of Energy has confirmed that "Mexico is the fourth world power in terms of reserves of shale gas."[1] The rating that Citigroup has extended to North America as the "New Middle East" in the world is no coincidence.

Pemex of Mexico has become the prototype of global subordination of the periphery to the center in a sense precisely contrary to the post-neoliberal trend in Latin America, where PDVSA of Venezuela and Petroecuador of Ecuador are entirely strategic state enterprises, even in contrast to a state like Colombia that has control over 88 percent of Ecopetrol. Mexico has been defeated regarding its classic nationalism that it had maintained throughout most of the twentieth century. In the twenty-first century Mexico has become an open country for an unprecedented transnational mastery of its strategic energy riches based on Pax Americana, without the necessity of asymmetric warfare.

In Mexico during the twenty-first century, the global subordination has also dramatically impacted the strategic core of food production and food reproduction for the nation. Just as with Pemex, the Mexican countryside has also become the object of strategic and aggressive underfunding. During the phase of the global

1 Secretary of Energy (SENER) of México, http://www.energia.gob.mx/portal/Default.aspx?id=2111.

food economy from the 1930s to the 1970s, Mexico maintained food sovereignty, principally in maize.

This has shifted, under contemporary capitalism, to the development of a delicate strategic food subordination. While from below, the Mexican countryside was the subject of an aggressive strategic underfunding that struck at national food self-sufficiency, from above, there was a growing openness to imports of food produced in the US, in even greater quantities than those originally stipulated by the NAFTA agreements. The outcome has shattered the "neoliberal" illusion that food sovereignty would be better replaced by comparative advantage, presumably because Mexicans would then have access to imported foodstuffs at much lower prices than it would cost to produce them internally.

However, global subordination has imposed on the Mexican countryside a drastic turn: according to USDA data, from the early eighties, Mexico has gone from a rate of 10 percent of imports of foodstuffs that are required for the social reproduction of the nation, up to 40 percent in the present day. By 2020, imports of hard grains (corn, sorghum, barley, rye and oats), could become more than 60 percent. The US estimates that by 2025, Mexico may depend almost 50 percent on the import of maize. The global subordination of the periphery to the center has impacted food reproduction in Mexico to such an extent that, according to the Food and Agriculture Organization (FAO), the country ranked as 3rd place in the importation of cereals and 4th in the importation of oilseed in the world. No doubt, global subordination generates an increasing food vulnerability of Mexico in the face of the contemporary global capitalist crisis.

Turning to the financial services sector, it can be clearly seen that, despite the massive bailout of banks made by the Mexican government through Fobaproa (Fondo Bancario de Protección al Ahorro), at present, 95 percent of the banking system is controlled by foreign firms. In Mexico, in the early nineties, only one foreign bank, Citibank, was authorized to operate in the local market, participating with less than 1 percent of total loans. After NAFTA, and even more after the 1995 banking crisis, the share of foreign banks grew rapidly to cover almost the entire Mexican banking system. As an economic mechanism for huge transfers of resources abroad, based on consumer loans with very high interest rates well above that apply to those foreign central banks in their countries of origin, in "neoliberal" twenty-first century Mexico, the bank does not provide credit to production or national techno-economic development; it is not a development bank. Rather, its function is ensuring the support of financial services to deepen the global subordination of the periphery to the center.[2]

Configured as a prototype of the new form of global subordination of the periphery to the center leaves Mexico exposed and highly vulnerable to the epochal crisis of capitalism of the twenty-first century. The subordination of its strategic energy deposits to transnational capital and the over-exploitation of one

2 Arthur Romo Guillén (2000) has developed a robust analysis of the impact of "neoliberalism" on the financial sector of the Mexican economy.

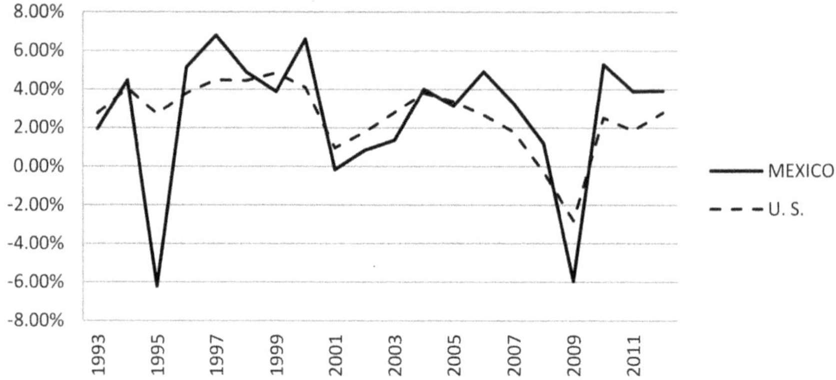

Figure 10.1 Annual growth rate of real GDP of US and Mexico, 1993–2011
Source: US = WORLD DATA BANK. MEXICO = INEGI, CONAPO, SHCP, SE, BANXICO, BDINEGI (elaborated by César Onofre).

of the cheapest labor forces in the world economy, along with the "neoliberal" subordination of the food reproduction of the nation and the foreign ownership of banks, have integrated in Mexico a set of channels of capitalist accumulation with extraordinary profits. Positioning the country in the worst political situation in Latin America, the global subordination in Mexico rapidly generated billionaires,[3] but at the price of transferring the costs of the contemporary crisis of the process of capital accumulation onto the processes of vital reproduction of the nation.

As shown in Figure 10.1, being the prototype of global subordination also leaves Mexico extremely exposed to the vagaries of economic cycles of the US such as that exhibited during the capitalist crisis of 2008. As confirmed especially for the years from 1995 to 2009, the fall in GDP in the US generates a multiplier effect in Mexico, which experienced a fall of -6 percent GDP. The abandonment of the project of economic and political sovereignty has created a high vulnerability of the social reproduction of the nation to the dynamics of capitalist globalization.

As extremely serious as this may be, this is not all. The inclusion of Mexico in the circuits of the criminal economy as one of the most powerful channels of the global accumulation of capital in the twenty-first century, is the most dramatic result of the crisis of the national project that has resulted in a new form of global subordination of the periphery to the center. Along with the birth of NAFTA, Mexican capitalism moved towards the creation of what may be called a *narco-political capitalism* (Arizmendi, 2012b: 31–34)—that is, towards the remodeling of capitalist accumulation that articulates with the criminal economy in alliance with the political class in all levels, including the federal government. But, during

3 The aggressive social recomposition of the Mexican ruling class, which redistributed the economic power of capital and produced the ranking billionaires of the world is analyzed by Jorge Zepeda Patterson (2007).

the second half of the twentieth century, Mexican capitalism has gone further with the formation of aggressive *necro-political capitalism* (see Fromm, 1973; Mbembé, 2003; Giroux, 2006; also Arizmendi, 2013: 129–134)—a form of capitalism in which the drug cartels make continuous use of terror as a basis for a decadent power. These cartels have literally enslaved migrant laborers in the southern part of Mexico to prevent their arrival at the northern border with the US; they have depopulated areas that contain strategic natural resources; and, they develop new and diverse sources of what may be called *criminal rent*. In addition to the extraordinary profits that attend the production and distribution of drugs and the trafficking in women, the necro-polítical capitalism has imposed, in certain areas under their control, the illegal payment of tribute for movement of goods and people. The intensification of the destructive political violence of necro-political capitalism in Mexico, as the historical form appropriate to the neoauthoritarian tendency in the twenty-first century, gives a decadent configuration to the class struggle in Mexico today.

Brazil: Circumscribed Post-neoliberalism and Subimperialism

At the start of post-neoliberal trend in Latin America, Brazil and Argentina seemed to stand at the head of the line, seemingly putting forward the project of a genuine liberal state for the twenty-first century. However, Brazil soon showed a deep ambivalence in its response to the historical cynicism arising from the *rapport de forces* in the class struggle, both nationally and globally.

There have been two fundamental differences, above all, that separate Brazil from the "neoliberal" trend that (given the Brady Plan, as in the case with Mexico) points towards the integration with the new form of global subordination: 1) the partial but effective configuration of liberalism in Brazil that has taken shape as a counterweight to the devastation created by the capitalist state, and 2) the resolute refusal by Brazil to be absorbed under the new form of subordination of the periphery to the center. This has been supported by Brazil's advancing initiatives such as the regional integration in South America, the reorienting of its international alliances toward China, using it as a counterweight to the US, and the relaunching of Brazil's project of establishing a regional subimperial state.

Perhaps the dimension which is more properly liberal has been the configuration of the Brazilian state, put forward by Lula Da Silva, that is concerned with the fight against hunger. The strategic objective of this configuration is to establish a protective measure against the global food crisis. Three coordinates intersect within this liberal role of the state: 1) Brazil has explicitly proposed to respond to the global food crisis by seeking to tap its huge output of cereals, primarily soybeans, to position itself as one of the main granaries of the world; 2) Brazil is a country in which 83 percent of the agricultural units are family farms. The Brazilian government has redirected its food purchases from food corporations to reinforce peasant production, and over the first decade of the twenty-first century, invested

2.7 billion *reales* in buying 2.6 million tons of food from domestic farmers. Even more notable was that 3) Brazil stimulated rural domestic industry, using it as a platform for the Zero Hunger Program, establishing stable prices for products to guarantee the supply of subsidized food to people living in food insecurity, people in hospitals, those in prisons, and to cover the school feeding programs. In sharp contrast to Mexico, the project of the liberal state in Brazil took place prior to the food crisis of the twenty-first century, funding peasant production of quality foods to give support to the struggle against food and nutritional insecurity. (Rosero, Carbonell, and Regalado, 2011: 25).

In order to resist—against the hegemony of the US—joining the global subordination and to counteract the external debt trap, Brazilian capitalism has reoriented its processes of reproduction and accumulation of capital with China. On the one hand, as shown in Table 10.2, since the last decade of the twentieth century but even more during the first decade of the twenty-first century, Latin America and the Caribbean have played a central role for Chinese exports, and are more than double the average Chinese exports to the other regions of the world.

Table 10.2 Average annual growth of Chinese exports by partners, 1990–2009

Regions\period	1990–1995	1995–2000	2000–2005	2005–2009
Latin America and the Caribbean	32.2	17.8	26.8	26.1
Asia-Pacific	26.5	9.3	20.3	11.6
US	36.7	16.1	25.6	10.2
European Union	26.3	15.0	28.8	14.9
Rest of World	8.6	7.1	26.6	14.3
World	19.1	10.9	25.0	13.4

Source: CEPAL, 2010. See Marcelo Dias Carcanholo and Alexis Saludjian, 2013: 57.

On the other hand, as shown in Figure 10.2, China has used its relationship with South America to drive what may be called the reprimarization of several South American economies. Between 1985 and 2009, given the joint growth of capitalist reproduction processes, China has prompted a shift, with exports of manufactured goods from South America declining from almost 70 percent to less than 10 percent, while during the same period, the exports of primary commodities from South America has risen from just over 30 percent to almost 90 percent.

But, as shown in Figure 10.3, also between 1985 and 2009, Brazil has changed the dynamics of its exports to South America: whereas at the end of the twentieth century the amount of Brazilian exports of primary commodities were very nearly the same as the exports of manufactured goods, in the twenty-first century the exports of manufactured goods have grown dramatically.

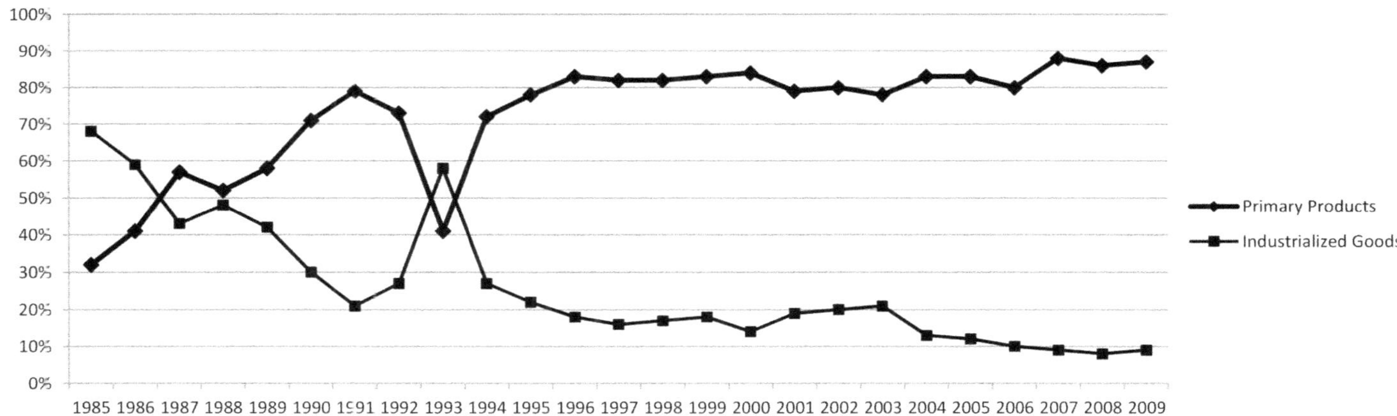

Figure 10.2 Exports from South America to China by type of product and technological level, 1985–2009
Source: UN-COMTRADE. See Marcelo Dias Carcanholo and Alexis Saludjian, 2013: 55.

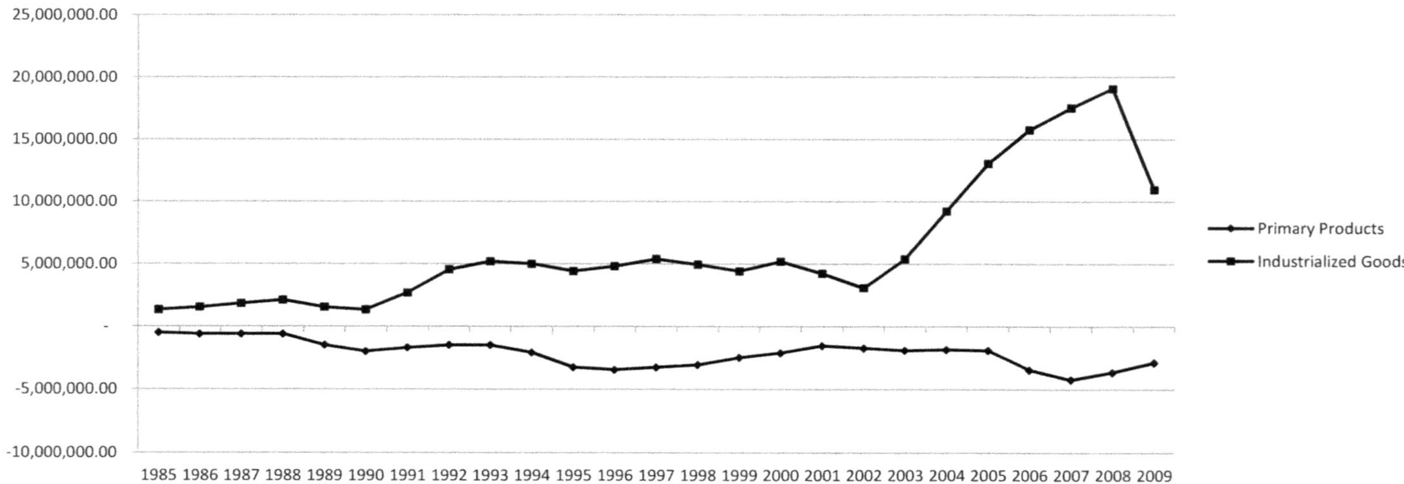

Figure 10.3 Exports from Brazil to South America, 1985–2009

Source: UN-COMTRADE. See Marcelo Dias Carcanholo and Alexis Saludjian, 2013: 60.

In the first decade of the twenty-first century, Brazilian capitalism has relaunched its project of *regional sub-empire*. Building upon a profound analysis of the concept of *subimperialism*, Ruy Mauro Marini (1977) has shown that it corresponds to a project of peripheral capitalism, whereby although the extent of technological productive forces lack the economic capacity to compete for global hegemony, the relatively greater development of the aspiring subimperialism, given the even more limited set of capitalist states that surround it, allows it to become the dominant power in the geo-historical space of a given region. In this sense, sub-imperialism is characterized by conforming to some extent to an international division of labor within a certain region of the world around it, which allows it to extract a technological rent from countries over which it exerts its relative economic power. While all peripheral capitalisms pay a tribute to the advanced capitalist states in the world economy, subimperial peripheral capitalism requires payment of a certain *regional technological rent*.

This explains the ambivalence of Brazil towards the historical cynicism. In principle, Brazilian capitalism exerts a "neoliberal" policy to some degree, towards the countries over which it exercises a certain subordination. Although it is no longer valid to say "wherever Brazil leans, so leans Latin America"—a formula expressed by Henry Kissinger to stress the role of the Brazilian military dictatorship in regional geopolitics—the strength of the geopolitics of anti-imperialism in Venezuela contrasts strikingly with the ambiguity of Brazil that, rather than naively submit to the US, underpins its commitment to its regional subimperial project. In 2013, influenced by the possibility of a geopolitical alliance with the US and the possibility of a permanent seat in the Security Council of the UN (even ahead of Japan, Germany and India who retain their seats only as non-permanent members), Brazil behaved ambiguously in relation to the regional integration projects, UNASUR and Mercosur. Not only that, and this is essential, Brazil is practicing a preventive policy to intervene in the *rapport de forces* of global geopolitics to protect its huge deepwater oil reserve—a reserve that has led to the statement that, in the twenty-first century, "God is Brazilian." But indeed the Brazilian subimperial project fosters chronic geopolitical tension within the regional unity.

While it may be characterized as circumscribed or limited in its historical setting as a post-neoliberal state, however, it was enough for Brazil to not fall into the feedback mechanism between debt cycle and the genesis of the new form of global subordination of the periphery to the center. As can be seen in Figure 10.4, which is based on moving averages of five years, comparing the evolution of the economies of the US and South America (Brazil, Uruguay, Argentina, Colombia, Chile, and Bolivia), it is evident that until the mid-nineties, cycles of debt caused a certain parallelism between them, but the post-neoliberal trend broke that parallelism in the first decade of the twenty-first century, polarizing on the one hand with the road towards the big crisis of 2007–08 for the US, while on the other hand South America moved toward a process of economic recovery and overcoming the debt trap.

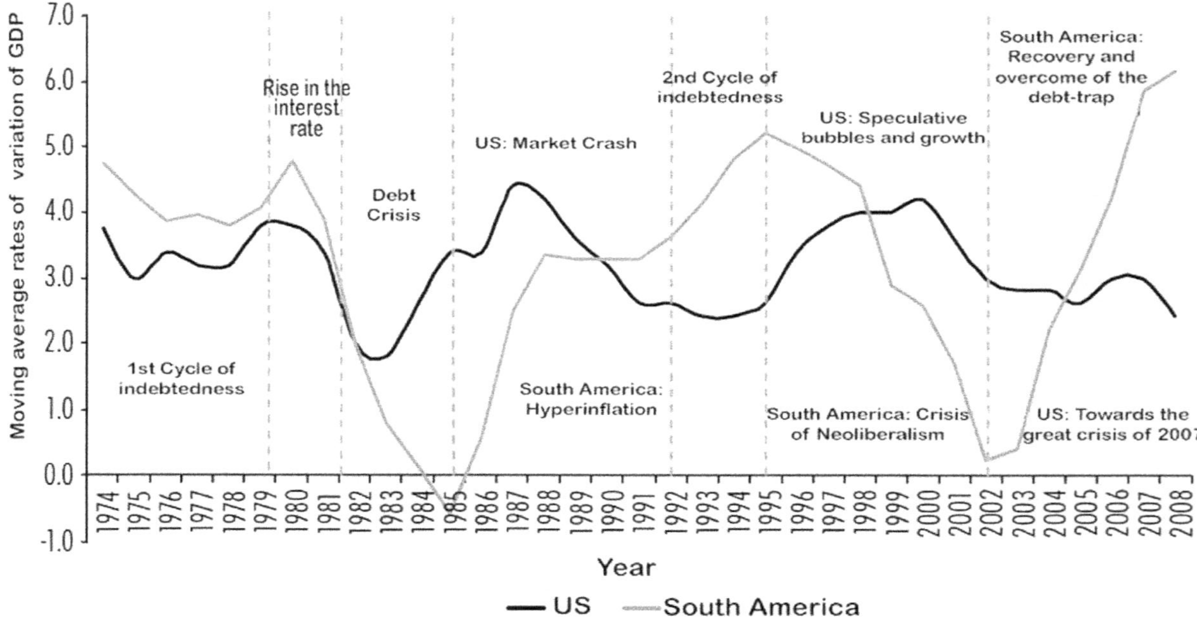

Figure 10.4 Comparison between economic cycles of US and South America, 1974–2008

Source: Database from *Global Development Finance*, elaborated by Mario Rapoport and Noemí Brenta, *Las grandes crisis del capitalismo contemporáneo* (ed.). Capital Intelectual, Argentina, 2010: 216.

However, despite its effective resistance against being incorporated, as Mexico has been, into global subordination, a huge limitation emerging from the circumscribed Brazilian post-neoliberalism is that it has no anti- or transcapitalist foundation, i.e. no basis from which to reject and transcend modern capitalism and to create an alternative to it. Thus *circumscribed post-neoliberalism not only is not synonymous with the direction of post-capitalism, it is a rejection of it.*

Along those lines we should understand the position of Brazil in the twenty-first century as the largest extractive economy in South America. In 2011, Brazil extracted more than 410 million tons of its major minerals (bauxite, coal, copper, iron, lead, tin, and zinc), while all other South American countries extracted just over 147 million tons. Brazil extracted mineral resources to an extent practically tripling the total of the other South American countries taken together: Argentina, Bolivia, Chile, Colombia, Ecuador, Guyana, Peru, Surinam, and Venezuela.

Of course, the vast devastation of the environment that capitalist accumulation in Brazil has caused is not limited to mining, but also occurs on a grand scale in agriculture and petrochemicals. The destructive course of the fossil fuel technoenergy industry has not stopped, despite unprecedented global overheating and the lessons manifested in the "accident" to the BP platform in the Gulf of Mexico in 2010. Brazilian capitalism is fully engaged in the era of "climate chaos." It is not going to stop searching for a huge petroleum rent derived from its enormous deepwater oil deposits. Similarly, Brazil has the greatest extractive agriculture in the region. It is ranked first in the global production and export of soybeans. In the 2011–12 harvest, Brazil produced more than 66 million metric tons, followed by Argentina with only 40 million.

Both these countries have become subordinated to the avariciousness of Monsanto and its complementary products, the transgenic crops and the herbicides. This extractive agriculture has required a huge increase in crop area, surpassing 24 million hectares. Far from responding to the possibility of modernization through alternative technology, the short-term extractivism of Brazilian capitalism determines its own weakness.

From Marini's conceptualization of subimperialism, one can understand the illusory nature of those geopolitical assessments that suggest that Brazil can be a contender in the race for global hegemony. Undoubtedly, its strategic alliances with Asia are relevant to the geopolitics of the twenty-first century, but they also respond to its project as a regional subimperialism. Thus the circumscribed post-neoliberalism of Brazil is based not on an anti-imperialist strategic project of an alternative national techno-economic development, but in the historical reprimarization of economic dynamics.

Post-neoliberalism and Transcapitalism: Ecuador, Venezuela, and Bolivia

Although it is inappropriate to characterize it as the historical realization of "Socialism of the Twenty-First Century"—a name appropriated from a myth of progress derived from the perspective of "liberation theology"—undoubtedly the scope of the projects of the state put forward by Ecuador, Venezuela and Bolivia are still substantial, because in these nations there is a tendency for post-neoliberalism and anti-capitalism that seeks not only to reconfigure capitalism in an anti-imperialist way, but actually to cast a challenge, achieving several victories and advances in their struggle to build alternative social order that are anti- and trans-capitalist.

The Sumak Kawsay Model (Good Living Model) of Rafael Correa,[4] the Communitarian Socialism of Hugo Chavez and the Andean Capitalism of Evo Morales—much more self-conscious of appropriate names at this stage of their project of historical social transformation—undoubtedly involve projects of another social order and a proper reconfiguration appropriate to the anti- and post-neoliberal state. Their historical force makes Latin America the only region of the world in which gradual but real alternatives are projected aginst the epochal crisis of capitalism of the twenty-first century.

To assess the full realization of the historical significance of post-neoliberalism in Ecuador, Venezuela and Bolivia demands that we account for the correlation and the contradictions between two trends that constitute important initiatives at each opening of new historical frontiers, especially when they tend to converge: the counter-hegemonic trend and the transcapitalist trend.

In order to recognize what is at stake in the counter-hegemonic post-neoliberalism project of these Latin American states, it is extremely important to emphasize that not only do they oppose this or that particular hegemon, but also the historical trend derived from the exercise of global hegemony in the twenty-first century. Demonstrating that it is possible to focus upon and to produce historical trajectories that are vigorously opposed to the new form of overall subordination of the periphery to the center and the tendency to extract a technological rent, the specifically post-neoliberal States have built a resistance—and even advanced a countercurrent—to the tendency of turn of the century capitalism to integrate and underpin what may be called a global proto-state. Looking to modify the *rapport de forces* in the global class struggle, they have demonstrated that another history is viable and feasible.

The trend towards the extraction of technological rent invariably accompanies the tendency to the formation of a global proto-state. Far from turning in on itself to form a kind of minimal state—that is a state that minimizes its intervention in the contemporary economy—state capitalism characterizes itself precisely to intensify the violent mode of its intervention in the economy. *Laissez faire, laissez passer* is a maxim that is by no means synonymous with the minimal state; rather, it corresponds to the conversion of the historical reality called "freedom of the market" to that which underpins global power in our era. Suspending

4 The name of the *Sumak Kawsay* project in Ecuador comes from the Quechua; it refers not to a "better life," not to a life that is "better than the others," or to a life that is continuously improving, but simply to a good life.

and snatching the sovereignty of peripheral states is nothing but a premise for what ends up being their refunctionalization as institutions at the service of the offensive of global capital against the vital reproduction of the peripheral nations themselves. Ensuring the "free play of market forces" is rather the exercise of anonymous-economic violence of global capitalist accumulation, requiring—to a greater or lesser extent, but undeniably—the exercise of political-destructive violence by the state system. The tendency to destroy the protective monopolies of peripheral states on behalf of the victory of the monopolies at the forefront of technological revolutions in the world economy, not only means that peripheral states, eroded and defeated, open the direct control of their exceptionally rich production resources and massive direct super-exploitation of their exceptionally cheap workforce by global capital. This also means that this way of turning the set of peripheral states into functional subordinates entails the confirmation, at once unstable but relentless, of a global proto-state.

In the era of the tendency toward the formation of a global proto-state, undoubtedly Ecuador, Venezuela and Bolivia are leading the counter-trend initiatives that propose—not the impossible return to the sovereignty of the nation-state in the style of the old developmentalism—but the struggle for the affirmation and advancement of the self-determination of the state in the sense of national or, better yet, plurinational self-determination. This is unlike the trends in both Mexico and Brazil. In Mexico the reconfiguration of the nation-state as anti-nationalist state reflects the fact that alliances by the political class with the metropolitan power and the dominant class with transnational capital generate a dizzying process of accumulation by dispossession that is also favorable to them. Also, unlike Brazil—where the relaunching of its own project as a subimperial state raises the ambivalence that combines opposition to, and unstable alliances with, the United States—in Ecuador, Venezuela and Bolivia the counter-hegemonic project of the state, in the framework of a *rapport of forces* openly adverse in the global class struggle, would simply be unfeasible and impossible without building alliances with different nationalities that make up their constituencies. Alliances of the state with various nationalities against global capital allow them to integrate a geo-economics and genuinely anti-imperialist regional geopolitics.

One of the major political forces in Ecuador, Venezuela and Bolivia—and this has been instrumental in promoting the massive support received by Correa, and earlier Hugo Chavez and Evo Morales—is the alliance of the urban poor, the semi-urban poor and the rural poor of the nation with the project of a post-neoliberal state. These three states are not advocating—as did the Latin American developmentalism of the last century—that the dominant class to be the primary beneficiary from the super-exploitation of the labor force—exceptionally low paid by a tradition of low system requirements—and the over-exploitation of the exceptionally rich natural resources of the country. Rather, as a counterpoint to that of the technological rent, this is the position to deactivate the historically transnational over-exploitation both of the labor force as well as of the country's own strategic natural resources. This march to counteract the global power of technological rent has realized itself in defending the historical-moral dimension of the process of reproduction of diverse nationalities and the internal use of the income from strategic natural resources. This is an historical reconfiguration of capitalism that resists and reverses the power of the transnationals, setting in place, to the greatest extent possible, the self determination of the state and the self determination of indigenous communities.

This involves resisting and reversing the super-exploitation of the workforce by establishing conditions, gradually but effectively, for improving the standard of living and the quality of the vital reproduction processes of their societies, by utilizing the petroleum rents or the rents from other strategic minerals—all snatched away to transnational capital. This involves making use of the various sources of ground rent in the struggle against the global power of technological rent; promoting the sovereignty of the post-neoliberal state in alliance with the entire nation or rather, with its diverse nationalities—that is the historical sense of the counter-hegemonic trend. A fair assessment of the scope and limits of the state projects of Ecuador, Venezuela and Bolivia can not be made without recognizing that from the depths of the counter-hegemonic trend rises, rightly and above all, the necessity of reversing the trend of capitalist globalization pressing for the victory of technological rent, as well as the state's self-determination over the various sources of ground rent. The counter-hegemonic postneoliberalism directs the states' self-determination regarding the disposition of strategic natural resources towards the struggle for countering the chronic mutilations, imposed by global capitalism, upon the vital reproduction processes of their societies.[5]

In this regard, Ecuador, Venezuela and Bolivia are struggling to project the post-neoliberal state as a real alternative over and against the epochal crisis of capitalism of the twenty-first century. They offer alternatives, of limited but effective scope, against the basis of the world food crisis, the globalization of poverty, the fourth crisis of globalized capitalist overproduction, and the worldwide environmental crisis (Arizmendi, 2010, 2014).

By subordinating the reproduction of foodstuffs of these nations to imports by imposing new channels of accumulation and of extraordinary windfalls through speculation including hunger, the configuration of capitalist accumulation generated a greater vulnerability of the poor to the rise in international food prices: this was one of the triggers of the emergence of the counter postneoliberalism in Latin America (see Vergopoulos, 2011; also Rubio, 2011).

In the case of the counter-hegemonic post-neoliberalism of Venezuela, emphasis must be put on three other converging lines of action with those of Ecuador, which are highly relevant because Venezuela's main strategic vulnerability lies precisely

5 In an incisive essay analyzing the scope of this offensive both in the periphery and the metropolis, James Russell (2014) shows that this economic violence was first unleashed by the Pinochet coup in Chile, which the Bush administration then brought to the US. Mexico is the country that has gone furthest in this regard, imposing aggressive wage reduction scenarios that in Chile required a coup.

in its national food dependency. Surely the petroleum rent has generated a strategic access to wealth, but also an almost totally urban setting of the national population that opens its vulnerable flanks to certain offensives of global capitalism. The fact that the rural population currently constitutes only 6 percent of the total, means that Venezuela faces serious limits to promote food sovereignty. This contrasts with Ecuador and Bolivia, where the rural population corresponds to 32 percent and 33 percent of the total, respectively.

The lines of action of the counter-hegemonic post-neoliberal Venezuelan state towards the global food crisis were: 1) strong containment of speculation in food prices by the transnationals; 2) the post-neoliberal reorganization of food distribution based on administration by the state; and 3) a project of land redistribution and therefore a post-neoliberal modification of the *rapport de forces* in the countryside to boost domestic food production.

In terms of a comparative analysis, arguably the counter-hegemonic post-neoliberal initiatives in Venezuela almost surpassed the programs in Ecuador in terms of these three lines of action, even though Venezuela was far from the conditions of food sovereignty that were possible for Ecuador (see Hidalgo Flor, 2011). In order to configure the counterhegemonic post-neoliberal flow of foodstuffs on a nationwide basis, regarding the post-neoliberal control of transnational corporations, under the leadership of Hugo Chavez, the state not only enacted harsh penalties, but also intervened against foreign companies to prevent speculation amidst soaring food prices. This strategic move strengthened the impact on the flow of foodstuffs to achieve—for 2007 based on the Mission Mercal project—state control of the national distribution of 40 percent of the foodstuffs, which were cheapened to ensure easy access to the population. And, indeed, a very serious step in the counter-hegemonic post-neoliberal food production was advancing redistribution of land amounting to nearly 3.5 million hectares to more than 78,000 small productive units, including the formation of cooperatives—not minifundias—with the prospect of counteracting the enormous food dependency (see Rubio, 2011: 112–113). Now while there is no Venezuelan equivalent to the Ecuadorean "human development bond," the counter-hegemonic configuration of the petroleum rent supports the broad impact of redefinition in the lowering of the system of prices of many commodities for popular consumption. In this sense, ground rents are counter-hegemonically used against the power of technological rent, improving the national social reproduction process. However, because food dependency in Venezuela is structural in nature, this leaves a major strategic vulnerability of the state and therefore, the Venezuelan food economy stands in stark contrast to the food sovereignty of many staples in Ecuador.

In the case of the postneoliberal counter-hegemony of Bolivia, four lines of action should be emphasized that are extremely important for a country that, since 2011—six years into its new historical trajectory—has ceased to be the poorest in South America.[6] The *New Constitution*, adopted in 2009, opens the way for a convergence in an extremely promising way of counter-hegemonic projects and anti-capitalist projects, articulating not only with the right to food, food sovereignty and the peasant economy, but plurinational self-management and the state.

The first line of action was that the Bolivian postneoliberal state responded by defending the plurality of ways that each nationality addressed the global food crisis. In 2008, before the explosion of this crisis, the state immediately designed a Fund for Reconstruction, Food Security and Production Support, channeling $600 million to counter scenarios of shortages and food insecurity (Rubio, 2011: 113). The first line of action to the global food crisis was defensive: it sought to protect food consumption.

The second line of action, equally defensive in character, was to reconfigure the post-neoliberal movement of foodstuffs, movement that remained within the capitalist framework. First, concerning exports governed by profit maximization regardless of food security—profit maximization which has no qualms about generating shortages—the state intervened by establishing limits: only after agricultural outputs have covered the domestic market were quotas assigned to authorize exports. Although there is an ongoing contradiction between corporate capital accumulation and the post-neoliberal state, the state managed to impose effective limits.

The third line of action—extremely important because it takes the initiative in the project of a counter-hegemonic offensive—has made significant progress in post-neoliberal land redistribution for peasant and indigenous communities. Even the strategic objective is to redefine structurally the *rapport de forces* in the class struggle in the countryside, considering that 50 percent of farmland remain under collective ownership and administration. This is a serious project of forming the peasant economy as the foundation of food sovereignty.

Finally, the fourth line of action—extremely promising because it expresses initiatives of the first order of the anti- and transcapitalist project in Bolivia—raises the development of the germinal and aggressive plurinational councils as the foundation of the historic reorganization of state government, making food sovereignty one of the spearheads of "good living." "Andean capitalism," therefore, is a self-conscious expression of the limitations as well as the constituent challenges of the current phase in which the Bolivian project is located.

Conclusion

As can be seen, in Latin America, the counter-hegemonic trend projects its greatest potential when it is able to converge with the transcapitalist trend. Unlike anti-capitalism which is a purely negative order, transcapitalism is a term that

6 See CEPAL, *Panorama Social 2012*, p. 14; also see William Neuman, "Turnabout in Bolivia as Economy Rises from Instability," *NY Times* (February 17, 2014).

serves to clarify that projects of alternative modernities emerge precisely from contemporary struggles, present and future, while the prospect of transcending capitalism necessitates the convergence of all sources of resistance. In the struggle for alternative solutions to counter the impact of the global capitalist crisis in Latin America, indigenous struggles are not struggles to return to the past, but the community in the past has many lessons to offer to the future. These are struggles that must converge with all other social struggles. In the historical-revolutionary struggle to transcend the domination of capitalism, that which is foremost is increasingly the conquering of spaces for the exercise of societal self-determination. This is opposed to neoliberal democracy as simulation—or what is the same, deterrent democracy ("democracia disuasiva")—which uses and abuses the electoral system to marginalize citizens from authentic intervention in decision making.

The communal power project in both rural and urban areas in Venezuela (Barreto Cipriani, 2011), the *Sumak Kawsay* project in Ecuador (Ramírez Gallegos, 2012) and the *Suma Qamaña* project of Bolivia[7] represent projects that, with various forms and scopes, are struggling to make the way for self-management or self-determination as an effective social basis of local and national government. These projects reject and seek to subvert the reduction of government to a *res publica*, i.e. a system of institutions, outside and above society and nationalities, which is limited to managing the modern class struggle in a fashion that is functional to one or another form of capitalism. These projects are seeking to constitute historical alternatives that are, to the extent that they assess new trajectories for the development of self-management in various forms, exploring unusual ways towards a transcapitalist revolution in the twenty-first century.

Of course, within the post-neoliberalism of Venezuela, Ecuador and Bolivia there are political forces that seek to reduce post-neoliberalism to a kind of welfare state project of the twenty-first century. These forces seek, in turn, to block the link between post-neoliberalism and post-capitalism. They are supporting and putting forward a new form of properly liberal capitalist modernity—that is, state intervention as a counterweight to the destructiveness of capitalist accumulation. Certainly, reducing post-neoliberalism to extractive neodevelopmentalism is a threat, potentially effective, in Ecuador, Venezuela, and Bolivia.

However, these political forces are not weakening the counter-hegemonic postneoliberalism that the transcapitalist trend is advancing in Latin America. Although other states around the world also hold firm anti-imperialist positions, their anti-imperialism may be combined with pre-capitalist foundations, which do not open the field of possibilities for the convergence with transcapitalist trends. The challenge of post-neoliberalism in Latin America rests in inventing agreements that address the *rapport de forces* of class struggles nationwide without losing sight

7 *Suma Qamaña* comes from the Aymara, from their ecological-communitarian basis, and refers directly to "good living," to the concrete utopian norm of good society for all with enough internal harmony (see De Marzo, 2010).

of the *rapport de forces* in the global class struggle. The challenge for Ecuador, Venezuela and Bolivia is to open the way for the power of the constituents and self-management in its various forms, advancing these without weakening the state's counter-hegemonic and post-neoliberal configurations. Therein lies the revolutionary potential to turn the global crisis of capitalism in the twenty-first century into a time of opportunity.

References

Aboites, Hugo. 1997. *Viento del Norte*, Plaza y Valdés, México.

Aboites, Hugo. 2012. *La medida de una nación*, UAM, México.

Arizmendi, Luis. 2010. "Concepciones de la pobreza en la fase del colapso del capitalismo neoliberal," *Mundo Siglo XXI*, Num. 21.

Arizmendi, Luis. 2011a. "La crisis epocal del capitalismo en el siglo XXI y sus disyuntivas," *Rebelion.*

Arizmendi, Luis. 2011b. "Crisis epocal del capitalismo y desmercantificación en el siglo XXI" *Horizontes de la vuelta de siglo*, CIECAS, IPN, Mexico.

Arizmendi, Luis. 2012a. "Soberanía económica y desmercantificación como principios estratégicos para un proyecto alternativo de nación," in Armando Bartra (ed.). *Los Grandes Problemas Nacionales*, Itaca, México.

Arizmendi, Luis. 2012b. "Los desafíos de las ciudades latinoamericanas y la modernidad barroca en la vuelta de siglo," *Búsqueda*, Revista del Instituto de Estudios Sociales y Económicos, Universidad Mayor de San Simón, Bolivia.

Arizmendi, Luis. 2013. "Crisis epocal del capitalismo, desafíos y encrucijadas del transcapitalismo," *Nuestra América y EU: Desafíos del siglo XXI*, Centro Internacional de Información Estratégica y Prospectiva/Instituto de Estudios de América, Argentina/Universidad Central de Ecuador.

Arizmendi, Luis. 2014. "Crisis ambiental mundializada y encrucijadas civilizatorias," *Crisis Global y Encrucijadas Civilizatorias*, Fundación Heberto Castillo, México.

Barreto Cipriani, Juan. 2011. *La Comuna, Antecedentes heroicos del gobierno popular*, Ministerio del Poder Popular para la Cultura, Venezuela.

Boltvinik, Julio. 2013. "Para reformar la reforma social neoliberal," *Revista Estado & Comunes*, IAEN, Ecuador.

Boltvinik, Julio and Luis Arizmendi. 2007. "Mundialización de la pobreza, autodeterminación y desarrollo," *Mundo Siglo XXI*, Num. 9, CIECAS, IPN, México.

Bourdieu, Pierre. 1998. "The Myth of 'Globalization' and the European Welfare State," *Acts of Resistance*, Cambridge, UK: Polity Press.

Carcanholo, Marcelo Dias and Alexis Saludjian. 2013. "Integración latinoamericana, dependencia a China y subimperialismo brasileño en América Latina," *Mundo Siglo XXI*, Num. 29, CIECAS, IPN, México.

De Marzo, Guiseppe. 2010. *Buen Vivir, Para una Democracia de la Tierra.* Editores Plural, Bolivia.
Douzinas, Costas. 2013. *Philosophy and Resistance in the Crisis*, Cambridge, UK, Polity Press.
Echeverría, Bolívar. 1998. "Violencia y modernidad," in *Valor de uso y Utopía*, Siglo XXI, Mexico.
Economic Commission for Latin America and Caribbean (CEPAL). 2010. *La República Popular China y América Latina y el Caribe: hacia una relación estratégica*, CEPAL, Santiago.
Fromm, Erich. 1973. *Anatomy of Human Destructiveness*, New York: Holt, Rinehart Winston.
Giroux, Henry. 2006. "Reading Hurricane Katrina: Race, Class, and the Biopolitics of Disposability," *College Literature*, Vol. 33, No. 3.
Harvey, David. 2007. *A Brief History of Neoliberalism*, New York: Oxford University Press.
Hidalgo Flor, Francisco. 2011. "Crisis alimentaria frente a soberanía alimentaria: el caso de Ecuador," *Mundo Siglo XXI*, Num. 26, CIECAS, IPN, México.
Hinkelammert, Franz. 1998. *El grito del sujeto*, San Jose, Costa Rico: Ed. DEI, Ch VI, "El capitalismo cínico y su crítica."
Horkheimer, Max. 2006. *Estado Autoritario*, Itaca, Mexico.
Jalife-Rahme, Alfredo. 2009. *La Desnacionalización de Pemex*, Orfila, Mexico.
Marini, Ruy Mauro. 1977. "La acumulación capitalista mundial y el subimperialismo," *Cuadernos politicos*, Num. 12, CIECAS, IPN, México.
Mbembé, Achille. 2003. "Necropolitics," *Public Culture*, Vol. 15, No. 1.
Ramírez Gallegos, René. 2012. *Socialismo del Sumak Kawsay*, Secretaría Nacional de Educación Superior, Ciencia, Tecnología e Innovación, Ecuador.
Rapoport, Mario, and Noemí Brenta. 2010. *Las grandes crisis del capitalismo contemporáneo*, Ed. Capital Intelectual, Argentina.
Romo Guillén, Arthur. 2000. *México hacia el siglo XXI*, Ed. Siglo XXI, México.
Rosero, Fernando, Karen Albuja Carbonell, and Fabián Regalado. 2011. *Hacia nuevas políticas alimentarias en América Latina y en Europa*, Policy Paper 12, Friedrich Ebert Stiftung.
Rubio, Blanca. 2011. "Soberanía alimentaria vs Dependencia: las políticas frente a la crisis alimentaria en América Latina," *Mundo Siglo XXI*, Num. 26, CIECAS, IPN, México.
Russell, James. 2014. "Expropiación de ahorros de jubilación de América Latina y EU," *Mundo Siglo XXI*, Num. 32, CIECAS, IPN, México.
Sader, Emir. 2009. *El Nuevo Topo: Los Caminos de la Izquierda Latinoamericana*, Editorial Siglo XXI, Argentina.
Saxe Fernandez, John. 2002. *La compra-venta de México*, Plaza & Janes, Mexico.
Vergopoulos, Kostas. 2011. "La crisis alimentaria: la tierra tiembla," *Mundo Siglo XXI*, Num. 26, CIECAS, IPN, México.
Zepeda Patterson, Jorge. 2007. *Los amos de México*, Edamsa, Mexico.

Chapter 11

"Africa Rising" or Africans Uprising? The Impact of the Global Capitalist Crisis on Africa

Patrick Bond

Introduction

The global capitalist crisis somehow passed Africa by, so they say. In contrast, the rest of the world experienced a hugely damaging downturn especially thanks to the outflow of portfolio flows to the "safe" US amidst crashing financial and speculative commodity markets during the second half of 2008, while real economies suffered a sharp rise in unemployment, dramatic slow-down in Gross Domestic Product (GDP) growth, austerity policies and a consequent rise in social unrest. Bank bailouts in 2008–09 and more general monetary profligacy seemed to band-aid the system as a whole, but many countries—e.g. the Portugal, Ireland, Italy, Greece and Spain (PIIGS) and later Cyprus, and in 2013 the "Fragile Five" middle-income economies of South Africa, India, Turkey, Brazil and Indonesia—continued to suffer extreme volatility. But, they say, aside from stagnation in the South and chaos in the North, most of Africa performed brilliantly throughout.

"Those billion Africans have just seen the biggest increase in wealth that the continent's ever experienced," according to London financial researcher Charles Robertson in the 2013 YouTube version of what might be the most extreme case of "Africa Rising" hype, *The Fastest Billion: The Story behind Africa's Economic Revolution.*[1] According to the multinational corporate "Renaissance Capital" team[2] led by Robertson, "Africa's growth could outstrip that of Asia" between now and 2050, with the former's GDP rising "from $2 trillion today to $29 trillion in today's money by 2050." Adds Nigerian finance minister Ngozi Okonjo-Iweala in the book's preface: "Just as Sub-Saharan Africa (SSA) has suffered through its despots and destitution, so the seedlings of transformation have pushed through the African soil. As an increasing number of economists, investors and financial policy makers have realized, SSA has emerged from its own malaise, into a dawn

1 http://www.youtube.com/watch?v=k1krRT3R9cc and http://www.fastestbillion.com.

2 Coauthors include Yvonne Mhango, Michael Moran, Arnold Meyer, Nothando Ndebele, John Arron, Johan Snyman, Jim Taylor, Dragan Trajkov, Sven Richter, and Bradley Way.

that promises growth to rival, if not surpass, that recorded by Asia's Tigers over the past two decades."

The hyperbole is in part irritating because Robertson understands a degree of political economy and explains post-independence poverty in familiar ways:

> Many of Africa's civil wars at this time were over valuable mineral resources and were supported, financed and armed by outside forces. Apartheid South Africa, acting as a Western outpost in Africa, caused considerable destabilization in Southern Africa through murderous wars and devastated national economies at all levels through the use of land mines, many of which remain hidden in place to this day. Even the best African leaders were inexperienced and easily duped by sharp practices from the developed world. IMF and World Bank policies, which were primarily designed to extract debt-service revenues through exports, damaged agriculture almost beyond repair and conditionalities that forced governments to cut spending on education and health. Growth figures from this era mask the fact that a good deal of it was debt. Grandiose white elephant projects ate up precious foreign revenues and income from resources were looted by local elites in conjunction with their foreign collaborators. Trillions of dollars were siphoned out of Africa. These were harsh lessons but Africans learnt them—some more quickly than others. (Robertson, 2013)

This chapter takes this perspective seriously but diverges 180 degrees when it comes to *which* Africans were educated by the last three decades of neoliberalism. Because "Africa Rising" rhetoric reproduces the kinds of banal, export-led, primary product-dependent and extractive orientation we have seen for so long, and because it continues to insert Africa into the volatile world economy on adverse terms, it is more appropriate to re-label the lesson Robertson *should have* taken forward as "Africa falling." Showing why this is the case in objective terms is the purpose of this chapter's second section, followed by thoughts on why the *world economy* is also falling. To some extent, an explanation for Africa's subservience is located in Pretoria, because South Africa has been the main legitimator, facilitator, predator and profiteer when it comes to the continent's underdevelopment. But likewise, a new threat—Brazil, Russia, India and China working with "gateway" South Africa (and its Development Bank of Southern Africa), known as BRICS—is on the horizon, not least because of a strategy to introduce more finance oriented to extractive infrastructure. This in turn requires a much richer sense of "uprising" than we have had since the early 1980s, and it is to a future in which both resistance to extraction and national protest can fuse in a genuine bottom-up Afro-optimism that we look in the concluding section.

Meanwhile, we must try to comprehend the central analytical argument in Robertson's narrative, namely the African elite's "learning by doing." His underlying assumption is that even without any change in power relations and incentive structures at the global scale, the continent's rulers weathered the global crisis because they learned the merits of orthodox Western structural adjustment

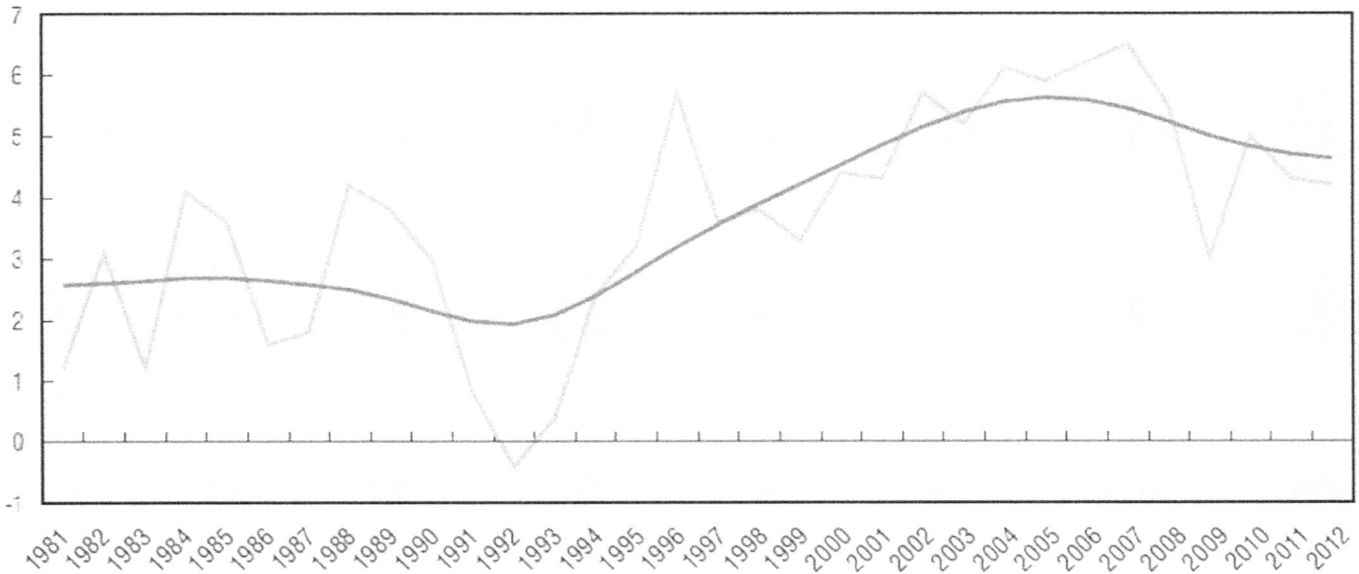

Figure 11.1 Africa's rising GDP (percentage real annual growth, 1981–2012, actual and trend)
Source: African Development Bank et al. (2013).

policies and no longer offered opposition: "While Africa has got its macro-economic management right, the heady heights envisioned for the continent will depend primarily on whether or not Africa can sustain its growth levels ... Africa is on track to deliver on all fronts," Robertson concludes.

The same argument is made by the economist most associated with revived Washington Consensus logic in Africa during the 2000s, the World Bank's Shanta Devarajan: "There's no question that the structural adjustment policies of the 1980s and early 1990s received a lot of criticism. But then ask the question, 'what changed?' As I was saying, the growth has accelerated since the 1990s. We can't hide from that fact. And you look at what changed. And it's that these countries adopted exactly the Washington Consensus policies in the mid-1990s" (quoted in Bond, 2010).

The main data used for celebrating "Africa Rising" are in Figure 11.1: GDP and per capita GDP has been increasing in Sub-Saharan Africa since around 1995, after fifteen years of decline.

This supposed economic growth, plus the claim of a massive new middle class and explosive increases in cellular telephone capacity, are the essence of the "Africa Rising" meme. Allegedly, "one in three Africans is middle class" and as a result, Africa is ready for "take-off," according to African Development Bank chief economist Mthuli Ncube, who defines middle class as those who spend between $2 (sic) and $20 per day, a group that includes a vast number of people considered extremely poor by any reasonable definition, given the far higher prices of most consumer durables in African cities. Actually, according to even his data, those spending between just $2 and $4 per day constitute a fifth of all Sub-Saharan Africans (and "float" in and out of poverty), while the range from $4 to $20 per day amounts to 13 percent, with only five percent of Africans spending more than $20 per day. Below the $2 per day level, 61 percent of Africans are mired in deep poverty (Smith, 2011).

As Jacques Enaudeau has pointed out, the "rising middle class" scam

> can be traced back to the strategic briefs and equity research notes published from 2010 onwards by Boston Consulting Group, McKinsey, Goldman Sachs or Deloitte, advertising 'the new African consumer,' finally in a position to spend some cash in brand new supermarkets. In a time when growth rates of industrialized countries stutter and when the Chinese and Indian engines of the global economy are somewhat slowing down, financial analysts and investment consultants can't get enough of the one thing that they have dismissed for so long: Africa. 'That's where the flavor is,' said Thabo Ncalo recently, manager of the Africa Fund for Johannesburg-based Stanlib, 'the frontier markets,' like Côte d'Ivoire, Nigeria or Rwanda. Close your eyes and let your imagination do the rest: hundreds of millions of purses loosening their strings ...
>
> Of course it's difficult to sell such a vision if 'Africa' remains associated with deadly conflicts, food crises and looming poverty. Thus baiting scaredy-cat

> investors and lobbying the media with the 'African middle class' is downright genius: there's enough actual change taking place all over the continent to make the notion look respectable, and it remains vague enough to accommodate any expectation and get traction across the board. This is where development organizations, in their quest for better aid efficiency and alternatives to aid, join forces with investors. (Enaudeau, 2013)

But no one should be fooled, argues Robert Bates:

> It is demand for the stuff underneath it—Africa's mineral and oil wealth—that is driving the economic growth behind all these 'Africa Rising' narratives. The BRIC economies, and China in particular, have fuelled a commodities boom that has benefitted state coffers across the continent though questions remain over the actual extent (and the equities) of this boom. But perhaps the central reason we are seeing all this 'good news' in Western media links back to the West's own idea of itself and of Africa. Africans are now, 'finally,' playing by the West's rules; as Professor Megan Vaughan, President of the African Studies Association of the UK, said in a recent speech, 'What is … striking is the fact that what is 'saving' Africa is the supposedly redemptive power of capitalism,' which, when coupled with the increasing adoption of liberal-democracy in Africa, vindicates the Western Way. Moreover, feelings of decline in the West—stubbornly low economic growth (or collapse), the threat of social upheaval, the rise of China, and so on—have made all these 'Africa Rising' narratives all the more breathless. *The Economist*, *Money Week*, and the rest seem to see in Africa's rise hope for the West's recovery. (Bates, 2012)

Ncube knows this, for as Enaudeau recalled, the African Development Bank economist

> gave it straight to CNN: 'it's a call to say "look, please invest in Africa."' Sure enough, if the new is made to look like the old, it gains the reassuring quality of being just the same. In that respect, the 'African middle class' is a means to an end, a programmatic concept: rationalize to normalize, normalize to legitimize.

Rick Rowden, too, finds a self-interested standpoint in the neoliberal celebration:

> Though African countries desperately need the policy space to adopt industrial policies, the rich countries are pushing loan conditions and trade and investment agreements that block them from doing so, all the while proffering a happy narrative about 'the rise of Africa.' (Rowden, 2013)

This is evident when considering how the World Bank's Devarajan rounds out his argument about how well neoliberalism works in Africa, and how durably the elites have learned by doing: "The difference is that they did it out of their own

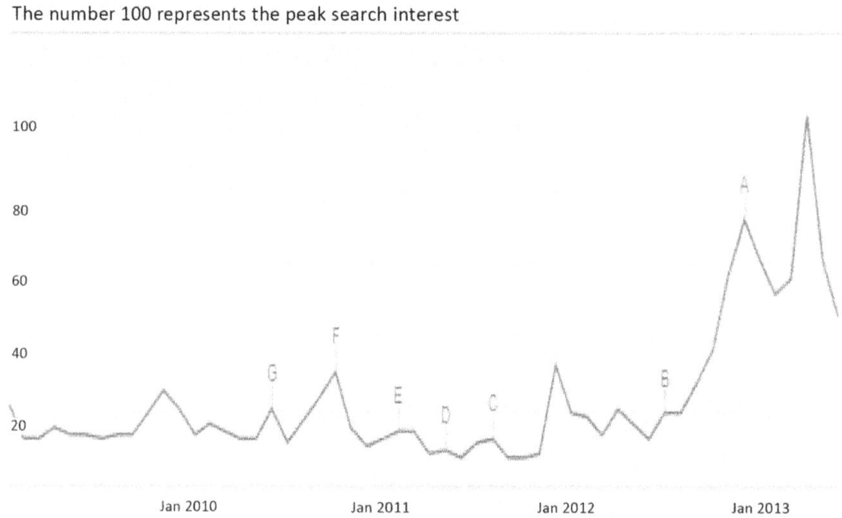

Figure 11.2 Google citation index of "Africa Rising," 2009–13
Source: Author's calculation using Google Citation Index, 4 January 2014.

accord, out of domestic political consensus, rather than imposed from Washington or Paris or London. And I think that's the point that people are not recognizing, that the actual policies that are generating the growth, are actually very similar to what was criticized in the structural adjustment era" (quoted in Bond, 2010).

Legitimizing the looting of Africa through the two words "Africa Rising" can be measured quantitatively using a Google citation index. It was especially after the *Time* front-page story in December 2012, as Figure 11.2 shows, that the two words spread rapidly.

The means of communication are terribly important, and indeed another major reason for the new Afro-optimism is increased cellular telephone access in many areas that were formerly off-grid for communications. The World Bank's main 2011 Africa policy paper, for example, argued that the "success of Information and Communications Technology (ICT), especially mobile phone penetration, shows how rapidly a sector can grow. It also shows how the public sector can set the conditions for the exponential growth of a vital industry that could transform the continent" (World Bank, 2011).

The reality is less encouraging. Although Africa is better off with cell phones than it was without (say, 20 years ago), the actual performance of the industry reveals profound weaknesses: the role of multinational capital in absorbing profits and dividends, the lack of genuine competition (collusion is notorious even in South Africa), relatively high prices for cell phone handsets and services, and limited technological linkages to internet service. Researchers Enrico Calandro, Alison Gillwald, Mpho Moyo and Christoph Stork have remarked on a host of ICT deficiencies: "the mobile market has experienced significant growth,

[but] outcomes have been sub-optimal in many respects" (Calandro, Gillwald, Moyo, and Stork, 2010).[3] For example, across nearly all of Africa, cell phone penetration rates "remain below the 40 percent critical mass believed to trigger the network effects associated with economic growth."[4] As for Africa's internet use, Calendro et al. conclude: "Large numbers of citizens across the continent still lack access to or cannot afford the kind of communication services that enable effective social and economic participation in a modern economy and society":

- broadband uptake trails even other developing regions in the world with a penetration rate below two percent;
- low penetration rates are mainly a result of the prohibitively high costs of internet services;
- the landing of several undersea cables and a number of terrestrial fibre investment projects have led to a significant reduction in the costs of accessing the internet. In some countries, the drop in wholesale prices has not, however, filtered to end-user prices; and
- digital literacy and the affordability of access devices like personal computers is expected to remain a challenge.

A final illustrative example of dubious "Africa Rising" hype comes from *Time* magazine's correspondent Alex Perry, in a December 2012 cover story:

> Africa owes its takeoff to a variety of accelerators, nearly all of them external and occurring in the past 10 years:

---

3 Cell phone penetration "figures tend to mask the fact that millions of Africans still do not own their own means of communication." Moreover:

- Africa continues to lag behind other regions both in terms of the percentage of people with access to the full range of communications services and the amounts and manner in which they can be used—primarily as a result of the high cost of services;
- the cost of wholesale telecommunication services as an input for other economic activities remains high, escalating the cost of business in most countries;
- the contribution of ICT to gross domestic product, with some exceptions, is considerably less than global averages;
- national objectives of achieving universal and affordable access to the full range of communications services have been undermined either by poor policies ... [or] regressive taxes;
- as a general trend across the continent, while the voice divide is decreasing, the internet divide is increasing and broadband is almost absent on the continent; and
- the fixed-line sector continues to show no signs of recovery ...

4 Even in mature markets (Ghana, Kenya, Nigeria, Tunisia and South Africa), "[t]he high 'penetration' figures result from the use of multiple-SIM cards, resulting in over-counting, often by several million."

- billions of dollars in aid, especially to fight HIV/AIDS and malaria;
- tens of billions of dollars in foreign-debt cancellations;
- a concurrent interest in Africa's natural resources, led by China; and
- the rapid spread of mobile phones, from a few million in 2000 to more than 750 million today.

Business increasingly dominates foreign interest in Africa. Investment first outpaced aid in 2006 and now doubles it. (Perry, 2012)

Africa Falling

Perry should have had an editor revise his words as follows:

> Africa owes its economic decline (running at more than 6 percent of gross income per year once nonrenewable resource depletion is considered) (World Bank, 2011) to a variety of accelerators, nearly all of them external and occurring in the past centuries during which slavery, colonialism and neo-colonialism locked in the continent's underdevelopment, but several of which—along with climate change—were amplified in recent years:
>
> - stagnant overseas development aid (Elliott, 2012)—around 60 percent "phantom" anyhow (ActionAid, 2006)—to most African countries, except to 14 "fragile states," (IMF, 2009) with Washington leading further cuts in funding to fight HIV/AIDS and malaria (Shaw, 2012);
> - tens of billions of dollars in foreign debt cancellation (of what was mainly unrepayable "Odious" loans to dictators in 2005) (CADTM, 2008) yet at the same time a squeeze on low-income African finance ministries that immediately afterwards caused a dramatic rise in debt repayments (from 5 to 8 percent of export earnings, according to IMF, 2009);
> - a concurrent looting of Africa's natural resources, led by China and the West, resulting in dramatic recent falls in mineral and petroleum wealth (when calculated as "Adjusted Net Saving" to incorporate resource-stripping); and
> - the rapid spread of mobile phones, which because of high costs and low internet connectivity, has done very little to solve the digital divide. (Calandro et al., 2010).
>
> Banking increasingly dominates foreign interest in Africa, as elite disinvestment into Western and Eastern financial markets continues to outpace aid and investment, amounting to an estimated $1.4 trillion in capital flight from the continent—both Sub-Saharan and North ends—from 1970–2010 (Ndikumana and Boyce, 2011, 2012a, 2012b).

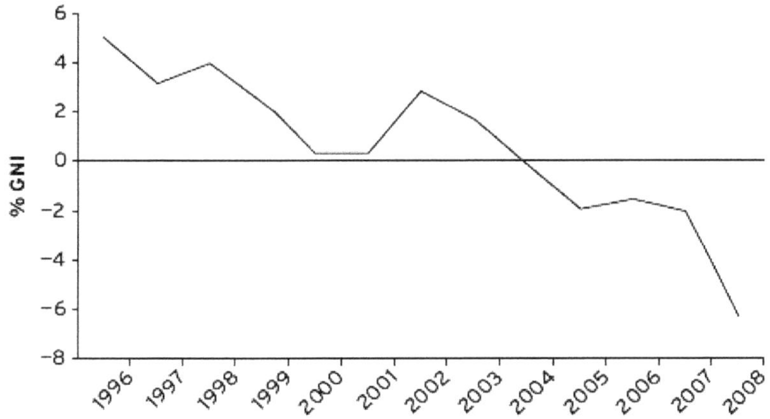

Figure 11.3 SSA adjusted net saving as percent of gross national income, 1995–2008

Source: World Bank, 2011.

To be blunt, the implication that *wealth* is being created by *rising GDP* in Africa is completely fallacious. The best way of thinking about the recent period is to negate Robertson's words completely: "Those billion Africans have just seen the biggest *decrease* in wealth that the continent has ever experienced." Robertson ignores the dramatic decline in Africa's broadest measure of wealth, including "natural capital" in the form of non-renewable minerals and petroleum, in contrast to those resource-rich countries (e.g. Norway, Australia and Canada) which ensure local reinvestment of the proceeds from extraction.[5] In Africa, once non-renewable resources are dug out of the soil by multinational corporations which repatriate the profits or transfer-price the revenues to their advantage, the permanent *debit* against genuine national savings (i.e. a decline in a country's natural capital stock, its "family silver") far exceeds the momentary *credit* to GDP.

By how much? It's impossible to say with any degree of accuracy, but it is substantial and getting worse. Since the commodity boom began in the early 2000s, according to the 2011 World Bank report *The Changing Wealth of Nations*, Africa has suffered negative "genuine savings" mainly because of non-renewable resource decay in the context of resource-cursed neo-colonial politics. Figure 11.3, from that book, shows that once non-renewable resources are removed from GDP

5 Most of the extractive corporations operating in Africa send profits to London, New York, Melbourne, Paris, Toronto, Rio de Janeiro, Shanghai or Beijing, with Johannesburg representing a 'branch plant' halfway house (no longer the site of accumulation for South African mining capital). The world's largest mining and metals house, BHP Billiton, is actively disinvesting, and Africa's largest company, Anglo American, continues its investment shift abroad.

(along with other small adjustments), the fall in "adjusted net savings" is sharp, to negative 6 percent of national income by 2008.

Reading the business press, one would not know that Africa is *losing* an estimated 6 percent of its wealth each year.[6] You would be forgiven for having the opposite impression when reading most reports from those with pro-globalization, export-oriented, petro-minerals-centric economic ideologies. Most multilateral financial institutions celebrate Africa's national economies as among the world's leading cases of post-meltdown economic "recovery."[7] Yet the neoliberal position neglects several features that have made Africa's supposedly resilient economies far more vulnerable to both global and local economic and environmental crises. These include excessive financial and trade integration into a volatile world economy, resource extraction costs, the "ecological debt" (as well as other non-remunerated value transfers) and climate change damage, as well as internal features of economies suffering from "Resource Curse" and processes of extreme uneven and combined development. The correlation of decline in Africa's real wealth—both in Sub-Saharan Africa and especially in North Africa (due to large volumes of oil extraction from Libya)—is *never* mentioned by "Africa Rising" advocates. But the GDP measure is especially pernicious when applied in Africa, because it treats all resource extraction as a positive, without factoring in the decline in natural capital—a country's "family silver"—which accompanies the extraction process.

This is no surprise, for Africa's exploitative trade, finance, investment and labor-migration relations within crisis-ridden world capitalism have intensified in recent years. From the early 2000s, ongoing resource extraction by Western firms was joined, and in some cases overtaken, by China, and as we see below, South Africa's role in the Brazil-Russia-India-China-SA (BRICS) bloc is as a gateway to yet more extraction, even at the risk of military chaos. Moreover, the phenomenon of "land grabbing" in Africa—especially by BRICS corporations—has also combined with larger-scale development of bio-fuels and genetic modification,

6 *The Changing Wealth of Nations* is rather conservative in calculating non-renewable resource depletion, leaving out several important minerals (including diamonds and uranium), and also neglecting the tax fraud and transfer pricing associated with transnational capital. These problems are documented by Khadija Sharife (2011) in *Tax Us If You Can* and by Leonce Ndikumana and James Boyce (2011, 2012a, 2012b) in various studies that deserve much more attention, e.g. their recent book on *Africa's Odious Debts* and updated 1970–2010 estimates of flight capital from Africa.

7 See, e.g., a report by the Washington-based International Institute of Finance (2012); the *African Economic Outlook 2011* from the Organisation for Economic Cooperation and Development, United Nations Economic Commission for Africa, United Nations Development Programme and African Development Bank (2011); the World Economic Forum's (2011) *Global Competitiveness Report*; the African Development Bank's (2011) discovery of a vast new middle class; the International Monetary Fund's (2011) *Regional Economic Outlook*; the World Bank's (2011) Africa strategy; and IMF (2011) research on African growth.

especially Western corporations. As for domestic economic dynamics, the process of financial liberalisation generated not only rising credit access, but also over-indebtedness.

Digging deeper into the data, it becomes obvious that Africa's alleged recovery is quite complex. As the world crisis unfolded in early 2009, for example, the continent's largest economy, South Africa, was recorded by *The Economist* as the riskiest among the world's 17 main emerging markets, largely due to its current account deficit (*The Economist*, 26 February 2009). That deficit had soared after 2001, thanks to capital flight by most of the largest companies formerly listed on the Johannesburg Stock Exchange (JSE). At that stage, in order to pay its overseas liabilities (especially profit and dividend outflows) as well as host the 2010 Soccer World Cup, South Africa's foreign debt increased by around a quarter to $140 billion by 2014—having begun at just US$25 billion in 1994 when Nelson Mandela was elected president. (Other African countries with dangerously high debt ratios were Ghana, Mauritius and Senegal.) The South African economy witnessed more than a million net job losses in 2009–10 plus worsening inequality, leaving it with the highest Gini coefficient among major countries, even worse than Brazil, in the wake of six currency crashes since 1994 and extreme stock market volatility. Yet, with minor exceptions (the promise of a National Health Insurance), there were no substantive changes in developmental or macroeconomic policy, not even with the potential that president Jacob Zuma would lean more to labor and even Communist influence. That proved elusive, and in late 2013, the largest union in Africa, the National Union of Metalworkers of SA (Numsa), formally broke away from the ANC mainly on grounds of Zuma's persistent neoliberalism.

In March 2014, Nigeria overtook South Africa as the continent's largest economy, through a statistical gimmick. Nigeria is also Africa's *fastest-shrinking* economy if measured by wealth, which includes the depletion of oil, degeneration of land, and departure of financial flows to offshore hideaways. Steve Omanufeme (2014) of Nigeria's *ThisDay* newspaper acknowledges that local elites are attempting quite a scam with their GDP "rebasing," a project that aligns national income account statistics to international norms: "The exercise was shelved in 2000 in order to pursue debt relief from the Paris Club [of Northern donor countries] and multilateral lenders. The thinking of the economic team then was that a revised GDP for the country would have pushed the economy into the category of the medium income economies." That move "would have made the country forfeit its eligibility for access to aid and grants from international organizations such as the IMF and the African Development Bank, as well as debt relief or forgiveness which was being considered at the time by the G8 group of industrialized nations. The strategy of delaying the rebasing worked as the Obasanjo administration's pursuit of debt relief was successful" (Omanufeme, 2014).

Finance minister Okonjo-Iweala, who during the 2000s also served as a World Bank managing director, was so successful arranging the deal that her South African counterpart Pravin Gordhan nominated her to be Bank president in 2012, though she didn't stand a chance against combined US and European votes. However, the fake-GDP scam and 2005 debt relief were not viewed so flatteringly by everyone, with experts like Nigeria Jubilee leader Rev. David Ugolor complaining: "The Paris Club cannot expect Nigeria, freed from over 30 years of military rule, to muster $12.4 billion to pay off interest and penalties incurred by the military. Since the debt, by President Obasanjo's own admission, is of dubious origin, the issues of the responsibilities of the creditors must be put on the table at the Paris Club" (AfricaFocus Bulletin, 2005). Remarked the Global AIDS Alliance (2005), "The creditors should be ashamed of themselves if they simply take this money. These creditors often knew that the money would be siphoned off by dictators and deposited in western banks, and the resulting debt is morally illegitimate. They bear a moral obligation to think more creatively about how to use this money."

The next step in the scam was for Obasanjo to agree to the reimposition of neoliberal economic policies. According to ActionAid's Soren Ambrose (2005), "The Paris Club requires that countries applying for relief be under an IMF program, but the prospect of agreeing to one is political dynamite in Nigeria. The Paris Club was, however, under great pressure to complete a landmark deal with Nigeria, where the legislature had threatened to simply repudiate the debts." The IMF snuck in through the back door as part of the debt deal. In short, the long-standing economic swindle was actually perpetrated against the Nigerian population by Washington financiers and allied local elites, especially Okonjo-Iweala. Later, in 2012, her neoliberalism catalyzed a national "Occupy Nigeria" strike that nearly overthrew the government because of a dubiously-formulated recall of a petrol subsidy (Adesamni, 2012). This was under direct pressure from IMF managing director Christine Lagarde (2011).

The final stage of the rebasing scam was the announcement that Nigeria has risen from a GDP of $262 billion in 2012 to become, after new counting techniques, the largest economy in Africa with $491 billion GDP in 2013 (compared to $384billion for South Africa) (Magnowsky, 2014), when in reality it is the *fastest-shrinking* in terms of wealth. As noted above, the term "wealth" is critical to interrogate because in addition to the financial assets, productive machinery, real estate, and "human capital" (educational accomplishments and skills) of a people, even the World Bank concedes that we should add "natural capital," i.e., resources, such as Nigeria's untapped oil and minerals, forests and agricultural land. Nigeria shrinks in wealth because natural capital is being stripped out of the Niger Delta by foreign oil companies without the kind of compensating investments that resource-rich Norway, Canada and Australia can brag, because their mining and oil companies are headquartered at home there.

The World Bank's (2011) *Changing Wealth of Nations* provides the latest available comparative data: in the year 2005 (when oil averaged $50/barrel), the average Nigerian lost $280—or in sum, 140 million Nigerians lost a net $39 billion—because the depletion of natural resources far outstripped the income gains from exploiting petroleum. This was not a one-year fluke, it amplified a trend the Bank observed for at least a decade earlier: "wealth in Nigeria declined by 15 percent." During the 14 years prior to 2008, say *Changing Wealth of Nations* authors, "clear trends emerge, with Adjusted Net Savings as well as per capita wealth increasing in Asia and ANS declining in Sub-Saharan Africa. In both instances, a few countries dominate the trend: the stellar performance of China and, more recently, India, drives the positive trends in Asia, and the poor performance of Nigeria and a handful of other countries outweigh the positive performance of many other African countries." Accurate updates are not available, but as oil prices rose to $145 per barrel through mid-2008, crashed to $32 for a short while later that year, and then rose to the $80–$100 range since 2010, Nigeria's wealth shrinkage became even worse. If all other factors remained roughly constant, 175 million Nigerians would have lost around $80 billion net in 2013.

Elsewhere in Africa, uneven development caused by adherence to the Washington Consensus in other smaller but higher-growth, resource-cursed economies, such as Equatorial Guinea (Appel, 2011), was even more extreme. In spite of rhetoric about a Keynesian turn in October 2008 under Strauss-Kahn's leadership, IMF staff reaction to the crisis in Africa was a reversion to Washington Consensus dogma. Out of 22 IMF programs on the continent underway in October 2009, according to the Center for Economic and Policy Research, 17 were contractionary orders and only five were expansionary (Weisbrot et al., 2009). Yet by late 2009, Africa's state deficits were exploding because a very slight spending increase was conjoined with a huge revenue drop as commodity prices crashed, resulting in a dramatic switch from a positive fiscal balance (six percent of GDP) to a huge deficit (minus six percent) between 2008 and 2009 (IMF, 2009). The crisis meant capital inflows shifted from an $80 billion inflow in 2007 to a $25 billion outflow of portfolio investments (mainly in South African financial assets), thus reflecting a net decline in total inflows. Although remittances held up, foreign direct investment fell back in 2009, leaving aid as the only rising financial inflow. But even this was conditional, with most flowing to 14 "fragile states": Burundi, the Central African Republic (CAR), Cote d'Ivoire, the Democratic Republic of Congo (DRC), Eritrea, Gambia, Guinea, Guinea-Bissau, Liberia, Sierra Leone, Sao Tome and Principe, Togo and Zimbabwe.

Under the circumstances, most of Africa experienced a rising fiscal deficit and higher public debt. Most central banks imposed lower interest rates after 2009 than prevailed in 2007. Most let their money supply rise, in part to compensate for private credit contraction. A few countries went further: new exchange controls helped Tanzania, Rwanda and Kenya fend off hostile financial forces. These classically Keynesian strategies also explain why Africa did not suffer as much as other regions during the crisis, even if the IMF harried so many weaker debtors with austerity directives. Slightly relaxed macroeconomic strategies help explain, partially, why in the wake of a huge commodities boom (2002–2008) and world-leading windfall profits for multinational extractive industries, a modicum of GDP growth was recorded in several African countries during the crisis period.

But the overall trajectory reflects ongoing dependency relations and underdevelopment. For in reality, contrary to Devarajan's protestations, Africa's economic policies were indeed "imposed from Washington." According to John

Weeks, "Over twenty years, 1990–2009, the governments of 46 Sub-Saharan countries sought to manage their economies under IMF programs during almost half the country years (417 of 920)" (Weeks, 2010). Weeks concludes of the IMF and World Bank: "The two international financial institutions played a major if not decisive role in policy making for all but a few countries of the region." Only a few countries escaped Bretton Woods Institutions' direct tutelage for extended periods (though most had long bouts of home-grown neo-liberalism): Angola, Botswana, Comoros, Equatorial Guinea, Eritrea, The Gambia, Liberia, Mauritius, Namibia, Nigeria, Seychelles, South Africa, Sudan, Swaziland and Zimbabwe. As for every other country, as Weeks reports, "[t]here is little evidence, rigorous or circumstantial, to believe that the "reforms" of the 1980s and 1990s lay the basis for that [2000s economic] recovery." Instead, behind the recent GDP growth was the combination of the post-conflict peace dividend and the 2000s rise of a commodity market super-cycle thanks to a last-gasp burst of sustained demand from Asian minerals and petroleum purchasers, as well as a modicum of internal domestic demand flawed by artificial characteristics, as we will observe in coming pages.

For example, Africa's long-deindustrialized manufacturing sector has been examined recently by Rowden (2013), and "despite some improvements in a few countries, the bulk of African countries are either stagnating or moving backwards when it comes to industrialization." As Table 11.1 shows, the proportion of GDP made up of manufacturing—a typical sign of maturing economic activity—has been shrinking in Africa, from a peak of 15.3 percent in 1990 to 10.5 percent in 2008.

Table 11.1 Manufacturing shrinkage and mining growth, by sector, 1970–2008

Economy type	Sector % share of GDP	1970	1980	1990	2000	2005	2008
DEVELOPING	Industry	27.3	41.1	36.8	36.3	38.9	40.2
ECONOMIES	Manufacturing	17.6	20.2	22.4	22.6	23.3	23.7
	Mining and utilities	5.7	14.7	8.9	8.3	10.1	10.9
AFRICAN	Industry	13.1	35.6	35.2	35.5	38.8	40.7
DEVELOPING	Manufacturing	6.3	11.9	15.3	12.8	11.6	10.5
ECONOMIES	Mining and utilities	4.8	19.3	15.2	18.4	23.0	25.8

Source: United Nations Conference on Trade and Development (UNCTAD) 2011.

Indeed from 1990–2010, manufacturing value added (MVA) per person fell in 23 African countries and was weak in 27 others (with only Namibia, Mozambique and Uganda above 5 percent annual growth) (UNCTAD, 2011). Of even greater concern, Rowden reports, "Africa is also losing ground in labor-intensive manufacturing: Its share of low-technology manufacturing activities in MVA fell from 23 percent in 2000 to 20 percent in 2008, and the share of low-technology manufacturing exports in Africa's total manufacturing exports dropped from 25 percent in 2000 to 18 percent in 2008." At the same time, Africa's total imports

Table 11.2 Manufacturing shrinkage and mining growth, global trade and Africa's share, 1980–2008

Year	Global trade (billions of tons)	Global trade volume (1980=100)	African trade (billions of tons)	African trade (1980 = 100)	Africa's share of global trade
1980	4.0	100	0.3	100	6.5
1985	3.9	96	0.2	91	6.2
1990	5.0	124	0.3	102	5.2
1995	6.1	152	0.3	121	5.1
2000	7.6	189	0.4	156	5.3
2005	9.6	232	0.5	188	5.1
2008	10.3	257	0.5	195	4.9

Source: United Nations Conference on Trade and Development (UNCTAD) 2012.

and exports were falling in relative terms, from 6.5 percent to 4.9 percent of world volumes from 1980 to 2008 (Table 11.2).

Seeking an understanding of Africa's economic plight thus requires much more serious inquiry than the multilateral institutions and their allies appear willing to consider. For example, the *internal* driver of growth in Africa during the 2000s was "private consumption."[8] One side effect, given African deindustrialization of even basic consumer-durable industries, was the rise of import bills. But it is instructive that private consumption across Africa was, from 2004 to 2008, well over twice as large a component of GDP growth as exports, as a result of the dramatic "financial deepening"—the rise of private sector bank credit as a percentage of GDP—from 14.3 percent in 2002 to 19.0 percent by 2008. The period from 1980 to 2004 was replete with bank failures and credit contraction across structurally-adjusted Africa, and hence according to John Karikari, "excluding the top 15 countries, the ratio of private sector bank credit to GDP declined by about 50 percent, on average, from 17.2 percent to 8.7 during this period" (Karikari, 2010). The uptick in credit availability after 2004 once the failed banks' assets had been written off and the new round of accumulation began, did indeed drive a degree of domestic consumption, but the critical question of repayment remained a concern.

The untenable rise of credit in Africa, especially South Africa where consumer default rates are at an all-time and very dangerous high, goes unremarked upon by most commentators, including Ncube at the African Development Bank. South Africa's consumer debt crisis sheds light on African macroeconomic and microeconomic problems, for one reason that rising debt for working-class and new middle-class consumers was untenable was the rise in real property prices by 389 percent between 1997 and 2008 (the highest in the world, with the second highest bubble, Ireland, at less than 200 percent). Meanwhile, wage levels had been outstripped by profits for most of the previous 17 years of post-apartheid neo-liberalism, leaving workers to rely upon higher rates of consumer credit to make up the gap. By late 2010, the main state credit regulator registered "impaired" status for 8.3 million South African borrowers, a rise from 6.1 million in 2007 (Davel, 2011). The role of over-indebtedness was central in the financial crisis experienced by workers at Lonmin's Marikana platinum mine in 2012, as well, as garnishee orders on salaries reduced paychecks to a bare minimum, resulting in very high militancy and demands for more than 100 percent wage increases

8 A degree of domestic economic reflation was recorded in most of Africa, including all oil exporters and middle- and low-income countries alike. Certainly, in the subsequent period, after 2008, when private sector decline was initially dramatic, African governments showed the ability to raise consumption using three Keynesian countervailing measures: budget deficits (so that falling tax revenues were not 'pro-cyclically' amplified throughout the economy), lower interest rates, and expanded money supplies. In spite of their overall orientation to the Washington Consensus, IMF staff were sufficiently worried about the depth of the world crisis in 2008 to 2009 in allowing large deficits, especially in regionally-powerful countries such as South Africa.

(Bond, 2013). While there are no reliable data on consumer credit systems in most African countries as a result of the great extent of informal and NGO lending, the overall world trend is highly disturbing. It offers no basis for claiming credit systems assist in "Africa Rising."

More recently, the trend in African financial markets has been for governments to mop up excessive savings in banks by issuing sovereign debt bonds, not just in South Africa but in ten other countries with growing domestic financial markets: Ghana, Gabon, the DRC, Côte d'Ivoire, Senegal, Angola, Nigeria, Namibia, Zambia, and Tanzania. According to Joseph Stiglitz and Hamid Rashid, "By February 2013, these ten African economies had collectively raised $8.1 billion from their maiden sovereign-bond issues, with an average maturity of 11.2 years and an average coupon rate of 6.2 percent. These countries' existing foreign debt, by contrast, carried an average interest rate of 1.6 percent with an average maturity of 28.7 years" (Stiglitz and Rashid, 2013). As a result of these yields and ongoing speculative funding flows emanating from northern financial centers, foreigners are seeking much higher lending rates available in Africa, according to Nairobi-based Stanlib banker David Makoni: "Judging from high levels of order book subscription at issue, African sovereign debt seems to be "flavor of the month" with international investors" (Thomas, 2013). From January-September 2013, the eurobond market hosted $8 billion in new African debt issuance, rewarding the governments of Egypt, Ghana, Nigeria, Rwanda and South Africa. But Stiglitz and Rashid warn, "Should oil and copper prices collapse, Angola, Gabon, Congo, and Zambia may encounter difficulties in servicing their sovereign bonds." Indeed, they remind, "the record of private-sector credit assessments should leave one wary" because when "shortsighted financial markets" combine "with shortsighted governments," this could lay "the groundwork for the world's next debt crisis," in countries which they term Africa's "subprime borrowers" (Stiglitz and Rashid, 2013).

In sum, "Africa Rising"? No, only the corporations which loot Africa and a very few comprador elites are prospering, and at great risk to both long-term and short-term prosperity, thanks to the extreme distortions they introduce. As Jumoke Balogun put it at the *Compare Afrique* blog site,

> Currently, the *top five* most unequal countries in the world are in Africa: Namibia, South Africa, Lesotho, Botswana, and Sierra Leone. Surprisingly, South Africa, the Continent's most influential and diversified economy, is slightly more unequal today than it was in 1993 shortly after apartheid ended. Further, three out of the twenty most expensive cities in the world are also on the continent: Luanda (2nd), N'Djamena (8th), and Libreville (20th)—all of which are more expensive than London … Considering that Africa is the poorest and most underdeveloped continent on the globe, these numbers provide a startling account of the current state of play: the few who have, have everything, and the majority who don't, have nothing. This is not to suggest that Africans who have amassed great personal wealth are culpable for the alarming disparity, but this is

> what *uneven development* looks like. This is where Africa is. This is what many deem worthy of celebration. (Balogun, 2013)

Another feminist writer, Ama Biney, has also debunked "Africa Rising" rhetorics:

> For whom does it rise? It rises for neoliberal and neo-colonial African governments selling off large tracts of land to outsiders for food or bio-fuel jatropha while their people go hungry and landless … It rises for a small African middle class whilst the 99 percent remain in the rural areas as farmers, unable to get subsidies like their European counterparts whose governments intervene on their behalf. Africa rises for those with forked tongue who 'talk left and walk right.' Africa is rising for the charismatic Christian preachers engaging in what they call 'prosperity preaching' to congregations obliged to pay one tenth of their miserly wages as tithes so the preacher can wear designer suits from Italy. Africa is rising for the continued exploitation of its enormous wealth by MNCs, tax evaders and those who engage in illicit wealth appropriation in a continued (not new) scramble for Africa. Africa is rising for a tiny black elite who believe in the New Partnership for Africa's Development and market fundamentalism alongside their governments committed to such policies. Africa is rising for those African women who equate economic freedom with the means to purchase Brazilian and Korean weave, false eyelashes and nails in their aspirations to resemble an African Barbie doll. Africa is rising for those few countries who have recently discovered oil: Uganda, Ghana, Ivory Coast—but will their people say the same in 20 years and not meet the same wretched fate as the peoples of the Niger Delta of Nigeria? (Biney, 2013)

The World Falling, too

Most importantly, Africa's subordinate position within the global economic order did not change. A year before the latest world financial meltdown began, in the book *Looting Africa* (Bond, 2006), I set out a full argument about how global capitalist crisis had unfolded over the prior four decades, and how Africa's vulnerability worsened. To summarize and update these concerns, it is first useful to go back to 1971 when the post-Second World War Bretton Woods system broke down. This was the beginning of a general rise in financial and monetary instability.[9] The

9 A series of speculative bubbles and panics ensued, reflecting uncontrolled financial turbulence. To some extent, these were offset or displaced by bailouts, but they generally destroyed more than 15 percent of the value of financial assets at stake within a short period of time: the dollar crash (1970s), gold and silver turbulence (1970s-80s), Third World debt crisis (1980s), US farmland collapse (1980s), energy finance shocks (mid 1980s), crashes of international stock (1987) and property (1991–93) markets, the long fall (from 1973–2002) in non-petroleum commodity prices and related securities, and after the dot.com crash of

2000s were the critical years, with low corporate fixed investment rates (especially after the dot.com software bubble burst), high debt loads and even bankruptcy threats to what were once some of the most powerful auto companies in the United States. Hence the restoration of profits for capital in general during the 2000s disguised the difficulty of extraction of surplus value, leaving most accumulation hollow, based increasingly upon financial and commercial activity rather than production. Although productivity increased and wage levels fell, profitability was mainly found outside the production process, especially in finance. Nevertheless, with much lower interest rates, low inflation and relatively low unemployment, resulting in steady GDP, a rising stock market and recovery from earlier outbreaks of currency volatility, it appeared to many investors that the US and global economies could continue along this trajectory.

This naiveté changed gradually from 2007 with the peaking of real estate speculation, and then evaporated in September 2008, as world capitalism began what initially (even after nine months) appeared to be an even worse crash than in 1929–30, in terms of decline in industrial output, trade, and stock market valuation. Commodity prices plunged by record amounts (e.g. oil from $150 to $35/barrel), and world GDP, industrial production and Foreign Direct Investment levels plummeted. The extreme financial panic underway in 2009 required several major interventions: very rapid increases in government debt, dramatic declines in interest rates and a vast inflow of new liquidity from the US Federal Reserve, which rapidly printed dollars and thus raised the global money supply. This was soon followed by similar measures in Europe and the 2009 International Monetary Fund issuance of new Special Drawing Rights to boost world liquidity.

In 2012, during another round of financial panics, more "Quantitative Easing" (money printing) and commitments to bailing out the lenders to southern Europe were announced by the US Federal Reserve, European Central Bank and Bank of England. In 2013, when the "tapering" (slowing down) of this strategy was announced by the Fed, it led to a dramatic outflow of capital from Brazil, Russia, India, South Africa, Indonesia and Turkey, amongst other emerging markets. Many neoliberal observers concluded, with *The Economist*, that "booming emerging economies will no longer make up for weakness in rich countries" (*The Economist*, October 12, 2013). Anders Aslund of the Peterson Institute for International Economics was scathing in a *Financial Times* article: "The BRICS

2000–2001, vast new devaluations of real estate, commodities, financial institutions and exposed sovereign securities in Europe (2007–13). Other examples of investment gambles gone sour include derivatives speculation, exotic stock market positions, and bad bets on currency, commodity and interest rate options, futures and swaps, with specific victims covering enormous losses. Even the fast-growing emerging markets offered spectacular examples of financial panic, including Mexico (1995), South Africa (1996, 1998 and 2001), Southeast Asia (1997–98), South Korea (1998), Russia (1998), Brazil and Ecuador (early 1999), Argentina (2001–02) and Turkey (2001–03). Trouble moved north, as far as Iceland (2008), Ireland (2009), Greece (2010), Portugal (2011), Spain (2011) and Cyprus (2013).

party is over. Their ability to get going again rests on their ability to carry through reforms in grim times for which they lacked the courage in a boom" (Aslund, 2013). Tempting as it is to write off the more schadenfreud-suffused and neoliberal of BRICS-pessimist commentators, their confidence grows from several countries' deep-seated problems, not just momentary financial fluctuations.

In the BRICS and across the world, powerful underlying forces associated with capitalist crisis tendencies are the main reason for such extreme turbulence. Stagnation characterized global capitalism for decades, as world per capita annual GDP increase fell from 3.6 percent during the 1960s, to 2.1 percent during the 1970s, to 1.3 percent during the 1980s, to 1.1 percent during the 1990s, followed by a rise to 2.5 percent for the first half of the 2000s, but then a crash in absolute terms at the end of the 2000s. To be sure, the character of goods measured over time has changed (high technology products enjoyed today were not available in the last century) and as noted, GDP is a very weak measure of surplus value much less genuine societal welfare. To correct GDP with a "Genuine Progress Indicator" would reveal even more pronounced stagnation.

Notwithstanding data caveats, the overall story of "overaccumulated capital" generating stagnation, uneven development, financialization and ultimately unprecedented crises remains convincing. This context gives a better sense of why the global financial architecture remains on the verge of collapse in 2014, and explains why national economies have been wrecked because of their excessive reliance upon international financial flows. In this global context, it is even more critical to be skeptical about the "Africa Rising" argument that was especially ascendant after 2010, because it simply feeds into notions that export-led growth and mineral extraction are the answer to poverty. At least one ruling elite within Africa is particularly well suited to take advantage of this neoliberal myth: South Africa's.

Africa Looted from Within

Amongst the world's 40 largest economies, South Africa suffered the world's second-highest loss in currency value from January-August 2013 (after Venezuela) and maintained the second highest current account deficit (after Turkey). And in order to cover the hard currency required to facilitate the vast capital flight by multinational corporations and banks, which had peaked at more than 20 percent of GDP in 2007,(Ashman, Fine, and Newman 2010), vast new foreign liabilities were taken on. The foreign debt soared from $25 billion 1994 to $70 billion by 2009 and $140 billion in 2013. To address the hard currency shortfall, South African mining and political elites appeared increasingly frantic about expanding their extractive capacities, especially in the African hinterland.

This problem has been brewing for more than a decade, once Johannesburg became the continent's premier hot-money centre after Pretoria bureaucrats began promoting financial liberalization. Exchange controls were lifted for non-residents in 1995 and in 1999, most of the largest SA corporations were allowed to relist their primary financial headquarters overseas. In mid-2002, South African finance minister Trevor Manuel had promised the Commonwealth Business Council he would "fast-track financial market integration through the establishment of an internationally competitive legislative and regulatory framework" for the continent (Manuel 2002). But without any Africa-wide progress to report two years later, Manuel's director-general Lesetja Kganyago announced a new "Financial Centre for Africa" project to amplify the financialization tendencies already evident in Johannesburg's exclusive new Sandton central business district: "Over the five years to 2002, the financial sector grew at a real rate of 7.7 percent per year, more than twice as fast as the economy as a whole" (Kganyago, 2004).

Such financial bubbling would ordinarily be understood as a sign of a parasitic and dangerous economy, but not by Pretoria financial officials. Responsible for a full quarter of post-apartheid South African GDP growth, the sector now required further room to expand, according to Kganyago: "What is needed is a financial hub especially focused on the needs and circumstances of the region, much in the same way that Singapore and Hong Kong cater for the capital needs of the Asian continent … International financial centers tend to have a foundation in common. Elements include political stability, free markets, and what is best described as the rule of commercial law. Pretoria's specific aims included "opening South Africa's markets to African and global issuers; global lowest trading costs and trading risk; global leadership in investor protection; and a global hub for financial business process outsourcing." Concluded Kganyago, "Africa's economies cannot wait the slow maturing of national financial markets to provide the necessary channel for large-scale foreign capital flows for development. Only a regional financial centre will be in a position to provide these services in the foreseeable future." Ironically, notwithstanding his own advocacy of liberalization, Thabo Mbeki soon reinvented himself as a leading critic of illicit capital flight from Africa—much of it routed via Sandton (Mbeki, 2012).

A telling incident in mid-2002 illustrated the responsibility that the South African government had taken on to police such world financial mechanisms in Africa. A Cabinet meeting in Pretoria concluded with this statement: "The meeting noted the provision by South Africa of a bridge loan to the Democratic Republic of the Congo of Special Drawing Rights (SDR) 75 million. This will help clear the DRC's overdue obligations with the IMF and allow that country to draw resources under the IMF Poverty Reduction and Growth Facility" (Republic of South Africa Government Communications and Information Service, 2002). In ensuring the rollover of the debt, Pretoria thus sanitized the earlier generation of IMF loans made to Mobuto Sese Seko, riven with corruption and capital flight to European banks. In fact, continuities with an earlier sub-imperial project were obvious, for the people of the DRC were previously victims of South Africa's apartheid-era allegiance with Mobuto, an arrangement that especially suited the ecology-destroying mineral extraction corporations headquartered in Johannesburg. Now the old "odious" Mobutu loans were honored and serviced with Pretoria's new credits. They should have been repudiated. In addition, IMF staff would be allowed back into Kinshasa with their own new loans, and with neoliberal conditionalities again applied to the old victims of Mobutu's fierce rule.[10]

At the same time, China was expanding its investment, financing and trading relations with Africa (indeed trade rose from around 5 to 20 percent of Africa's total from 1994–2012, with China replacing the US as the main partner). Rationalizing and facilitating tighter continental economic relationships with BRICS countries thus became one of Pretoria's leading objectives, according to deputy foreign minister Marius Fransman: "South Africa also presents a gateway for investment on the continent, and over the next 10 years the African continent will need $480 billion for infrastructure development" (Fransman 2013). Not just a gateway, but a vanguard, for as SA foreign minister Maite Nkoana-Mashabane correctly observed, "In 2012, South Africa invested in the rest of Africa more than any other country in the world" (Mataboge, 2013). In 2010, 17 out of Africa's top 20 companies were South African, even after the capital flight a decade earlier (Laverty, 2011). As Ernst & Young's *Africa Attractiveness Survey* recorded, thanks to predictable mining houses and MTN cell phone service, Standard Bank, Shoprite retail, and Sanlam insurance, SA's foreign direct investment in the rest of Africa had risen 57 percent since 2007 (Ernst and Young, 2013).

Johannesburg capital's drive to accumulate up-continent was already moving at a rapid rate, especially in mining, retail, banking, breweries, construction, services and tourism. The largest South African corporations benefited from the African financial liberalization that Pretoria had long promoted, so they could repatriate profits with increasing ease. However, most of the money did not stop in Johannesburg, as was the case prior to 2000. The financial flight went mainly to London, where Anglo American Corporation, DeBeers, Old Mutual insurance, South African Breweries, Liberty Life insurance and other huge South African firms had relisted at the turn of the Millennium.

To sum up the argument so far, the myth that Africa is "rising" has become widespread as a result of the commodity boom that began in 2002 (albeit with interruptions in 2008 and 2013) and the cessation of conflict in some countries (albeit others—the CAR, DRC, Mali, Nigeria, Somalia and South Sudan—continue as resource-related battlefields in 2014). But the context is a long global economic slump in which stagnation tendencies were only temporarily displaced through

10 A similar process was repeatedly offered to regimes such as Mugabe's Zimbabwe and King Mswati's Swaziland, again for the purpose of repaying the IMF first and foremost, without a care to human rights and other non-economic values. In several of these cases, South African president Jacob Zuma's own relatives and the African National Congress' investment arm, Chancellor House, have been involved in the equation linking financing and Pretoria's geopolitical moves.

financial speculation and globalization. In Africa, a far-reaching Resource Curse still ensures unequal ecological exchange drains Africa of far more *wealth* each year than is earned, in income measures based upon standard GDP accounting. This means the kind of brief, Keynesian-based credit-driven recoveries in many African economies after 2008–09 were not durable. Nor were the much-hyped strategies reliant upon cellular technology.

Africa's Early Uprisings Against "Africa Rising"

The beginnings of a Polanyian "double-movement"—i.e. excessive market penetration of society countered by social activism, as identified by Karl Polanyi in *The Great Transformation*—stirred in Africa around 2010, beginning in three North African countries but also evident south of the Sahara, including in South Africa's platinum mines where the Marikana massacre of August 2012 was one result, and in December 2013 the cleavage of the main trade union, Numsa, from the ruling party was another. But a central challenge remains in most countries: nascent economic justice movements could follow the Latin American road in which "IMF Riots" during the 1980s paved the way for more sustained leftist activism and even changes in government. Aside from ongoing progressive mobilisations in Egypt and Tunisia in reaction to IMF and fundamentalist Islamic repression, only in South Africa is that process apparently ascendant. But the potential remains great, as witnessed in the heady days of 2011 when "Africa Rising" was best considered in terms of the numbers of social protests, as Figure 11.4 shows.

According to the African Development Bank and other sponsors of the continental protest research, "Public protests in North Africa in 2012 had a political undertone that reflected an extension of the Arab Spring revolts. The protests were primarily motivated by calls for further and deeper political reforms … Protests in sub-Saharan Africa were mostly over economic concerns. More than half of public protests were to demand salary increases or to complain against the increasing cost of living" (Agence France Press data reported in African Development Bank et al., 2013). In 2011, the Bank added, "nearly all African countries faced increased protests" while the 2012 experiences were concentrated in fewer, larger countries. Of concern, however, is that these protest figures—only 250 in 2011, for example—are vast underestimates, given that in South Africa alone, the number of *violent* protests in 2012–13 was recorded by police as 1882, with more than 10 000 additional non-violent "Gatherings Act" incidents (Mthethwa, 2013). There, police minister Nathi Mthethwa observed that "Over the past four years, a total of 46 180 incidents were attended to and all were successfully stabilized, with 14,843 arrests effected"—although debate continues on how successful the police were in Marikana, as a result of incontrovertible evidence (most supplied from their own computers after

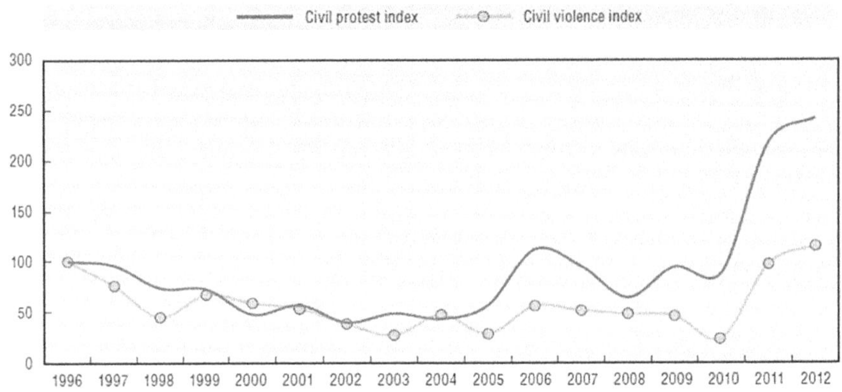

Figure 11.4 Public protest and civil violence in Africa, 1996–2012
Source: Agence France Press data reported in African Development Bank et al., 2013.

clumsy cover-ups) that their massacre of mineworkers was premeditated, and entailed planting of weapons on mineworker corpses. Nationally, it is difficult to identify decisive trends and correlate these to particular political causalities, but it is evident that a higher level of violent incidents occurred after 2008, perhaps due to the combination of the global economic crisis (leaving more than one million South Africans newly unemployed) and the rise in electricity rates by 128 percent that occurred over the subsequent four years.

The varied nature of these local gatherings makes them difficult to quantify, but according to official police "crowd management" statistics from 2009–13, between 8 and 15 percent of the more than 10 000 protests per year, on average, were classified as "unrest" incidents, in which police intervene (often using force) where they perceive threats to security or damage to property. "Peaceful" incidents are defined as those where there is co-operation between the police and the convener and where no police intervention is necessary. The many more incidents of protest where there are fewer than 15 people are not recorded by the police, as such events are not considered applicable under the Gatherings Act (yet in many cases, larger protests occur with participants placing themselves in groups of 14 or more at a 50 meter distance in the event they did not obtain police permission).[11] Data of this sort should be considered valid only insofar as reliable trends can be discerned, and this is a matter of subjectivity when it comes to protest, given that definitions vary dramatically and that those

11 One of the main studies based on IRIS, by Bilkis Omar, 'confirmed that protest marches between 2002 and 2005 had increased from 6 757 in 2002 to a high of 10 162 in 2005—an increase of 50 percent,' with 'violent incidents' peaking in 1998 at 1185 and rising again from 562 in 2004 to 932 in 2005. Statistics are discussed in more detail in Bond and Mottiar, 2013.

recording the events—especially journalists—do so in a manner that fluctuates over time. Protests become regular and hence no longer of news value.

The resurgence of regular mass protest on the continent dates to the 2011 uprisings, which occurred not only in North Africa where socio-economic grievances were central to the revolts in even the (neo-liberally) best-performing of African countries, e.g., Tunisia, but also in Sub-Saharan Africa, where after years of ineffectual IMF riots, growing unrest had a surprisingly powerful effect in crucial sectors and geographical spaces from Senegal in the west, to Uganda in the east to Swaziland in the south. Since the Washington Consensus narrative was unchanged in all important respects, contradictions grew more extreme. There was even awareness in Egypt's military, for example, that neoliberal reforms carried out by Mubarak were responsible for the revolts insofar as they compelled a core working-class constituency—independent trade unions—to view their struggles in political terms (Mekay, 2011). However, it is equally certain that the counter-revolutionary forces in Egypt, including the army leadership, would not be able to deliver the socio-economic progress demanded in Tahrir Square, and in 2013, their coup against the fundamentalist Islamic regime was due in part to the latter's IMF deal, yet the army continued the same process in late 2013.

Perhaps the most acute observer of the potential for emancipation in Africa is Sokari Ekine. Her June 2011 review of developments in several countries is illustrative:

> Uganda, Swaziland, Kenya, and Botswana actions are in response to concerns over food security, rising unemployment particularly amongst youth, political marginalisation, corruption of government officials and a pushback against the entrenched leadership of the circle of 'rulers for life.' Military dictators have been replaced by democracy dictatorships under militarised states. (Ekine, 2011)

In Kampala, wrote Ekine, "The government has blamed inflation on external factors out of their control, obviously believing Ugandans are so ill-informed as to not make the connection between the $740 million spent on fighter jets and tanks ... Museveni who, in a show of militarism, chose to wear military fatigues during the recent swearing in of MPs," complained that his guests, President Kabila of the DRC and Goodluck Jonathan of Nigeria, "were pelted with stones by people."

"In Nairobi, grassroots movements such as 'Bunge La Mwananchi' [The People's Parliament] and the 'Unga Revolution' [a collection of civil society groups including Bunge La Mwananchi] campaigning for economic and social rights have been formed in response to the rising cost of living and loss of social benefits."

In Manzini, "The Swazi pro-democracy uprisings which began on 12 April 2013 were met with beatings, teargas and hundreds of arrests. Many of the protesters were driven 100 miles into the country where they were dumped by the police. Student leader Maxwell Dlamini and Musa Ngubeni of the Swaziland Youth Congress were arrested, tortured and remain in detention."

In Gaborone, "Botswana, much revered in the west as 'Africa's success story,' public sector workers—transport, schools, clinics and government staff—began striking on 18 April 2013. The ruling party has been in power for 45 years and people are calling for a change. The leader of the opposition, Duma Boko has called for an 'Egypt-style uprising.'"

In Harare in February 2011, Robert Mugabe's forces arrested 45 attendees of an International Socialist Organisation Zimbabwe meeting who were reviewing footage from Tahrir Square and Tunisia. In Dakar, Senegal's well-respected mass movements rose up in late June, burning down the country's national electricity building and tax authority, and protesting at cabinet ministers' houses to force both a resolution of an energy crisis and a withdrawal of President Abdoulawaye Wade's proposed legislation that would have seen him extend his neoliberal political rule. That protest was successful, as was the January 2012 "Occupy Nigeria" protests against the doubling of the fuel price mandated by IMF Managing Director Christine Lagarde. Millions of Nigerians took to the streets, and it became evident to President Goodluck Jonathan that he would have to concede on the socio-economic front, or be ousted from power.

In addition to movements to democratize societies, which are invariably drawn from and compel further struggles for socio-economic justice, innumerable micro-struggles continue. These include community campaigns to preserve natural resources and rethink the merits of extractive industries (especially minerals, fossil fuels and river sources), in places like the Niger Delta, Zimbabwe's diamond fields and South Africa's platinum and titanium belts. Others are national initiatives of labor and its allies to meet basic needs and balance local economies through domestic ("import-substitution") production, with South Africans the most active.

The ability of labor to move from micro-shop floor and industry-level demands to national policy will be crucial to Africa's future uprisings. For optimists, the World Economic Forum's September 2013 *Global Competitiveness Report* demonstrated that Africa's labor protesters are easily the world's most militant, even if not yet most effective. In one questionnaire given to representative samples of corporate managers, the topic of "Cooperation in labor-employer relations" is quantified on a scale of 1 to 7, from "generally confrontational" to "generally cooperative." The mean for the worlds' working classes was 4.3, i.e. with a bias towards quiescence. Table 11.3 shows the results of a selection from 148 countries, of which 39 are African: northern and Asian workers are most pliable, and African (especially South African) are most militant. Of the 39 African countries surveyed, 30 were higher than (or at) the world mean level of militancy. South Africa was by far the most militant working class, for the second year in a row.

Table 11.3 Africa's working-class militancy, 2013: Ranking of 148 countries

1 Switzerland 6.0	63 Sierra Leone 4.4	116 Tanzania 3.9
2 Singapore 6.0	66 Madagascar 4.4	117 Egypt 3.8
3 Denmark 5.8	67 Zambia 4.3	118 Cape Verde 3.8
4 Norway 5.8	69 Ghana 4.3	119 Tunisia 3.8
5 Netherlands 5.7	73 Kenya 4.2	121 Ethiopia 3.8
6 Sweden 5.7	78 Liberia 4.2	122 Lesotho 3.8
7 Qatar 5.6	85 Libya 4.2	123 Zimbabwe 3.7
8 Hong Kong SAR 5.6	91 Morocco 4.1	126 Cameroon 3.7
9 Japan 5.6	93 Uganda 4.1	127 Benin 3.7
10 Austria 5.5	95 Malawi 4.1	130 Mozambique 3.6
28 Gambia, The 5.0	100 Nigeria 4.1	137 Algeria 3.4
32 Rwanda 4.9	102 Guinea 4.0	141 Chad 3.3
36 Côte d'Ivoire 4.8	104 Namibia 4.0	142 Mauritania 3.3
38 Mauritius 4.8	108 Botswana 4.0	143 Burundi 3.2
45 Seychelles 4.6	110 Burkina Faso 4.0	145 Angola 3.1
54 Mali 4.5	114 Gabon 3.9	148 South Africa 2.6
57 Senegal 4.5		

Note: Top 10 pliable working classes are shown, followed by 39 African countries, rated 1–7.
Source: World Economic Forum, 2013.

This degree of anger must, at some stage, result in a more effective double movement than has happened to date. The earlier era of protests did not derail neoliberalism in Africa, even though in 1983 World Bank president A.W. Clausen was worried enough to tell a board meeting, "We must ask ourselves: How much pressure can these nations be expected to bear? How far can the poorest peoples be pushed into further reducing their meagre standards of living? How resilient are the political systems and institutions in these countries in the face of steadily worsening conditions? I don't have the answers to these important questions." (Clausen, 1983).

More recently, the world's elites have been aware of the potential for more sustained critique, for in 2011, the IMF's then managing director, Dominique Strauss-Kahn, was asked by a journalist, "Do you have any fears that there is perhaps a far left movement coming through these revolutions that want more, perhaps, closed economies? I mean, there have been a lot of pictures of Guevara there." His answer:

> Good question. Good question. There's always this risk, but I'm not sure it will materialize. Look, during the global financial crisis we went just through, at the beginning many were afraid of the possibility of an increase in protectionism. It didn't happen. Why? Because, I think, that most governments, maybe not all of them, but most governments and most people, man on the street, have understood that there was no good solution in this direction. I'm not saying that everybody agrees with this, but most had understood that the closed economy were not the way to benefit from global growth and certainly from investment.

> And we're in a globalized world, so there is no domestic solution. (International Monetary Fund, 2011a)

To make the case that we need not worry about Africans inspired by Che—whose mid-1960s fight against Mobutu alongside (briefly) the father of current DRC president Joseph Kabila, was utterly miserable—Strauss-Kahn used as a proxy "protectionism." In the case of South Africa, normally amongst Africa's most aggressively neoliberal regimes, Strauss-Kahn should have been worried, for in 2009, a Communist Party member, Rob Davies, was made trade minister, and by 2013 he had begun widespread cancellation of free trade deals, and even imposed an 82 percent tariff on import of Brazilian chickens. The "domestic solution" Strauss-Kahn despises is also to be found in the reimposition of capital controls, defaults on Odious Debt, state-directed investment and favorable interest rates (Asian "developmental state"-style), Keynesian reflation and more social spending. These strategies are all gaining steam, leading *The Economist* to worriedly headline its 12 October 2013 special issue on the world economy, "The Gated Globe."

What the IMF leader should also have considered was a deeper set of critical reactions to the era of African neoliberalism in which financialization has fused with extractivist accumulation, and in which the "Africa Rising" argument is increasingly revealed as rubbish. If so, then the "far left movement" seeking "closed economies"—i.e., those protected from especially the ravages of deregulated global finance—would find a much more compelling Polanyian double movement which has emerged in civil (and often uncivil) society. As we have seen, the resistance stiffened especially beginning in 2011. This is true not only in North Africa, but also in Sub-Saharan Africa. Most crucially, the South African bottom-up rupture with the African neoliberal-nationalist script is worth following; indications in late 2013 were that connectivities can be found in sites of grassroots and labor struggle, offering hope for stronger alliances of poor and working people than we have ever known here, perhaps also beyond South Africa's borders. The question in coming months and years is whether the Numsa metalworkers broaden out into the general working class, and simultaneously reach downwards into the unemployed and especially youth, for support and linkage to the communities' service delivery protests.

If such protests can coagulate and move from local to national to continental to global scales in coming years, what would they be potentially articulating, as an antidote to "Africa Rising" rhetoric? According to Balogun,

> African governments hold the solution to a more equitable society. By closing the skills gap, initiating a more progressive corporate tax system, and providing subsidies for public services that protect the bottom percentile, many countries can begin to turn the tide. However, we must all first admit that most Africans are not rising with Africa, and that wealth disparity is a major obstacle to overall development. (Balogun, 2013)

Once that admission is accepted, further words of counsel are provided by Ama Biney, *Pambazuka News* editor:

> Ultimately, fundamental to Africa genuinely 'rising' must be a critical examination of what this 'rising' will entail. What kind of development do we envisage for Africa? Does it only lie in economic development and progress? What about social and cultural development? What about the psyche and aesthetics that a people adhere and aspire to? What kind of economic development will ensure that the economy is controlled by the greatest number of ordinary people rather than the minority? If Africa is to rise, surely it must rise for the greatest majority of its people—particularly the unemployed youth in many African countries; those living with disabilities ostracized and stigmatized by cultural taboos and attitudes; albino individuals who also face similar stigmatization; women; the poor; those in need of ARV drugs to prolong the quality of their lives as they live with HIV/AIDS as well as LBGTI individuals persecuted in many African countries?

However, at the moment it seems the type of development the "Africa is rising" evangelists envisage is that which Fanon warned us against: an imitation of Europe and a desire to catch up with Europe. There appears little desire or will to seek an alternative to capitalism, one that is centered on the ideas and interests of ordinary people. There was no blueprint for capitalism yet it was constructed on the backs of African slaves and wage laborers around the world. Similarly, there is no model nor blueprint for socialism yet many are seduced by TINA (There is No Alternative to Capitalism) which maintains the neoliberal status quo. If Africa is to rise, it must heed Thomas Sankara and "dare to invent the future" based on a new egalitarian economic system that puts people before profits and in which ordinary people critically control the production of what they produce and how they produce it (Biney, 2013).

References

Action Aid. 2006. *Real Aid.* London. http://www.actionaid.org/sites/files/action aid/real_aid.pdf.

Adesanmi, P. 2012. Occupy Nigeria: Ngozi Okonjo-Iweala, Paul Collier, and Some Troublesome Nigerian Professors!, *Sahara Reporters*, Lagos, 20 January, http://saharareporters.com/column/occupy-nigeria-ngozi-okonjo-iweala-paul-collier-and-some-troublesome-nigerian-professors.

AfricaFocus Bulletin. 2005. Nigeria: Debt Deal Views, 10/27/05. http://www.africa.upenn.edu/afrfocus/afrifocus102705.html.

African Development Bank, OECD Development Centre, UN Development Programme and Economic Commission for Africa. 2013. *African Economic Outlook*, Tunis. www.africaneconomicoutlook.org.

Ambrose, S. 2005. IMF Adds a New Tool to its Bag of Tricks, Washington, International Debt Observatory. http://www.oid-ido.org/article.php3?id_article=136.

Appel, H. 2011. *Futures: Oil and the Making of Modularity in Equatorial Guinea.* Doctoral dissertation. Stanford University, Department of Anthropology, Palo Alto, California.

Ashman, S., B. Fine and S. Newman. 2010. "The Crisis in South Africa: Neoliberalism, Financialization and Uneven and Combined Development," in L. Panitch, G. Albo and V. Chibber (eds) *The Crisis This Time: Socialist Register 2011.* London: Merlin Press; New York: Monthly Review Press.

Aslund, A. 2013. "Now the Brics Party is Over, They Must Wind Down the State's Role. *Financial Times*, 22 August. http://www.ft.com/intl/cms/s/0/0147b43c-040b-11e3-8aab-00144feab7de.html#axzz2keJpWM2W.

Balogun, J. 2013. "Africa is Rising. Most Africans are Not." *Compare Afrique*, 15 February, http://www.compareafrique.com/africa-is-rising-most-africans-are-not/.

Biney, A. 2013. "Is Africa Really Rising?" Pambazuka News, 31 July and 4 September. http://pambazuka.org/en/category/books/88474 and http://pambazuka.org/en/category/features/88748.

Bates, R. 2012. "Africa Through Western Eyes: The World's Dark Continent or Capitalism's Shining Light?" *Think Africa Press*, 31 October 2012. http://thinkafricapress.com/culture/africa-through-western-eyes-worlds-dark-continent-or-capitalisms-shining-light.

Bond, P. 2006. *Looting Africa.* London: Zed Books.

Bond, P. 2010. "Is Africa Still Being Looted? World Bank Dodges its Own Research," *Links*, 15 August 2010. http://links.org.au/node/1843.

Bond, P. 2013. "Subimperialism as Lubricant of Neoliberalism: South African 'Deputy Sheriff' Duty within BRICS." *Third World Quarterly*, 34, 2.

Bond, P. and S. Mottiar. 2013. "Social Protest in South Africa." *Journal of Contemporary African Studies*, 31(2), 283–302.

CADTM Commission to Annul Third World Debt. 2008. "Topicality of Odious Debt." Brussels, 8 August. http://cadtm.org/Topicality-of-the-odious-debt.

Calandro, E., A. Gillwald, M. Moyo and C. Stork. 2010. *Comparative Sector Performance Review 2009/2010: Towards Evidence-based ICT Policy and Regulation*, volume 2, policy paper 2. http://www.researchictafrica.net/publications/Policy_Paper_Series_Towards_Evidence-based_ICT_Policy_and_Regulation_-_Volume_2/Vol_2_Paper_2_-_Comparative_Sector_Performance_Review_2009_2010.pdf.

Clausen, A.W. 1983. Speech by the World Bank President to Board of Directors. Washington, DC: World Bank.

Davel, G. 2011. *Debt Stress: A Harmless Cold or a Deadly Virus?* Consultative Group to Assist the Poor, 14 February. http://microfinance.cgap.org/2011/02/14/debt-stress-%E2%80%93-a-harmless-cold-or-a-deadly-virus/.

Ekine, S. 2011. "Defiant in the Face of Brutality: Uprisings in East and Southern Africa." *Pambazuka News*, 532, 2 June. http://pambazuka.org/en/category/features/73738.

Elliott, L. 2012. Aid to Africa Dwindles as Euro Crisis Rages On." *Mail & Guardian*, 29 June. http://mg.co.za/article/2012-06-29-aid-to-africa-dwindles-as-euro-crisis-rages-on.

Enaudeau, J. 2013. "In Search of the African Middle Class." *Africa is a Country*, 1 May 2013. http://africasacountry.com/2013/05/01/in-search-of-the-african-middle-class/.

Ernst & Young. 2013. *Africa Attractiveness Survey.* New York. http://www.ey.com/ZA/en/Issues/Business-environment/Africa-Attractiveness-Survey.

Fransman, M. 2012. *South Africa: A Strong African Brick in BRICS.* Stellenbosch: University of Stellenbosch, 21 November.

Global Aids Alliance. 2005. Nigeria's Creditors Should be Ashamed, Says Global AIDS Alliance: Nigeria to Send $12.4 Billion to World's Richest Nations, Washington, http://www.prnewswire.com/news-releases/nigerias-creditors-should-be-ashamed-says-global-aids-alliance-55483812.html.

International Monetary Fund. 2009. *Africa: Regional Economic Outlook.* Washington, DC: IMF.

International Monetary Fund. 2011a. Press conference, 6 April. Washington, DC: IMF.

International Monetary Fund. 2011b. Statement by IMF Managing Director Christine Lagarde at the Conclusion of her Visit to Nigeria, Washington, DC: IMF Press Release No. 11/478, 20 December. http://www.imf.org/external/np/sec/pr/2011/pr11478.htm.

Karikari, J. 2010. *Governance, Financial Liberalization, and Financial Development in Sub-Saharan Africa.* Washington, DC: US Government Accountability Office.

Kganyago, L. 2004. "South Africa as a Financial Centre for Africa." Speech to the Reuters Economist of the Year Award Ceremony, Johannesburg, 11 August.

Laverty, A. 2011. "Globalization in Emerging Markets: How South Africa's Relationship to Africa Serves the BRICS." *The African File*, 2 May. http://theafricanfile.com/public-diplomacy/international-relations/globalization-in-emerging-markets-united-how-south-africa%E2%80%99s-relationship-to-africa-serves-the-brics/.

Magnowsky, D. 2014. Nigerian Economy Overtakes South Africa's on Rebased GDP, *Bloomberg*, 7 April. http://www.bloomberg.com/news/2014-04-06/nigerian-economy-overtakes-south-africa-s-on-rebased-gdp.html.

Manuel, T. 2002. *Mobilizing International Investment Flows: The New Global Outlook.* Speech to the Commonwealth Business Council, Johannesburg, 24 September.

Mataboge, M. 2013. "Nkoana-Mashabane: South Africa is not Looting the Continent, We're Cultivating Peace and Trade." *Mail and Guardian*, 15 November.

Mbeki, T. 2012. "Tackling Illicit Capital Flows for Economic Transformation." Thabo Mbeki Foundation, Johannesburg, South Africa. http://www.thabombeki foundation.org.za/Pages/Tackling-Illicit-Capital-Flows-for-Economic-Trans formation.aspx.

Mekay, E. 2011. "Privatization Aided Egypt Revolt, Army Says." *InterPress Service*, 8 April. http://www.ips.org/africa/2011/04/privatisation-aided-egypt-revolt-army-says/.

Molatlhwa, O. 2012. "DBSA Not Backing Down on Mo." *Sunday World*, 13 August. http://www.sundayworld.co.za/news/2012/08/13/dbsa-not-backing-down-on-mo.

Mthethwa, N. 2013. Remarks by the Minister of Police at the Release of the SA Police Services 2012/2013 National Crime Statistics." Pretoria, South Africa. http://politicsweb.co.za/politicsweb/view/politicsweb/en/page71656?oid=405 740&sn=Detail&pid=71656.

Ndikumana, L. and J. Boyce. 2011. *Africa's Odious Debts*. London: Zed Books.

Ndikumana, L. and J. Boyce. 2012a. *Capital Flight from North African Countries*. University of Massachusetts/Amherst Political Economy Research Institute. http://www.peri.umass.edu/fileadmin/pdf/ADP/NAfrica_capitalflight_Oct 15_2012. pdf.

Ndikumana, L. and J. Boyce. 2012b. *Capital Flight from Sub-Saharan African Countries: Updated Estimates, 1970—2010*. University of Massachusetts, Amherst Political Economy Research Institute. http://www.peri.umass.edu/ fileadmin/pdf/ADP/SSAfrica_capitalflight_Oct23_2012.pdf.

Omanufeme, S. 2014. Why Nigeria delayed GDP rebasing for 24 years, *ThisDay*, 6 April. http://www.thisdaylive.com/articles/why-nigeria-delayed-gdp-rebasing-for-twenty-four-years/175494/.

Paton, C. 2013. "Are the Right People Leaving DBSA." *Business Day*, 10 April. http://www.bdlive.co.za/business/financial/2013/04/10/are-the-right-people-leaving-dbsa.

Perry, A. 2012. Africa Rising, *Time*, 3 December.

Republic of South Africa Government Communications and Information Service. 2002 Statement on Cabinet Meeting. Pretoria, South Africa, 26 June.

Robertson, C. 2013. "Why Africa Will Rule the 21st Century." *African Business*, 7 January 2013. http://africanbusinessmagazine.com/features/profile/why-africa-will-rule-the-21st-century.

Rowden, R. 2013. "The Myth of Africa's Rise: Why the Rumors of Africa's Explosive Growth Have Been Greatly Exaggerated." *Foreign Policy*, 4 January 2013. http://www.foreignpolicy.com/articles/2013/01/04/the_myth_ of_africa_s_rise.

Sharife, K. 2011. *Tax Us If You Can.* Oxford: Fahamu Books. http://www. taxjustice.net/cms/upload/pdf/tuiyc_africa_final.pdf.

Shaw, A. 2012. "Experts: African Countries Lose AIDS Funding." Associated Press, 19 July. http://news.yahoo.com/experts-africa-countries-lose-aids-fund ing-120711764.html.

Smith, D. 2011. "One in three Africans is Now Middle Class, Report Finds." *The Guardian*, 5 May. http://www.guardian.co.uk/global-development/2011/may/05/one-three-africans-middle-class.

Stiglitz. J. and H. Rashid. 2013. "Sub-Saharan Africa's Subprime Borrowers." *The Global Dispatches*, 1 July. http://www.theglobaldispatches.com/articles/sub-saharan-africas-subprime-borrowers.

United Nations Conference on Trade and Development. 2011. *Economic Development in Africa*, Geneva: UNCTD.

United Nations Conference on Trade and Development. 2012. *Economic Development in Africa*, Geneva: UNCTD.

World Bank. 2011. *The Changing Wealth of Nations.* Washington, DC: World Bank.

Chapter 12

The Structural Crisis of Global Capitalism and the Prospects for World Revolution in the Twenty-First Century[1]

Chris Chase-Dunn and Anthony Roberts

The recent waves of social unrest coupled with the weak performance of global markets have demarcated a turning point in the trajectory of global capitalism. Rising income inequality, public debt insolvency, declines in global output, chronic structural unemployment, financial instability, and the political oppression of pro-democracy movements are showing the natural limits of the current regime of global capitalism. During the crises of the 1930s and 1970s, the systemic contradictions of declining profits and social unrest was resolved with the global dispersion of capital, the incorporation of new lands and populations into the system, and the establishment of Fordist-Keynesian regimes of accumulation. However, the current structural crisis of profit accumulation and social unrest has shown the limits of these solutions while signifying a transitional moment in the capitalist world-system.

The important question is whether this new wave of unrest and market failure represents a transition into a new phase of capitalist development or the end of capitalism. According to the 'systemic cycles of accumulation' (SCA) perspective (Arrighi 1994, 2006), the recent financial crisis signified the end of the US regime of accumulation and the transition toward a new mode of capitalist accumulation based on a global market-system regulated by emerging global institutions. However, according to the recent work of Immanuel Wallerstein (2003), the current systemic crises are indicative of an "Age of Transition" and the end of the capitalist mode of accumulation. Given this disagreement over the trajectory of the capitalist world-system, we aim to evaluate the current structural crises and the emergence of anti-systemic movements to determine whether capitalism is undergoing another transformation into a new regime of capitalist accumulation or whether the modern world-system itself is ending and being replaced by a new mode of accumulation.

1 Thanks to Roy Kwon for help with an earlier version of this chapter. Our research on trade globalization trends has been supported by National Science Foundation Grant #NSF-HSD SES-0527720.

In this chapter, we review the structural crisis of global capitalism and the nascent constellation of anti- systemic movements (the New Global Left) to evaluate the possibility of evolutionary change in the modern world-system. Given the relatively short lifespan of global capitalism, we argue that recent structural contradictions are likely to produce a new phase of capitalist development, which establishes a global Keynesian regime to manage global economic instabilities. While current crises and movements provide the sociopolitical opportunity for a transition from capitalism into a more egalitarian mode of accumulation, the New Global Left would need to become much more organized and effective in order to motivate significant and collectively rational solutions to the contradictions of capitalism within the next few decades.

The Emergence of Capitalism

Predominant form of modern capitalism was born in semiperipheral Europe. Similar to previous world-system transformations, the structural conditions of the semiperiphery facilitated the increased predomination of a different logic of accumulation (Chase-Dunn and Hall, 1997). Because of this institutional development, Europe was able to move to the core of the modern world-system and to expand its control of other continents. The forereaching states that further evolved capitalism were former semiperipheral polities that rose to hegemony. These semiperipheral polities were able to develop and implement new institutional models for resolving the systemic crises brought on by previous hegemonic regimes located in the core of the modern system. Therefore, economic crises and world revolutions have been important elements in the evolution of capitalism and global governance institutions for centuries.

In between periods of hegemony in the world-system were periods of hegemonic rivalry in which several contenders strove for global power. The core of the modern world-system has remained multicentric, meaning that a number of sovereign states ally and compete with one another. Earlier regional world-systems sometimes experienced a period of core-wide empire in which a single empire became so large that there were no serious contenders for predominance. This did not happen in the modern world-system until the United States became the single super- power following the demise of the Soviet Union in 1989.

The sequence of hegemonies can be understood as the evolution of global governance in the modern world-system. The system of theoretically sovereign states was expanded to include the peripheral regions in two large waves of decolonization in the 1830s and mid-1900s, eventually resulting in a situation in which the whole modern system became composed of sovereign national states. East Asia was incorporated into this system in the nineteenth century, though aspects of the earlier East Asian tribute-trade state system were not completely obliterated by that incorporation (Hamashita, 2003).

Each of the hegemonies was larger as a proportion of the whole system than the earlier one had been. And each developed the institutions of economic and political-military control by which it led the larger system such that capitalism increasingly deepened its penetration of all the areas of the earth. And after the Napoleonic Wars in which Britain finally defeated its main competitor, France, global political institutions began to emerge over the tops of the international system of national states. The first proto-world-government was the Concert of Europe, a fragile flower that wilted when its main proponents, Britain and the Austro-Hungarian Empire, disagreed about how to handle the world revolution of 1848. The Concert was followed by the League of Nations and then by the United Nations and the Bretton Woods international financial institutions (The World Bank, the International Monetary Fund and eventually the World Trade Organization).

The political globalization evident in the trajectory of global governance evolved because the powers that be were in heavy contention with one another for geopolitical control and for economic resources, but also because resistance emerged within the polities of the core and in the regions of the non-core. The series of hegemonies, waves of colonial expansion and decolonization and the emergence of a proto-world-state occurred as the global elites tried to compete with one another and to contain resistance from below. Other important forces of resistance were slave revolts, the labor movement, the extension of citizenship to men of no property, the women's movement, and other associated rebellions and social movements.

These movements affected the evolution of global governance in part because the rebellions often clustered together in time, forming what have been called "world revolutions" (Arrighi et al., 1989; Martin et al., 2008).[2] The Protestant Reformation in Europe was an early instance that played a big role in the rise of the Dutch hegemony. The French Revolution of 1789 was linked in time with the American and Haitian revolts. The 1848 rebellion in Europe was both synchronous with the Taiping Rebellion in China and was linked with it by the diffusion of ideas, as it was also linked with several new Christian Sects in the United States. In 1917 a constellation of anti-world capitalist movements emerged with the Bolsheviks in Russia, the Chinese Nationalist revolt, the Mexican Revolution, the Arab Revolt of 1916, and the General Strike in Seattle led by the Industrial Workers of the World. Responding to previous anti-systemic movements, a "New Left" emerged in 1968 with the student revolts in the US, Europe, Latin America and the Red Guards in China. Since the collapse of the Soviet Union in 1989 anti-systemic

2 The important book on world revolutions by Giovanni Arrighi, Terence Hopkins and Immanuel Wallerstein (1984) pointed out that revolutionaries rarely attain their demands immediately. Rather what happens is that "enlightened conservatives" implement the demands of an earlier revolution in order to cool out the challenges of a current world revolution. This is the way in which world revolutions produce the evolution of global governance.

movements have learned important lessons about the value of civil rights beyond justification for capitalist democracy, which has led to a nascent global civil society challenging world- capitalism.

The current world revolution of 20xx (Chase-Dunn and Niemeyer, 2009) will be discussed in this chapter as the global countermovement that is occurring during the period of the contemporary crisis. The big idea here is that the evolution of capitalism and of global governance is importantly *a response to resistance and rebellions from below*. This has been true in the past and is likely to continue to be true in the future. Boswell and Chase-Dunn (2000) contend that capitalism and socialism have dialectically interacted with one another in a positive feedback loop similar to a spiral. Labor and socialist movements were obviously a reaction to capitalist industrialization, but also the US hegemony and the post-Second World War global institutions were importantly spurred on by the World Revolution of 1917 and the waves of decolonization. The emergence of self-determination movements in European colonies caused the expansion of the institution of sovereignty and the incorporation of new lands and people into the capitalist world-system. More importantly, the emergence of labor movements in the core and communist revolution in Eastern Europe and Asia spurred the social reform of capitalist accumulation in these by instituting strong welfare regimes and social provisions at the national-level (Arrighi, Hopkins, and Wallerstein 1989). The constellation of anti-systemic movements during the early 20th century was a major factor in the development of the current regime of accumulation based on US hegemony.

In the current moment of systemic crisis, nascent global movements have emerged in response to the structural failure of global capitalism. For example, while new territories were recognized as sovereign states during the first half of the 20th century, several of these countries continue to be controlled by non-democratic regimes which obtained power through the support of Western Europe and the United States. Additionally, since the 1970s, the social pact between capital and labor in the core has been under attack by neoliberal reform instigated by the Reagan and Thatcher regimes to combat declining profit rates caused by the economic crises of the 1970s and 1980s. More importantly, the recent financial collapse and global economic recession have compounded these structural failures as states try to manage public spending and debt solvency while stimulating economic growth. In response to the recent systemic crisis, a new constellation of movements and political regimes have begun to challenge the capitalist world-system with renewed demands for democratic reform, social spending, and greater economic equality. The more critical question of whether this new constellation is the harbinger of a new regime of capitalism or the end of capitalism itself remains to be answered.

Stages of World Capitalist Development: Systemic Cycles of Accumulation

Giovanni Arrighi's (1994) account of "systemic cycles of accumulation" (SCA) has solved some of the problems of the notion that world capitalism started in the long sixteenth century and then went through repetitive cycles and trends. Rather than positing "stages of capitalism" that national societies each go through (as most of the older Marxists did), Arrighi posits somewhat overlapping global cycles of capitalist accumulation in which finance capital and state power take on new forms and increasingly penetrate the whole system. In this sequence of global cycles and regime formation, Arrighi identifies two general events that distinctly mark the transition between phases within cycles and the transition between cycles themselves. More specifically, *signal crises* are events which mark the current regime of accumulation switch from investing in trade and production to investing in financial instruments. *Terminal crises* are the major event when regimes of accumulation collapse and are incapable of reproducing themselves (Arrighi, 1994: 215). In applying the SCA approach to the current crisis, it is critical to identify whether current structural instability and social unrest is a terminal crisis and the beginning of a new regime of accumulation or the end of capitalism itself.

Systemic cycles of accumulation are more different from one another than are Wallerstein's cycles of expansion and contraction and upward secular trends. And Arrighi (2006) made more out of the differences between the current period of US hegemonic decline and the decades at the end of the nineteenth century and the early twentieth century when British hegemony was declining. The emphasis is less on the beginning and the end of the capitalist world-system and more on the evolution of new institutional forms of accumulation and the increasing incorporation of modes of control into the logic of capitalism. For example, Arrighi (2006), taking a cue from Andre Gunder Frank (1998), saw the rise of China as portending a new systemic cycle of accumulation in which "market society" would eventually come to replace rapacious finance capital as the leading institutional form in the next phase of world history.[3] However, Arrighi (1994, 2006) never discussed the end of capitalism and the emergence of another basic logic of social reproduction and accumulation. But he did explicitly analyze how the current world situation was similar to, yet importantly different from, the period of declining British hegemonic power before the First World War (see a detailed summary in Chase-Dunn and Lawrence, 2011: 1471–1451).

3 Arrighi sees the development of market society in China as a consequence of the differences between the East Asian and Europe-centered systems before their merger in the nineteenth century, and as an outcome of the Chinese Revolution. His discussion of Adam Smith's notions of societal control over finance capital is interesting, but he is vague as to what are the forces that can counter-balance the power of finance capital. In China it is obviously the Communist Party and the new class of technocratic mandarins. This is somewhat similar in form to Peter Evans's discussion of the importance of technocrats in Brazilian, Japanese and Korean "developmental states."

In case of British hegemony, the two primary factors leading to its inevitable fall were the emergence of the German state as a military contender in the European and global balances of power and the emergence of the United States as an economic contender in the world economy (Arrighi, 1994: 39). The culmination of these factors erupted into the terminal crisis of British hegemony: the first and second World Wars, which left the British Empire in shambles and created both a political and economic power vacuum in the word-system for the rise of US hegemony. Additionally, in response to the instability of British hegemony during this period, a cluster of social movements emerged to challenge the British regime of accumulation (Martin et al., 2008).

Unlike the decline of British hegemony, in the current world- system no military or economic contender has emerged to replace US hegemony. Even though the US SCA has entered its autumn with the Vietnam War and the economic crisis of the mid-1970s, there has been no legitimate hegemonic contender capable of instituting a new global regime to resolve both social and economic contradictions of global capitalism. This fundamental difference between British and US hegemony have led to diverging opinions on the next phase of capitalist development.

Arrighi argues that the commercial and industrial rise of China, coupled with its growing economic interdependence with United States, has led to a "bifurcation" of political and economic power in the world-system. In terms of political power, the US and its European and Asian allies continue to dominate global geopolitics and international institutions. However, in terms of global economic power, the United States continues to slowly fall from the "commanding heights" of the world economy. Overall, Arrighi argues that the next cycle of capitalist accumulation will be built upon a system of market exchange, in which economic power is multi-polar and global political power is constrained by economic interdependence in the world-system (Arrighi, 2006). Given the global effect of the most recent financial crisis in the US and the European Union, it is becoming increasingly clear that the current regime of US hegemony is incapable of resolving the contradictions of capitalist accumulation. This may indicate that the world-system is experiencing the terminal crisis of US hegemony and the beginning of a new regime of capitalist accumulation.

For Immanuel Wallerstein (2003) the decline of US hegemony and the absence of a powerful hegemonic contender indicate the terminal *end* of capitalism rather than a moment of transition between regimes. From this perspective, the end of capitalist accumulation is primarily driven by the inability of a new system to resolve three structural contradictions of capitalist accumulation:

1) rise of real wages; 2) rising costs of material inputs; and 3) rising taxes. Overall, these trends perpetually reduce the average rate of profit, thus, making the current structure of capitalism unsustainable for profit maximizing. In the past, new regimes have devised strategies for combating these trends (automation, capital flight, job blackmail, attacks on the welfare state and unions, etc.), but these strategies have

become ineffective.[4] Therefore, Wallerstein calls the next five decades "The Age of Transition" (Hopkins and Wallerstein, 1996; Wallerstein, 2003), where the world-system will either institutionalize a new mode of accumulation or fall into a long-term state of instability.

In general, Wallerstein's version is more apocalyptic and more millenarian compared to Arrighi's evolutionary perspective. The old world is ending. The new world is beginning. In the coming systemic bifurcation what people do may be prefigurative and causal of the world to come. And he agrees with the students of the New Left in 1968 and many activists in the current global justice and anti-austerity movements that the tactic of taking state power has been shown to be futile because of the disappointing outcomes of the World Revolution of 1917 and the decolonization movements. However, given the systemic contradictions and the inevitable structural crisis of world-capitalism, he argues that new movements have ample opportunity to fundamentally transform the modern world-system.

Economic Globalization: A New Regime of Accumulation?

Regarding the issue of whether or not the recent financial meltdown is itself a structural (or terminal) crisis or the beginning of a long process of system-wide transformation, it is relevant to examine recent trends in economic globalization. Is there yet any sign that the world economy has entered a new period of deglobalization of the kind that occurred in the first half of the twentieth century during the decline of British hegemony?

Globalization, in the sense of the expansion and intensification of larger and larger economic, political, military and information networks, has been increasing for millennia, albeit unevenly and in waves (Chase-Dunn, Kawano and Brewer 2000). And globalization is as much a cycle as a trend (see Figure 12.1). The wave of global integration that has swept the world in the decades since the Second World War is best understood by studying its similarities and differences with the waves of international trade and foreign investment expansion that have occurred in earlier centuries, especially the last half of the nineteenth century.

Figure 12.1 is an updated version of the trade globalization series published in Chase-Dunn et al. (2000). It shows the great nineteenth century wave of global trade integration, a short and volatile wave between 1900 and 1929, and the post-1945 upswing that is characterized as the "stage of global capitalism." The figure indicates that globalization is both cyclical and volatile . Accordingly, there have

4 For example, the "spatial fix" of outsourcing and off-shoring production has caused deindustrialization in the core, which decreases real wages in industrial labor markets in the core, but leads to industrialization and the emergence of labor movements in the semiperiphery and periphery, which increases real wages of industrial workers in the semiperiphery and periphery (Silver, 2003; Firebaugh, 2003).

Figure 12.1 Trade globalization: World imports as a percentage of world GDP, 1820–2012

Source: Chase-Dunn et al. (2000); World Bank (2014).

been significant periods of deglobalization in the late nineteenth century and in the first half of the twentieth century.

During the 2008–09 recession the level of world trade globalization (imports/GDP) experienced a steep decline to a pre-2000 level, but quickly recovered in 2010 and 2011. The 2012 level declined again. Trade integration is still at a very high level, but may be showing signs of instability that might be the beginning of another period of deglobalization. Investment globalization has also shown a decrease since 2008 (Ip, 2013).

The long-term upward trend since 1945 has been relatively volatile compared to previous periods, with occasional downturns in response to global recessions such as the one shown in the 1970s. Since 1945, however, short-run decreases in trade globalization have all been followed by upturns that restored the overall upward trend of trade globalization. The large decrease of trade globalization in the wake of the global financial meltdown of 2008 represents a 21 percent decrease from the previous year, the largest reversal in trade globalization since the Second World War. Even with the modest recovery since 2009, the outlook for global trade integration appears bleak with the persistence of economic recession since 2007. The question is whether or not this sharp decrease and partial recovery represents a reversal in the long upward trend observed over the past half century. Is this the beginning of another period of deglobalization? According to a recent study, the trajectory of trade globalization is primarily determined by the stability of hegemonic power within the world-system (Kwon, 2012). Given the decline of US hegemony over the last 30 years, one would expect a corresponding decline in the level of trade globalization. However, as seen in Figure 12.1, there has been a steady increase, which suggests that an alternative factor is stabilizing the world-economy. One possibility is the emergence of a new regime of global capital accumulation based on increasing internationalized circuits of commodity production. The geographic dispersion of manufacturing processes to new areas of the world-system seems to have bolstered global trade during the recent global recession. As production process continue to fragment, international trade will become an increasingly integral component to capital accumulation through manufacturing.

A critical feature of contemporary capitalism has been the transnationalization of production, which has been a significant driver of the upward trend in trade globalization since 1945. As observed in Figure 12.1, the overall value of global imports, relative to the value of world production, has steadily increased over the last 60 years. During this period, a significant structural transformation of the world economy has been the rapid geographic dispersion of production processes to the semiperiphery and periphery (Dicken, 2003; Feentstra, 1998). As firms increasingly offshore and outsource production to these countries, both imports and exports are expected to grow because of the increase in intermediate goods and service trade between firms within circuits of transnational production. The emergence of these transnational circuits of production, in which firms in different geographic locations are linked together by their constituent production of a single commodity or service, limits the possibility of a reversal in the trend of trade globalization.

In fact, this new form of economic production and growing transnational interdependency between firms lends support to Arrighi's perspective on an emerging multi-polar, market-based regime of accumulation. Compared to previous periods of hegemonic rise, industrial activities are less geographically concentrated in dominant core countries as global production circuits increasingly replace national circuits of production. For example, over the last 20 years, the rate of offshoring in the garment, electronics, and transportation equipment industries has steadily increased (Mahutga, 2012) with the integration of firms in low-wage, industrializing countries into low-value activities of global production. More so than any other developing country, China has embraced this new form of production by promoting export-oriented manufacturing and attracting foreign investment via preferential governmental policies for local industrial firms and foreign companies (Pan, 2009). The rapid growth in manufacturing in China is indicative of the increasingly important role of China in maintaining these vast new global production networks. Indeed, over the 1998–2006 period, Chinese industrial productivity increased by an average rate of 7.7 percent (Brandt et al., 2009) while the size of the Chinese manufacturing sector has grown by an

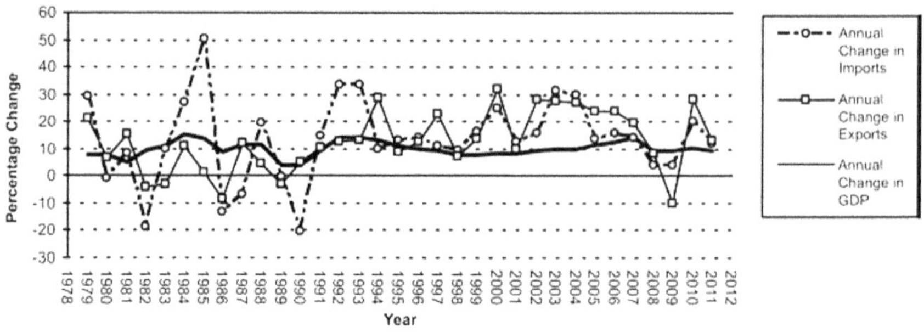

Figure 12.2 Annual growth of Chinese trade and economic development, 1979–2011

Source: World Bank (2011).

average of 10 percent per year over the last ten years (World Bank, 2011). This rapid growth in manufacturing productivity and value-added has led many to view China as the new "World Factory" (Zhang, 2006).

As discussed in Arrighi (2006), the Chinese economy is a strong empirical case for this interrelationship between globalized production and the industrial development of emerging semiperipheral countries. Indeed, as shown in Figure 12.2, over the last 30 years, the Chinese economy has managed an average growth rate of about 10 percent through the rapid growth of imports and exports. During this period, Chinese exports and imports grew by an average of about 13 percent, which has outpaced the rate of growth in the domestic economy. Since the 1990s this rate has only increased, where both exports and imports have grown ata rate of about 15 percent per year. As the value of trade increases relative to the value of domestic production, it is becoming increasingly necessary for the Chinese state to promote an export-strategy for development, which increases the dependency of the Chinese economy on the world economy (namely consumer markets in core economies) and fosters the growth of neoliberal reform in Chinese economic policy. Additionally, as seen in Figure 12.2, the volatility in exports and imports creates a degree of instability in the development of the Chinese economy, where periods of decreasing trade corresponds to declines in the rate of economic growth.

Given the central importance of international trade and investment for Chinese growth, it is important to examine how the industrialization of the semiperiphery and periphery is becoming a major force behind increasing integration of the world economy and the possibility of a "market-society" regime of accumulation. More specifically, as industrial production shifts toward the developing world, the formation and persistence of global circuits of production appears to be largely contingent on the capabilities of firms in semiperipheral and peripheral economies. China, as an example of "development through globalization," provides direct insight to how economic performance is tied to integration into global production circuits. But how are other developing countries performing?

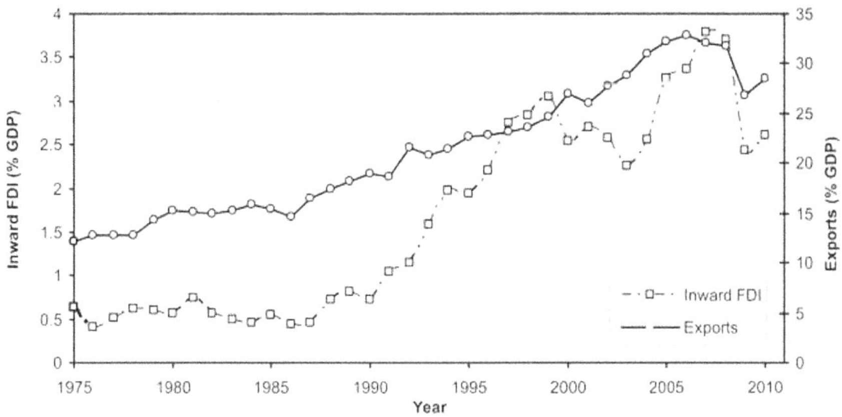

Figure 12.3 Inward foreign direct investment and total exports in low and low-middle income countries, 1975–2010

Source: World Bank (2011).

Figure 12.3 shows the trends in foreign direct investment and exports for developing countries over the past 35 years. Since the 1990s, inward foreign direct investment as dramatically increase in developing countries, where in 1980 the flow of inward FDI was valued at only .5 percent of GDP, by 2007 it increased to 3.5 percent of GDP. Similarly, exports from developing countries were valued around 13 percent of GDP, but by the mid 2000s, they climbed to over 30 percent of GDP. It appears that, as foreign capital flows into the semiperiphery and periphery, these developing economies are increasingly integrated into circuits of global production. This "development through globalization" process is becoming one of the most central features of the world economy and provides some evidence for the continuance in the upward trend of trade globalization and the increasing dominance of global capitalism.

Until the logistic and transportation costs of global production exceed the requisite rate of profit within global circuits, it appears that globalization will be a continuing feature of contemporary capitalism. The critical question, however, is whether the globalization of production, and, in general, economic globalization are capable of resolving the decline of US hegemony and the current social and economic contradictions of global capitalism. Further, in what ways has the expansion of capitalist production to the developing world amplified or suppressed the timing of the terminal crisis of US hegemony and of corporate capitalism? Lastly, is economic globalization facilitating the development of a "market-society" phase of global capitalism? In order to answer these questions, it is essential to analyze the counter-movement of society against this global intensification of capitalist production.

Financialization and Global Recession: Terminal Crisis?

A central argument of the SCA approach is that hegemonic transitions are punctuated by the growth of financial activities at the expense of productive activity in core countries during periods of declining profit rates in manufacturing sectors (Arrighi 1994). This "signal crisis" marks the transition in the systemic cycle of accumulation between hegemonic rise and decline. For the US regime of accumulation, the current growth of the financial sector appears to signify the decline of US hegemony. This rapid growth in financial activity since the 1980s was the response of US capital to the perceived threats to profits in the 1970s: 1) surging oil prices; 2) growth in real wages; and 3) global manufacturing competition (Harvey, 2005; Tomaskovic-Devey and Lin, 2011; Miller and Tomaskovic-Devey, 1983). Indeed, over the last ten years, several studies have provide evidence on the rapid growth of the financial sector in the United States and a dramatic deregulation of financial activities (Epstein and Jayadev, 2005; Krippner, 2005, 2011; Davis, 2009; Tomaskovic-Devey and Lin, 2011; Lin and Tomaskovic-Devey, 2013). According to this literature, since the 1980s the share of profits from the financial sector has steadily increased (Krippner, 2005; Tomaskovic-Devey and Lin, 2011) while the relative compensation of employees in the financial sector has substantially grown compared to other sectors (Philippon and Reshef, 2009; Tomaskovic-Devey and Lin 2011). As a consequence of this growth in financial investment and wages in the financial sector, income inequality has steadily increased in the US while the labor share of income has steadily declined. As the US economy becomes increasingly dominated by financial capital, has the rest of the world-system undergone a similar process? As seen in Figure 12.4, the banking and stock markets have rapidly grown across the world since the 1980s.

While the banking sector has steadily increased, the stock market has been relatively volatile and unstable because of a series of bubbles and bursts. Since 1960, domestic credit from the banking sector has increased by 106 percent while the market capitalization of publically traded firms (e.g. price of company stocks by the number of shares) has grown by 7 percent from 1985 to 2011. However, between 1985 and 1999, market capitalization grew by 102 percent, but declined by 70 percent over the next five years because of the tech bubble burst. This decline was soon followed by the real estate bubble which caused a rapid growth in market capitalization. However, this growth was followed by another rapid decline which was caused by the recent financial collapse instigated by the burst of the real estate bubble. The instability of financial accumulation and the growth of the financial market appears to have created a degree of volatility in capitalist accumulation, which puts the world economy in a perpetual state of crisis.

The recent financial collapse has signified the end of US hegemony and the current regime of capitalist accumulation. However, whether the current regime is being replaced by a new regime based on transnational production depends on whether transnational capital will implement a new strategy that resolves the structural crises induced by processes of globalization and financialization. More

Figure 12.4 Global trends in banking and stock market value, 1960–2010
Source: World Bank (2011).

importantly, a new regime of accumulation needs to address the demands of the nascent constellation of anti-systemic movements. The rest of this chapter is aimed at reviewing this "new Global Left."

The World Revolution of 20xx

World history has proceeded in a series of waves. Capitalist expansions have ebbed and flowed, and egalitarian religious and humanistic counter-movements have emerged in a cyclical dialectical struggle. Polanyi (1944) called this the double-movement. Boswell and Chase-Dunn (2000) have termed it the "spiral of capitalism and socialism." This spiral of capitalism and socialism describes the undulations of the global economy that have alternated between expansive commodification throughout the global economy, followed by resistance movements on behalf of workers and other oppressed groups. The Reagan/Thatcher neoliberal capitalist globalization project extended the power of transnational capital. During the 1980s and 1990s, the United States and Western Europe underwent a series of economic reforms aimed at removing capital and trade controls while promoting greater labor market flexibility through the dismantling of social policies. Coupled with the export-oriented developmental strategy of East Asia and other developing countries, this neo-liberal reform in the core initiated the rapid growth in international trade, investment, and financial sectors across most areas of the world-system. However, this project has reached its ideological and material limits. It has increased inequality within some countries, exacerbated rapid urbanization in the Global South (so-called *Planet of Slums* [Davis, 2006]), attacked the welfare state and institutional protections for the poor, and led to global financial crisis

(Harvey, 2005; Kotz, 2009). This trajectory of social and economic development has induced a new world counter-movement dedicated to dismantling neoliberal globalization (Santos, 2008). Whether this new counter-movement will induce a system-wide revolution toward a new mode of accumulation or a system-wide evolution to new stage of capitalist accumulation remains unanswered. By analyzing the constellation of the "New Global Left" we can begin to understand the revolutionary potential of this new world counter-movement.

The contemporary world revolution is similar to earlier ones, but also different in important ways. Our conceptualization of the New Global Left includes civil society entities: individuals, social movement organizations, labor unions, non-governmental organizations (NGOs), but also political parties and progressive national regimes.[5] In the remainder of this section we discuss the relationships among the transnational global justice movements and the progressive populist regimes that have emerged in Latin America in recent decades.[6] We also consider the Arab Spring that began in Tunisia in December of 2010 and the anti-austerity movements that have emerged in Europe and the United States.

The boundaries of the progressive forces that have come together in the New Global Left are fuzzy and the process of inclusion and exclusion is ongoing (Santos, 2006). The rules of inclusion and exclusion that are contained in the Charter of the World Social Forum, though still debated, have not changed much since their formulation in 2001.[7] The Charter defines the World Social Forum as a "movement of movements" with the general goal of opposing forms of discrimination, exclusion, and oppression. Rather than define the World Social Forum using traditional modes of political and social organization, the Charter establishes the World Social Forum as an inclusive, deliberative, and democratic organization which aims to facilitate interaction between local,

5 We conceptualize global civil society and the realm of world citizens as all those who intentionally try to have an impact on the world-system as a whole. This includes some actors whose goals are not compatible with the groups we identify as part of the New Global Left. We have in mind some of the global elite actors whose main goal is to protect their privileges and property as well as some fundamentalist religious movements.

6 We understand the Latin American "Pink Tide" regimes to be an important part of the New Global Left, though it is well known that the relationships among the movements and the regimes are both supportive and contentious.

7 The Transnational Social Movement Research Working Group at the University of California-Riverside has studied the movements participating in the World Social Forum since 2005. The project web page is at http:// www.irows.ucr.edu/research/tsmstudy.htm8. We argue that, the WSF is embedded within a larger socio-historical context that is challenging the hegemony of global capital. It was this larger context that facilitated the founding of the WSF in 2001. The anti-IMF protests of the 1980s and the Zapatista rebellion of 1994 were early harbingers of the current world revolution that challenged the neoliberal capitalist order. And the World Social Forum was founded explicitly as a counter-hegemonic project vis-à-vis the World Economic Forum (an annual gathering of global elites founded in 1971).

national, and international movements representing a myriad of interests. Given this orientation, the World Social Forum has established itself as a 'new' social movement based on principles of inclusion in both its scale and interests (Santos, 2009: 251). Since the New Global Left includes a diverse set of movements, the World Social Forum is an important democratic institution for unifying global civil society against neo-liberalism and other contemporary forms of political and economic oppression.

The New Global Left has emerged as resistance to, and a critique of, global capitalism (Lindholm and Zuquete, 2010). It is the old social movements that emerged in the nineteenth century (labor, anarchism, socialism, communism, feminism, environmentalism, peace, human rights) and movements that emerged in the world revolutions of 1968 and 1989 (gay rights, anti- corporate, fair trade, indigenous) and even more recent movements such as the slow food/food rights, global justice/alterglobalization, antiglobalization, health-HIV and alternative media (Reese et al., 2008). The explicit focus on the Global South and global justice is somewhat similar to some earlier instances of the Global Left, especially the Communist International, the Bandung Conference and the anticolonial movements. The New Global Left contains remnants and reconfigured elements of earlier Global Lefts, but it is a qualitatively different constellation of forces because: 1) there are new elements; 2) the old movements have been reshaped; and 3) a new technology (the Internet) is being used to mobilize protests in real time and to try to resolve North/ South issues within movements and contradictions among movements.

There has also been a learning process in which the earlier successes and failures of the Global Left are being taken into account in order to not repeat the mistakes of the past. Many social movements have reacted to the neoliberal globalization project by going transnational to meet the challenges that are obviously not local or national (Reitan, 2007). But some movements, especially those composing the Arab Spring, are focused mainly on regime change at home. Additionally, the relations within antisystemic movements and among the Latin American Pink Tide populist regimes are both cooperative and competitive. The issues that divide potential allies need to be brought out into the open and analyzed in order that cooperative efforts may be enhanced and progressive global collective action may become more effective. We review the components of the New Global Left to determine whether this constellation of anti-systemic movements and political regimes are unifying and demanding an alternative to neoliberal global capitalism.

The "Pink Tide" and Progressive National Regimes in Latin America

A global network of progressive transnational social movements has arisen to challenge neoliberalism, neoconservatism and corporate capitalism in general. This network is composed of increasingly transnational social movements as well as a growing number of populist governments in Latin America—the so-called "Pink Tide." The Pink Tide is composed of populist leftist regimes that have come to state power in Latin America, some of which advocate dramatic structural transformation of the global political economy. The failure of neoliberal reforms implemented by conservative regimes in the 1980s and 1990s, which were aimed at increasing privatization through promoting free trade and state deregulation, induced voters to elect progressive regimes based on their platforms of nationalization and social welfare reform (Hershberg and Rosen, 2006; Roberts, 2008). For example, between 1980 and 1995, countries in Latin America grew by 1.5 percent to 2.5 percent annually while the rest of the world grew by an average of 3 percent to 4 percent annually over this period. Additionally, during the 1990s, the unemployment rate grew from 6.8 percent to over 10 percent in 1999 (World Bank, 2011). The poor economic performance of Latin America during a period of neoliberal reform that was directed at promoting international trade and investment seems to be the underlying catalyst for the emergence of the Pink Tide in Latin America.

The early Structural Adjustment Programs imposed by the International Monetary Fund in Latin America in the 1980s were instances of "shock therapy" that emboldened domestic neoliberals to attack the "welfare state," unions, and workers' parties. In many countries these attacks resulted in downsizing and streamlining of urban industries, and workers in the formal sector lost their jobs and were forced into the informal economy, swelling the "planet of slums" (Davis, 2006). This is the formation of a globalized working class as described by William I. Robinson (2008). In several countries the swollen urban informal sector was mobilized by political leaders into new populist movements and parties, and in some of these, the movements were eventually successful in electing their leaders to national power, creating the Pink Tide regimes. Thus neoliberal Structural Adjustment Programs provoked counter-movements that eventuated in the Pink Tide regimes (Chase-Dunn, Garita, and Pugh, 2012).

An important difference between these and many earlier Leftist regimes in the non-core, such as the Castro regime in Cuba, is that they used democratic means (popular election) to obtain power rather than civil war or revolution. This signifies an important difference from earlier world revolutions. The spread of electoral democracy to the non-core has been part of a larger political incorporation of former colonies into the European interstate system. This development of the global political system has mainly been caused by the industrialization of the non-core and the growing size of the urban working class in non-core countries (Silver, 2003). While much of the "democratization" of the Global South has consisted mainly of the emergence of "polyarchy" in which elites manipulate elections in order to stay in control of the state (Robinson, 1996), in some countries the Pink Tide Leftist regimes have been voted into power through their populist platforms dedicated to social spending and justice. This is a very different form of regime formation than the road taken by earlier Leftist regimes in the non-core. With a few exceptions earlier Left regimes came to state power by means of civil war or revolution.

The ideologies of the Latin American Pink Tide regimes have been both socialist and indigenist, with different mixes in different countries. The acknowledged leader of the Pink Tide as a distinctive brand of leftist populism is the Bolivarian Revolution led by Venezuelan President Hugo Chavez. But various other forms of progressive political ideologies are also heading up states in Latin America. Indigenist and socialist Evo Morales is president of Bolivia. The Fidelistas in Cuba remain in power. The Brazilian Workers' Party is still an important player, though its elected presidents have been pragmatic politicians rather than revolutionary leaders. In Chile social democrats are in power. Sandinistas in Nicaragua and the FMLN in El Salvador have elected national leaders. Argentina bravely and unilaterally restructured its own debt obligations in 2005. The President of Peru is a leftist. And several European-style social democrats lead some of the Caribbean islands. The common feature of these different regimes and ideologies is a resistance to neoliberalism, which calls for greater state austerity and privatitization.

Most of these regimes are supported by the mobilization of historically subordinate populations including the indigenous, poor, and women. The rise of the voiceless and the challenge to neoliberal capitalism seemed to have its epicenter in Latin America before the emergence of the Arab Spring. While there are important differences of emphasis among these Latin American regimes, they have much in common, and as a whole they constitute an important bloc of the New Global Left. We agree with William I. Robinson's (2008) assessment of the Bolivarian Revolution and its potential to lead the global working class in a renewed challenge to transnational capitalism.

The rise of the populist left has engulfed nearly all of South America and a considerable portion of Central America and the Caribbean. Why has Latin America been the site of both populist Leftist regimes and most of the transnational social movements that have contested neoliberal capitalist globalization up until recently? We suggest that part of the explanation is that Latin America as a world region has so many semiperipheral countries. These countries have more options to pursue independent strategies than the mainly peripheral countries of Africa do. But some of the Pink Tide countries in Latin America are also peripheral. There has been a regional effect that did not seem to be operating in either Africa or Asia. The Pink Tide phenomenon and the anti-neoliberal social movements may have been concentrated in Latin America because the foremost proponent of the neoliberal policies has been the United States. Latin America has long been the neocolonial "backyard" of the United States. Most of the people of Latin America think of the United States as the "colossus of the North." The US has been the titular hegemon during the period of the capitalist globalization project, and so the political challenge to neoliberalism has been strongest in that region of the world. Both Africa and Asia have a more complicated relationship with former colonial powers and with US hegemony.

President Hugo Chavez of Venezuela is perhaps the most vocal advocate of an alternative to global capitalism, and his advocacy is greatly aided by the massive

Venezuelan oil reserves. The *Banco del Sur* (Bank of the South) that Chavez founded, for example, has been joined by many Pink Tide nations and seeks to replace the International Monetary Fund and the World Bank in sponsoring development projects throughout the Americas. The goal is to become independent of the capitalist financial institutions headquartered in the Global North.

In fact, the very existence of the World Social Forum (WSF) owes much to the Pink Tide regime in Brazil. The Brazilian transition from authoritarian rule in the 1980s politicized and mobilized civil society, contributing to the elections of leftist presidents. One of these was Fernando Henrique Cardoso, a famous Brazilian sociologist who was one of the founders of dependency theory. The Brazilian city of Porto Alegre, where the first World Social Forum meetings were held, had been a stronghold for the Brazilian Workers' Party. The World Social Forum was born in Porto Alegre with indispensable help from the Brazilian Workers' Party and its former leader who had been elected President of Brazil, Luis Inàcio da Silva. The political trend of the Pink Tide was an important element in context and conditions that allowed for the rise of the World Social Forum.[8]

The relations between the progressive transnational social movements and the regimes of the Pink Tide have been both collaborative and contentious. We have already noted the important role played by the Brazilian Workers' Party in the movements see involvement in struggles to gain and maintain power in existing states as a trap that is likely to simply reproduce the injustices of the past. These kinds of concerns have been raised by anarchists since the nineteenth century, but autonomists from Italy, Spain, Germany and France now echo these concerns. And the Zapatista movement in Southern Mexico, one of the sparks that ignited the global justice movement against neoliberal capitalism, has steadfastly refused to participate in Mexican electoral politics. Indeed the New Left led by students in the World Revolution of 1968 championed a similar critical approach to the old parties and states of the Left as well as involvement in electoral politics. This antipolitics-as-usual has become embodied in the Charter of the World Social Forum, where representatives of parties and governments are theoretically proscribed from sending representatives to the WSF meetings.

The older Leftist organizations and movements are often depicted as hopelessly Eurocentric and undemocratic by the neo-anarchists and autonomists, who instead prefer participatory and horizontalist network forms of democracy and eschew leadership by prominent intellectuals as well as by existing heads of state. Thus when Lula, Chavez and Morales have tried to participate in the WSF, large crowds have gathered to protest their presence. The organizers of the WSF have found

8 The charter of the World Social Forum does not permit participation by those who attend as representatives of organizations that are engaged in, or that advocate, armed struggle. Nor are governments, confessional institutions or political parties supposed to send representatives to the WSF. See World Social Forum Charter http://wsf2007.org/process/wsf-charter/.

various compromises, such as locating the speeches of Pink Tide politicians at adjacent, but separate, venues. An exception to this kind of contention is the support that European autonomists and anarchists have provided to Evo Morales's regime in Bolivia (e.g. López and Iglesias Turrión, 2006). Many of the activists in the Occupy movement that began in New York City in the Fall of 2011 have a similar attitude toward formal organization and hierarchy. The movement has described itself as "leaderless" and has focused on direct democratic decision-making in face-to-face groups.

Latin America was the epicenter of the contemporary world revolution until the rise of the Arab Spring and the anti-austerity protests. If the movements and the progressive regimes in Latin America could work together this would be an energizing model for the other regions of the globe. The challenges are daunting but the majority of humankind needs organizational instruments with which to democratize global governance and the World Social Forum has been designed to be the venue within which such instruments could be forged. Whether progressive regimes in Latin America and other developing countries engage with other anti-systemic movements remain to be seen.

Arab Spring, European Summer, Occupy Fall and Anti-austerity Movements

The most significant threat to the current US-led regime of accumulation and global capitalism and its structural crises is the recent wave of civil unrest in Europe, the United States, and the Arab world. Since the financial meltdown, a series of new and old movements have mobilized for social and economic reform aimed at promoting democratic political participation and reducing economic inequality . More specifically, the eruption of civil unrest and non-violent protest across North Africa and the Middle-East, which became known as the Arab Spring, was primarily directed at implementing free elections for the purpose of regime change., Recent protests and demonstrates in the US, Greece, Spain, and other Western European countries, such as the Occupy and Anti-Austerity movements have been aimed at raising awareness on the substantial growth in income inequality over the last two decades and making demands on the state to increasing social spending. Even though these movements have different interests and orientation, the proximity in time of these movements appears to be attributable to two structural contradictions of the US hegemonic regime and global capitalism—the persistence of structural unemployment amongst the youth and the persistence of structurally induced poverty and inequality. Given the exclusive focus of state policy toward financial stability and neoliberal reform over social equity and the continued push for state retrenchment, these counter-movements are symptomatic of deep structural flaws of global capitalism and the inability of the state to resolve these problems.

The movements that have swept the Arab world since December of 2010 are also part of the world revolution of 20xx and they may play a role in the New Global Left. As in earlier world revolutions, contagion and new technologies of communication have been important elements. And as in earlier world revolutions, rather different movements stimulated by different local conditions converge in time to challenge the powers that be (Martin et al., 2008). The Arab Spring movements have been rather different from the global justice movements. Their targets have mainly been authoritarian national regimes rather than global capitalism. Youthful demonstrators have used *Facebook* to organize mainly peaceful protests that have succeeded in causing several old entrenched regimes to fall. And these rebellions have been strongly supported by labor unions and Islamist parties. The countries in which these movements have succeeded are not the poorest countries in Africa and the Middle East. Rather they have been semiperipheral countries in which a large mobilizable group of young people have access to social media. In many cases the old autocrats had been trying to implement austerity programs in order to be able to borrow more money from abroad and this set the stage for the mass movements. But the Arab Spring movements have not explicitly raised the issues of austerity and global financial dependency.

However, even though the Arab Spring never directly addressed state austerity, it shares a common characteristic with the anti-austerity movements in Europe and the Occupy movement in the United States. In all national contexts, there has been a substantial segment of the youth population (ages 15–24) unemployed. For Western Europe and the United States, the growth in youth unemployment has been primarily explained by skill mismatch, where youth are either under-qualified or over-qualified for positions (ILO, 2013). The restructuring of national economies in the Global North induced by the globalization of production has reduced the demand for semi-skilled industrial labor, which, in the past, absorbed the large surplus of uneducated youth. Additionally, while uneducated youth are unable to obtain standard work in unskilled occupations, educated youth are often unable to find work in skilled occupations because these occupations require a skill set that youth never received in formal education.

For North African and Middle Eastern countries, the growth in youth unemployment is due to the limited availability of standard and formal work (ILO, 2013). Since youth are more likely to drop out of school in these developing countries, they are often forced into the informal sector and/or irregular work in the formal sector. The relocation of manufacturing processes to these countries have only amplified this problem by increasing the demand for subcontracted labor and semi-skilled labor.

Indeed, as seen in Figure 12.5, on average, people between the ages of 15 and 24 are almost three times more likely to be unemployed than other age groups. Over the last seven years, the average youth unemployment rate has increased from 15 percent to nearly 25 percent. For example, in 2005, the unemployment rate for youth in Tunisia and Egypt exceeded 30 percent, where in the United States the rate was around 11 percent and around 20 percent in the European Union (both higher than the national average). Since 2005, the unemployment rate has increased and remained the same in all of these countries. In fact, in 2010, in the general region of North Africa and the Middle East the employment-to-

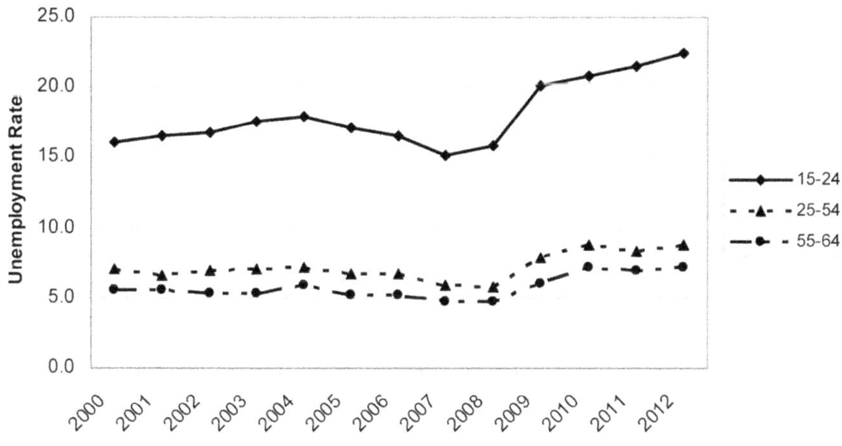

Figure 12.5 Global trends in unemployment rate by age group, 2000–2012
Source: ILO (2012).

population ratio of youth was only around 46.6 percent (ILO, 2011). For the United States, during the last few years, the youth unemployment rate climbed to 18.4 percent, while in Europe, the rate climbed to 22 percent. Even though the Arab Spring was primarily addressing the need for democratic reform, it appears that one of the motivators for reform, amongst the youth, was increasingly dire conditions in domestic labor markets.

The issues raised by the Arab Spring movements have mainly been about national democracy, not global justice. But the example of masses of young people rallying against unpopular regimes spread rapidly to the second-tier core states of Europe. Spain and Greece have seen large anti-austerity demonstrations that were inspired by the Arab Spring. These were directed at unpopular national regimes, but also at the global financial structure that has been pushing draconian austerity and further privatization in the context of the global financial crisis. The austerity programs are the conditions imposed by global finance capital for re-inflating the accumulation structures of these counties of the European second-tier core. The popular anti-austerity rebellions could yet provoke an even deeper financial collapse if investors and their institutional agents lose faith in the ability of the system to reproduce the existing structures of accumulation. The anti-austerity movements also spread to some of the core states where severe fiscal crises have led to the dismantling of public services. The rise of the Occupy Wall Street movement in New York City and its rapid spread to even small towns in the US and to cities all over the world shows that popular resistance to global finance capital is indeed widespread (Chase-Dunn and Curran-Strange, 2012). Further, while the anti-austerity protest of the "European Summer" were primarily directed at preventing state austerity, the Occupy movement has focused on broader themes of income inequality and economic justice. Even though these movements differed

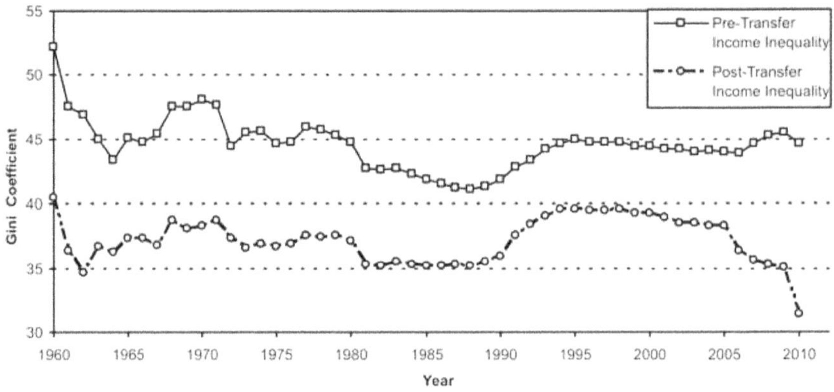

Figure 12.6 Global trend in pre-transfer and post-transfer income inequality, 1960–2010

Source: Solt (2009), updated in 2011.

in their mobilizing issues, these issues are interrelated, where redistribution programs, especially in Europe, have the strongest impact on mitigating growing income inequality in these countries.

Indeed, as seen in Figure 12.6, these American and European movements against state austerity and income inequality are directly addressing one of the biggest socioeconomic problems of contemporary capitalism: the expected growth of income inequality due to state retrenchment. Figure 12.6 presents the average trends in pre-transfer and post-transfer income inequality for countries over the last 50 years. For pre-transfer income inequality, which exclude government transfers, the mean income inequality has grown to pre-1980s level in 2009–10. As earnings inequality increasingly become more paramount for the overall distribution of incomes in core countries (Kenworthy, 2007), it is imperative that government transfers mitigate this potential socioeconomic crisis. In fact, as shown in Figure 12.6, once government transfers are included in estimates of income inequality, the average trend in income inequality has declined since the mid-1990s. Further, between 2005 and 2010, the average post-transfer trend in income inequality has declined to its lowest level in the last 50 years. However, given the recent push for state retrenchment as states deal with insolvent public debt, it is quite possible for these transfers to be significantly reduced and, as a consequence, leading to a growth in income inequality.

Overall, the rapid growth of income inequality and the persistent structural unemployment of the youth have caused the emergence of three distinct social movements. Even though these movements are oriented toward different political and economic objectives, they all share a common characteristic—the mobilization of youth. Since the youth of these countries are more adversely affected by changes in the labor market, social spending, and relative deprivation, they have begun to mobilize against injustice. However, until these movements are able to gain a sense of solidarity by recognizing their common causes, it is unlikely that they will be able to bring their issues and missions to the global stage and cause a system-wide revolution.

The Financial and Ecological Meltdown and Counter-movements

Starting in the early 1980s, the US financial system has substantially grown in complexity and volume as new financial instruments and services were increasingly integrated into a dense global network of financial markets. Following Arrighi's SCA framework, this is not surprising. For Arrighi (1994), a common reaction, in all regimes of accumulation, to the decline of profits in trade and production has been the investment into finance. For the US regime of accumulation, in reaction to the economic recession of the mid-1970s, US and other core capitalists pursued a financial strategy of accumulation (Arrighi, 1994; Krippner, 2005). This "financialization" of the core reached its apex in 2006–07, followed by the US housing bubble burst and the dramatic failure of global security markets. As a consequence, US and European banks lost more than a trillion dollars in value while the median American household lost the equivalent of 18 years of wealth with the dramatic fall in housing prices. However, not only the US and Western European countries were significantly impacted by the financial crisis, but developing countries, especially the "BRICs," saw substantial slowdown in exports because of their dependence on consumer markets in the developed countries (Aloui et al., 2011).

What have been the effects of the global financial meltdown on the counter-movements and the progressive national regimes? The World Social Forum slogan that "Another World Is Possible" seems far more appealing now than when the capitalist globalization project was booming. Critical discourse has been taken more seriously by a broader audience. Marxist geographer, David Harvey, has been interviewed on the BBC. The millenarian discourses of the Pink Tide regimes and the radical social movements seem to be at least partly confirmed. The "end of history" triumphalism and theories of the "new economy" seem to have been swept into the dustbin. The world-systems perspective has found greater support, at least among earlier critics such as the more traditional Marxists. The insistence of Wallerstein, Arrighi, and others that US hegemony is in long-term decline has now found wide acceptance.

While heterodox economics have started to gain a foothold in the public discourse on the financial crisis, how have the general populace reacted to the recent financial crisis? The social consequence of the financial crisis in the United States has been the dramatic rate of residential foreclosures caused by the insolvency of subprime mortgages. Since 2006, the value of homes has dropped by 36 percent while the average rate of mortgage delinquency reached a high of 10 percent in 2009 (Mian et al., 2011). This dramatic shift in household assets has become a major topic in the general political discourse since 2006. Correspondingly, as more and more people have lost their homes, local organizations have started to mobilize to address these issues. In particular, organizations such as the Campaign to Restore National Housing Rights and Causa Justa, have started nation-wide campaigns advocating for tenants' rights in response to foreclosures and subprime mortgages. More generally, movements such as the Occupy campaign have not only advocated against issues of socioeconomic inequality, but also have expanded their agenda to include the rights of tenants and the prevention of foreclosures. Therefore, while public discourse has shifted to include more radical perspectives on the capitalist system, organic movements are emerging to directly challenge the negative consequences of the financial crisis.

In addition to a renewed interest in socioeconomic justice, movements and NGOs,on a more practical level have had difficulty raising money, but this has been counterbalanced by increased participation (Allison et al., 2011). The environmental movement has received some setbacks because the issue of high unemployment has come to the fore. The Copenhagen and Rio summits were mainly failures to reach binding agreements regarding greenhouse gas emissions. The wide realization that energy costs are likely to continue to go up has increased the numbers who support the further development of nuclear energy, despite its long-run environmental costs. But the Japanese earthquake, tsunami and nuclear meltdown of March 2011 led to the declaration of a non-nuclear future by the German government. And the radical alternative of indigenous environmentalism has gotten a boost. The World People's Conference on Climate Change and the Rights of Mother Earth, held in Cochabamba, Bolivia in April of 2010, discussed a Universal Declaration of the Rights of Mother Earth, a World People's Referendum on Climate Change, and the establishment of a Climate Justice Tribunal. The meeting was attended by 30,000 activists from more than 100 countries and was financially supported by the governments of Bolivia and Venezuela.

Conclusion

Do recent developments constitute the beginning of the terminal crisis of capitalism or the beginning of another systemic cycle of accumulation? As mentioned above, predominant capitalism has not been around very long from the point of view of the succession of qualitatively different logics of social reproduction. But capitalism itself has speeded up social change. The contradictions of capitalism will eventually reach levels that cannot be accommodated. But when will that happen? Declarations of an imminent transformation to a qualitatively different more humane and sustainable mode of accumulation are useful for mobilizing social movements. Yet, the diversity of anti-systemic movements in the contemporary world-system have not coalesced into a unified force against the intensification of global capitalism. Even though these movements have been spurred by a set of structural crises, initiated by the decline of US hegemony and the contemporary regime of accumulation, they have yet to develop sense of collective identity necessary for unified action at the global level. The World Social Forum and its organizational design are best equipped to develop and promote a collective identity that can be shared across these diverse anti-systemic movements. More importantly, the World Social Forum continues to provide a deliberative space for movements to exchange ideas and to engage with other movements.

We think both a new stage of capitalism and a qualitative systemic transformation are possible within the next three decades. If US hegemonic decline is slow, as it has seemed to be, and if financial and ecological crises are spread out in time and conflicts between ethnic groups and nations are also spread out then there may be a chance for enlightened progressives to reform the system that is still capitalist but meets the current challenges at least partially. But if a perfect storm of calamities (Kuecker 2007) should all come together in the same period, the movements and progressive regimes of the New Global Left will have the chance to radically change the mode of accumulation to a form of global socialism.In the meantime, and either way, the movements need to clarify what is wrong with capitalism and what might be done to replace it. Even if the transformation to a collectively rational global commonwealth does not occur anytime soon, pushing the ideas and the demands will move things in the right direction.

References

Allison, Juliann, et al. 2011. "Is the Economic Crisis a Crisis for Social Justice Activism?" *Policy Matters* (Spring), 5(1), http://policymatters.ucr.edu.

Aloui, Riadh, Mohamed Safouane Ben Aissa, and Duc Khoung Nguyen. 2011. "Global Financial Crisis, Extreme Interdependences, and Contagion Effects: The Role of Economic Structure?" *Journal of Banking and Finance*, 35, 130–141.

Arrighi, Giovanni. 1994. *The Long Twentieth Century*. London: Verso.

Arrighi, Giovanni. 2006. *Adam Smith in Beijing*. London: Verso.

Arrighi, Giovanni, Terence K. Hopkins, and Immanuel Wallerstein. 1989. *Antisystemic Movements*. London: Verso.

Boswell, Terry and Christopher Chase-Dunn. 2000. *The Spiral of Capitalism and Socialism: Toward Global Democracy*. Boulder, CO: Lynne Rienner.

Brandt, Loren, Johannes Van Biesebroeck, and Yifan Zhang. 2009. "Creative Accounting or Creative Destruction? Firm-level Productivity Growth in Chinese Maufacturing." *NBER Working Paper*, no. 1515.

Chase-Dunn, Christopher. 1998. *Global Formation: Structures of the World-Economy*. Lanham, MD: Rowman and Littlefield.

Chase-Dunn, Christopher and Michaela Curran-Strange. 2012. "The Diffusion of the Occupy Movement in California" *IROWS Working Paper*, no. 74. http://irows.ucr.edu/papers/irows74/irows74.htm.

Chase-Dunn, Christopher and Thomas D. Hall. 1997. *Rise and Demise: Comparing World Systems*. Boulder, CO: Westview.

Chase-Dunn, Christopher, Angie L. Garita, and David Pugh. 2012. "Latin America in the World-system: World Revolutions, Semiperipheral Development and the Evolution of Global Governance." Paper present at the International Sociological Association Forum on "Social Justice and Democratization," Buenos Aires, August 1. http://irows.ucr.edu/papers/irows76/irows76.htm.

Chase-Dunn, Christopher, Yukio Kawano, and Benjamin Brewer. 2000. "Trade Globalization Since 1795: Waves of Integration in the World-System." *American Sociological Review*, 65(1), 77–95.

Chase-Dunn, Christopher, Roy Kwon, Kirk Lawrence, and Hiroko Inoue. 2011. "Last of the Hegemons: U.S. Decline and Global Governance" *International Review of Modern Sociology*, 37(1), 1–29.

Chase-Dunn, Christopher and Kirk Lawrence. 2011. "The Next Three Futures, Part One: Looming Crises of Global Inequality, Ecological Degradation, and a Failed System of Global Governance." *Global Society*, 25(2), 137–153. http://irows.ucr.edu/papers/irows47/irows47.htm.

Chase-Dunn, Christopher and R.E. Niemeyer. 2009. "The World Revolution of 20xx," pp. 35–57, in Mathias, Albert, Gesa Bluhm, Han Helmig, Andreas Leutzsch, Jochen Walter (eds). *Transnational Political Spaces*. Campus Verlag: Frankfurt.

Davis, Gerald. 2009. *Managed by the Markets: How Finance Re-Shaped America*. Oxford: Oxford University Press.

Davis, Mike. 2006. *Planet of Slums*. London: Verso.

Davis, Mike. 2011. "Spring confronts Winter." *New Left Review* (72), 5–15.

Dicken, Peter. 2003. *Global Shift: Reshaping the Global Economic Map in the 21st Century*, 4th Edition. London: Sage.

Epstein, Gerald and Arjun Jayadev. 2005. "The Rise of Rentier Incomes in OECD Countries: Financialization, Central Bank Policy, and Labor Solidarity." pp. 46–74, in Gerald Epstein (ed.). *Financialization of the World Economy*. Northampton: Elgar.

Feenstra, Robert. 1998. "Integration of Trade and Disintegration of Production in the Global Economy." *Journal of Economic Perspectives*, 12(4), 31–50.

Harvey, David. 2005. *A Brief History of Neoliberalism*. Oxford: Oxford University Press.

Harvey, David. 2010. "The Crisis of Capitalism." http://davidharvey.org/2010/05/video-the-crises-of-capitalism-at-the-rsa/.

Hopkins, Terry and Immnauel Wallerstein (eds). 1996. *The Age of Transition: The Trajectory of the World-System, 1945–2025*. London and New Jersey: Zed Books.

International Labour Organization. 2011. *Global Employment Trends for Youth: 2011 Update*. Geneva: ILO.

International Labour Organization. 2013. *Global Employment Trends for Youth: 2013 Update*. Geneva: ILO.

Ip, Greg. 2013. "The Gated Globe." *The Economist*, October 12.

Kotz, David M. 2009. "The Financial and Economic Crisis of 2008: A Systemic Crisis of Neoliberal Capitalism." *Review of Radical Political Economy*, 41(3), 305–317.

Krippner, Greta. 2005. "The Financialization of the American Economy." *Socio-Economic Review*, 3, 173–208.

Krippner, Greta. 2011. *Capitalizing on Crisis: The Political Origins of the Rise of Finance*. Cambridge: Harvard University Press.

Kuecker, Glen. 2007. "The Perfect Storm." *International Journal of Environmental, Cultural and Social Sustainability*, 3.

Kwon, Roy. 2012. "Hegemonic Stability, World Cultural Diffusion, and Trade Globalization." *Sociological Forum*, 27(2), 324–347.

Lin, Ken-Hou and Donald Tomaskovic-Devey. 2013. "Financialization and U.S. Income Inequality." *American Journal of Sociology*, 118(5), 1284–1329.

Lindholm, Charles and Jose Pedro Zuquete. 2010. *The Struggle for the World: Liberation Movements for the 21st Century*. Palo Alto, CA: Stanford University Press.

Mahutga, Matthew. 2012. "When Do Value Chains Go Global? A Theory of the Spatialization of Global Value Chains." *Global Networks*, 12(1), 1–21.

Martin, William G. et al. 2008. *Making Waves: Worldwide Social Movements, 1750–2005*. Boulder, CO: Paradigm.

Mian, Atif, Amir Sufi, and Francesco Trebbi. 2011. "Foreclosures, House Prices, and the Real Economy." *NBER Working Paper*, no. 16685.

Miller, Seymour and Donald Tomaskovic-Devey. 1983. *Recapitalizing America: Alternatives to the Corporate Distortion of National Policy*. Boston: Routledge & Kegan Paul.

Moghadam,Valentine. 2012. "The Arab Spring, MENA Democratization and the World-system: The Good, the Bad and the Ugly." Paper preseented at The Left Forum, New York (March 16–18).

Pan, Chengxin. 2009. "What is Chinese About Chinese Businesses? Locating the 'Rise of China' in Global Production Networks." *Journal of Contemporary China*, 18(58), 7–25.

Philippon, Thomas and Ariell Reshef. 2009. "Wages and Human Capital in the US Financial Industry, 1909–2006." *NBER Working Paper*, no. 14644.

Polanyi, Karl. 1944. *The Great Transformation*. New York: Farrar & Rinehart.

Reitan, Ruth. 2007. *Global Activism*. London: Routledge.

Robinson, William I. 1996. *Promoting Polyarchy: Globalization, US Intervention and Hegemony*. Cambridge: Cambridge University Press.

Robinson, William I. 2008. *Latin America and Globalization*. Baltimore: Johns Hopkins University Press.

Santos, Boaventura de Sousa. 2006. *The Rise of the Global Left*. London: Zed Press.

Santos, Boaventura de Sousa. 2008. "The World Social Forum and the Global Left." *Politics & Society*, 36(2), 247–270.

Smith, Jackie, et al. 2007. *Global Democracy and the World Social Forums.* Boulder, CO: Paradigm Publishers.

Silver, Beverly J. 2003. *Forces of Labor: Workers' Movements and Globalization Since 1870.* Cambridge: Cambridge University Press.

Silver, Beverly J. 2010. "Contradictions in the Latin American Left." Commentary No. 287 (August 15), http://www.iwallerstein.com/contradictions-in-the-latin-american-left/.

Solt, Frederick. 2009. "Standardizing the World Income Inequality Database." *Social Science Quarterly*, 90(2), 231–242.

Tomaskovic-Devey, Donald and Ken-Hou Lin. 2011. "Income Dynamics, Economic Rents, and the Financialization in the U.S. Economy." *American Sociological Review*, 76(4), 538–559.

World Bank. 2014. *World Development Indicators* [online]. Washington, DC: World Bank.

Zhang, Kevin Honglin (ed.). 2006. *China as the World Factory*. New York: Routledge.

Chapter 13
The Global Capitalist Crisis and the End of Empire

Martin Orr

The reign of the last of the great Western empires, that of the United States, is over. Although for many this would seem a preposterous statement, the US bears all the marks of a fallen power. The domestic population is more impoverished, unhealthy, illiterate and disenfranchised than that of any other major industrialized nation. At all levels of government, democratic constraints upon the powerful have been gutted, corruption and corporate collusion are the norm, and the people's faith in their government and other institutions are at unprecedented lows. The media is thoroughly corporatized and dominated by mindless diversions, while what passes for journalism is simply the parroting of White House and Pentagon press releases, punctuated by calls to bomb other nations or by cries to persecute whistleblowers. Police forces are militarized, the armed forces are increasingly involved in protecting the "homeland," and a monstrous system of surveillance is in place—the loyalty to empire is in doubt, and all of the world's citizens are suspects. Most telling, despite driving the nation into debt with military spending in excess of that of the rest of the world combined, the United States Armed Forces have not won a war in almost 70 years. The rattling of the Empire's saber is muted by a growing chorus of global opposition. This is what a fallen empire looks like.

This chapter offers a critical analysis of the rise and fall of the United States as a global imperial power. The rise of US capital to world dominance was a direct outcome of the second inter-imperialist oil war. Emerging victorious from this war, the US ruling class had the power to impose an international financial order and trade system made possible by its vast wealth, protected by its unrivaled military. As long as it was able to supply its own energy needs, the economy of the United States could grow enough to enable modest reductions in economic inequalities, and to respond, at least symbolically, to the growing demands for civil and human rights. Once the US reached peak domestic oil production in the 1970s and as the empire subsequently began to decline, the social contract was increasingly declared null and void. Growing budget and trade deficits, rapid inflation in the cost of basic needs, exploding inequality, contagious capital flight, and the wanton neglect of public services and infrastructure characterized the 1970s and 1980s. In the 1990s and the first half of the last decade, the disintegration of the Soviet Union enabled the United States to reassert its leadership temporarily through neoliberal trade policy and neoconservative foreign and domestic policies. In response to popular opposition, both of these strategies failed.

Over the past four decades, class polarization and stagnant wages have been masked by growing indebtedness. The bursting of the real estate bubble amid rapid energy inflation prevented further indebtedness, destroyed demand, and the economy collapsed. The "Great Recession" marks an epochal transition in many ways—nations are increasingly ignoring neoliberal dogma in favor of nationalist, populist and socialist alternatives, and people worldwide are showing an increasingly vocal contempt for the policies and actions of the United States. While it is impossible to predict with confidence the contours of the emerging global order, it is beyond doubt that it won't be dominated by the US Empire. Given an ineffective military, an inability to control world events, and having generated a global financial meltdown, US capital may find it necessary to concentrate its efforts on maintaining its domestic power and turn inward to focus on its own national territory.

The Origins and Triumph of the US Empire

The United States is the product of imperialism, and imperialism continues to be the organizing feature of United States history. A loose amalgam of European colonies was freed in the first modern war of national liberation, and then quickly adopted its own colonial enterprise. By 1850 it had conquered the continent, and with its defeat of Spain a half century later it not only dominated the Western Hemisphere, but had established footholds in the Pacific and Asia. The United States emerged from the First World War the equal of any colonial power in Europe, and in the aftermath of the Second World War it supplanted the UK as the dominant capitalist power, checked from establishing a world empire only by the existence of the Soviet Union. Its supremacy among capitalist nations was cemented both by its preeminent military power as well as by the financial and trade protocols established by the Bretton Woods agreements, which established the World Bank and the International Monetary Fund (IMF). As is typical of empires, the United States immediately engaged in imperial overreach and squandered its wealth, and by the early 1970s it was in every respect in decline. The collapse of the Soviet Union briefly gave the United States an opening to make US domination global and permanent—a "New World Order" and a "New American Century" were promised by advocates of "nation building," "humanitarian interventions," and "free trade." Absent the pretext of defending against the "Soviet menace," neoliberal and neoconservative policies were quickly and successfully challenged at home and abroad.

The rise of the United States is generally attributed to some ideal force. "Manifest Destiny," "American Exceptionalism," the character or ingenuity of the "American People," or the putative advantages of the uniquely libertarian nature of US capitalism have all been offered as explanations for the ascendance of the United States in the twentieth century. Material forces are of course more significant—most especially a huge resource base (and superexploited slave, indentured and immigrant labor). Although land, iron and coal were the basis for many fortunes, a single resource—oil—has been at the center of wealth and political power from J.D. Rockefeller to Halliburton. Vast oil wealth forced the West to accept US leadership. The world wars that led to the high-water mark of US. Empire were fought over oil and with oil. The victors were those who could deprive the enemy of oil.

The inter-imperialist oil wars from which the United States emerged triumphant can be traced to 1912, when First Lord of the Admiralty Winston Churchill ordered the transition of his battleships from coal to oil—soon thereafter, in part to fuel its navy, the British government bought a majority share of the Anglo-Persian Oil Company, now BP (Klare, 2001: 30). The United Kingdom's desire to block Germany's access to oil through the Berlin to Baghdad railway set the stage for the First World War (Engdahl, 2004), and 80 percent of the Allies' petroleum was supplied by the US—"The Allied cause [floated] to victory on a wave of oil" (Yeomans, 2004: 9–10). The United States quickly joined Europe in the scramble for Middle Eastern oil. Saudi Arabia granted oil concessions to Standard Oil of California in 1933, and in 1943 the US government began providing military aid to the Saudis. In the Second World War, Hitler's inability to reach the oilfields of Baku contributed to the German defeat, the United States' blockade of Japanese oil and steel imports precipitated the attack on Pearl Harbor, and destroying their oil tankers cut off the islands from the one material essential for an industrial war economy (Klare, 2001: 31). Months before the end of the war in Europe, President Franklin Delano Roosevelt met with King Abdul Aziz ibn Saud in February 1945 aboard the USS *Quincy* to at least implicitly link US protection of the Saudi regime with access to Saudi oil. With President Truman's subsequent letter to King ibn Saud in 1948 there was no mistake as to the arrangement: "No threat to your Kingdom could occur that would not be a matter of immediate concern to the United States" (Yeomans, 2004: 16). By the end of the Second World War the United States was producing two-thirds of the world's oil. As a result, it also had half of the world's manufacturing capacity and held 70 percent of the world's gold reserves. The United States used its wealth and power to make Europe and its former colonies economically and militarily dependent.

The relationships and institutions that would characterize the period of US ascendancy following the Second World War began with negotiations between bankers and industrialists in the United States, the United Kingdom, and Germany in the 1930s regarding how to prevent the approaching war from interfering with trade (Seldes, 1943). Following the US victory the modern international order took shape. The United Nations (UN) and the North Atlantic Treaty Organization (NATO), both by design dominated by the United States, remain central to this system of political and military control. The basis of US financial control was established by Bretton Woods institutions—the World Bank, the International Monetary Fund, and the General Agreement on Tariffs and Trade (GATT). US capital was checked only by the need to compete with the Soviet Union for the "hearts and minds" of people in other nations, and to demonstrate to domestic audiences the advantages for working people of capitalism. As long as there was a material basis for its power, this system served US capital well.

But this material basis was being extracted and consumed at accelerating rates. In 1970, with the United States already importing a third of its oil, the annual rate of domestic production of crude peaked. The following year, President Richard Nixon took the US Dollar off of the gold standard, abrogating the central tenant of the Bretton Woods agreements. World governments quickly followed suit, and "market confidence" (i.e., the interests of wealthy investors) has subsequently determined the value of a nation's currency. At roughly the same time, the Organization of Petroleum Exporting Countries (OPEC) emerged to challenge the major oil corporations, and demonstrated its economic power to protest US support for Israel during the 1973 Arab-Israeli War. Also before mid-decade, it was clear that the war in Vietnam was lost, that Nixon was indeed a crook, and that, despite some meaningful social reforms and levels of inequality lower than any point since the Great Depression, the movements of the previous decades would not fundamentally rein in a self-destructive corporate capitalism.

Opposition and Decline of the US Empire

Reagan's campaign promise to restore "Morning in America" reflected the unconscious realization that in the 1970s the US was in decline. Under his administration, the levels of inequality began the upward climb that has continued for three decades. Taxes on the wealthy were reduced, military budgets increased dramatically, the social safety net was redefined as the subsidization of sloth, and deficit spending exploded. During the 12 years of Reagan-Bush, the national debt rose from a third of GDP to nearly two-thirds (US Census Bureau, 2010). Capital flight was encouraged, and industry relocated from unionized labor markets in the "Rust Belt" to the US South, to Maquiladoras in Mexico, and to "Free Trade Zones" in the Philippines. In the 1980s, due to lingering domestic and foreign opposition to the Vietnam War, the US faced increasing obstacles to its ability to project power. Iran had been lost, our favored dictator in Nicaragua had been overthrown, and attempts to bring these and other nations into line failed despite the criminality of the Iran-Contra conspiracy. The best Reagan could do is to topple an already unstable government on the tiny Caribbean island of Granada. Although George H.W. Bush was able to invade Panama and remove Manuel Noriega from power, his war against Iraq ended only in containment and the imposition of economic sanctions. The only major foreign policy "success" of the Reagan-Bush era was helping Afghani warlords stalemate the Soviet Union. Although it contributed to the dissolution of the "Evil Empire," it also set the stage for the dissolution of that of the United States.

The collapse of the Soviet Union and the restoration of capitalism in the Warsaw Pact nations appeared, briefly, to give the remaining "lone superpower" the opportunity to reassert global leadership. But absent the pretext of the "red menace" the US was compelled to take a less belligerent and a more multilateral approach. Neoliberalism and globalization became the centerpiece of a proposed international order that, although allegedly premised on consensus and mutual benefit, was no less intended to provide Western capital with unfettered access to Third World markets than was direct colonialism. The 1994 North American Free Trade Agreement (NAFTA) was the most significant early effort toward this end, and in 1995, linked to the Bretton Woods institutions and the culmination of GATT negotiations, the World Trade Organization was established.

The World Trade Organization (WTO) is nominally charged with administration of trade agreements, arbitration of trade disputes, and facilitating continuing negotiations. In practice, the WTO serves to penalize governments that impede "free trade" through tariffs, bans on imports and exports, and other "trade restrictive" laws that protect workers, consumers, and the environment. Laws that limit the length of the workweek or prohibit child labor, equal pay, minimum wage and workplace safety provisions, consumer safety, product labeling and environmental protection requirements, and public services including education and health care can be challenged as "distorting markets" and impeding trade. IMF "structural adjustment" policies, which also serve to dictate governments' control of domestic economic policy, have come under attack. These policies have had such direct and immediate impacts on communities that an anti-globalization movement quickly gathered momentum around the world. A watershed in this movement in this struggle was the 1999 "Battle in Seattle," in which over 40,000 people gathered in opposition to neoliberal globalization, blocked intersections and off-ramps leading to the Seattle Convention Center, and delayed the opening sessions of the WTO. Delegates representing Third World governments opposed to WTO proposals were emboldened by the support for their positions in the streets (Weissman, 1999). The following year, the 133 members of the G77 group of developing nations expressed support for the anti-globalization movement and, in what one observer called the "Seattle effect," the meetings of the IMF in Prague the following year "turned into a contest over which fat cat could show the most contrition for capitalism's shortcomings and evince the greatest sympathy for the poor" (Zachary, 2000). Seattle gave momentum to the movement—over the next years similar demonstrations were held against the IMF and the World Bank in Washington, DC and in Prague, against meetings in Miami devoted to a proposed Central American Free Trade Agreement, against meetings of the G-8 group of major industrial economies, and against the conventions of both the Republican and Democratic Parties in the summer of 2000. The level of state surveillance against the movement was immediately compared to the "red squads" and the FBI's COINTELPROs of decades past (Scher, 2001), and demonstrations against the institutions of global power have become routine. Any meeting of the Bretton

Woods institutions or their political enablers requires a militarized perimeter around the site.

The anti-globalization movement helped derail neoliberalism, exposed state repression and the corporate bias of media, forced "public" meetings behind increasingly militarized police lines, and compelled the WTO and international capital more generally to concede legitimacy to other nations and to global publics. And while negotiations continue and a few bilateral trade agreements have been concluded, little progress has been made in expanding the WTO agenda, and the United States is still unable to perpetuate its dominance through the ostensibly peaceful means of trade policy. Still, despite these successes, much of the early potential of the movement was lost as world events conspired against it.

The attacks on the World Trade Center and the Pentagon shifted world attention from critics of neoliberalism and from the anti-globalization movement. Furthermore, it provided the "evildoers" who could be employed to justify neoconservative and unilateralist policies. Amidst the catastrophic consequences of neoliberalism, and with US dominance challenged by an international movement calling into question these policies, September 11th offered the Bush Administration the perfect pretext to launch a final bid to dominate the distribution of oil and natural gas from the Middle East and South Asia, and to clamp down on domestic dissent in the process. The attacks constituted the "new Pearl Harbor" that the neoconservative Project for a New American Century had hoped would rally the US public to support their agenda.

The invasion of Afghanistan was accepted as a legitimate response to the attacks by most, but its place in energy politics was clear. Afghanistan was in the path of a proposed pipeline to transport natural gas from the Caspian Sea Basin. The Taliban government, apparently unwilling to accept the terms offered them, was targeted for regime change months before 9/11 (Brisard and Dasquie 2002). The invasion of Afghanistan was followed by a massive international public relations effort to draw the Bush Administration's preferred target of Iraq into the "War on Terror" (Rampton and Stauber, 2003). Approximately 650,000 Iraqis died in the first three years of the occupation (Burnham et al., 2006), and for the survivors conditions deteriorated (Parenti, 2004). Two million Iraqis were internally displaced and 2.2 million left Iraq altogether (Cockburn, 2007). For the Iraqi people, the motives behind this aggression were unmistakable (Bacon, 2007). In October 2000, the Iraqi government had demanded compensation for its oil in Euros—one of the first consequences of the occupation was to return to the US dollar for oil transactions. Although the Bush Administration, with the eager help of corporate media, was able to convince most Americans that Iraq was a front in the "War on Terror," the war was condemned by most European allies, and tens of millions of people demonstrated against the war in cities all over the world. Revelations of torture and other atrocities at Guantánamo and Abu Ghraib, the claims of Iraqi chemical and biological weapons capabilities proven false by their absence, and the wholesale carnage let loose upon the Iraqi people made the nature of this war glaringly obvious, the world became increasingly united in opposition to US foreign policy—by 2007, 32 percent of those surveyed in five major European countries responded that the United States government is the greatest threat to world peace. Neoconservativism proved a disaster. It led only to genocide, torture and other war crimes abroad, to media propaganda, governmental secrecy and heightened surveillance domestically, to neoliberalism without the pretense of consensus. It was ultimately rejected by its victims, by US allies, and by the American people.

The "Great Recession" and the Crisis of Empire

Neoliberalism and neoconservatism sought to project American "leadership" into the distant future, but both ignored the consequences of impoverishing workers, neglecting social services and public infrastructure, and financing the military through deficit spending. The "Great Recession" was the result of this myopia. Domestic inequalities were exacerbated by neoliberal capital flight and the transfer of public wealth into private hands. Class polarization led to the workers' increasing reliance upon debt, the financial sector encouraged this trend, and a rapid rise in oil prices over the preceding several years finally broke the budgets of households, businesses, and governments, destroying demand. Rather than embrace the reforms necessary to save capitalism from itself, ruling classes have demanded more austerity for the many and more bailouts for themselves so as to make every effort to return to business as usual. Regardless of the ability of publics in the US and the EU to challenge the domestic policies of their own governments, other publics and other world powers are asserting their right to be heard. The US government is bankrupt, and is in no position to dictate terms over others.

Officially, the Great Recession began in the fourth quarter of 2007 (Business Cycle Dating Committee 2008), but as the most significant global economic crisis since the Great Depression—it will probably be remembered as beginning with the liquidity crisis on Wall Street that culminated in the stock market crash of October 2008. Although an international crisis of capitalism, the epicenter of the recession was the United States. The Great Recession is the result of the growing gap between the fortunes of capital and labor in the United States. Neoliberalism encouraged the transfer of unionized manufacturing jobs to repressive labor markets, the off-shoring of service and professional work, and the superexploitation of migrants fleeing the ravages of NAFTA upon rural Mexico. Real wages have been stagnant since the mid-1970s as the percentage of income received by the best paid five percent of households increased from 14.8 percent in 1974 to 22.6 percent in 2006 (US Census Bureau, 2010). Inflation, especially of the basic needs upon which most people spend almost the entirety of their income—food, energy, shelter and health care—has further eroded the purchasing power of workers. In addition, effective tax rates on the rich and their estates have been dramatically reduced, regressive taxes and "user fees" on working people have been increased, and social services have been slashed. Finally, the skyrocketing cost of the neoconservative's preemptive wars has contributed to deteriorating public services. But since technological developments continue to increase the productivity of US workers, there is a widening chasm between the value of the commodities produced by labor and the purchasing power of workers. Over the last three decades, this gap has been closed by the growing indebtedness of households (Foster, 2006; Wolff, 2009). Since 1975, the ratio of household debt to income has more than doubled.

With the manufacturing sector largely dismantled, US capital touted the emergence of an "information economy," and investment flowed toward internet startup firms. Although a few of these went on to become giants in retail and media, most had no tangible assets and no prospect for profitability. When the dot-com bubble burst in 2000, many investors turned to the more lucrative real estate market, driving up prices. As the value of their homes rose in this market, many workers took advantage of the opportunity to borrow against their home equity to finance home improvements, pay medical bills, or simply maintain their standard of living in the midst of stagnant wages. Beginning in 2005, as real estate values began to fall, workers lost equity to borrow against to pay for unanticipated expenses, and the rate of foreclosure began to increase. Adding to the crisis, many buyers had agreed to "sub-prime mortgages" with initially low "teaser rates" offered by "predatory lenders"—often subsidiaries of the major banks. Often these borrowers lacked sufficient income to justify the mortgage, and as their adjustable rates rose they found themselves unable to make the higher payments. In addition to the systemic problem of class polarization, widespread corruption among mortgage lenders on Wall Street contributed to the collapse (Petras, 2009; Taibbi, 2009).

Rising inequality, the real estate bubble and the Ponzi-scheme capitalism of Wall Street had assembled a house of cards. The final blow came in the form of energy inflation. Spikes in oil prices have routinely triggered recessions—as with those following the 1973 Israeli-Arab War, the 1979 Iranian Revolution, and Iraq's invasion of Kuwait in 1990. Between 1988 and 2003, the inflation-adjusted, annual average price of oil didn't quite double (and it was at the same price it was in 1983). Between 2003 and 2008 the annual average price quadrupled, and spiked in the summer of 2008, six times higher than the 1988 average, at nearly $147 per barrel. In order to keep pace with rising global demand, stagnant production of light sweet crude has led to increasing reliance upon more expensive sources and technologies—heavy crudes, tar sands and deep-water drilling. As returns on real estate investment diminished, the more tangible energy market became more attractive, and speculators contributed to driving prices to their peak. Given the role of fossil fuels as central inputs for industrial agriculture, food prices followed energy prices closely, sparking food riots, rationing, and export bans around the world. Rising inequality and the collapse of the housing bubble had pushed workers to the brink, and then energy inflation pushed them over the edge, destroying consumer demand. As the foreclosure rate continued to soar, "exotic investment instruments" like "collateralized debt obligations" that bundled and sold homeowners' debt to investors became "toxic assets" with no market value. In October 2008 the US economy collapsed, dragging the world economy with it.

European banks were heavily exposed to these toxic assets and were immediately drawn into the liquidity crisis, and contagion led to ongoing sovereign debt crises throughout Europe. Of greatest concern is the solvency of governments on the periphery of Europe, derisively called by bankers the "PIIGS"—Portugal, Ireland, Italy, Greece and Spain. Declining tax revenues and rising unemployment insurance and welfare costs have led to increasing budget deficits. But the monetary policies usually available to governments to manage a debt crisis—devaluation of the nation's currency and cutting interest rates—are in the hands of the European Union (EU) and the European Central Bank. As confidence in the ability of these governments to reduce their deficits waned (and as entire nations were effectively "shorted" by Wall Street), borrowing to service their debt became more difficult and more expensive, precipitating crisis. In April 2010, ratings agencies reduced Greek bonds to "junk" status, threatening the major European banks that held this debt. The EU and IMF lent Greece the funds to service its debt, but as always given neoliberalism conditional on "structural adjustment"—flattening taxes, reducing public spending, and liquidating government assets. This crisis led to the devaluation of the Euro by about ten percent in a matter of weeks, and, despite repeated bailouts since, nations throughout Europe remain at risk of default. As a result of the Great Recession, the long-term viability of the Euro itself has been called into question, and should the sovereign credit defaults spread, even the most solvent nations in Europe will find it increasingly difficult to continue to borrow the money necessary to service their debt.

Facing huge budget and trade deficits itself, the ability of the United States to service its external debt may soon be called into question. Neoliberalism led to the export of the United States' manufacturing capacity, and the attempt to crush resistance requires the expenditure of 60 percent of the federal government's discretionary budget on defense of empire, leading to massive deficit spending. Given the status of the US dollar as the world's reserve currency and as the medium of exchange for oil transactions, other nations have been willing to finance these deficits. But central banks and investors worldwide are moving away from the dollar as support for US fiscal and foreign policies erodes. Iran has proposed establishing an oil bourse that would compete with those of the US and England, and in 2006 China opened its own petroleum exchange. Many oil exporters have proposed trading oil in Euros, Rubles, or through a "basket of currencies," and Russia and China have agreed to abandon the dollar for their bilateral trade (Qiang and Xiaokun, 2010). The dollar has lost its monopoly status as the medium of international exchange, and will likely become increasingly valueless as a reserve currency. Like the rest of its economy, the US military is funded by the rest of the world. Other governments will not be willing to prop up the United States so that it can project military power indefinitely.

Despite the threat to capitalism, capitalists have become even more shortsighted and rapacious. Rather than closing deficits by raising taxes to preserve the consumer demand generated by the public sector, the bankers are imposing on their own people the IMF structural adjustment policies that before they were only able to impose upon the Third World. The National Commission on Fiscal Responsibility and Reform (2010) made this agenda explicit. Among its proposals were reducing the number of federal employees by 10 percent, reducing corporate taxes, reducing payments to Medicare, introducing copayments for Veteran's Administration medical care, privatizing public property, cutting funding for education and public broadcasting, and increasing the retirement age. For capital, on the other hand, public austerity has led to private fortune. The bankers and their bonuses were saved, preserving their ability to successfully lobby against meaningful financial reform, and US corporate profits have reached record highs (Rampell, 2010).

Austerity—whether imposed by overtly political decisions or by what seems the anonymity of the market—has not gone unchallenged. Widespread cuts to social spending led to continuing protests in Greece, a proposal to restrict pension benefits to protests in France, tuition increases to protests throughout Great Britain, and the Irish won early elections hoping to unseat those responsible for accepting the latest EU/IMF-imposed austerity program (Burns, 2010). In the US, the most visible "movement" was for a time the misdirection of anger by the Koch-funded, Murdock-promoted Tea Party, but unions, students and community groups also continue to engage in protest, activism, and mutual assistance. Repeated releases of classified US military and State Department documents by the whistleblowers' outlet Wikileaks have contributed to eroding what remains of United States' reputation globally and domestically. And since young adults are often at the vanguard of any movement, the desperation visited upon them by this recession should give capital pause. In the United States, the unemployment rate for people aged 16–24 is about twice that of the general population, and studies demonstrate that entering the workforce during a recession leads to reductions in one's income over a lifetime (Ratner, 2009). Despite voting in record numbers to protest the foreign and domestic policies of the Bush Administration in 2008 and tipping the election to Obama, the abstention of disgusted young people led to Republican victories in the mid-term elections of 2010.

The End of Empire and the Crisis of America

At the end of the empire, the remaining question is: What will become of constitutional law in the United States? The Obama Administration has made the outrages of the George W. Bush Administration normal and "legal." Indeed, his first act as President was to commit a war crime. Immediately after taking the Oath of Office, in order to uphold the Constitution (including, as required, enforcing the treaties to which the US is signatory), he was obligated to place under arrest the main actors of the Bush cabal, with the concurrent order to end all such criminality. Instead, of course, something quite different happened. He urged us to magnanimously "looked forward, not back," and continued without pause the wars, the torture and the assaults upon domestic civil liberties.

Every President lays the groundwork for his Administration with his Cabinet appointments, and so from the beginning it was clear that any hope that there would be substantive change was misguided. His first Chief of Staff, Raum Emmanuel, is noted for saying "never let a crisis go to waste" (i.e., the Great Recession should be used as a pretext to cut social services). Now mayor of Chicago, he has shown similar contempt for teachers' unions and community groups as they attempt to prevent his racially-motivated school closures. In the midst of overwhelming evidence of collusion and criminality on Wall Street, Obama appointed Wall Street insider Timothy Geitner, former New York Reserve Board Chair, and protégée of Bush's Treasury Secretary Henry Paulson (formerly CEO of Obama's top campaign contributor, Goldman Sachs). Larry Summers, architect of the Clinton-era deregulation that set the stage for the financial meltdown, was brought on to pick up the pieces of an economy that he had helped destroy.

Despite having campaigned on making a break with neoconservative foreign policy, Obama retained Bush's Defense Secretary, Robert Gates, to ensure continuity with that policy. Despite defeating Hilary Clinton by having questioned her support for Bush's war on Iraq, he appointed her Secretary of State to lead our "diplomatic" efforts (which, thanks in part to Wikileaks, we know conclusively to have included directly undermining democracies, shilling for Monsanto, and maintaining CIA stations at US embassies worldwide). His military team was also composed of holdovers—the now disgraced Generals Petraeus and McCrystal continued the murderous counterintelligence programs of the Bush years. So too with domestic affairs: For example, Arne Duncan was tapped (and retained) as Secretary of Education. Thus the union-busting, corporate welfare scheme of Bush's No-Child-Left-Behind has been expanded, complete with for-profit high-stakes standardized exams. (Note that when Wisconsin Governor Scott Walker pushed through legislation intended to gut the teachers' union, no meaningful support was offered by the Obama Administration.) Former Monsanto V.P. for Public Policy Michael R. Taylor was appointed to the Food and Drug Administration. In a previous stint at FDA in the early 1990s he contributed to the approval of the use of bovine growth hormones, and now he is charged with hawking genetically-modified seed to Africa (Kenfield 2009). Given this cast of characters the "accomplishments" of the Obama Administration remain those of an empire in its death throes: Squeezing the populace to pay the debts incurred by an increasingly impotent defense of the realm.

Although the US economy resumed modest growth in mid-2009, the economic crisis continues. The unemployment rate in the United States, as official underreported, continues to hover at historically high levels, moderated only by the fact that so many have left the labor market. No one is predicting a return to pre-recession employment levels over the foreseeable future. While consumer confidence has improved somewhat, and while a new housing bubble appears to be forming (and being manipulated), the fundamentals of the US political economy have not changed. The recession has only exacerbated inequality, "structural readjustment" will only increase the impact of poverty, and people are being pushed out of the credit market that for a time facilitated this class polarization. In addition, the energy crisis that triggered the recession has and will only continue to grow worse. While many tout modest increases in the volume of overall fossil fuel extraction, the rate of production of light, sweet crude—the easy to access energy-rich basis of the modern era, peaked in 2005. Growth in US and world production of "total liquids" since that time has been made possible, temporarily, by expensive sources like deepwater, tar sands, and fracked reserves. This modest growth will of course be unsustainable for reasons of simple geophysics, is vigorously opposed by communities worldwide as a result of its environmental impact, and will ultimately be unprofitable. Most ominous, Saudi Arabia, the world's "swing producer," recorded between 2005 and 2009 a decline in its rate of production of over 12 percent (BP, 2010: 8). Access to oil is no longer simply a matter of seizing it militarily or through free trade. No matter how supplies are distributed, there is not enough energy to fuel even a stagnant economy indefinitely. Regardless of economic conditions in the US, continued growth in the emerging powers will inevitably generate new spikes in oil prices and further destructions of demand.

As the sun sets on the American Empire, other powers are on the rise. China has absorbed much of the United States' manufacturing base and is the federal government's largest foreign creditor, holding over 26 percent of this debt (US Department of the Treasury, 2010). Although its export economy cannot remain stable in the absence of global demand, China has thus far weathered the Great Recession (IMF, 2010)—while energy consumption in the US, Europe and Japan decreased between 2008 and 2009, China's petroleum consumption increased over 6 percent and its coal consumption increased by nearly 10 percent (BP, 2010). A resurgent Russia was able to ignore hypocritical US protestations of its alleged violation of the former Soviet republic of Georgia's sovereignty, continues to leverage Europe's dependence on its natural gas in its ongoing disputes with Belarus and Ukraine, has given asylum to the National Security Administration whistleblower Edward Snowden, and has thus far blocked direct Western intervention in Syria. In acquiescence to another emerging power, President Obama has supported India's bid to become a Permanent Member of the UN Security Council. In Latin America, once a relatively secure realm of empire, recent elections in Argentina, Bolivia, Brazil, Chile, Ecuador, Nicaragua, El Salvador, and of course Venezuela have been won by candidates who rejected neoliberal free-trade and who promised to use the wealth of their nations to eliminate the poverty imposed by the long history of US intervention. In an ongoing rebuff of the Anglo-American alliance, Ecuador continues to give refuge to WikiLeaks co-founder Julian Assange in its London embassy. Moreover, without the ability of the US to force nations to the table, regional rivalries have become more intense—Pakistan's role in both Afghani and Indian terrorism becomes increasingly impossible to ignore, and Israel's continuing blockade of Gaza and "settlement" of the West Bank turns ever more brazen. It has become a multipolar world, in which the interests of other nations, and their publics, cannot be ignored.

Conclusion

Made possible by their seizure of the nation's oil wealth, the founding families of US capital rose to a position of global supremacy within a century. For the three decades following the Second World War, the US dominated the global financial system. Declining oil production, defeat in Vietnam, the challenge of OPEC, and the repression of a domestic dissent that might have revitalized the nation marked the onset of decline. Neoliberalism and neoconservatism constituted attempts to shore up US capitalist hegemony, but both succumbed to domestic and international opposition. The "Great Recession," born of this failure—of inequality, debt, corruption and energy inflation—marks the end of US dominance. Other major world powers are emerging, smaller nations are asserting their independence, and workers globally are increasingly unwilling to accept austerity as defined by the US, the EU, the IMF or subservient governments.

There is no basis for the delusion of "American exceptionalism." Domination was instead made possible by quirks of geophysics and geopolitics, and was prolonged only by the failed practices of neoliberalism and neoconservatism. As a result of these last ditch efforts, the United States remained at the head of the table until the end of the twentieth century. But attempting to dictate the affairs of other peoples and other nations, through either trade agreements or at the barrel of a gun, has inevitably led to opposition. The collapse of the global economy has exacerbated class conflict. Capital, at its own peril, is attacking the most fundamental aspects of the social contract, and a growing global movement continues to challenge a disastrous and unsustainable status quo that will in the end cost the Empire its very existence.

At home and elsewhere in the developed world, the cold comfort of consumerism and the hollow rewards of careerism cannot hold the attention of people whose jobs have been eliminated, wages have been cut, and homes foreclosed. Thus, America is moving in a direction where more and more of its people are calling into question the burdens of Empire, protesting its costs shouldered by its working people for so long. But the end of Empire is also sign of a new beginning—the emergence of a new social order responsive to the needs of its people. But such an order can only be brought about by the struggles of working people against the system that has kept them down for so long.

References

Bacon, David. 2007. "Iraqi's Oil Should Stay in Public Hands." Truthout.org, accessed online at http://www.truthout.org/docs_2006/071007C.shtml.

BP. 2010. "Statistical Review of World Energy," accessed online at http://www.bp.com.

Brisard, Jean Charles and Guillame Dasquie. 2002. *Forbidden Truth: U.S.-Taliban Secret Oil Diplomacy and the Failed Hunt for bin Laden*, translated by Lucy Rounds. New York: Thunder's Mouth Press.

Burnham, Gilbert, Riyadh Lafta, Shannon Doocy, and Les Roberts. 2006. "Mortality After the 2003 Invasion of Iraq: A Cross-sectional Cluster Sample Survey." *The Lancet*, 368(9545), 1421–1428.

Burns, John F. 2010. "Thousands in Dublin Protest Irish Austerity Plan." *The New York Times*, November 28, A13.

Business Cycle Dating Committee. 2008. "Determination of the December 2007 peak in Economic Activity." National Bureau of Economic Research, accessed online at http://www.nber.org/cycles/dec2008.html.

Cockburn, Patrick. 2007. "UN Warns of Five Million Iraqi Refugees." *The Independent* (July 17), accessed online at http://news.independent.co.uk/world/middle_east /article2640418.ece.

Engdahl, F. William. 2004. *A Century of War: Anglo-American Oil Politics and the New World Order.* London: Pluto Press.

Foster, John Bellamy. 2006. "The Household Debt Bubble." *Monthly Review*, 58(1), 1–11.

International Monetary Fund. 2010. *World Economic Outlook: Rebalancing Growth*. Washington, DC: International Monetary Fund.

Kenfield, Isabella. 2009. "Monsanto's Man in the Obama Administration." *Counterpunch* (August 14–16), accessed online at http://www.counterpunch.org/2009/08/14/monsanto-s-man-in-the-obama-administration/.

Klare, Michael T. 2001. *Resource Wars: The New Landscape of Global Conflict*. New York: Henry Holt and Company.

National Commission on Fiscal Responsibility and Reform. 2010. *Draft of CoChairs' Proposal*, accessed online at http://www.fiscalcommission.gov/sites/fiscalcommission.gov/files/documents/Illustrative_List_11.10.2010.pdf.

Parenti, Christian. 2004. *The Freedom: Shadows and Hallucinations in Occupied Iraq*. New York: The New Press.

Petras, James. 2009. *Global Depression and Regional Wars*. Atlanta, GA: Clarity Press.

Qiang, Su and Li Xiaokun. 2010. "China, Russia Quit Dollar." *China Daily*, November 24, accessed online at http://www.chinadaily.com.cn/china/2010-11/24/content_11599087.htm.

Rampell, Catherine. 2010. "3rd Quarter was Record for Profits in U.S. Firms." *The New York Times*, November 23, B2.

Rampton, Sheldon and John Stauber. 2003. *Weapons of Mass Deception: The Uses of Propaganda in Bush's War on Iraq*. New York: Tarcher/Penguin.

Ratner, Lizzy. 2009. "Generation Recession: Young People Have Lost 2.5 Million Jobs to the Crisis, Making them the Hardest-hit Age Group." *The Nation*, November 23, 23–26.

Scher, Abby. 2001. "The Crackdown on Dissent." *The Nation*, February 5, 23–24.
Seldes, George. 1943. *Facts and Fascism.* New York: In Fact, Inc.
Taibbi, Matt. 2009. "The Big Takeover." *Rolling Stone*, March 11, 66–97.
US Census Bureau. 2010. *Statistical Abstract of the United States*, 129th edition, accessed online at http://www.census.gov/statab/www/.
US Department of the Treasury. 2010. "Major Foreign Holders of Treasury Securities," accessed online at http://www.ustreas.gov/tic/mfh.txt.
Weissman, Robert. 1999. "Welcome to Seattle: Ministerial Meeting Debates the World Trade Organization's Agenda for the 21st Century." *Multinational Monitor*, October/November, 9–13.
Wolff, Richard D. 2009. "Capitalism Hits the Fan." In *The Economic Crisis Reader* (ed.). Gerald Friedman, Fred Moseley, Chris Sturr, et al. Boston, MA: Dollars and Sense.
Yeoman, Matthew. 2004. *Oil: A Concise Guide to the Most Important Product on Earth.* New York: The New Press.
Zachary, G. Pascal. 2000. "The New Imperialism: A Year After the 'Battle in Seattle,' the Rich are Embracing Their Critics. Watch out." *In These Times*, December 25, 30.

Conclusion: The Global Capitalist Crisis and Class Struggle

Berch Berberoglu

The ongoing global capitalist crisis that we are experiencing today is a product of three decades of neoliberal capitalist policies of privatization, deregulation, tax cuts for the wealthy, speculative investments, financialization, and profiteering of unimaginable proportions. Through these practices many capitalists became very wealthy and amassed great fortunes during this period, while working people were super-exploited through extremely low wages in the sweatshops of the giant capitalist corporations that have spread their tentacles across the globe.

In my recent book *Globalization in the 21st Century: Labor, Capital, and the State on a World Scale*, published by Palgrave Macmillan in 2010, I pointed out that "neoliberal globalization … has come under severe criticism and opposition from movements around the world that have waged (and continue to wage) a successful struggle against it" (Berberoglu 2010: 199). I went on to document that

> Movements made up of workers, peasants, indigenous peoples, environmentalists, intellectuals, students, and others have come together in a broad coalition of forces to oppose corporate globalization that has advanced the interests of the dominant classes in society to profit from the exploitation and oppression of the great majority of the people, while forcing millions into poverty and destitution. From sweatshop slavery to global warming, from mass unemployment to military interventions, and from speculative profiteering to ethnic cleansing, the capitalist powers have used the neoliberal cover to justify every shady imperialist activity to the benefit of their global empire that is now crumbling in the face of the worst economic collapse since the Great Depression. Thus, the era of neoliberalism, that is, of neoliberal capitalist globalization, is coming to an end. And people across the globe are coming together to form a powerful coalition of forces to resist the global capitalist system and reverse its course in a last-ditch effort to save the planet from those who are intent on destroying it. (Berberoglu, 2010: 199)

Global capitalism, in fact, came very close in 2008 to destroying the very system that it had created not so long ago. Cyclical crises of recessions and depressions, economic rivalry, political and military conflict, war, and other forms of disruptions and catastrophes have been the characteristic of global capitalism ever since its inception a few centuries ago. In my latest book *Beyond the Global Capitalist Crisis: The World Economy in Transition*, published by Ashgate in 2012, I pointed out that "Tracing the evolution of the capitalist economy and the capitalist business cycle historically, it becomes clear that the ups and downs—"booms and busts"—of the capitalist economy is the result of the "normal" process of evolution of the capitalist system, and that economic crises (i.e., recessions and depressions) are a recurrent aspect of capitalism at the national and now the global level" (Berberoglu, 2012: 179). I went on to argue that therefore "the crisis-ridden business cycle of capitalism—one that is to be found *only under capitalism*—is the life-blood of the capitalist system in that capitalism cannot grow and prosper without such a 'correction' (crisis) in the economy every few years. And this can be seen as part of the process of capitalist expansion and contraction over its life-course" (Berberoglu, 2012: 179).

The current continuing global capitalist crisis that originated in the Great Recession of 2008–2009 is but one serious crisis in a series of capitalist crises that have erupted over the past few centuries as capitalism developed and expanded from Europe to North America and elsewhere across the globe over this period. The dynamics and contradictions of this process of recurrent crises of the capitalist system leading to the crisis of global capitalism have been documented very clearly and in great detail in a wide array of literature (Berberoglu, 2003, 2010, 2012; Petras, 2009; Sherman, 2010; Bivens, 2011; Calhoun and Derluguian, 2011), and the nature and depth of its most recent capitalist crisis has been examined at length in various chapters of this book by a team of progressive political economists who have exposed the inner workings of this moribund and decaying economic system with great precision and care.

The continuing global capitalist crisis is a manifestation of capitalism and capitalist globalization at this (imperialist) stage of the globalization of capital. Thus, to go beyond the crisis of global capitalism and imperialism, we need to address a variety of issues that emanate from the system itself—issues that are directly linked to the very nature of neoliberal capitalist globalization and the global capitalist crisis in the age of imperialism. And this raises further questions as to the nature and sources of the changes that are necessary to take us beyond this epochal predicament: who (which social class) shall lead the process of transformation, and in which direction? It is here that we benefit from analyses of capitalist imperialism that not only lay out the process at work that has taken us to the point where we are today, but help us move forward and go beyond the contradictions and crises of this exploitative and oppressive system.

In his *Imperialism: The Highest Stage of Capitalism*, Vladimir Lenin addressed this very question precisely and showed the way forward by identifying not only the source of the crisis (capitalist imperialism), but the class agents that will bring about its final downfall and transformation. Thus he wrote: "Imperialism is the eve of the social revolution of the proletariat … on a world wide scale" (Lenin,

[1917] 1975: 640). And Karl Marx and Frederick Engels had similarly eulogized capitalism when they referred to the workers as the "grave diggers" of capitalism and urged them to come together across the world (hence their slogan "Workers of the World, Unite!") to rise up and overthrow the global capitalist system (Marx and Engels, 1972). Clearly, exploited and oppressed under capitalism, the working class is the only class that is destined to lead humanity in transforming society toward a new social order that provides true liberty through collective social expression that is democratic, egalitarian, and socially responsible—an economic, political, and social system that can only be achieved under socialism—i.e., a state and society ruled by the working class in alliance with all other oppressed classes and groups in society.

The economic crisis brought by the 2008 financial meltdown is a direct outcome of the operations of the very same capitalist system that has dominated the global economy to this day. And the ramifications of this latest and deepest economic crisis since the Great Depression of the early twentieth century will be felt for a long time to come. While this means the impact of the crisis on the working class will be significant, it is also the case that this may lead to greater class- consciousness among workers who will increasingly become aware of the system's fault lines, as its unequal and exploitative nature becomes visible and obvious for all to see. This process would surely assist in the development of sufficient class- consciousness that would call into question the very premises and legitimacy of the capitalist system. It is this unfolding process that in time comes to inform the working class of the necessity to organize and engage in class struggle for state power (Lenin [1916] 1975; Gramsci, 1971). While this is a long process and requires much work and determination on the part of the workers to wage such struggle, the dynamics of the class struggle under capitalism will of necessity force workers to take the required steps to achieve this eventuality through organized collective political action (Polet, 2007; Berberoglu, 2009).

In looking at the history of the US labor movement over the past two centuries, one finds a vibrant movement of workers who came together to wage struggle against capital in both the nineteenth and twentieth centuries that showed a high level of class consciousness, thanks to the radical leadership of organized labor from the Industrial Workers of the World (IWW) to the Congress of Industrial Organizations (CIO) and beyond. As the Great Depression unfolded, US labor began to become more visible through increased union membership and expanded labor organization and activism in the form of mass demonstrations, protests, and strikes (Boyer and Morais, 1986). With union membership having reached 35 percent of the labor force, organized labor became a powerful force to be reckoned with in their historic struggle against capital in the United States.

Today, the politicization of the working class through various forms of struggle against global capitalism is already beginning to take hold across the world. Movements led by workers and their class-conscious organizations, in alliance with a variety of popular forces, are beginning to proclaim "another world is possible" and indeed *necessary*. And it is with this concern for the future of working people, and indeed of humanity in general, that the progressive forces rallied around labor are urgently mobilizing their ranks to take the leadership to address and overcome these challenges through revolutionary social and political action that will involve struggles to take state power to set the economy and society on a path that will allow the oppressed and the exploited—above all the working class across the globe—to take charge of their destiny in building a just and egalitarian society.

As once proclaimed by two well-known champions of the working class, Marx and Engels, "the history of all hitherto existing society is the history of class struggles," and such struggles are the engines of social change and transformation that working people have effected through the historic path that they have taken and will continue to take to move us forward to the future (Marx and Engels, 1972). In the closing lines of the book that I published a few years ago, titled *Globalization of Capital and the Nation-State: Imperialism, Class Struggle, and the State in the Age of Global Capitalism*, I wrote: "What the future holds for the dominant forces of modern-day conquest and plunder that have imposed their class rule onto the rest of the world, history and the working classes of the world will ultimately determine," and added, "and thus, it is not unreasonable to expect that, like everything else in history, the globalization of capital and the capitalist state may in fact one day be a thing of the past!" (Berberoglu, 2003: 137). And that continues to be the case today, but the question still remains: Where do we go from here in order to secure for us—and for future generations—a society and a social order that is beyond global economic crises and serves the interests of all of humanity? The answer to this question will undoubtedly come from those who are most severely affected by the continuing global capitalist crisis—the global working class, allied with all other exploited and oppresses classes and groups around the world—who are conscious of their predicament and are able to organize to take the lead to change the course of history and society which we are bound to witness in the coming period.

References

Berberoglu, Berch. 2003. *Globalization of Capital and the Nation State: Imperialism, Class Struggle, and the State in the Age of Global Capitalism.* Lanham, MD: Rowman and Littlefield.

Berberoglu, Berch. 2009. *Class and Class Conflict in the Age of Globalization.* Lanham, MD: Lexington.

Berberoglu, Berch. 2010. *Globalization in the 21st Century: Labor, Capital and the State on a World Scale.* New York: Palgrave Macmillan.

Berberoglu, Berch. 2012. *Beyond the Global Capitalist Crisis: The World Economy in Transition.* Farnham: Ashgate.

Bivens, Josh. 2011. *Failure by Design: The Story Behind America's Broken Economy.* Ithaca, NY: ILR Press.

Boyer, Richard O. and Herbert M. Morais. 1986. *Labor's Untold Story*, 3rd Edition. Seattle, WA: United Electrical, Radio and Machine Workers of America.
Calhoun, Craig and Georgi Derluguian (eds). 2011. *Aftermath: A New Economic Order?* New York: New York University Press.
Gramsci, Antonio. 1971. *Prison Notebooks*. International Publishers.
Lenin, Vladimir I. [1916] 1975. The State and Revolution. In V.I. Lenin, *Selected Works in Three Volumes*. Moscow: Progress Publishers.
Lenin, Vladimir I. [1917] 1975. *Imperialism: The Highest Stage of Capitalism. Selected Works. Vol. 1.* New York: International Publishers.
Marx, Karl and Frederick Engels. 1972. "Manifesto of the Communist Party." In Karl Marx and Frederick Engels, *Selected Works*. New York: International Publishers.
Petras, James. 2009. *Global Depression and Regional Wars*. Atlanta: Clarity Press.
Polet, Francois. 2007. *The State of Resistance: Popular Struggles in the Global South*. London: Zed Books.
Sherman, Howard. 2010. *The Roller Coaster Economy: Financial Crisis, Great Recession, and the Public Option*. Boston: M.E. Sharpe.

Select Bibliography

Abdelal, Rawi. 2009. *Capital Rules: The Construction of Global Finance.* Cambridge, MA: Harvard University Press.

Adejumobi, Said. 2013. "Europe: The Failure of Structural Adjustment?" *New African*, 58–60.

Aldcroft, Derek H. 1993. *The European Economy, 1914–1990*, 3rd Edition. London: Routledge.

Allen, Franklin and Elena Carletti. 2010. "An Overview of the Crisis: Causes, Consequences, and Solutions." *International Review of Finance*, 10(1), 1–26.

Amaladoss, Michael (ed.). 1999. *Globalization and its Victims as Seen by its Victims*. Delhi, India: Vidyajyoti Education and Welfare Society.

Amin, Samir. 2003. *Obsolescent Capitalism: Contemporary Politics and Global Disorder*. New York: Zed Books.

Amoroso, Bruno. 2001. *On Globalization: Capitalism in the 21st Century.* New York: St Martin's.

Ashman, S., B. Fine, and S. Newman. 2010. "The Crisis in South Africa: Neoliberalism, Financialization and Uneven and Combined Development," in L. Panitch, G. Albo, and V. Chibber (eds). *The Crisis This Time: Socialist Register 2011.* London: Merlin Press; New York: Monthly Review Press.

Baker, Dean. 2009. *Plunder and Blunder: The Rise and Fall of the Bubble Economy.* New York: Berrett-Koehler Publishers.

Batra, Ravi. 1988. *The Great Depression of 1990*. New York: Dell.

Batra, Ravi. 2005. *Greenspan's Fraud: How Two Decades of His Policies Have Undermined the Global Economy*. New York: Palgrave Macmillan.

Baylis, John, Steve Smith, and Patricia Owens. 2008. *The Globalization of World Politics*, 4th Edition. New York: Oxford University Press.

Bello, Walden. 2005. *Deglobalization: Ideas for a New World Economy*, revised edition. London: Zed Books.

Bello, Walden. 2006. "The Capitalist Conjuncture: Overaccumulation, Financial Crises, and the Retreat from Globalization." *Third World Quarterly*, 27(8), 1345–1367.

Bello, Walden. 2009. "The Global Collapse: A Non-orthodox View." *MRZine*, February 20. Available at http://www.monthlyreview.org/mrzine/bello200209.html.

Bello, Walden, Shea Cunningham, and Bill Rau. 1994. *Dark Victory: The United States, Structural Adjustment, and Global Poverty*. Oakland: California, Institute for Food and Development Policy.

Berberoglu, Berch. 1992. *The Legacy of Empire: Economic Decline and Class Polarization in the United States*. New York: Praeger.

Berberoglu, Berch (ed.). 2002. *Labor and Capital in the Age of Globalization.* Lanham, MD: Rowman and Littlefield.

Berberoglu, Berch. 2003. *Globalization of Capital and the Nation-State.* Lanham, MD: Rowman and Littlefield.

Berberoglu, Berch (ed.). 2005. *Globalization and Change: The Transformation of Global Capitalism.* Lanham, MD: Lexington Books.

Berberoglu, Berch. 2009. *Class and Class Conflict in the Age of Globalization.* Lanham, MD: Lexington Books.

Berberoglu, Berch (ed.). 2010. *Globalization in the 21st Century.* New York: Palgrave Macmillan.

Berberoglu, Berch (ed.). 2012. *Beyond the Global Capitalist Crisis: The World Economy in Transition.* Farnham: Ashgate.

Bergman, Gregory. 1986. "The 1920s and the 1980s: A Comparison." *Monthly Review* (October), 38(5).

Birnbaum, Norman. 2010. "The Economic Crisis, US Progressivism, and West European Socialism and Social Democracy." *Social Europe: The Journal of the European Left*, 5, 5–10.

Bivens, Josh. 2011. *Failure by Design: The Story Behind America's Broken Economy.* Ithaca, NY: ILR Press.

Blau, Judith and Marina Karides (eds). 2009. *The World and U.S. Social Forums.* Lanham, MD: Rowman & Littlefield.

Bluestone, Barry and Bennett Harrison. 1982. *The Deindustrialization of America.* New York: Basic.

Blum, William. 2001. *Rogue State: A Guide to the World's Only Superpower.* London: Zed.

Boltho, A. and Corbett, J. 2000. "The Assessment: Japan's Stagnation—Can Policy Revive the Economy?" *Oxford Review of Economic Policy*, 16(2), 1–17.

Bonacich, Edna, Lucie Cheng, Norma Chinchilla, et al. (eds). 1994. *Global Production: The Apparel Industry in the Pacific Rim.* Philadelphia: Temple University Press.

Bond, Patrick. 2006. *Looting Africa.* London: Zed Books.

Bond, Patrick. 2010. "Is Africa Still Being Looted? World Bank Dodges its Own Research." *Links*, August 15, 2010. Available at http://links.org.au/node/1843.

Bond, Patrick. 2013. "Subimperialism as Lubricant of Neoliberalism: South African 'Deputy Sheriff' Duty within BRICS." *Third World Quarterly*, 34(2).

Bond, P. and S. Mottiar. 2013. "Social Protest in South Africa." *Journal of Contemporary African Studies*, 31(2), 283–302.

Bottelier, Peter. 2010. "China: Is the Recovery Too Strong?" *International Economic Bulletin* (March).

Braby, Don. 2008. *The Greatest Depression of All Time.* CreateSpace.

Braun, Denny. 1991. *The Rich Get Richer: The Rise of Income Inequality in the United States and the World.* Chicago: Nelson-Hall.

Brecher, Jeremy, Tim Costello, and Brendan Smith. 2000. *Globalization From Below: The Power of Solidarity*. Cambridge, MA: South End.

Brenner, Robert. 2000. *The Economics of Global Turbulence*. London: Verso.

Brenner, Robert. 2003. *The Boom and the Bubble: The U.S. in the World Economy.* London: Verso.

Broome, Andre. 2010. "The International Monetary Fund, Crisis Management and the Credit Crunch." *Australian Journal of International Affairs*, 64, 37–54.

Bureau of Economic Analysis (BEA). US Department of Commerce. Available at www.bea.gov.

Burns, John F. 2010. "Thousands in Dublin Protest Irish Austerity Plan." *The New York Times*, November 28: A13.

Bustillo, Inés and Helvia Helloso. 2009. *The Global Financial Crisis: What Happened and What's Next*. Washington, DC: ECLAC, Washington Office, February.

Calhoun, Craig and Georgi Derluguian (eds). 2011. *The Deepening Crisis: Governance Challenges after Neoliberalism*. New York: NYU Press.

Callari, Antonio. 2010. "2008: A New Chapter for U.S. Imperialism." *Rethinking Marxism: A Journal of Economics, Culture & Society*, 22(2), 210–218.

Campbell, Colin. 2004. *The Coming Oil Crisis*. Brentwood, UK: Multi-Science Publishing Company, Ltd.

Campbell, John L. 2010. "Neoliberalism in Crisis: Regulatory Roots of the U.S. Financial Meltdown." *Research in the Sociology of Organizations*, 30(B), 65–101.

Carroll, William, K. 2010. *The Making of a Transnational Capitalist Class: Corporate Power in the 21st Century*. London: Zed.

Chew, Sing C. 2006. *The Recurring Dark Ages: Ecological Stress, Climate Changes, and System Transformation*, Lanham, MD: Alta Mira Press.

Chossudovsky, Michel and Andrew Gavin Marshall (eds). 2010. *The Global Economic Crisis: The Great Depression of the XXI Century.* Quebec: Global Research Publishers.

Chu, Kathy. 2010. "China Posed to Replace Japan as World's No. 2 Economy." *USA Today*, August 16, 2010. Available at http://www.usatoday.com/money/world/2010-08-16-china-japan-gdp_N.htm.

Cohen, Daniel. 2007. *Globalization and Its Enemies*. Cambridge, MA: The MIT Press.

Connolly, Richard. 2009. "Financial Vulnerabilities in Russia." *Russian Analytical Digest*, No. 65, October 6, 2–6.

Correa Leite, Jose. 2005. *The World Social Forum: Strategies of Resistance*. Chicago: Haymarket Books.

Danaher, Kevin and Roger Burbach (eds). 2000. *Globalize This! The Battle Against the World Trade Organization and Corporate Rule.* Monroe, ME: Common Courage.

De la Barra, Ximena and Richard A. Dello Buono. 2008. *Latin America After the Neoliberal Debacle.* Lanham, MD: Rowman and Littlefield.

Desai, Padma. 2010. "Russia's Financial Crisis: Economic Setbacks and Policy Responses." *Journal of International Affairs* (Spring–Summer) 63(2), 141–151.

Devine, Jim. 1982. "The Structural Crisis of U.S. Capitalism." *Southwest Economy and Society* (Fall), 6(1).

Diamond, Jared. 2005. *Collapse: How Societies Choose to Fail or Succeed.* New York: Penguin.

Dickenson, Torry D. and Robert K. Schaeffer. 2001. *Fast Forward: Work, Gender, and Protest in a Changing World.* Lanham, MD: Rowman and Littlefield.

Dorn, Nicholas. 2011. "Regulatory Sloth and Activism in the Effervescence of Financial Crisis." *Law & Policy*, 33(3), 428–448.

Duboff, Richard B. 1989. *Accumulation and Power: An Economic History of the United States*. Armonk: M.E. Sharpe.

Duménil, Gérard and Dominique Lévy. 2011. *The Crisis of Neoliberalism.* Cambridge, MA: Harvard University Press.

Duncan, R. 2012. *The New Depression.* Singapore: John Wiley & Sons.

Dymsky, Gary A. 2009. "The Political Economy of the Subprime Meltdown." Paper presented at the symposium, Financial Crisis and Globalization, Institute for Global Cooperation and Conflict (IGCC), University of California at Riverside (13 January).

Eichengreen, Barry. 2008. *Globalizing Capital: A History of the International Monetary System*. 2nd Edition. Princeton, NJ: Princeton University Press.

Eichengreen, Barry. 2011. *Exorbitant Privilege: The Rise and Fall of the Dollar and the Future of the International Monetary System*. New York: Oxford University Press.

Engdahl, F. William. 2004. *A Century of War: Anglo-American Oil Politics and the New World Order.* London: Pluto Press.

Epitropoulos, Mike-Frank. 2010. "Greece as a Demonstration Project: Will the Black Sheep Bite Back? Will the PIIGS? What about US?" *Dollars&Sense* (May/June), 9–11.

Evans, Ben. 2010. "O'Donnell said China Plotting to take over U.S." *The Associated Press* (October 4).

Falk, Richard. 1999. *Predatory Globalization: A Critique.* Malden, MA: Blackwell.

Faux, Geoffrey P. 2006. *The Global Class War*. Hoboken, NJ: Wiley.

Filger, Sheldon. 2009. *Global Economic Forecast 2010–2015: Recession into Depression.* Available at www.GlobalEconomicCrisis.com.

Financial Crisis Inquiry Commission. 2011. *The Financial Crisis Inquiry Report.* Washington, DC: US Government Printing Office.

Fisher I. 1933. "The Debt-Deflation Theory of Great Depressions." *Econometrica* (October), 1(3), 337–357.

Foran, John (ed.). 2002. *The Future of Revolutions: Rethinking Political and Social Change in the Age of Globalization*. London: Zed.

Foran, John. 2005. *Taking Power: On the Origins of Third World Revolutions.* Cambridge: Cambridge University Press.

Foster, John Bellamy. 2006. "The Household Debt Bubble." *Monthly Review*, 58(1), 1–11.

Foster, John Bellamy. 2010. "The Age of Monopoly-Finance Capital." *Monthly Review* (February). Available at http://monthlyreview.org/2010/02/01/the-age-of-monopoly-finance-capital.

Foster, John Bellamy and Hannah Holleman. 2010. *The Financial Power Elite. Monthly Review* (May). Available at http://monthlyreview.org/100501foster-holleman.php.

Foster, John Bellamy and Fred Magdoff. 2009. *The Great Financial Crisis: Causes and Consequences*. New York: Monthly Review Press.

Friedman, Gerald, Fred Moseley, and Chris Sturr (eds). 2009. *The Economic Crisis Reader*. Boston, MA: Dollars and Sense.

Friedman, Jonathan (ed.). 2002. *Globalization, the State, and Violence.* Lanham, MD: Rowman and Littlefield.

Gaddy, Clifford G. and Barry W. Ickes. 2010. "Russia after the Global Financial Crisis." *Eurasian Geography and Economics*, 51(3), 281–311.

Galbraith, John Kenneth. 1988. *The Great Crash, 1929*. New York: Houghton-Mifflin.

Garson, Barbara. 2013. *Down the Up Escalator: How the 99 Percent Live in the Great Recession*. New York: Doubleday.

Gavin, Francis J. 2003. *Gold, Dollars, and Power—The Politics of International Monetary Relations, 1958–1971*. Charlotte: The University of North Carolina Press.

Ghotge, Sanjeev. 2009. "Financial Meltdown: An Intriguing Silence at the Core." *Capitalism, Nature, Socialism* (December), 20(4), 85–88.

Gills, Barry (ed.). 2011. *Globalization in Crisis.* London and New York: Routledge.

Glasner, David. 1997. "Crisis of 1873," in David Glasner and Thomas F. Cooley (eds). *Business Cycles and Depressions: An Encyclopedia*. New York: Garland Publishing.

Glipin, R. 2000. *The Challenge of Global Capitalism.* Princeton University Press: New York.

Goldman, Michael. 2005. *Imperial Nature: The World Bank and Struggles for Social Justice in the Age of Globalization.* New Haven, CT: Yale University Press.

Gordon, Greg. 2010. "How Goldman secretly bet on the U.S. housing crash." *McClatchy*. Available at http://www.mcclatchydc.com/2009/11/01/77791/how-goldman-secretly-bet-on-the.html.

Gosh, B.N. and Halil M. Guven (eds). 2006. *Globalization and the Third World: A Study of Negative Consequences*. New York: Palgrave Macmillan.

Gowan, Peter. 1999. *The Global Gamble: Washington's Faustian Bid for World Dominance*. New York: Verso.

Gowan, Peter. 2010. *A Calculus of Power: Grand Strategy in the Twenty-First Century*. London: Verso.

Guthrie, Doug. 2006. *China and Globalization: The Social, Economic and Political Transformation of Chinese Society.* New York: Routledge.
Habermas, Jürgen. 2012. *The Crisis of the European Union : A Response.* Trans by Cronin Ciaran. Cambridge, UK: Polity.
Halevi, J. and Lucarelli, B. 2002. "Japan's Stagnationist Crisis." *Monthly Review,* 53(9), 24–36.
Halliday, Fred. 2001. *The World at 2000.* New York: St Martin's Press.
Harman, Chris. 2009. *Zombie Capitalism: Global Crisis and the Relevance of Marx.* London: Bookmarks Publications.
Harman, Chris. 2010. *Zombie Capitalism: Global Crisis and the Relevance of Marx,* reprint edition. Chicago: Haymarket Books.
Harris, Jerry. 2003. "Transnational Competition and the End of U.S. Hegemony." *Science and Society,* 67(1).
Hart, Jeffrey A. 1992. *Rival Capitalists: International Competitiveness in the United States, Japan, and Western Europe.* Ithaca, NY: Cornell University Press.
Hart-Landsberg, Martin. 2010. "The U.S. Economy and China: Capitalism, Class, and Crisis." *Monthly Review,* 61(9), 14–31.
Harvey, David. 2003. *The New Imperialism.* New York: Oxford University Press.
Harvey, David. 2005. *A Brief History of Neoliberalism.* New York: Oxford University Press.
Harvey, David. 2006. *The Limits to Capital.* London: Verso.
Harvey, David. 2010a. *The Enigma of Capital and the Crises of Capitalism.* New York: Oxford University Press.
Harvey, David. 2010b. "Organizing for the Anti-Capitalist Transition." *Radical Perspectives on the Crisis* (August 30).
Harvey, David. 2011. *The Enigma of Capital and the Crises of Capitalism.* New York: Oxford University Press.
Harvey, David. 2014. *Seventeen Contradictions and the End of Capitalism.* New York: Oxford University Press.
Hedley, R. Alan. 2002. *Running Out of Control: Dilemmas of Globalization.* West Hartford: Kumarian.
Held, David and Anthony McGrew. 2002. *Governing Globalization: Power, Authority and Global Governance.* Cambridge, UK: Polity.
Held, David and Ayse Kaya (eds). 2007. *Global Inequality: Patterns and Explanations.* Cambridge, UK: Polity.
Hertz, Noreena. 2002. *Silent Takeover: Global Capitalism and the Death of Democracy.* New York: The Free Press.
Ho, Karen. 2009. *Liquidated; An Ethnography of Wall Street.* London: Duke University Press.
Hook, Glenn D. and Hasegawa Harukiyo (eds). 2001. *Political Economy of Japanese Globalization.* New York: Routledge.
Hooks, Gregory. 1991. *Forging the Military-Industrial Complex. World War II's Battle of the Potomac.* Urbana-Champaign, IL: University of Illinois Press.

Hoshi, T. and Kashyap, A. 2004. "Japan's Financial Crisis and Economic Stagnation." *Journal of Economic Perspectives*, 18(1), 3–26.

Houtart, Francois and Francois Polet (eds). 2001. *The Other Davos Summit: The Globalization of Resistance to the World Economic System.* London: Zed Books.

Hudson, Michael. 2003. *Super Imperialism: The Origin and Fundamentals of U.S. World Dominance*, revised edition. Herndon, VA: Pluto.

Hudson, Michael. 2010. "'Drop Dead Economics': The Financial Crisis in Greece and the European Union: The Wealthy Won't Pay Their Taxes, So Labor Must Do So." *GlobalResearch.ca: Center for Research on Globalization.* Available at http://www.globalresearch.ca/index.php?context=va&aid=19107.

Hughes C.H. 2000. "Japanese Policy and the East Asian Currency Crises: Abject Defeat or Quiet Victory?" *Review of International Political Economy*, 7(2), 219–253.

Hung, Ho-Fung. 2009. "America's Head Servant? The PRC's Dilemma in the Global Crisis." *New Left Review*, 60, 5–25.

Hytrek, Gary and Kristine M. Zentgraf. 2008. *America Transformed: Globalization, Inequality and Power*. New York: Oxford University Press.

James, Harold. 2002. *The End of Globalization: Lessons from the Great Depression.* Cambridge, MA: Harvard University Press.

James, Harold. 2009. *The Creation and Destruction of Value: The Globalization Cycle.* Cambridge, MA: Harvard University Press.

Jenkins, Holman W., Jr. 2008. "How to Shake Off the Mortgage Mess." *Wall Street Journal* (July 30). Available at http://online.wsj.com/article/SB121737434767195077.html?mod=todays_columnists.

Jessen, Corinna. 2010. "Entering a Death Spiral?: Tensions Rise in Greece as Austerity Measures Backfire." *Der Spiegel.* Available at http://www.spiegel.de/international/europe/0,1518,712511,00.html.

Johnson C. 1998. "Economic Crisis in East Asia: The Clash of Capitalisms." *Cambridge Journal of Economics*, 22(6), 653–661.

Johnson, Simon. 2010. "Creating the Next Crisis." *Project Syndicate* (June 15). Available at http://www.project-syndicate.org/commentary/johnson9/English.

Jones, Alun, Julian Clark, and Angus Cameron. 2010. "The Global Economic Crisis and the Cohesion of Europe." *Eurasian Geography & Economics*, 51, 35–51.

Klein, Naomi. 2008. *Shock Doctrine: The Rise of Disaster Capitalism.* New York, NY: Metropolitan Books.

Kliman, Andrew. 2012. *The Failure of Capitalist Production: Underlying Causes of the Great Recession.* New York: Pluto Press.

Kagarlitsky, Boris. 2000. *The Twilight of Globalization: Property, State, and Capitalism.* Herndon, VA: Pluto.

Katsiaficas, George and Eddie Yuen (eds). 2002. *The Battle of Seattle: Debating Capitalist Globalization and the WTO.* New York: Soft Skull.

Kennedy, Paul. 1987. *The Rise and Fall of the Great Powers*. New York: Random House.

Keynes, John Maynard. 1965. *The General Theory of Employment, Interest, and Money.* New York: Harcourt, Brace, and World.

Klak, Thomas (ed.). 1997. *Globalization and Neoliberalism.* Lanham, MD: Rowman and Littlefield.

Klare, Michael T. 2001. *Resource Wars: The New Landscape of Global Conflict*. New York: Henry Holt and Company.

Konings, Martijn (ed.). 2010. *Beyond the Subprime Headlines: Critical Perspectives on the Financial Crisis*. London: Verso.

Koo R.C. 2008. *The Holy Grail of Macroeconomics: Lessons from Japan's Great Recession.* Singapore: Wiley & Sons.

Koo R.C. 2011. "The World in Balance Sheet Recession: Causes, Cures and Politics." *Real World Economics Review*, 58, 19–37.

Kotz, David M. 2009. "The Financial and Economic Crisis of 2008: A Systemic Crisis of Neoliberal Capitalism." *Review of Radical Political Economy*, 41(3), 305–317.

Kotz, David M. 2013. "Can China's Rise Continue?" *China Policy Review* (November) (In Chinese, English language version is available from the author on request.)

Kotz, David M. 2014. *The Rise and Fall of Free-Market Capitalism*. Cambridge, MA: Harvard University Press.

Kotz, David M. and Fred Weir. 2007. *Russia's Path from Gorbachev to Putin: The Demise of the Soviet System and the New Russia.* London and New York: Routledge.

Kozul-Wright, Richard and Robert Rowthorn (eds). 1998. *Transnational Corporations and the Global Economy.* New York: St Martin's.

Krippner, Greta R. 2005. "The Financialization of the American Economy." *Socio-Economic Review*, 3, 173–208.

Krippner, Greta R. 2011. *Capitalizing on Crisis: The Political Origins of the Rise of Finance.* Cambridge, MA: Harvard University Press.

Krugman, Paul. 2009. *The Return of Depression Economics and the Crisis of 2008.* New York: W.W. Norton and Company.

Kuroda, Haruhiko. 2009. "China's Policy Response to the Global Financial Crisis." *China Development Forum* (March 22, 2010).

Kushlis, Patricia. 2010. "The Greek Financial Crisis through a Political Lens Darkly." *Whirled View*, September 10, 2010. Available at http://whirledview.typepad.com/whirledview/2010/03/the-greek-financial-crisis-through-a-political-lens-darkly.html.

Lapavitsas, Costas et al. 2012. *Crisis in the Eurozone*. London/New York: Verso.

Lechner, Frank J. and John Boli (eds). 2007. *The Globalization Reader.* 3rd Edition. Oxford: Wiley-Blackwell.

Lewis, Michael. 2010. "Beware of Greeks Bearing Bonds." *Vanity Fair*, October 10, 2010. Available at http://www.vanityfair.com/business/features/2010/10/greeks-bearing-bonds-201010.

Lenin, V.I. [1917] 1975. *Imperialism: The Highest Stage of Capitalism. Selected Works. Vol. 1*. Moscow: Foreign Languages Publishing House.

Leonhardt, David. 2009. "A Bold Plan Sweeps Away Reagan Ideas." *New York Times*, February 26. Available at www.nytimes.com/2009/02/27/business/economy/27policy.html.

Levine, Richard. 2009. "Growing Out of Crisis." *Development Outreach*, World Bank Institute (December).

Levitt, Theodore. 1983. "Globalization of Markets." *Harvard Business Review*.

Li, Minqi. 2008. *The Rise of China and the Demise of the Capitalist World Economy*. New York: Monthly Review Press.

Lindholm, Charles and Jose Pedro Zuquete. 2010. *The Struggle for the World: Liberation Movements for the 21st Century.* Palo Alto, CA: Stanford University Press.

Lippit, Victor. 2010. "Social Structure of Accumulation Theory." In T. McDonough, M. Reich, and D. Kotz (eds). *Contemporary Capitalism and its Crises: Social Structure of Accumulation Theory for the 21st Century*. New York: Cambridge University Press.

Loftsdóttir, Kristín. 2010. "The Loss of Innocence: The Icelandic Financial Crisis and Colonial Past." *Anthropology Today*, 26, 9–13.

Lucarelli, B. 2002. "The East Asian Financial Meltdown." *Journal of Contemporary Asia*, 32(4), 500–516.

Lucarelli, B. 2011. *The Economics of Financial Turbulence*. Cheltenham, UK: Edward Elgar.

MacEwan, Arthur. 1991. *Debt and Disorder: International Economic Instability and U.S. Imperial Decline*. Monthly Review Press: New York.

Magdoff, Fred and Michael Yates. 2009. *The ABCs of the Economic Crisis: What Working People Need to Know.* New York: Monthly Review Press.

Magdoff, Harry and Paul M. Sweezy. 1981. *The Deepening Crisis of U.S. Capitalism*. New York: Monthly Review.

Marazzi, Christian. 2010. *The Violence of Financial Capitalism*, Los Angeles: Semiotics(e).

Marquand, Robert. 2010. "Crisis in Ireland tests Eurozone Vision of Common Currency, Common Interests." *The Christian Science Monitor* (November 23), 1.

Marx, Karl and Frederick Engels. 1972. "Manifesto of the Communist Party," in K. Marx and F. Engels, *Selected Works*. New York: International Publishers.

Mason, Edward S. and Robert E. Asher. 1973. *The World Bank Since Bretton Woods*. Washington, DC: The Brookings Institution.

Massey, Douglas S. 1996. "The Age of Extremes: Concentrated Affluence and Poverty in the Twenty-First Century," *Demography*, 33(November).

Mavroudeas, Stavros. 2010. "The Greek External Debt and Imperialist Rivalries: 'One Thief Stealing from Another'." *MRZine, A Project of the Monthly Review Foundation.* Available at http://mrzine.monthlyreview.org/2010/mavroudeas 200210.html.

McDonough, Terrence, Michael Reich, and David M. Kotz (eds). 2010. *Contemporary Capitalism and Its Crises*. New York: Cambridge University Press.

McNally, David. 2010. *Global Slump: The Economics and Politics of Crisis and Resistance.* Oakland, CA: P.M. Press.

Melander, Ingrid. 2010. "Greek parliament passes austerity bill." *Reuters.* Available at http://in.reuters.com/article/idINIndia-46690820100305.

Meszaros, Istvan and John Bellamy Foster. 2011. *The Structural Crisis of Capital*, New York: Monthly Review Press.

Mitchell, Wesley C. 1951. *What Happens During Business Cycles: A Progress Report*. New York: National Bureau of Economic Research.

Mizruchi, Mark. 2010. "The American Corporate Elite and the Historical Roots of the Financial Crisis of 2008." In *Markets on Trial: Pt. B: The Economic Sociology of the U.S. Financial Crisis.* Lounsbury, Michael and Paul Hirsch (eds) (pp. 103–139). Bingley, UK: Emerald Group Publishing Ltd.

Morris, J. (ed.). 1991. *Japan and the Global Economy.* New York: Routledge.

Morrison, Wayne M. 2009. "China and the Global Financial Crisis: Implications for the United States." Congressional Research Service: CRS Report for Congress.

National Bureau of Economic Research, available at http://www.nber.org/cycles/cyclesmain.html

National Bureau of Economic Research (NBER). 2008. "Determination of the 2007 Peak in Economic Activity." Business Cycle Dating Committee. December 11.

Nonini, Donald M. 2008. "Is China becoming NeoLiberal?" *Critique of Anthropology*, 28(2), 145–176.

Odekon, Mehmet (ed.). 2010. *Booms and Busts: An Encyclopedia of Economic History from the First Stock Market Crash of 1792 to the Current Global Economic Crisis*. Armonk, NY: M.E. Sharpe Reference.

Omadeon Worldpress. 2010. "Max Keiser on the Greek Debt Crisis—Video 1." *Al-Jazeera news segment translation and subtitle (English).* May 5, 2010. Available at http://www.youtube.com/watch?v=AbH1JsOTInk.

Panitch, Leo and Colin Leys (eds). 2003. *The New Imperial Challenge*. New York: Monthly Review Press.

Panitch, Leo, Greg Albo, and Vivek Chibber (eds). 2010. *The Crisis This Time: Socialist Register 2011*. New York: Monthly Review Press.

Perelman, Michael. 2008. "The Corrosive Qualities of Inequality: the Roots of the Current Meltdown." *Challenge*, 51(5), 40–64.

Perlo, Victor. 1988. *Super Profits and Crises: Modern U.S. Capitalism*. New York: International.

Perrucci, Robert and Carolyn C. Perrucci. 2007. *The Transformation of Work in the New Economy: Sociological Readings*. Los Angeles: Roxbury.

Petras, James. 2007. *Rulers and Ruled in the U.S. Empire.* Atlanta: Clarity Press.

Petras, James. 2009. *Global Depression and Regional Wars*. Atlanta, GA: Clarity Press.
Petras, James and Henry Veltmeyer. 2001. *Globalization Unmasked: Imperialism in the 21st Century*. London: Zed Books.
Petras, James and Henry Veltmeyer. 2003. *System in Crisis: The Dynamics of Free Market Capitalism*. London: Zed Books.
Petras, James and Henry Veltmeyer. 2007. *Multinationals on Trial: Foreign Investment Matters*. London: Ashgate.
Petras, James and Henry Veltmeyer. 2011. *Social Movements in Latin America: Neoliberalism and Popular Resistance.* New York: Palgrave Macmillan.
Phillips, Brian. 1998. *Global Production and Domestic Decay: Plant Closings in the U.S.* New York: Garland.
Pieterse, Jan Nederveen. 2007. *Globalization or Empire?* London: Taylor and Francis.
Polet, Francois (ed.). 2007. *The State of Resistance: Popular Struggles in the Global South*. London: Zed.
Pollin, Robert. 2003. *Contours of Descent: U.S. Economic Fractures and the Landscape of Global Austerity*. London: Verso.
Pollin, Robert. 2008. "How to End the Recession." *The Nation* (November 24).
Prasch, Robert E. 2010. "'Disaster Capitalism' Comes to Ireland." CommonDreams.org. December 3, 2010. Available at http://www.zcommunications.org/disaster-capitalism- comes-to-ireland-by-robert-e-prasch.
Prashad, Vijay and Teo Ballve (eds). 2006. *Dispatches from Latin America: On the Frontlines Against Neoliberalism*. Boston: South End Press.
Psimitis, Michalis. 2011. "The Protest Cycle of Spring 2010 in Greece." *Social Movement Studies*, 10, 191–197.
Quinn, Ben. 2010a. "Amid Greek debt crisis, Iceland still recovering from its own collapse." *The Christian Science Monitor.* September 18, 2010. Available at http://www.csmonitor.com/World/Europe/2010/0217/Amid-Greek-debt-cri sis-Iceland-still-recovering-from-its-own-collapse.
Quinn, Ben. 2010b. "Iceland financial crisis: Voters reject debt repayment plan." *The Christian Science Monitor.* September 18, 2010. Available at http://www.csmonitor.com/World/Europe/2010/0307/Iceland-financial-crisis-Voters-reject-debt-repayment-plan.
Rajan, Raghuram G. 2010. *Fault Lines: How Hidden Fractures Still Threaten the World Economy.* Princeton, NJ: Princeton University Press, 2010.
Rajan, Raghuram G. 2010. "Let Them Eat Credit: How Inequality is at the Root of the Great Recession." *The New Republic* (August 27). Available at http://faculty.chicagobooth.edu/raghuram.rajan/research/articles_files/Let%20them%20e at%20credit%20new%20republic.pdf.
Ratner, Lizzy. 2009. "Generation Recession: Young People Have Lost 2.5 Million Jobs to the Crisis, Making them the Hardest-hit Age Group." *The Nation*, November 23: 23–26.

Reifer, Thomas E. (ed.). 2002. *Hegemony, Globalization and Anti-systemic Movements.* Westport, CT: Greenwood.

Ritholtz, Barry and Aaron Task. 2009. *Bailout Nation: How Greed and Easy Money Corrupted Wall Street and Shook the World Economy*. Hoboken, NJ: John Wiley & Sons, Inc.

Roberts, Michael. 2009. *The Great Recession: Profit Cycles Economic Crisis*. London: lulu.com.

Robinson, William I. 2004. *A Theory of Global Capitalism: Production, Class, and State in a Transnational World.* Baltimore, MD: The Johns Hopkins University Press.

Robinson, William I. 2008. *Latin America and Global Capitalism: A Critical Globalization Perspective.* Baltimore: Johns Hopkins University Press.

Roberts, Michael. 2009. *The Great Recession: Profit Cycles, Economic Crisis—A Marxist View.* London: lulu.com.

Rosen, Ellen Israel. 2002. *Making Sweatshops: The Globalization of the U.S. Apparel Industry*. Los Angeles: University of California Press.

Rosenthal, John. 2012. "Germany and the Euro Crisis." *World Affairs*, 175, 53–61.

Ross, Robert J.S. 1995. "The Theory of Global Capitalism: State Theory and Variants of Capitalism on a World Scale." In *A New World Order? Global Transformations in the Late Twentieth Century* (eds), David Smith and Jozsef Borocz. Westport, CT: Praeger.

Ross, Robert J.S. and Kent C. Trachte. 1990. *Global Capitalism: The New Leviathan*. Albany: SUNY Press.

Roubini, Nouriel and Stephen Mihm. 2010. *Crisis Economics: A Crash Course in the Future of Finance.* New York: Penguin.

Rowbotham, Sheila and Stephanie Linkogle (eds). 2001. *Women Resist Globalization.* London: Zed.

Sanfey, Peter. 2011. "South-Eastern Europe: Lessons Learned from the Global Economic Crisis in 2008–10." *Journal of Southeast European & Black Sea Studies*, 11, 97–115.

Santos, Bonaventura de Sousa. 2006. *The Rising of the Global Left: The World Social Forum and Beyond.* New York: Zed Books.

Santos, Bonaventura de Sousa. 2008. "The World Social Forum and the Global Left." *Politics & Society*, 36(2), 247–270.

Sassen, Saskia. 2009. "Too Big To Save: The End of Financial Capitalism." *Open Democracy News Analysis*, April 2.

Schumpeter, Joseph A. 1939. *Business Cycles; A Theoretical, Historical, and Statistical Analysis of the Capitalist Process*. New York/London: McGraw-Hill Book Company, Inc.

Schwartz, Nelson. 2009. "Asia's Recovery Highlights China's Ascendance." *The New York Times*, August 23, 2009.

Shambaugh, David. 2009. "Is China ready to be a global power?" *Global Times* (November 11).

Sherman, Howard. 1991. *The Business Cycle: Growth and Crisis Under Capitalism*. Princeton, NJ: Princeton University Press.

Sherman, Howard. 2003. "Institutions and the Business Cycle." *Journal of Economic Issues*, 3, 621–642.

Sherman, Howard. 2010. *The Roller Coaster Economy: Financial Crisis, Great Recession, and the Public Option.* Armonk, NY: M.E. Sharpe.

Shore, Cris. 2012. "The Euro Crisis and European Citizenship: The Euro 2001–2012 –Celebration or Commemoration?"*Anthropology Today*, 28, 5–9.

Silver, Beverly J. 2003. *Forces of Labor: Workers' Movements and Globalization Since 1870.* Cambridge: Cambridge University Press.

Silver, Beverly J. 2010. "Contradictions in the Latin American Left." Commentary No. 287 (August 15). Available at http://www.iwallerstein.com/contradictions-in-the-latin-american-left/.

Sklair, Leslie. 2002. *Globalization: Capitalism and Its Alternatives*. New York: Oxford University Press.

Sklar, Holly. 2010. "Wall Street Has Already Voted." *Common Dreams*, October 26, 2010. Available at http://www.commondreams.org/view/2010/10/26-6.

Smith, Jackie G. and Hank Johnston (eds). 2002. *Globalization and Resistance: Transnational Dimensions of Social Movements*. New York: Routledge.

Smith, Jackie and Marina Karides, et al. 2008. *Global Democracy and the World Social Forums*. Boulder, CO: Paradigm Publishers.

So, Alvin Y. 2003. "The Making of a Cadre-Capitalist Class in China." In *China's Challenges in the Twenty-First Century*, edited by Joseph Cheng. Hong Kong: City University of Hong Kong Press.

So, Alvin Y. 2010. "Globalization and China: From Neoliberal Capitalism to State Developmentalism in East Asia." In *Globalization in the 21st Century*, edited by Berch Berberoglu. New York: Palgrave Macmillan.

So, Alvin. 2010a. "Post-Socialist State, Transnational Corporations, and the Battle for Labor Rights in China at the turn of the 21st Century." *Development and Society*, 39, 97–118.

So, Alvin. 2010b. "Globalization and China: From Neoliberal Capitalism to State Developmentalism in East Asia." (pp. 133–154) in *Globalization in the 21st Century: Labor, Capital, and the State on a World Scale*, edited by Berch Berberoglu. Palgrave Macmillan.

So, Alvin Y. 2012. "The Global Capitalist Crisis and the Rise of China to the World Scene." (pp. 123–144) in *Beyond the Global Capitalist Crisis: The World Economy in Transition*, edited by Berch Berberoglu. Farnham: Ashgate.

Stephens, Philip. 2009. "A Summit Success That Reflects a Different Global Landscape." *Financial Times*, April 3, 9.

Stevis, Dimitris and Terry Boswell. 2008. *Globalization and Labor: Democratizing Global Governance.* Lanham, MD: Rowman and Littlefield.

Stiglitz, Joseph E. 2002. *Globalization and Its Discontents*. New York: W.W. Norton.

Stiglitz, Joseph. 2010. "A principled Europe would not leave Greece to bleed." *The Guardian*. December 11, 2010. Available at http://www.guardian.co.uk/commentisfree/2010/jan/25/principled-europe-not-let-greece-bleed.

Stiglitz, Joseph. 2010. *The Stiglitz Report: Reforming the International Monetary and Financial Systems in the Wake of the Global Crisis*. New York: The New Press.

Stiglitz, Joseph. 2011. *Freefall: America, Free Markets, and the Sinking of the World Economy*. New York: W.W. Norton.

Sutela, Pekka. 2010. "Russia's Response to the Global Financial Crisis." *Carnegie Endowment for International Peace Policy Outlook*. July 29. Available at http://carnegieendowment.org/files/russia_crisis.pdf.

Sweezy, Paul M. and Harry Magdoff. 1988. "The Stock Market Crash and Its Aftermath." *Monthly Review*, 39, 10(March).

Tabb, William. 2012. *The Restructuring of Capitalism in Our Time*. New York: Columbia University Press.

Taggart-Murphy R. 2000. "Japan's Economic Crisis." *New Left Review*, 1(second series), January/February, 25–52.

Taggart-Murphy R. 2009. "Is Japan Heading for a Fiscal Doomsday?" *The Asia-Pacific Journal*, 46(4), 1–4.

Tanzer, Michael. 1974. *The Energy Crisis: World Struggle for Power and Wealth*. New York: Monthly Review.

Tanzer, Michael. 1991. "Oil and the Gulf Crisis." *Monthly Review*, 42(11).

Thomas, Janet. 2000. *The Battle in Seattle: The Story behind the WTO Demonstrations*. Golden, CO: Fulcrum.

Tyers, R. 2012. "Japanese Economic Stagnation: Causes and Global Implications." *Economic Record*, 88(283), 517–536.

United States Government Accountability Office. 2011. *Federal Reserve System: Opportunities Exist to Strengthen Policies and Processes for Managing Emergency Assistance*. Washington, DC: US Government Accountability Office.

Veltmeyer, Henry (ed.). 2008. *New Perspectives on Globalization and Antiglobalization: Prospects for a New World Order?* Burlington, VT: Ashgate.

Wade, Robert and Veneroso, Frank. 1998. "The Asian Crisis: The High Debt Model vs. The Wall Street-Treasury-IMF Complex." *New Left Review* (March-April), 3–23.

Wagner, Helmut (ed.). 2000. *Globalization and Unemployment*. New York: Springer.

Wallerstein, Immanuel. 1974. "The Rise and Future Demise of the World Capitalist System." *Comparative Studies in Society and History*, 16(4) (September).

Wallerstein, Immanuel. 2002. "The United States in Decline?" In *Hegemony, Globalization, and Anti-Systemic Movements* (ed.) Thomas E. Reifer. Westport, CT: Greenwood.

Wallerstein, Immanuel. 2003. *The Decline of American Power: The United States in a Chaotic World*. New York: New Press.

Wallerstein, Immanuel. 2010. "Structural Crises." *New Left Review*, 62, 133–142.

Weinberg, Meyer. 2003. *A Short History of American Capitalism*. Chicago: New History Press.

Wiseman, Paul. 2011. "A Boom in Corporate Profits, A Bust in Jobs, Wages." *Associated Press* (July 22).

Westbrook, David A. 2010. *Out of Crisis: Rethinking Our Financial Markets*. Boulder, CO: Paradigm Publishers.

Whittaker D.H. and Kurosawa Y. 1998. "Japan's Crisis: Evolution & Implications." *Cambridge Journal of Economics*, 22(7), 761–771.

Wolf, Martin. 2012. "Confronting the Eurozone Crisis." *Brown Journal of World Affairs*, 18, 11–16.

Wolff, Richard. 2009. *Capitalism Hits the Fan: The Global Economic Meltdown and What to Do About It*. Olive Branch.

Xinbo, Wu. 2010. "Understanding the Geopolitical Implications of the Global Financial Crisis." *Washington Quarterly*, 33, 155–163.

Yao Shujie and Dan Luo. 2010. "Chinese Economy 2009: Leading the World Economy out of Crisis." The University of Nottingham, China Policy Institute, *Briefing Series*, Issue 59.

Yates, Michael D. 2003. *Naming the System: Inequality and Work in the Global Economy*. New York: Monthly Review Press.

Yoshikawa H. 2001. *Japan's Lost Decade*. Tokyo: International House of Japan.

Yuen, Eddie, George Katsiaficas, and Daniel Burton Rose (eds). 2002. *The Battle of Seattle: The New Challenge to Capitalist Globalization*. New York: Soft Skull.

Zhu, Andong and David M. Kotz. 2011. "The Dependence of China's Economic Growth on Exports and Investment." *Review of Radical Political Economics*. Special Issue on "China and Global Capital Accumulation," 43(1), Winter, 932.

Zoelick, Robert. 2009. "After the crisis." *Development Outreach*, World Bank Institute (December), 1–3.

Zohlnhöfer, Reimut. 2011a. "Between a Rock and a Hard Place: The Grand Coalition's Response to the Economic Crisis." *German Politics*, 20, 227–242.

Zohlnhöfer, Reimut. 2011b. "The 2009 Federal Election and the Economic Crisis." *German Politics*, 20, 12–27.

Index

For Product Safety Concerns and Information please contact our EU representative GPSR@taylorandfrancis.com
Taylor & Francis Verlag GmbH, Kaufingerstraße 24, 80331 München, Germany

www.ingramcontent.com/pod-product-compliance
Ingram Content Group UK Ltd.
Pitfield, Milton Keynes, MK11 3LW, UK
UKHW022008180926
475701UK00003B/266

* 9 7 8 0 3 6 7 6 0 0 1 9 8 *